Lebanon: a History of Conflict and Consensus

Edited by
NADIM SHEHADI
and
DANA HAFFAR MILLS

The Centre for Lebanese Studies

in association with

I.B. Tauris & Co Ltd
Publishers
London

Published by
The Centre for Lebanese Studies
in association with
I.B.Tauris & Co Ltd
3 Henrietta Street
Covent Garden
London WC2E 8PW

British Library Cataloguing in Publication Data

Lebanon : a history of conflict and consensus
1. Lebanon. Political events, history
I. Shehadi, Nadim   II. Mills, Dana Haffar
956.92

ISBN 1–85043–119–1

Printed and bound in Great Britain by
Redwood Burn Limited, Trowbridge, Wiltshire

Contents

Notes on Contributors

Engin Akarli is Associate Professor at the Department of History, Yarmouk University, Jordan. He has written several articles on the nineteenth-century socio-political history of Turkey, Lebanon, and Syria. He is currently working on the history of Lebanon, 1850–1920, and the artisans of Istanbul, 1750–1850.

Nabil Beyhum is Research Assistant at the Institut de recherche sur le monde arabe contemporain in Lyon.

Edmund Burke III is Professor of Middle Eastern History and Chairman of the Board of Studies in History at the University of California, Santa Cruz. He is the author of numerous articles on the history of the Maghrib, French orientalism, and Islam and world history. He is currently working on a book entitled *The Making of the Modern Middle East: Protest and Resistance in the Emergence of Modern Politics, 1750–1950*.

Dominique Chevallier, currently Professor at the University of Paris, Sorbonne, lived in Lebanon from 1958 until 1964 and was Professor at the University of Tunis (1964–8). His published works include *La Société du Mont-Liban à l'époque de la révolution industrielle à l'Europe* (1971; 3rd edition in preparation) and *Renouvellements du monde arabe 1952–1982*.

Youssef Choueiri holds a Ph.D. from Cambridge. A revised version of his thesis, *Arab Historians and the Rise of the Nation-State, 1820–1980*, is being prepared for publication. He is currently writing a book on *Islamic Fundamentalism*.

Georges Corm, economist and writer, is author of *Géopolitique du conflit libanais* (1986).

Guilain Denoeux is a Doctoral Candidate in the Department of Politics at Princeton.

Leila Fawaz holds a dual appointment as Associate Professor of History and of Diplomacy in the History Department and the Fletcher School of Law and Diplomacy at Tufts University. She is the author of *Merchants and Migrants in Nineteenth Century Beirut* (1983), of contributions to collected works, and of several articles. She is currently working on a book on the civil war of 1860 in Mount Lebanon and Damascus.

Michael C. Hudson is Professor of International Relations and Government and Seif Ghobash Professor of Arab Studies at Georgetown University in Washington, DC. He is also Director of the Georgetown University Center for Contemporary Arab Studies. He is author of *The Precarious Republic: Political Modernization in Lebanon* (1968), *Arab Politics: the Search for Legitimacy* (1977), and other works.

Samir Khalaf is Visiting Professor of Sociology and Near Eastern Studies jointly at Princeton and NYU. His most recent book is *Lebanon's Predicament* (1987).

Ali el-Khalil is former Minister of Finance, Minister of State for Administrative Reform and Member of Parliament for Tyre and South Lebanon, and Lecturer in Political Science at the American University of Beirut.

Fadia Kiwan holds a Doctorat d'état in Political Science from the University of Paris, I Sorbonne. She is Lecturer in Political Sociology at the Faculty of Law and Political Sciences at St Joseph University, Beirut. She has published articles in French journals on Lebanon and on Syria.

Boutros Labaki is Associate Professor in Economic and Social History of Lebanon and the Arab World and in the Economy and Sociology of Development at the Institut des sciences sociales de l'Université libanaise. His publications include *Introduction à l'histoire économique du Liban* (1984), and several contributions to collective works. He is currently writing a book on the economy of the Lebanese migration.

Antoine Nasri Messarra is Professor at the Lebanese University. He is the author of three books on Lebanon published by the Lebanese University Press. *Approche comparative du système politique libanais: la société post-communautaire* is currently in preparation.

Joseph Abou Nohra is currently Professor of Modern History of Lebanon at the Lebanese University's Faculty of Letters. He is a founder member and Secretary of the Lebanese Association for Ottoman Studies.

Ghassan T. Raad is Assistant Professor of International Relations and Political Science at the Lebanese University, and Research Associate at the Institute of Strategic Studies for Peace in Lebanon. He was Visiting Fellow at the Center for International Development and Conflict Management, University of Maryland.

Kamal Salibi is Professor of History at the American University of Beirut. He is the author of several books, including *Crossroads to Civil War: Lebanon 1958–1976* (1976) and *The Bible Came From Arabia* (1985). His most recent books are *Secrets of the Bible People* (1988) and *A House of Many Mansions: the History of Lebanon Reconsidered* (1988). From January until June 1988 he was Visiting Fellow at the Centre for Lebanese Studies.

Raghid Solh is a free-lance writer on Arab affairs. He received a D.Phil. from St Antony's College, Oxford, in October 1986.

John Spagnolo is Professor of History at Simon Fraser University. He received an MA from the American University of Beirut and holds a D.Phil. from Oxford. He is the author of *France and Ottoman Lebanon, 1861–1914* (1977).

Acknowledgements

It was a challenge to produce this volume on time and it would not have been possible without the help of many people, of whom we can only mention a few.

Margaret Owen has our deepest gratitude for editing the French papers and keeping to our hectic schedule with good humour and patience. Special thanks to Jonathan Livingstone who survived all our demands with good spirit. His help in the production of the book was invaluable. To John Cooper our thanks for keeping to a tight schedule for the typesetting.

Many thanks also to Anne Enayat, whom we often consulted on the politics and economics of publishing; Nabil Beyhum, who was our co-ordinator in France; Catherine Secretan, for typing the French manuscripts; and Chibli Mallat, for his help with proof-reading. Lavinia Brandon oversaw the co-ordination of the project from its inception as a conference.

Foreword

To re-examine and reassess a historical process can be particularly important in times of crisis. For those who are concerned with the tragedies and future of Lebanon, such a reappraisal is essential, because the events of the years since 1975 inevitably pose the question of whether the view of Lebanese history which had generally been held until then can any longer be accepted.

Until the outbreak of the civil war, it was customary to think of the modern history of Lebanon as the history of a success, even of a triumph. Gradually over the centuries, it was believed, there had developed a social and political order in Lebanon within which members of different communities, separated as they were by inherited beliefs and traditions, could live together in peace, amity and co-operation. The order had broken down in the three decades between 1830 and 1860, because of a combination of internal and external factors, but had then been restored in more explicit form: the traditional symbiosis became embodied in formal institutions, first those of the *mutasarrifiyya* and then those of the Lebanese republic.

The last years, however, have witnessed a spectacular breakdown of the civil order, once more because of internal and external factors, and inevitably this has raised new questions. Is discord rather than harmony the normal state of relations between the different communities? Was the apparent harmony of an earlier period illusory? Why did it come to an end, and what are the conditions that will restore it?

The papers in this volume are the outcome of a conference organized by the Centre for Lebanese Studies in Oxford in September 1987. The aim of the conference was to investigate the nature, causes and limits of the alternations of harmony and breakdown (or of apparent harmony and apparent breakdown) in the history of Lebanon from 1830 to 1975. The first date was chosen because it marks the beginning of the Egyptian occupation of Lebanon and the surrounding region, and the active interest of the European powers in them; the beginning of the civil war was taken as the terminal date, although some of the writers have found it necessary to look at more recent events.

The chapters have been written by historians, social scientists and other specialists in Lebanese matters. No attempt has been made to treat all aspects of the subject comprehensively, and the book should be seen as a historical introduction to the complexities of the Lebanese problem.

The Centre for Lebanese Studies, by organizing the conference, hopes to have contributed to the process of rethinking which is inevitable in difficult periods such as the one Lebanon is experiencing.

Albert Hourani
Nadim Shehadi

LEBANON: A History of Conflict and Consensus

INTRODUCTION

The Historical Perspective

KAMAL SALIBI

In the historical study of modern Lebanon, it would be useful to keep a number of matters in mind.

First, the modern history of Lebanon has been studied considerably more than the history of most other parts of the Eastern Arab world during the same period. There is an advantage and a disadvantage in this. The advantage: many details regarding the last two centuries of the Lebanese past have been thoroughly researched time and again, and the available knowledge of the subject, though still somewhat uneven, is extensive. The disadvantage: because not as much detail is known about the history of other parts of the Arab East during the same centuries, one often tends to study modern Lebanese history without adequate regard to the regional perspective.

Second, the concept of Lebanon as a historical country has been a highly controversial one ever since the State of Greater Lebanon, which is today the Lebanese Republic, was created within the present borders in 1920. Here again, there are advantages and disadvantages. The principal advantage: the controversy over the historicity of Lebanon has provided much of the incentive for the study of the Lebanese past. The principal disadvantage: the same controversy has frequently tended to make Lebanese history a subject of polemics rather than of proper scholarly investigation.

Third, the precise definition of what constitutes Lebanese history, inclusively and exclusively, is not easy. In all living history, one studies the past with a view to gain better insight into the present. Consequently, the past can often be given attributes of the present which do not legitimately belong to it. In the case of Lebanon, we have a country which did not come into political existence as a territorial state until 1920. Before that time, there was a political entity called Mount Lebanon which was constituted as a privileged administrative unit of the Ottoman empire under international guaranty; but this *mutasarrifiyya* of Mount Lebanon, as it was called, had no existence before 1861. Earlier on, 'Mount Lebanon', or 'the Lebanon', was a geographical expression which did not acquire internationally recognized political usage until the 1830s. This point is pertinent in a special way to the subject of the present conference on conflict and consensus in Lebanon between 1830 and 1975. What is involved, at least to some degree, are two different subjects: one relating to the old Mount Lebanon; and the other to the present Greater Lebanon. And the two are not the same thing. There is certainly a connecting thread between the two subjects. It is important, however, to determine precisely the nature of this connecting thread, if one is to remain on firm historical ground.

Fourth, when speaking historically of Lebanon, past or present, it is worth bearing in mind that one is not speaking necessarily of one historical script relating to a fully coherent body of territory and population. To a great extent, one is speaking of a number of separate and distinct scripts which happen to have been played historically on the same stage: sometimes independently; sometimes in conjunction with one another. Each of these various Lebanese scripts belongs to a different historical territory or community, has a special theme, tells a special story, and demands full recognition for what it is on its own, before it is related to the others. Lebanese history, in short, does not have one story line; nor is it a saga or epic consisting of a succession of episodes relating to the same general motif. Rather, it is more like a novel: a highly complex narrative with a contrapuntal structure in which different motifs intrude from different directions at different points to fuse into a whole, each motif reasserting its individuality time and again in the process of the fusion.

One might indicate a fifth point in this connection. Had Lebanon not been in existence today, there would not have been such a thing as Lebanese history. There would have been, of course, a number of historical subjects relating to the present Lebanese territory which could attract antiquarian interest among specialists: for example, the history of local religious communities such as the Maronites and the Druzes; or the history of the local administrative developments—the government of the Ma'an and Shihab amirs; the Dual *qa'imaqamiyya* (*qa'imaqamiyyatan*); the *mutasarrifiyya*—fitting within the broader context of the history of Ottoman administrative irregularity. It is only because Lebanon does exist today that whatever happened on its territory in the past which bears on the present, or which helps explain this present, acquires living significance and becomes understandable and valid as Lebanese history.

What all this means is the following: in studying the history of Lebanon, as in studying any history, or any other subject for that matter, one ought to be fully aware of precisely what one is doing.

Otherwise, there is bound to be confusion. The realities of history are by their very nature elusive, and they become even more intractable when historians do not know exactly what they are searching for. When we study living history, we not only search for knowledge of what actually happened in the past; we also try to understand relationships between different situations of the past, and most important of all, relationships between the past and the present. The records will not tell us what these relationships are. We have to speculate about them as best we can; and in speculation, no two people can be of exactly the same mind. This is why different interpretations of the same historical subject are always possible.

Before we try to determine the main line of historical connection between the old Mount Lebanon and the present Greater Lebanon, it is important to consider how what today we call Lebanese history fits into the general context of the modern history of the Arab world. To keep the subject manageable for the present purpose, we might arbitrarily keep Egypt and North Africa out of the picture. This leaves us with the following sketch.

In the nineteenth century, the Ottoman state was making determined efforts to maintain the integrity of its territory by tightening its grip, particularly on the Syrian, Mesopotamian and Arabian provinces which still formed part of the Islamic core of the Ottoman empire. At the same time, European powers were encroaching on the lands of the Arab East from every direction. Britain nibbled at Arabia, where by gradual stages between 1819 and 1916 a system of British protectorates of varying forms came to be established all the way from the mouth of the Red Sea to the northern end of the Persian Gulf. From another direction, Britain and France intervened as rivals in the affairs of Ottoman Syria. Other Western powers were no less avid to gain political access to all these regions. And wherever there was a European intrusion of any kind, no matter how directly successful or unsuccessful, a process of local political developments was set in motion. The social raw material for these developments was nowhere actually created by the intervening European powers, or by the Ottomans who tried to stop or contain the foreign interventions. In every case, this raw material already existed, its different elements fused in one combination or another: tribes locked in traditional hostilities; local potentates coveting one another's territories, yet all equally concerned to perpetuate their individual autonomies, angling for ways and means to stay in power; religious and ethnic minorities in different regions living in obsessive fear of majorities and nervously searching for security; parochial merchant establishments anxious to promote their commercial interests; traditional local economies disrupted by the impact of the industrial economy of Western Europe;

interlopers seeking protection for whatever dubious enterprise they
were engaged in, and prepared to place their services at the disposal of
whoever was willing to protect them. In every case, there were
sufficient political and social ingredients to create a potential for
conflict; and this potential was exploited by the Ottomans from one
direction, and by the European powers from another. The circumstances almost invited exploitation.

To this extent, the history of Mount Lebanon in the nineteenth
century was not much different in its broad lines from other Arab
stories of the same period. In it one finds most of the elements just
alluded to. From the outside, there was Western intervention colliding
with Ottoman resistance, coupled with a rivalry of interests within the
ranks of the Western intervention. On the inside, there were
Maronites and Druzes behaving as tribes and eyeing one another with
atavistic hostility; Christians feeling insecure as a minority in
overwhelmingly Islamic surroundings and searching for ways and
means to feel more secure; a variety of social tensions arising from
accelerating economic change; individuals here and there with
personal ambitions, out for adventure; and at the same time, a
tradition of local political and administrative privilege within the
Ottoman system which had become particularly meaningful to the
Christians, and more particularly to the Maronites, who sought to
perpetuate and enhance it for their own interests, without much regard
for the Druzes.

The potential for conflict existed and was open to external
exploitation; therefore, it was exploited. We need not go into more
detail at the present moment: keeping the main lines of the story in
mind will be sufficient. Once the internal conflict in Mount Lebanon
reached the point where it became counter-productive to the interests
of the external parties concerned, a settlement was imposed, with
guarantees to make it work. The outcome was the Lebanese
mutasarrifiyya.

After the destruction of the Ottoman empire with the end of the
first world war, Britain and France were able to redraw the political
map of the Eastern Arab world. In a number of cases, new countries
which had no earlier historical existence in any recognizable form were
created virtually from scratch. In other cases, traditional tribal or
regional autonomies were preserved which ultimately emerged as
states. The case of Lebanon lay somewhere in between. The State of
Greater Lebanon which emerged in 1920 was a created one, in the
sense that it represented no actual continuity of structural institutions
from the preceding period. On the other hand, there was a continuity
of a different kind. The historical territory of the Lebanese
mutasarrifiyya which was already in existence before the war, and

which approximately conformed to the older historical territory of the Shihab amirs, was preserved to serve as a territorial nucleus for the creation of the new Lebanese state.

In 1861, it was France who had taken the military and political initiative which resulted in the establishment of the *mutasarrifiyya* of Mount Lebanon. The State of Greater Lebanon, in 1920, was created by the same French initiative. Had matters stopped there, the principal historical connection between the old Mount Lebanon and the new Greater Lebanon would have been the continuity of French policy in the area. In the initiative of 1861, however, as in that of 1920, an important indigenous factor was also involved. The French action in both cases was geared to serve the political interests of a particular community of the local population, who were the Maronites. In the case of Greater Lebanon, it was even more than that: the territory of the new Lebanese state was put together by France under Maronite political pressure, and in accordance with a Maronite blueprint which had already been worked out in considerable detail earlier on. It is at this point that the story of modern Lebanon begins to differ from other Arab stories and acquire a special character.

In the story of modern Lebanon, the principal line of historical continuity between the Mount Lebanon of the nineteenth century and the Greater Lebanon of the twentieth, certainly at the internal political level, was the Maronite connection. And the Maronites were not a restricted establishment such as a dynasty. They were a community with a sense of special identity, composed of individuals and groups of various kinds but sufficiently disciplined to act on certain issues as a political body working systematically to achieve common aspirations. Lebanon already existed in the Maronite imagination before it became a political reality. To understand the historical nature of modern Lebanon, one must begin with the Maronites, because it was the Maronites who wanted to have Lebanon in the first place. What applies to Lebanon in this respect does not apply in the same way to other Arab situations. This statement involves an oversimplification. For the moment, however, it will be useful to oversimplify in order to grasp the essentials.

This conference is concerned with conflict and consensus in Lebanon. The subject commands our attention today because Lebanon is now in a state of conflict which awaits resolution; and it is strongly felt that the only way this conflict can be resolved without the country being destroyed is by some form of consensus. We intend to treat the subject historically because we recognize that the present conflict in Lebanon has historical antecedents. There is something else, however, that needs to be recognized. In every conflict situation that is historically related to present-day Lebanon, one thing was constant: the Maronites invariably represented one of the two sides involved. Again we will have to simplify in order to understand; so we may begin by attempting to reduce the historical information we have in our hands into a skeletal model. Subsequently, we can put this model to the test to discover the degree to which it is valid.

First, we have the territory of present-day Lebanon. On this territory we have a population composed of different communities, among them the Maronites. Each of these communities has a special sense of identity and set of loyalties, and some among them are better organized than others. The Maronites, however, differ from the rest because they represent a concentration of organized social energy focusing on a specific aim. The Maronites have a political programme. They want to see things happen in a particular way in the territory they inhabit. The problem is, they do not inhabit this territory alone; so their political programme impinges on other parties and provokes reactions whenever it is activated. In the nineteenth century, the Maronite political programme only involved the Christian-Druze territory of Mount Lebanon, where the reaction to it, when it was activated, came from the Druzes. Later, the Maronite programme came to involve a larger area and other communities, which made things more complex. In both situations, however, the Maronite political programme was the constant, and the reactions to it were the variables.

At this point, we must elaborate a little further. The Maronites, being Christians, conceived of their political programme not only in strictly Maronite terms, but also in broader Christian terms. Sometimes, they even managed to energize other Christians and involve them to some degree in what they did or proposed to do—normally as auxiliaries rather than full associates. Historically, the Maronites had always shared the fears of other Christians of the overwhelmingly Islamic Arab world. As Christians, they had managed to fare remarkably well under Islamic rule; but this only served to whet their political appetite. Moreover, they remained seriously concerned about the future. In Mount Lebanon, as later in Greater Lebanon, they pressed the issue of Christian political security, and this naturally aroused suspicions and feelings of insecurity and apprehension on the Islamic side.

Our model, however, is not complete yet. Before the nineteenth century, the Maronites and other Christian Arabs of Mount Lebanon and the broader neighbourhood had been living in the traditional world of Ottoman Syria. There were influences from the West at the time, but they were limited. With the nineteenth century, these Western influences became virtually irresistible, and changes began to occur. The Christian communities on the present Lebanese territory—and we shall restrict ourselves to this territory, to keep sight of our model—were naturally more receptive to the Western influences than the Islamic communities, so they changed faster. As a result, social and cultural disparities between the Christians and the Muslims developed, which further complicated the situation.

Something more must be added here. The Western influences which began to produce changes in Ottoman Syria in the nineteenth century were not only social, economic and cultural. Behind them stood the political and military might of the West, which made a great deal of difference. On the one side, it gave the local Christians the feeling that they had strong backing, so their demands for political security were pressed harder. On the other side, it made the Muslims increasingly apprehensive and suspicious of the Christians. After the destruction of the Ottoman empire, the West arrived in the area in full force, and the Christian–Muslim tensions were compounded. On the Christian side, the Maronites from the very beginning were the most indiscreet in seeking political support from the West for what they wanted to achieve. This made their political programme—and more so its success—appear all the more obnoxious from the general Islamic point of view. There were also many Christians who were apprehensive about it, because they feared it would ultimately prove counter-productive to the general Christian interest. Once the direct Western presence in the Arab world began to taper off after the second world war, the Maronite political achievement in Lebanon became the target for concerted attack.

We must stop to consider something else. Inhabited territories do not become countries unless certain conditions are met. These conditions, as in the case of Lebanon, involve concentrations of organized social energy building up to the critical level where political precipitations can take place. The agency for the buildup of the social energy required for such precipitation varies from one situation to another. It can be an individual of special charisma and ambition who lives long enough; a conclave or caucus of some kind; a tribal or regional dynasty; a clerical establishment; a party or a gang; a community of economic interests; or any combination of such elements.

To achieve its ultimate end, which is the transformation of a territory and a population into a country or state, the active agency, at some point, has to destroy existing social loyalties which are incompatible with the requirements of the state. It has to break the eggs to make the omelette. This can be achieved with relative facility when the agency is in a position to claim that it represents a common interest, because the population on which it acts happens to be sufficiently homogeneous. The same end cannot be achieved as easily when the active agency is in no position to make such a claim, because the primordial loyalties of the population on which it acts happen to be highly divergent. In such situations, the agency for political development normally emerges out of one loyalty group from which it derives its motive power. Its vision is restricted to the attitudes and interests of the special constituency it represents, so that it starts out with a distinct social disadvantage. Unless it can manage to involve the other constituencies in its political programme on an equal basis, no national vision can build up around this programme, and whatever success is achieved remains highly precarious.

Lebanon presents a pre-eminent case of this kind. Here, since roughly the middle of the last century, the Maronites have known what they wanted for themselves, and have worked systematically towards the achievement of set aims. At any given moment, they could assess political situations for what they were—at the internal, regional and international levels—and manipulate them in one way or another to their advantage. They have consistently maintained specific political aspirations, while the aspirations of other communities with whom they came to be involved tended to be more diffuse, and generally reactive rather than active. The Maronite aspirations did reflect a general Christian interest alongside the narrower Maronite interest. This, in time, made their political programme acceptable more widely as a Christian programme. On the other hand, the required degree of empathy for the sensitivities of the Islamic communities in the country was generally lacking.

On the whole, Christians only understood these Islamic sensitivities at the political level, which was the level at which they were actually expressed. The unarticulated social anxieties and frustrations that lurked behind them were not fully appreciated. The reverse was equally true. The Muslims, by and large, showed little understanding for the fears of the Christians. These Christian fears were not restricted to Lebanon. The Islamic anxieties and frustrations, in their turn, existed all over the Arab world, being of the sort that develops wherever traditional societies find themselves forced to abandon their old ways and accommodate to change. In Lebanon, however, these frustrations and anxieties were highlighted by the glaring imbalance in the accommodations made by the Christians on the one hand, and the Muslims on the other, to the ways of the modern world. Islamic opinion commonly blamed the Christian political programme in the country for this imbalance, which made this programme unacceptable to the Islamic communities as a national one in which they could be fully involved. Moreover, the conviction persisted for a long time that there were in fact alternatives to Lebanon as a state—viewed as being essentially a Christian political achievement—which could serve the interests of the Islamic communities better. It was only as these alternatives began to vanish under changing regional and international circumstances that the worth of the Lebanese political achievement to all the parties concerned started to attract increasing recognition, until all began to demand their rightful shares in it, as is the situation today.

Returning to the subject of the present conference, the history of Lebanon since the 1830s, as I see it, does not present cycles of alternation between conflict and consensus. What it does present, in my view, is a succession of collisions between one organized political force concentrating inexorably on set aims, and running against the general grain, and various other social forces of the grain joining together to form a resistance whenever there was an opportunity for this to happen. There never was a point in the past when the two sides saw the same things in the same way. During the nineteenth century, the Maronite–Druze conflict did not resolve into a consensus. The Druzes were not consulted about the establishment of the Lebanese *mutasarrifiyya*. The Maronites, in a way, were also not consulted. The arrangement was simply imposed on both sides, though initially more to Maronite than Druze political satisfaction. It worked for more than half a century because it was adequately provided with the internal machinery and external guarantees to make it work; not because the Maronites and the Druzes, after two decades of intermittent warfare, decided to bury the hatchet and live together under one government in peace. When Greater Lebanon was created in 1920, only the Maronites were consulted. No other community really was. The Druzes were taken for granted, because they had already been living quietly in the Lebanese *mutasarrifiyya* since 1861, without voicing any special political demands or grievances. The Shi'is at the time were not yet in a position to express an opinion on the matter. Where the Sunnis were concerned, the new Lebanese state was actually created against their declared wishes.

The entente arrived at between the Christians and Muslims of Lebanon in 1943—the *sous-entendu* agreement called the National Pact—did in fact represent a sort of consensus; however, it was a consensus arrived at principally at the level of standing political leaderships, which did not readily reach all the social levels of the Lebanese population. For this reason, if for no other, it remained highly precarious. In 1958, the latent conflict in the country which had been there from the beginning broke out into the open, and an external military and political intervention was needed to resolve it. This time, things were patched up by consultation with all the parties concerned. The outcome was that Maronites and other Christians were left nursing feelings of psychological frustration, because they had grown accustomed to being consulted alone; while the communities on the

Islamic side, partly but not entirely satisfied by their achievement, awaited opportunities to score further psychological triumphs. In 1975, the conflict between the two sides broke out again on a more massive scale, and the same conflict continues to the present moment. External forces have intervened politically or militarily from different directions to resolve it in different ways, in each case to suit a special regional and international concept of what the future of Lebanon ought to be. So far, however, these interventions have only served to compound the internal complexities of the problem.

Whether or not the present conflict in Lebanon will ultimately lead to a Lebanese consensus remains to be seen. One may venture the guess that unless Lebanon is actually removed from the political map of the world, some settlement of the outstanding conflict in the country is bound to come sooner or later, and any such settlement would have to involve some kind of national consensus if it is to last. Certainly, there is no real historical precedent for the sort of consensus that would be needed for a happy ending to the Lebanese story, now that things have reached the point that they have reached. To this extent, history has nothing to say on the matter.

On the other hand, history can explain how Lebanon came to exist, to what extent it succeeded, and to what extent it failed, and why. To resolve the Lebanese question, the realities of Lebanese history would have to be understood and admitted. Lebanon was created by the political ambition of the Maronites. Once it came to exist, however, it did not legitimately belong to the Maronites alone, but also to many other communities: both those who initially wanted it and those who did not. Today all the Lebanese seem to want it, but each community in a different way. This is no real consensus. It is simply a new variation of the old conflict theme.

Actually, the chances of whether Lebanon survives as a country depend on whether or not the Lebanese Republic can break with its history to become truly a commonwealth involving *citizens'* rather than *community* rights. For this to happen, some practical formula must be devised which takes into account the realities of Lebanese society in their full regional perspective, without surrendering to the dictates of these realities where they go beyond the reasonable limits. Historically, modern Lebanon has been to a great degree a Maronite or Christian political experiment which came to involve the Islamic sector of the country more by accident than by design. Nevertheless, the experiment did succeed in bringing Lebanon into existence, and in keeping it going for some time. The point has been reached, however, where this situation cannot continue along the same lines. For Lebanon to be recreated as a commonwealth, a fresh historical departure is needed, initiated by a new concentration of organized social energy transcending the traditional interests and loyalties of diverse communities, and representing a common national vision instead. This, of course, is much easier said than done.

In a commonwealth, the partners would have to participate as equal citizens rather than as members of communities performing traditional roles. People who get accustomed to playing roles according to set scripts do not easily give up the habit, even when it becomes necessary for them to do so. This by itself would make the break with history in Lebanon difficult, let alone the fact that the present Lebanese conflict is not being played out in a closed political arena where no outside participants intervene. Yet, at some point, the difficulties will have to be surmounted and the transition to the commonwealth attempted; otherwise, there can only be a parting of ways in the country, none of them to any predictable destination. When the transition is in fact attempted, and only then, can history finally begin to speak of consensus in Lebanon—not as part of the story of the Lebanese past, but as the only possible theme for a story of Lebanese future. Conflict, it is true, creates more interesting historical reading than consensus; but consensus certainly has the advantage over conflict as a way of life.

1

Rural Collective Action
and the Emergence of Modern Lebanon
A Comparative Historical Perspective

EDMUND BURKE III

The peculiarities of the Lebanese

Until the last decade, scholars tended to see modern Lebanon as a uniquely successful example of modernization in the Middle East, in which sectarian strife had been held at bay by the ability of most Lebanese to compromise for the higher good—and because it was good for business. Thus Lebanon was portrayed as the one successful secular state in the Arab world, the Switzerland of the Middle East.

Beginning in the late 1960s, as the social consequences of the blocked development of the Lebanese state became increasingly evident, this view began to be challenged. A more critical explanation was propounded, in which the Maronite-dominated political stasis was seen as the inevitable result of the manner of Lebanon's incorporation into the capitalist world economy. In this view, the real story is of underdevelopment—of stunted economic growth, blighted political development, and the modernization of tradition. However, the resurgence of religious sectarianism following the civil war of 1975–6 did not match revisionist expectations of the direction of historical change. It also weakened the credibility of non-cultural explanations of the Lebanese historical experience. Instead, explanations that stress a putative Lebanese exceptionalism, and that emphasize the role of endogenous causes in the making of modern Lebanon, are once again in the ascendancy.[1]

Without denying the many evident common features of Lebanese culture and society, modes of explanation that stress 'the peculiarities of the Lebanese' are in some measure unsatisfactory. If what counts is national character, or supposedly innate traits like religious sectarianism and familism, then the scope for historical thinking and social analysis is drastically constrained. However, it is the similarities of the Lebanese experience to that of other Middle Eastern and mediterranean societies that I, as a comparative historian of collective action in the modern Middle East, find particularly striking.[2]

One way to begin to make sense of the Middle Eastern (and Lebanese) experience lies precisely in placing it in comparative historical context. As Barrington Moore Jr and Theda Skocpol have shown, the entry into the modern age of states like France, Russia and China was the occasion of intense rural conflict, which under certain conditions could give rise to social revolutions.[3] Whether they did or not, they argue, the manner in which old agrarian structures were transformed permanently shaped the sort of modern state that emerged in each, and the coalition of forces that would sustain it. Much the same thing is true for Lebanon, and for Middle Eastern societies more generally. Accordingly, I would like to explore some of what would seem to be the central features of Lebanese development in comparative historical perspective, focusing upon the role of rural collective action in the transformation of the Middle East in the long nineteenth century (1750–1919).

Why this concern with agrarian protest? In part, because societies like Lebanon were overwhelmingly peasant societies, in which the weight of rural forces predominated. Imperial efforts to extend control over the countryside from the cities, as Albert Hourani has argued, were limited in their impact until well into the nineteenth century.[4] In agrarian bureaucracies like the Ottoman empire, the study of rural conflict places in sharp relief the chief structural features of the society. In studying social protest, in a sense, we study the society in action.

This paper presents first a survey of the recent literature on agrarian protest in the Middle East, while trying to provide an interpretive framework for understanding the complex processes of change that Middle Eastern societies underwent during the period 1750 to 1919. This is followed by an overview of the literature on rural collective action in the Middle East since 1750, in an attempt to show not only that rural protest was a recurrent feature of modern Middle Eastern history, but also that there were patterns to this protest. Finally, situating the history of rural collective action in modern Lebanon in comparative historical perspective, I will attempt to show that the outcomes of its rural struggles helped shape the political and economic contexts within which local elites operated, and thus the kind of polity that emerged.

Rural collective action: some preliminary considerations

Contrary to prevailing scholarly opinion, peasant rebellions and agrarian protest movements were recurring features of rural politics in the Middle East during the period 1750–1950.[5] The historical literature has emphasized the non-revolutionary character of the Middle Eastern peasantry, stressing the fatalism of peasants and the oppression of corrupt governments and landowners. The elite bias of the sources and orientalist stereotypes about the nature of Islamic societies to a considerable extent account for this view.[6]

Recently there have been signs of the crumbling of this orthodoxy. A survey of rural protest in Egypt and Bilad al-Sham for example, concludes that 'throughout the last 200 years there was no generation which did not witness a fellah rebellion.'[7] Peasant protests were also important in the Maghrib, where their occurrence is somewhat better documented.[8] In some cases, as we shall see, peasant revolts could give rise to challenges to the established agrarian order.

Yet the overall situation is best characterized not by the presence of rural protest, but by its relative absence. The alternation between protest and passivity, it now seems clear, as well as the changing patterns of peasant revolts in the Arab world over the period were both connected to the transformation of the agrarian structures. When and how these changes came about, as well as which groups benefited from them, and which ones suffered, are topics which must be explored in order to understand more fully their genesis.

We are on the threshold of a new understanding of the processes of rural change in the Middle East and North Africa. In part, this is due to the accumulation of new research, which called into question many of the old assumptions about the ways Middle Eastern rural society was transformed.[9] In part, it is due to the significant changes which have occurred in the social science literature on rural society and peasant protest, which has evolved from an infatuation with peasant revolution to a more complex and nuanced grasp of the realities of peasant protest and avoidance.[10] In this paper, it is not possible to do more than sketch in some of the major themes.

Nineteenth-century changes: an interpretive framework

For purposes of analysis, one can say that since 1750 social movements in the Middle East have emerged as a result of the intersection of three main kinds of change. The first was the indigenous self-strengthening movement in the region. Under its aegis the state bureaucracy tried to increase its control over the society; modern armies were established;

and modern schools and methods of communication were developed. In the Ottoman provinces this process was known as the *tanzimat* movement. It inevitably led to a collision between reform-minded state bureaucrats and local elites eager to defend their traditional rights and liberties. The *tanzimat* also stimulated conflict with peasants and artisans, for whom the encroachment of the state was experienced primarily in the form of military conscription and increased taxation.

The incorporation of the Middle East into the world economy stimulated a second and in some ways more far-reaching type of change, which affected even relatively isolated regions with weak states. Its effects, however, were differentially greater upon those societies, such as Egypt and the Arab East, which stood astride major world communications links. Economic incorporation led to the rise of a new urban middle class whose fortunes were linked to Europe, and to the emergence of an urban-based class of landowners engaged in commercial agriculture for export. It also resulted in the decline of artisans and peasants unable to adapt to the changing economic tides. To the fiscal and other pressures of the centralizing state were added, therefore, additional ones based on incorporation in the capitalist world market.

Where the experience of the Middle East diverges from that of Europe and joins that of the rest of the Third World is in the colonial context of its coming to modern politics. The establishment of European hegemony challenged basic cultural values even as it distorted the impact of change in significant ways, and set in motion deeply rooted responses throughout the region. One place to evaluate the extent of Western dominance upon Middle Eastern societies is in its influence on internal processes of political change, where collaboration with imperialism worked to undermine the legitimacy of local elites even as it increased their power. In this ambiguous context, the national struggle tended to take precedence over the class struggle. Thus European dominance shored up the precarious power of old elites, who successfully capitalized upon their position to maintain control of the nationalist movement, and ensured that when new classes made their long-deferred emergence on the political scene after the second world war, their impact would be muffled. This era is only now showing signs of drawing to a close.

Each of these vectors of change worked in favour of certain groups in the society, and against others. Those possessing privileged ties to the state or to European business interests were often in a position to profit disproportionately, while urban artisans and rural agriculturalists found themselves squeezed from all sides. Following the establishment of European political control, groups willing to serve as intermediaries gained substantially, while overt opponents suffered from various forms of political and economic discrimination. The complex sequence of changes thus set in motion intersected with one another, generating powerful cross-currents and back eddies which eroded old established interests and remoulded new ones. Social protest and resistance found fertile ground in the circumstances thus created.

The phases of peasant protest, 1750–1925

In a previous study, I have attempted to sketch the changing patterns of protest across the region in the long nineteenth century.[11] Looking at the changing forms of rural collective action over the period as a whole, one can observe that they tend to correspond to the phases of the transformation of rural society. As the centralization of the state and the commercialization of agriculture progressively undermined the old agrarian society over the nineteenth century, different social solidarities were invoked by insurgents. By the twentieth century, the European drive for political hegemony had increasingly begun to define the forms of protest. At the risk of being schematic, the patterns of rural collective action may be seen to fall naturally into three phases.

The first phase covers the period from the 1750s to the 1840s. In response to the increasing fiscal demands of the state upon the rural populations, a series of revolts broke out in Egypt and Bilad al-Sham (Greater Syria). These began in the 1770s and 1780s in Egypt and Lebanon. Following the establishment of the Muhammad 'Ali regime in 1805 (and comparable regional dynasts in Lebanon and Palestine), there was another wave of peasant uprisings including the 1821 rebellion of peasants in Mount Lebanon, the 1821–3 peasant insurgency in Qina province in Upper Egypt, and other, lesser Egyptian rebellions in the 1820s and 1830s. In Palestine and Syria there were significant uprisings in 1834 and 1837–8 respectively.[12]

A finer-grained analysis than that which is possible here reveals the crucial importance not only of the new, more systematized demands of the Muhammad 'Ali dynasty, but also responses to the commercialization of agriculture; the transformation of landholding arrangements; the increased role of urban money-lenders; and, as has been suggested for the Egyptian rebellions of the 1820s, the decline of rural artisans and craftsmen threatened by the incorporation of hitherto largely autonomous provinces into a national economy linked to the capitalist world economy.[13] The local elites proved to be central in all of these uprisings, in most instances reaching compromises with the established governments that safeguarded their interests, or even increased their control locally.

From the 1840s to the early 1880s a second phase of protest intervened in response to the impact of the commercialization of agriculture and Ottoman self-strengthening movement. A key problem was that there was no security of land tenure anywhere in the region. The system of land rights was based on the enjoyment of usufructuary rights by farmers, and the payment of land rents to various inter-mediaries, with the rest forwarded to the central treasury. As a consequence, surplus revenues were placed in commerce, rather than in land. The changes introduced from the 1840s onwards exploded the old agrarian structures. Private property on the European model was introduced, and the bonds between the cultivator and the land, and the cultivator and the village community were loosened. The old class of tax-farmers was abolished, and in its place a variety of different new social groups emerged, including a class of urban-based absentee landowners in Lebanon and Greater Syria.[14]

By the 1850s the agrarian structures of the Middle East entered a phase of sustained crisis. In several places, especially Lebanon (1858–61), Tunisia (1864–5), and Algeria (1871–2), rebellions broke out which challenged the very basis of the system itself, before they were put down with European assistance.[15] By their scale and radical demands, these mid-century rebellions mark a break with those that had occurred earlier. More significantly, I would argue, their suppression led to the crystallization of the particular coalitions of rural, urban, and state forces within which agricultural development proceeded until the twentieth century.

If we look at the peasant rebellions mid-century, beyond the many obvious differences among them, several common features emerge. One is their opposition to crushing government fiscal impositions and to the intervention of the state and its agents. The increasing ambitions of government, and hence the need for more revenues to pay for them, resulted in a sharply increased tax burden on the peasantry. A second feature is the encroachment on local autonomy of reform-minded governments intent upon developing an efficient provincial administration.

Around 1880, a third phase of rural collective action began which was to last until the 1920s. One of the first indications of the changing patterns of rural insurgency was the 1882 agricultural labour strike that occurred in Sharqiya province in Egypt. Sharecroppers in the district of Zankalun struck against a large landlord and forced him to give up his lease.[16] The old repertoire of peasant protest, based on the traditional Islamic moral economy and defence of local rights gradually disappeared, to be replaced by new forms of social movements keyed to the new market relations: rent strikes, agricultural worker strikes, boycotts, and an epidemic of rural banditry.

These changes signalled the transformation of agrarian relations, and marked the beginning of a new phase in the history of the Middle East. For the first time, the state was able to exercise a degree of control over the countryside. With the development of a rural constabulary, the settlement of the nomads, the extension of modern means of communication (railroads and telegraph) into the country-side, and the development of modern property relations, the terrain on which the old struggles were enacted was transformed.[17]

The social movements of the liberal age (1880–1925) reflect not only the tightening grip of state authorities and the heightened pace of economic change, but also the looming shadow of the West. A key feature of this period was an experimentation with new forms and ideologies of collective action. Increasingly, the remnants of the old system were bypassed by the emergence of new social groups with distinctively different economic bases, cultural reference points, and social experiences. In the countryside, peasant jacqueries began to give way to rent strikes, and attacks on local estate agents and usurers. Most importantly, as portions of the Arab world came under European domination, experiments with new forms of identity and social cohesion, notably secular nationalism, began to emerge.

Lebanese agrarian change in comparative historical perspective

In the preceding pages, I have argued that while it has been but little recognized, the transformation of Middle Eastern society in the nineteenth century was accompanied by substantial rural conflict. I have also stressed that far from being timeless and unchanging, over the course of the long nineteenth century the forms of rural collective action in the Middle East underwent an important transformation from local peasant jacqueries to large-scale regional insurrections, rent strikes and anti-usurer movements. With certain variations, these patterns can be observed in Lebanon as well.

A central question that runs through much of the writing about Lebanon is whether the course of Lebanese history should be explained primarily as the result of features internal to the society (a weak state, religious sectarianism, familism, and the persistence of archaic rural structures into the twentieth century); or as the result of the operation upon Lebanese society of external forces which had broadly similar consequences elsewhere in the region. Obviously, in some respects, it is both. Comparative historical analysis has much to offer in attempting to resolve this question, for many of the features of the Lebanese case may be found elsewhere within the Middle Eastern and mediterranean world. In particular, the histories of Sicily and of Kabilya in Algeria offer the example of societies similarly affected by a weak state, familism, endemic peasant protest, archaic agrarian structures, retarded economic development and substantial emigration.

If we look at the patterns of rural conflict in the Lebanon over the nineteenth century in comparative historical perspective, what is most striking is the shifting role of local elites, in response to the gradual expansion of the scale of rural protest, from the 1821 and 1840 *'ammiya* revolts, to the 1858–61 *thawra* (uprising), and to the post-1861 *Règlement* period. In each case, Lebanese local elites played a decisive role in altering or maintaining features of the existing agrarian system. Let us turn to a brief consideration of the history of Lebanese rural collective action.

The first major rural rebellion in modern Lebanese history was the 1821 *'ammiya* uprising. A popularly based movement, the *'ammiya* developed in Maronite districts in response to the extraordinary tax levies by 'Abdullah Pasha, the Ottoman governor of Sidon. Rebellious Maronite peasants, in alliance with members of the Shihab family and elements of the Maronite clergy (including Bishop Yusuf Istfan), were encouraged to elect village representatives (*wakil*s) to act as spokesmen with government authorities. They drew up covenants in which they pledged to remain united against the unjust taxes and to support their representatives.[18] An incipient tension between the quasi-feudal *muqata'ji* amirs and the upper Maronite clergy on the one hand, and the lower clergy and the peasants on the other hand, provided an opportunity for the rebellion to develop. However, because neither the *tanzimat* reforms nor capitalism had yet progressed very far toward undermining the old system, when the rebel coalition splintered, Ottoman authorities were able to work through the *muqata'ji* amirs to re-establish order. The old agrarian structures remained essentially intact.

A second major upsurge of agrarian disturbances occurred in 1840. In the interim, a number of intersecting changes had begun to transform the old society—although their full impact came only in 1858. First, the development of Lebanese silk exports brought prosperity to some rural districts, and helped to weaken economically some of the old *muqata'ji* families. Within the Maronite church, an articulate, popularly recruited lower Maronite clergy had begun to challenge the church hierarchy. Finally, the beginnings of sectarian politics based on assertions of the primacy of religious or communal identity date from this period as well. Increasingly, the move to sectarianism became enmeshed in the growing challenge to the authority of the *muqata'ji*s by peasants and urban merchants.

In 1840 all of this might still have been accommodated. But more than 15 years of Egyptian occupation and fiscal oppression had substantially altered the landscape on which the old system was based. Intensified government control, reorganization of land tenure, and closer integration into the world market sharply increased the incidence of taxation and of government encroachment upon traditional liberties. As in 1821, the rebellion was led by Maronite peasants in alliance with elements of the clergy, but this time also included some *muqata'ji*s, urban notables, and members of other religious communities. They rebelled against excessive government fiscality, as well as against the efforts of the Egyptian administration to disarm the local Maronite population, and to impose the corvée and military conscription.

The outcome of the 1840 *'ammiya* rebellion was shaped by the role of the local elites, both Druze and Maronite amirs, in much the same fashion as in 1821. They also played a key role in dampening the more radical demands of the peasants. The context was however different. Widespread dissatisfaction with Egyptian rule merged with other sources of discontent to produce a more explosive situation. It occurred against the background of an abortive Druze revolt against the Egyptian authorities in 1839, which had been suppressed with the support of some Maronite amirs, and the shifting economic balance between the two communities in the interim period. Property disputes between the two groups, and the defiant political stance of the Maronite elite, further exacerbated the situation. Intercommunal violence flared up at Dayr al-Qamar and Zahle in 1841. Inter-ethnic tensions ran high, and were not dispelled until the dispatch of an Anglo-Austrian-Turkish expeditionary force in November 1841. The expulsion of the Egyptians and the cooling of social radicalism marked the final phase of the protest.

As in 1821, while divisions in ruling circles fanned the flames of revolt, there were clear limits on how far the peasant rebels were permitted to go. Contesting the rule of the *muqata'ji* amirs was not yet on the agenda. By 1858, however, this situation had changed.[19] The increased integration of Lebanon into the world economy during the 1840s and 1850s as a result of the rise in exports of Lebanese silk through Beirut, gradually undermined the positions of the *muqata'ji* amirs. The position of the old landed class came under increased pressure, especially in districts like Kisrawan where the Khazin amirs ruled over an increasingly fractious peasantry.[20] Significantly, the districts affected by the 1858 revolt were among those most involved in the silk trade.

In the spring of 1858 a rebellion broke out in Kisrawan. Maronite peasants, taking advantage of the political isolation of their Khazin lords, demanded the abolition of feudal exactions and forced obligations such as the corvée. Rebel demands gradually escalated in the succeeding weeks. Symptomatically, however, they did not attempt to expropriate Khazin lands. Instead, their campaign focused upon eliminating feudal privileges. *Shaykh shabab*s, popular local village committees elected by the insurgents, named Taniyus Shahin, a blacksmith, to be their leader. Significantly, the rebels enjoyed the support of younger members of the Maronite clergy, as well as of Christian merchants and money-lenders in Beirut. By early 1860 the revolt had spread to other Maronite districts, as well as to mixed Druze–Maronite villages in Kisrawan. This last development propelled the conflict into a new phase. Alarmed Druze lords, in an effort to preserve their class position and rally the Druze peasantry, presented the fighting as a Maronite threat. Intercommunal fighting soon erupted, with atrocities perpetrated by both sides. The sectarian fighting continued off and on until the dispatch of a joint Ottoman–European expeditionary force in 1861 restored order.

In retrospect, it seems clear that the 1858 uprising was primarily an assault upon the quasi-feudal privileges of the *muqata'ji* class, though it soon evolved in other directions. Initially, the rebels took up arms in defence of the allegedly self-sufficient peasant village, selecting their leaders from among the local elites and better-off peasants, and drafting political demands aimed at forcing a roll back of intrusive government reform measures. But—revolution in the revolution— radical peasants sought to broaden the insurgency into an attack upon the remnants of the old agrarian structures, as well as against government fiscal oppression. As the revolt consolidated its gains, this radicalization lost the rebels the support and sympathy of urban groups. The opposition of the urban landowners and big merchants entailed the opposition, eventually, of the Maronite upper clergy. With these defections, the balance of social forces shifted and the rebellion was repressed.

While the economic crisis provided the window of opportunity for the Kisrawan rebels, the need for a speedy resolution stimulated the involvement of the Beirut-based money-lenders.[21] In some ways, therefore, the contradictions in the old system helped to guarantee this outcome. But as the fighting spread and degenerated into intercommunal violence, the structural limits on an attempted agrarian revolution in Lebanon were underscored. What was different in 1858 from the earlier 'ammiya uprisings was not only the temporary existence of an opening for revolt, but also the changed situation of the local actors. By 1858 the social fracture lines were more deeply etched, and as a result the 1858 movement was a far more significant event.

The abortive 1858–61 Lebanese revolution casts interesting shadows on the changing structure of rural society, and the limitations of rural collective action. While the Khazin amirs were temporarily dispossessed of their lands in Kisrawan, they eventually reclaimed them. Although the 1858 *thawra* overturned feudalism in its administrative/juridical forms, it left intact the social and economic power of the great families in most of Lebanon outside of Kisrawan. The Beiruti money-lenders and would-be capitalists were unable fully to pry open the old agrarian structures to the world market. In the ensuing compromise, the control over the means of violence in the countryside remained in the hands of the great and not-so-great families locally, and reinforced their dominance over the labour market. The *de facto* alliance between Maronite and Sunni leaderships sanctioned by the 1861 *Règlement* crystallized a new status quo, based upon a complicated sharing out of the spoils.[22] Structural tensions were not resolved, just redistributed. In the 1861 settlement, the local agrarian structures retained much of their previous character, and the old families their power. The development of new agrarian relations was thus largely channelled within the old social forms, overlapping them and interpenetrating them.

The 1858–61 events primarily affected the Maronite amirs, leaving the Druze areas largely untouched. International trade furthered the opening of Lebanon in the years that followed, and the silk industry went through a significant transformation. The Druze areas (the Hawran and Jabal Druze) also became more integrated into the world market, though it was for grain production rather than silk that they were known. The expanding administrative power of the state also impinged increasingly. By the 1880s the Ottoman administration was able to intervene even in Jabal Druze, provoking dangerous ripples of opposition. Though muffled and delayed, the social consequences of these changes were soon apparent.

In 1889–90, Druze peasants rose up against their Atrash lords in the last great mid-century rebellion.[23] The Druze peasants, who previously had owned neither their fields nor their homes and could be evicted at will with no compensation, endured undeniably harsh circumstances. In alliance with anti-Atrash clan heads, they managed in 1889 to wrest ownership of the land from their quasi-feudal Atrash overlords. An important and little-studied instance of rural collective action in the pre-1914 Arab East, the 1889–90 revolt resembles the 1858 revolution which led to the abrogation of the legal structures of feudalism in the Maronite districts of Lebanon. The resolution of the conflict, while permitting the untrammelled extension of new relations of production into the heart of the Jabal, in interestingly parallel ways to the 1858 rebellion resulted in recementing the alliance of Druze peasants with their chiefs in opposition to Ottoman policy. As with the 1861 *Règlement* one result of the settlement was to restructure sectarianism into the system.

Lebanon was not the only mountainous mediterranean land to confront the challenge of an explosive agrarian hinterland. In the course of the nineteenth century Sicily also experienced endemic peasant insurrections which challenged the very basis of the system.[24] Primarily a wheat-farming and wine-producing area, Bourbon Sicily had a quasi-feudal system which found itself in difficulty as a result of the abolition of the feudal regime in 1820 and the opening of Sicily to the world market. As in Lebanon, the introduction of steamship navigation drastically altered its competitive position in the world market in the first half of the nineteenth century. Peasant protests flared in 1820, 1837, 1848, 1860, 1866 and 1875. In the conditions of rural insecurity that flourished, massive emigration not surprisingly was a major response, as it had been in Lebanon. Again, as in Lebanon, forms of what the Schneiders have called 'broker capitalism' tended to predominate, rather than more modern forms of capitalism.[25]

The other face of peasant revolt, as Anton Blok observes with reference to Sicily, is the intimidation of peasants who might be tempted to rebel by the landlord's agents, or those of the state. Blok was attempting to explain the sociogenesis of that peculiarly Sicilian institution, the Mafia.[26] Historically, as Blok has shown, mafia was the practical Sicilian remedy for an explosive countryside. The term *mafia* refers to the leaseholders (*gabelloto*) and field guards (*campiere*) who controlled rural estates on behalf of their absentee landowners. (Only later did the term acquire its present connotation of a criminal gang.) If we look at Lebanon through Sicilian spectacles, it is striking the extent to which the countryside was controlled by similar social forces: the Lebanese *zu'ama* (leaders) and *qabadayat* ('tough men'). In Lebanon as in Sicily, the remedy for peasant insurgency was political violence by estate managers and their agents.

Violent political middlemen, in a myriad of social forms, flourished in the niche created between governments which were weak and uncertain of their power, and a restive and rebellious peasantry. Through their control over the means of local coercion, they were able to dominate the countryside into the twentieth century. Through their control over kinsmen, clients and confederates, they were able to dominate the labour market and make themselves indispensable to urban absentee landlords and the state, as their Sicilian counterparts were doing in the same period. The ability of the Lebanese local elites to control the labour force (notably the largely female silk workers) prevented the penetration of the state into the interstices of local society.[27] Following the 1861 *Règlement* rural elites were able to penetrate the emerging state administration in Beirut. As in the Sicilian case, they were able to capitalize upon this to preserve their control by barring the access of rivals to the major patronage networks controlled by the state apparatus. Would-be peasant rebels simply had no opportunity for action with the rural elite firmly in command both in Beirut and in the local arena.

Although violent political middlemen were found from one end of the mediterranean to the other, they thrived in Lebanon, with its intense confessional rivalries, oppressive agricultural system, and weak state. The antidote to an explosive countryside was a repressive local landlord class. The perpetuation of archaic political and social forms is to be understood in this context.

As in Sicily, the viability of the old structures was maintained not only by coercion, but also by the availability of emigration as a safety valve in the explosive countryside. Here we come to the under-studied subject of peasant avoidance protest.[28] If Middle Eastern agrarian structures have managed to preserve the shreds and tatters of the old forms, it is due more to peasant avoidance than to landlord oppression. Again, the Lebanese example is telling. Tens of thousands of Lebanese (3,000 per year from 1860 to 1900) of all sects took the road of voluntary expatriation as the alternative to continued misery in the impacted agrarian setting of their homeland.[29] While the dimensions of the movements of agriculturalists remain largely hidden, we know enough from the fragmentary statistics available on Lebanon to get a sense that it was cumulatively substantial. Much the same process appears to have occurred in Kabylia where the maintenance of archaic structures has been linked historically to massive emigration.[30]

If, unlike the densely settled peasant societies of China and India, the Middle East entered the modern world with a thinly settled countryside, then the dilution of this base by migration is surely an important explanatory variable in determining the patterns of collective action in the region. Violent political middlemen in growing numbers helped police the rural truce. As in these other impacted agrarian settings, the development of large-scale emigration completed the disarming of the agrarian time bomb. Without a sea in which to swim, the fish are easily caught.

The final feature of Lebanese society that requires explanation is religious sectarianism. Although it has often been portrayed as 'natural', in fact like other so-called primordial ties religious sectarianism was historically created. Clearly, it was linked to the emergence of violent political middlemen, rural migration, and the ways the society was restructured following the 1861 settlement. But in what ways? Again, comparative history can be invoked to help explain how this came about. The example of Ireland seems informative, as it has only two major religious communities, Protestant and Catholic—unlike Lebanon with its four major religious groups (Maronite, Druze, Sunni and Shi'i) and numerous minor ones. In neither society does the historical record support the received impression of endless religious strife. Rather, in each, ethnicity has been culturally produced: it has been historically structured as part of the emerging state, as a result of *de facto* ethnic divisions of labour, political arrangements, and the retrospective invention of cultural traditions.

Only in modern times did religious sectarianism become significant in Lebanon and in Ireland. In both societies religious ethnicity became a key marker in the nineteenth century primarily as a result of the kind of state that was created and how it came about.[31] In particular, it may be helpful to view the politicization of ethnicity in the two societies in the context of the parallel quasi-colonial situation of the Maronites and Protestants. The ability of the Maronite elite—clergy, *muqata'ji*s, and merchants—to benefit from French capitulatory status as its privileged local agents, set in motion a process of separate development that culminated by 1914 in the crystallization of a quasi-colonial franco-phone elite, as jealous of its privileges and prerogatives as any Orangeman. In the meantime, Muslims and Druzes were assuming a different (and subordinate) position in the regional economy, and becoming incorporated into the nascent state structures. Despite contrary currents, like the Arab *nahda*, which bound a minority of the chiefly non-Maronite Christian elite to the Muslim minority, it is the evolving *structural* position of the Maronite community as a privileged minority that commands attention. As is argued in some recent studies of the development of sectarianism in Ireland, the overlap of privilege, political allegiance and religion worked to divide Maronites from Druzes and Sunni Muslims.[32] As in Ireland as well, externally brokered solutions to agrarian unrest, like the French-sponsored *Règlement* of 1861, worked to reinforce religious ethnic affiliation as a central political marker.[33] Ultimately, of course, Lebanon was not Ireland. The role of external powers in structuring relations between its communities goes back to Ottoman times and beyond. The *Règlement* and the forms by which power sharing between Druzes and Maronites were worked out structured religious ethnicity into the emerging Lebanese state in its cradle.

The Lebanese case, while by no means typical, reveals many of the basic mechanisms that operated in the transformation of the agrarian structures throughout the Middle East. I have argued that the collision of social forces in peasant protest in Lebanon helped shape the emerging new structures by reinforcing certain societal features, and ignoring others. The transformation of Lebanese rural society was an

uneven process, in which some of the trappings of the old feudal
system were maintained, while the new state structures were
penetrated from the outset by the great families. Because of the
ethnically complex and ecologically varied setting of Lebanon, rural
forces were divided and lacked the power to overturn the system. But
they were occasionally able to force a redistribution of the cards, or a
grudging alteration in the weighting of the elements in the social
balance.

In the end, capitalism, the *tanzimat* reforms, new methods of
communication and new technologies of warfare made possible the
domination of the cities over the countryside for the first time in
modern history. Rural collective action continued to affect the political
evolution of Lebanese society in the twentieth century, although the
patterns it assumed, and the context in which it operated were
decisively different. This, however, is another story.

Notes

1. Samir Khalaf, *Lebanon's Predicament* (New York, 1987). According to Khalaf, the
peculiar pattern of Lebanese development is best explained by the dialectics of tradition and
modernization. However, such views remain firmly rooted in the paradigm of modernization
theory and shed insufficient light on the manner in which the political and economic
structures of modern Lebanon evolved.

2. This paper is derived from my *Making of the Modern Middle East: Protest and Resistance
in the Emergence of Modern Politics* (in progress).

3. Barrington Moore Jr, *Social Origins of Dictatorship and Democracy* (Boston, Mass., 1966) and
Theda Skocpol, *States and Social Revolutions* (Cambridge, 1979).

4. Albert Hourani, 'Political Society in Lebanon: a Historical Introduction', Papers on
Lebanon no. 1, Centre for Lebanese Studies, Oxford, 1986, p. 5.

5. See for example the work of Gabriel Baer, notably his 'Fellah rebellion in Egypt and the
Fertile Crescent', *Fellah and Townsman in the Middle East* (London and Totowa, NJ, 1982).
For Baer and Haim Gerber, *The Social Origins of the Modern Middle East* (Boulder, Co.,
1987), the 1858 Kisrawan rebellion was the unique example of an authentic peasant revolt in
the region. However, neither shows much awareness of recent research on peasant protest,
and both take their models of rural collective action from a misreading of the European
(especially French) experience.

6. For a summary and critique of this literature, see Bryan S. Turner, *Marx and the End of
Orientalism* (London, 1978).

7. Gabriel Baer, 'Fellah rebellion'.

8. See for example Muhamed Cherif, 'Les mouvements paysans dans la Tunisie du xixe
siècle', *Revue de l'Occident musulman et de la Méditerrannée* 30 (1980); Peter Von Sivers,
'Rural uprisings as political movements in early colonial Algeria (1851–1914)', in Edmund
Burke III and Ira M. Lapidus eds, *Islam, Politics and Social Movements* (Berkeley, 1988);
and Edmund Burke III, *Prelude to Protectorate in Morocco: Precolonial Protest and Resistance,
1860–1912* (Chicago, Ill., 1976).

9. See, among others, Charles Issawi, *An Economic History of the Middle East and North
Africa* (New York, 1982); Roger Owen, *The Middle East in the World Economy* (London,

1981); Tarif Khalidi ed., *Land Tenure and Social Transformation in the Middle East* (Beirut, 1984); and Lucette Valensi, *Fellahs tunisiens* (Paris and The Hague, 1977).

10. Joel Migdal, *Peasants, Politics and Revolution* (Princeton, NJ, 1974); Jeffery Paige, *Agrarian Revolution* (New York, 1975); Samuel Popkin, *The Rational Peasant* (Berkeley, Calif., 1979); James Scott, *The Moral Economy of the Peasant* (New Haven, Conn., 1976).

11. See my 'Changing patterns of peasant protest in the Middle East, 1750–1950', presented at the annual meeting of the Middle East Studies Association (November, 1986).

12. Gabriel Baer, 'Fellah rebellion'.

13. On the Egyptian rebellions, see Gabriel Baer, 'Submissiveness and revolt of the fellah', in his *Studies in the Social History of Modern Egypt* (Chicago, Ill., 1973), pp. 93–108. Also Fred H. Lawson, 'Rural revolt and provincial society in Egypt, 1820–1824', *IJMES* 13.2 (1981) 131–53; and Judith Tucker, *Women in Nineteenth Century Egypt* (Cambridge, 1985), ch. 4.

14. For a summary of our present understanding, see Roger Owen, *The Middle East in the World Economy, 1800–1914* (London, 1981). Also Dominique Chevallier, 'Western development and Eastern crisis in the mid-nineteenth century: Syria confronted with the European economy', in W. R. Polk and Richard Chambers eds, *The Beginnings of Modernization in the Middle East* (Chicago, Ill., 1968), pp. 205–22.

15. There is a voluminous literature on the Kisrawan rebellion. See, among others, Dominique Chevallier, 'Aux origines des troubles agraires libanais', *Annales E.S.C.* 14 (1959) 35–64. Also Abdallah Hanna, *Qadiyat al-zira'iyyah wa-harakat al-fallahiya fi Suriya wa-Lubnan, 1820–1920*; Malcolm Kerr, *Lebanon in the Last Years of Feudalism, 1840–1868* (Beirut, 1959); Yeheshua Porath, 'The peasant revolt of 1858–61 in Kisrawan', *Asian and African Studies* 2 (1966) 77–157; and I. M. Smilianskaya, *Al-harakat al-fallahiya fi lubnan* (Beirut, 1972).

On Tunisia, the 1864 rebellion is treated by Bice Slama, *L'Insurrection en 1864 en Tunisie* (Tunis, 1967). See also the articles of Mohamad Cherif, notably his 'Expansion européenne et difficultés tunisiennes de 1815 à 1830', *Annales E.S.C.* 25.3 (1970) 714–45; and Lucette Valensi, *Fellahs tunisiens: l'économie rurale et la vie des campagnes* (Paris, 1977).

The Algerian rebellion of 1871 is analysed by Charles-Robert Ageron, *Les Algériens musulmans et la France*, 2 vols (Paris, 1968). Also Louis Rinn, *Histoire de l'insurrection de 1871* (Algiers, 1891); and Col. N. Robin, *L'Insurrection de la Grande Kabylie en 1871* (Paris [1901]).

16. Gabriel Baer, 'Submissiveness and revolt', p. 101.

17. On the development of Ottoman provincial administration, Andrew Gould, 'Pashas and brigands: Ottoman provincial reform and its impact upon the nomadic tribes of southern Anatolia, 1840–1885', Ph.D. thesis (unpublished), University of California, LA, 1973. On the settlement of nomads, see Norman N. Lewis, *Nomads and Settlers in Syria and Jordan, 1800–1980* (Cambridge, 1987); on the land question, see the articles by Peter Sluglett and Marion Farouk-Sluglett, Albertine Jwaideh, Abdul-Karim Rafeq and Michael Gilsenan, in Tarif Khalidi ed., *Land Tenure and Social Transformation in the Middle East* (Beirut, 1984).

18. These have been analysed by Ilya Harik, *Politics and Change in a Traditional Society, Lebanon, 1711–1845* (Princeton, NJ., 1968), pp. 213–14.

19. Recently we have learned a great deal about the ways by which 'the Lebanon that was' was transformed, and at what cost. Studies of the impact of the silk industry upon the making of modern Lebanon include most notably, the work of Dominique Chevallier, *La Société du Mont Liban à l'époque de la révolution industrielle en Europe* (Paris, 1971). See also Toufik Touma, *Paysans et institutions féodales chez les Druzes et les Maronites du Liban du XVII siècle à 1914*, 2 vols (Beirut, 1971); and more recently Boutros Labaki, *La Soie dans l'économie du Mont Liban*, 2 vols (Paris, 1979).

20. Recent research helps us trace the material origins of the 1858 revolution. For a summary see Axel Havemann, *Rurale Bewegungen im Libanongebirge des 19. Jahrhunderts* (Berlin, 1983), and Porath, 'The peasant revolt'. Also Roger Owen, *The Middle East*, ch. 5;

Abdullah Hanna, *Qadiyat al-zira'iyyah*; Rick Joseph, 'The material origins of the Lebanese conflict of 1860', B.Litt. thesis (unpublished), Oxford; and Paul Saba, 'The development and decline of the Lebanese silk industry', B.Litt. thesis (unpublished), Oxford.

21. On this see the theses of P. Saba and R. Joseph, op. cit.

22. On this period see John Spagnolo, *France and Ottoman Lebanon, 1861–1914* (London, 1977). See also Mohammad Said Kalla, 'The role of foreign trade in the economic development of Syria, 1831–1914', Ph.D. thesis (unpublished), American University, 1969; Leila Fawaz, *Merchants and Migrants in Nineteenth Century Beirut* (Cambridge Mass., 1983).

23. On the rebellion see David McDowell, *The Druze Revolt, 1925–1927, and its Background in the Late Ottoman Period*, B.Litt. thesis (unpublished), Oxford. Also Shakeeb Salih, 'The British–Druze connection and the Druze rising of 1896 in the Hawran', *Middle Eastern Studies* 13 (1977) 251–7; and Linda Schatkowski-Schilcher, 'Violent confrontations in rural Syria of the 1890s', paper presented at the annual meetings of the Middle East Studies Association, November 1986.

24. On Sicily see Roderick Aya, *The Missed Revolution: the Fate of Rural Rebels in Sicily and Southern Spain, 1840–1950*, Papers on European and Mediterranean Societies no. 3 (Amsterdam, 1975), and Anton Blok, 'Mafia and peasant rebellion as contrasting factors in Sicilian latifundism', *European Journal of Sociology* 10 (1969) 95–116.

25. Jane Schneider and Peter Schneider, *Culture and Political Economy in Western Sicily* (New York, 1976).

26. Anton Blok, *The Mafia of a Sicilian Village* (New York, 1974).

27. See Owen, *The Middle East*, and Akram Khater, 'Silk, shaykhs, peasants and merchants: the impact of silk production on the society of Mount Lebanon in the 19th century', MA thesis (unpublished), University of California, Santa Cruz, 1986.

28. On avoidance protest, see the special issue of *The Journal of Peasant Studies* 13/2 (1986): 'Everyday forms of peasant resistance in south-east Asia'. Also Michael Adas, 'Market demand vs. imperial control: colonial contradictions and the origins of agrarian conflict in south and southeast Asia', in E. Burke ed., *Global Crises and Social Movements: Artisans, Peasants, Populists and the World Economy* (Boulder Co., 1988), pp. 89–116; and James C. Scott, *Weapons of the Weak: Everyday Forms of Peasant Resistance* (New Haven, Conn., 1985).

29. Boutros Labaki, 'L'Emigration libanaise en fin de période Ottomane', *Hannon* 19 (1987) 7–32. Also Kemal Karpat, 'The Ottoman emigration to America, 1860–1914', *IJMES* 17.2 (1985) 175–209; and Elie Safa, *L'Emigration libanaise* (Beirut, 1976).

30. On Algeria, see Pierre Bourdieu, *The Algerians* (Boston, Mass., 1962) and *Esquisse d'une théorie de la pratique* (Paris and Geneva, 1972).

31. See Kamal Salibi, *A House of Many Mansions* (London, 1988), for a magisterial elucidation of this process.

32. Michael Macdonald, *Children of Wrath: Political Violence in Northern Ireland* (Cambridge, 1986), and Katherine O'Sullivan, *First World Nationalisms: Class and Ethnic Nationalisms in Northern Ireland and Quebec* (Chicago, Ill., 1986). Also Samuel Clark, *Social Origins of the Irish Land War* (Princeton, NJ, 1979).

33. Khalaf, *Lebanon's Predicament*, esp. ch. 3.

2

L'Evolution du système politique libanais dans le contexte des conflits régionaux et locaux (1840–1864)

JOSEPH ABOU NOHRA

The dramatic set of circumstances in Lebanon, which has lasted for almost 13 years, is oddly evocative of the troubled years of the nineteenth century. An examination of the historical evolution of the country reveals the close connection between its political and religious destinies which contributed, during the last century, to the elaboration of the confessionalism of the Dual *qa'imaqamiyya* (*qa'imaqamiyyatan*) and of the *mutasarrifiyya*.

In the first half of the nineteenth century, a series of demographic, social and political evolutions had already made its mark on the regime of the emirate; the effect on Lebanon, with regard to the development of its community structure and the formation of its political spirit, was profound: a large demographic shift—the Maronites as opposed to the Druzes; emigration of Christians to the Mountain; Christian expansion in the Druze regions; conversion to Christianity by the ruling Shihab family and the great Druze family of Abi Lama'; weakening of feudal links in favour of community allegiance; the anti-Druze policy of the two amirs, Bashir II and Bashir III, and its inauspicious consequences; the Egyptian conquest of Syria and the beginning of the Druze–Maronite struggle; far-reaching social transformations among the Maronites and the feudal conservatism of the Druzes; intervention by the European powers who incited internal dissension under the pretext of protecting one or another religious community.

Because of the internal conflicts and the external interference, Lebanon experienced its first civil war in 1841; this cost the abolition of the emirate and the loss of autonomy. The Sublime Porte removed Amir Bashir III from office and declared the direct attachment of Lebanon to the Ottoman administration with 'Umar Pasha as governor-general.

The unity of the Mountain was susequently destroyed by the adoption of the Dual *qa'imaqamiyya* which was, originally, a Turko-European, not a Lebanese, idea.

A second armed conflict between Maronites and Druzes in 1845 gave the Porte another opportunity to intervene and modify the Dual *qa'imaqamiyya*: the reforms of Shakib Efendi made the *wali* of Sidon the effective governor of the Mountain.

The third conflict of 1860 ended in intervention by the European powers who passed a special statute for Mount Lebanon. The unity of the Mountain was re-established by the *Règlement Organique* of 1861 and the Protocol of 1864, but Mount Lebanon was governed from then on by a *mutasarrif*.

Thus, in the nineteenth century, the fate of Lebanon was bound up with that of the
Great Powers. In their cupidity they confronted each other in the tiny arena of
Lebanon and cultivated internal dissensions which placed in peril the unity of the
Lebanese people and the integrity of their territory.

Le Liban, montagne refuge pour des minorités persécutées en Orient,
a abrité dans ses vallées profondes et ses versants escarpés,
des communautés chrétiennes et musulmanes en quête de liberté.
Une société pluricommunautaire s'est constituée dans son espace géographique restreint où les relations harmonieuses se sont parfois
transformées en affrontements conflictuels à dimensions locales et
internationales.

L'histoire du Liban au milieu du dix-neuvième siècle montre bien
que les conflits intercommunautaires n'ont jamais abouti à la victoire
définitive d'une des parties en cause. Vu l'équilibre de forces entre les
différentes communautés, une telle victoire n'est possible qu'avec
l'appui d'une puissance externe qui n'interviendrait que pour assurer
ses propres intérêts aux dépens de l'unité du Liban et de sa
souveraineté. L'évolution historique du pays révèle l'intime connexion
qui unit ses destins politiques et religieux, et qui a contribué, au siècle
dernier, à l'élaboration des statuts confessionnels des deux *qa'imaqamiyya (qa'imaqamiyyatan)* et de la *mutasarrifiyya*.[1]

Après un aperçu rapide sur la situation intérieure du pays
jusqu'au milieu du dix-neuvième siècle, sur la politique de la Sublime
Porte et l'intervention européenne dans ce qu'il est convenu d'appeler
'l'héritage de l'Homme Malade', nous étudierons l'évolution du
régime politique libanais dans le contexte des conflits internes et de la
concurrence européenne en Orient.

L'Autonomie du Mont-Liban à l'intérieur
de l'Empire ottoman

Depuis la conquête ottomane au début du seizième siècle, le
Mont-Liban a joui d'une autonomie administrative à l'intérieur de
l'Empire. Après sa victoire sur les Mamlouks en 1516, le sultan Selim
1er confirma aux chefs locaux de la Montagne les privilèges
traditionnels dont ils avaient joui sous les Mamlouks, tout en donnant
aux émirs Maan une prééminence de fait et de droit par rapport aux
autres membres de l'aristocratie féodale.[2] C'est ainsi que s'est
instaurée une autonomie administrative coutumière qui a permis aux
Libanais de poursuivre leur vie communautaire dans le cadre du
régime de l'émirat, sous l'autorité de leurs seigneurs.

A la tradition d'autonomie interne dont jouissait le Mont-Liban, appelé à l'époque 'Montagne des Druzes', s'est ajoutée une volonté de vivre ensemble entre Druzes et Maronites, amorcée sous le gouvernement de Fakhreddine II Maan (1590–1633). C'est la première fois dans l'histoire de l'Orient que deux communautés de religion différente s'entendent pour former une patrie.[3]

En 1697, les émirs Chehab ont succédé aux émirs Maan dans le gouvernement de la Montagne. Leur choix a été fait par une assemblée de notables libanais, tenue à Simqaniyya après le décès de l'émir Ahmad Maan, mort sans descendant mâle. Grâce à leur influence auprès des pachas de Tripoli et de Sidon, les émirs Chehab arrivèrent graduellement à unifier la Montagne et à lui conserver son autonomie.[4]

A la première moitié du dix-neuvième siècle, le régime politique de l'émirat reposait encore sur la féodalité qui, malgré des similitudes avec le système seigneurial de l'Occident, portait des contours particuliers. Le fait essentiel qui caractérisait la féodalité libanaise c'est qu'elle n'avait pas connu le servage tel qu'il existait en Occident. Au Mont-Liban, le métayer n'était pas rivé à la terre qu'il cultivait pour le compte du propriétaire. D'ailleurs, beaucoup de paysans de la Montagne jouissaient de la pleine propriété foncière et cultivaient leur propre terre.

Etant propriétaires, les paysans payaient, de ce fait, l'impôt foncier (*miri*) et se sentaient directement concernés par la gérance des affaires de l'émirat, puisqu'ils contribuaient à en assurer les deniers publics.

En effet, la paysannerie libanaise a fait preuve, sous le régime de l'émirat, d'un éveil politique assez poussé, qui était de nature à empêcher le despotisme des chefs locaux ou celui de l'émir gouverneur. La répartition du pouvoir entre les mains des chefs locaux qui jouissaient d'une égalité relative, a créé des conditions favorables au changement politique. Ce changement n'a pas été opéré au sommet de la pyramide féodale, mais il s'est fait, le plus souvent, au niveau de la masse paysanne qui donnait de temps en temps un souffle nouveau de liberté aux us et coutumes régissant le système de gouvernement.[5]

Les princes du Liban n'ont jamais pu assurer un pouvoir centralisateur fort comme celui de Mohamad Ali en Egypte, même au temps de son allié l'émir Bechir II Chehab, bien connu pour sa grande autorité. Les voyageurs européens qui visitaient l'Orient, ne cachaient pas leur admiration pour le climat de liberté et de démocratie qui régnait dans la région du Liban, à la différence des autres contrées arabes de l'Empire. Ce fait a été relevé par Lamartine, au début du dix-neuvième siècle: 'Si dans telle ou telle contrée de l'Orient, il y a un homme, au Liban il y a un peuple', avait-il écrit.[6] L'observation de Lamartine est d'autant plus significative qu'elle a été faite au temps de Bechir II, le plus autoritaire des émirs que la Montagne ait connus.

Les habitants du Liban ont fait preuve, dès le début du dix-huitième siècle, d'une conscience populaire à caractère national où des sujets chrétiens et musulmans étaient unis pour s'opposer au despotisme des gouverneurs ottomans ou à l'arbitraire des émirs libanais. Cette conscience a été concrétisée par des soulèvements populaires tout au long du dix-huitième siècle.

L'éveil politique qui prime l'appartenance confessionnelle est caractérisé par la bipolarisation politique qu'a connue la Montagne malgré la diversité des communautés religieuses. Dès les premiers temps de leur constitution au Liban, les deux partis Qaysite et Yamanite groupaient chacun des partisans appartenant aux différentes communautés chrétiennes et musulmanes. Après le triomphe des Qaysites à 'Ayn Dara, en 1711, et la disparition définitive du parti Yamanite de la scène politique libanaise, il y eut constitution de deux nouveaux partis nés de rivalités politiques druzes: le parti Jumblati et le parti Yazbaki où chrétiens et musulmans, aux côtés des druzes, défendaient les couleurs de l'un ou de l'autre parti.[7]

Les Grands Changements du dix-huitième siècle

Dans la première moitié du dix-neuvième siècle, une série d'évolutions démographiques, sociales et politiques avaient déjà marqué le régime de l'émirat; le Liban s'en est profondément ressenti dans l'évolution de sa structure communautaire et la formation de son esprit politique:

1 Une grande poussée démographique maronite

C'est surtout au dix-neuvième siècle que l'équilibre démographique entre druzes et maronites a révélé ses premiers signes d'instabilité. Le nombre des maronites s'élevait à 95 360 habitants alors que celui des druzes n'était que 35 600 habitants, ou 37,33 pour cent par rapport aux maronites. Pour la même époque, les autres communautés de la Montagne offraient les chiffres suivants: orthodoxes: 28 500 habitants, melkites : 12 330 habitants, chiites: 12 330 habitants, et juifs: 200 habitants, sur un total général de 213 070 habitants.[8]

2 Une émigration chrétienne, de la Syrie vers la Montagne

Au dix-huitième siècle, des communautés chrétiennes sont venues s'installer au Mont-Liban à la suite de leur union avec Rome: les Melkites, les Syriens et Arméniens catholiques. Ces communautés ont fondé, dans le Kesrouan surtout, des séminaires et des couvents doublés d'écoles qui serviront de pôles d'attraction pour les chrétiens de l'intérieur.

3   Une expansion chrétienne dans les régions druzes

Cette expansion s'est surtout faite au Metn et dans le Chouf. Ce mouvement qui remonte à l'époque de Fakhreddine II avait pris de l'ampleur aux dix-huitième et dix-neuvième siècles. Des agglomérations exclusivement chrétiennes, telles que Dayr el-Qamar et Jezzine, se sont formées au Chouf et au Sud. Par ailleurs, les druzes avaient encouragé la constitution d'une filière de villages chrétiens s'étalant entre Sidon et Jezzine car ils cherchaient à ce que les chrétiens forment comme une ceinture de sécurité entre eux et les chiites du Sud. Les relations druzo-chiites étaient souvent tendues, alors que les chrétiens étaient bien reçus par l'une ou par l'autre partie.

Au début du dix-neuvième siècle, les chrétiens formaient déjà avec les druzes, les chiites et les sunnites, beaucoup de villages mixtes, aussi bien dans la région méridionale que dans la région septentrionale du pays. Il était évident que les chrétiens qui étaient devenus de grands propriétaires terriens dans ces régions mixtes, prenaient une influence politique aux dépens de l'élément druze.

4   Adoption du christianisme par les familles Chehab et Abi Lama'

Les deux grandes familles ont adopté le - christianisme par leur agrégation à la communauté maronite. Ce fait sur lequel peu d'historiens se sont arrêtés, a eu une portée politique considérable puisqu'il a permis aux maronites d'accéder, pour la première fois, au gouvernement de l'émirat.

5   Affaiblissement des liens féodaux en faveur de l'appartenance communautaire

Ce changement s'est surtout opéré au sein de la communauté maronite après la disparition du pouvoir des *muqaddam*s et l'affaiblissement de celui des cheikhs en faveur du pouvoir du clergé. La renaissance de l'Eglise maronite a eu lieu après la fondation du Collège maronite de Rome (1584) et s'est concrétisée par la réforme du Synode libanais (1736). Au début du dix-neuvième siècle, le patriarche maronite a comblé le vide créé par le recul de la féodalité pour apparaître sur la scène politique comme le chef incontesté de sa communauté.

La renaissance de l'Eglise maronite a eu aussi pour corollaire l'accession des prêtres d'appartenance sociale modeste, aux hautes charges ecclésiastiques. Au milieu du dix-neuvième siècle, le clergé était formé, en majorité, de fils de pays. Au dix-huitième siècle, sur les 20 évêques maronites 15 appartenaient à la classe des notables (75 pour cent), et sur 8 patriarches élus, 6 étaient des notables (75 pour cent). Au dix-neuvième siècle, il n'y avait plus que 7 évêques notables sur un total de 17 (41 pour cent) et 2 patriarches sur 6 (33 pour cent).[9]

Pour faire face à l'influence politique des maronites et au pouvoir grandissant de leur clergé, les druzes ont consolidé leurs propres institutions féodales. Ces attitudes contradictoires dues à la dissemblance de l'évolution sociale au sein des deux communautés, vont retarder la chute du régime féodal au Liban. L'abolition de la féodalité était considérée dangereuse par les druzes tant que l'accord sur un nouveau régime qui leur assurerait leur autonomie, eu égard à leur droits ancestraux, n'était pas conclu.

6 La conquête égyptienne et ses conséquences sur les relations druzo-maronites

Sous l'occupation égyptienne, Ibrahim Pacha a eu recours à l'émir Bechir II pour soumettre les druzes révoltés de Hasbaya et de Rachaya. Bechir II s'est servi, pour la première fois, de troupes chrétiennes pour réduire la révolte, obligeant certains druzes à se réfugier au Houran et à Constantinople.[10]

Plus tard, lors de la révolte druze du Houran en 1838 et son triomphe contre Ibrahim Pacha, l'émir Bechir fit intervenir une armée exclusivement chrétienne contre les druzes. La révolte a été étouffée mais 'les conséquences de cette politique furent désastreuses, car un abîme de haine sépara ainsi les deux communautés'.[11]

Les druzes vont saisir l'occasion de la crise de 1841 pour avoir leur revanche, considérant leur lutte contre les chrétiens comme un simple règlement de compte politique. Dans une requête adressée à Mohamad Ali, le 8 mai 1840, les maronites pressentaient déjà les conséquences néfastes de la politique de Bechir II: 'Nous avons été dans le Houran . . . nous y avons combattu les druzes nos amis . . . Nous sommes haïs par tous nos voisins et particulièrement par les druzes.'[12]

Bechir II avait usé de tous les moyens pour abattre les notables druzes. Après s'être débarassé de son redoutable adversaire le cheikh Bechir Jumblat, ce fut ensuite le tour des familles Arslan, Abd el-Malak, Nakad et Imad qu'il fit déposséder de leurs biens et du gouvernement de leur district.[13]

Il est à noter que vers 1840, sur les quatorze *muqata'a*s du Chouf qui étaient initialement gouvernés par des chefs druzes, il n'en restait que deux, les douze autres ayant été cédés par l'émir à certains membres de sa famille ou à des gouverneurs chrétiens.

Après la destitution de Bechir II, son successeur l'émir Bechir III a essayé de poursuivre la destruction de la féodalité druze. Mais à cause de sa faible personnalité, et de la complexité des conjonctures locale et régionale, Bechir III ne put empêcher l'éclatement de la situation intérieure qui a abouti à l'abolition définitive de l'émirat.

La Question du Liban et les intérêts européens

A l'époque de l'émirat, chaque communauté avait le droit d'appliquer ses lois et ses coutumes sur des matières relevant du statut personnel, entendu en son acceptation la plus large et embrassant l'entier réseau de la vie familiale et spirituelle. De ce particularisme ont surgi des moeurs hétérogènes et des tendances politiques qui n'ont pas manqué de s'exprimer dans la vie publique par l'apparition de fractions gravitant autour de leaders antagonistes.

Ce fait s'est accentué dans la première moitié du dix-neuvième siècle où l'intervention des puissances européennes sur la scène libanaise est devenue plus énergique à travers les différentes communautés dont chacune était protégée par un pays déterminé. Dans le langage diplomatique de l'époque, la communauté était assimilée à une nation, de sorte que les dépêches signalent 'la nation druze' et 'la nation maronite' ou autres. Au Liban, le fait d'être protégé par une puissance européenne était considéré comme un privilège et une nécessité 'sans laquelle on ne croit pas ici qu'il y ait d'existence assouvie'.[14]

Les conflits d'intérêts européens étaient tellement évidents sur la scène libanaise que les pays protecteurs ne se faisaient pas solliciter pour offrir leurs services. Des Méloizes, consul de France à Beyrouth, pouvait écrire en 1841: 'En ce pays-ci ce ne sont plus les protégés qui recherchent la faveur des protecteurs, ce sont, au contraire, ceux-ci qui se disputent les bonnes grâces des protégés.'[15]

La France usait de son influence religieuse et de la protection séculaire qu'elle assurait aux maronites et aux autres chrétiens unis à Rome, pour défendre ses intérêts contre toute concurrence européenne en Orient. C'est dans cette perspective que la France a appuyé son allié Mohamad Ali dans la conquête et la domination de la Syrie et du Mont-Liban (1832–1840).

En 1840, le gouvernement de Thiers a fait la sourde oreille aux protestations des Libanais de la Montagne qui réclamaient leur émancipation du joug égyptien. Pour la France, l'enjeu de sa politique en Orient passait bien avant les intérêts de ses protégés chrétiens.[16]

En effet, plus que le protectorat des Maronites, c'est l'importance stratégique de l'Egypte et de la Syrie que la France disputait à ses partenaires européens et particulièrement à l'Angleterre. Les objectifs stratégiques de l'Angleterre sont exprimés par le colonel Churchill, son envoyé au Mont-Liban: 'Si l'Angleterre voulait maintenir son pouvoir en Orient, elle devrait, d'une façon ou d'une autre, entrer en Syrie et en Egypte dans le cadre de ses zones d'influence et de domination . . . Qu'en est-il du Mont-Liban, cette grande forteresse naturelle qui se dresse entre l'Orient et l'Occident?'[17]

Les Anglais, lassés par les obstacles de tout genre que leurs agents et missionnaires ont rencontrés auprès des chrétiens, et découragés par un éventuel rapprochement avec les maronites, se tournèrent alors vers les druzes. Le colonel Rose, consul anglais à Beyrouth, avait écrit à son gouvernement: 'Les Maronites sont voués corps et âme à la France et l'Angleterre n'a plus le choix; il lui est irrévocable de soutenir les druzes.'[18]

Parallèlement à la protection des druzes, les Anglais avaient accordé leurs faveurs aux juifs en donnant caution à leur retour en Palestine pour y instituer le 'Royaume d'Israël'.[19] Ils avaient aussi donné leur appui aux missionnaires protestants qui, sur ordre du patriarche maronite Youssef Hobeïche, furent maltraités et chassés des villages chrétiens. Ce fait devait exaspérer les Anglais et créer entre eux et les maronites un abîme profond.[20]

La Russie était la protectrice des orthodoxes qui priaient dans leurs églises pour le tsar et la gloire de son empire. Sa protection profitait aussi aux syriaques, aux juifs et même aux chiites sans prendre pour autant un caractère officiel. La politique de la Russie qui était plus engagée dans la région des Balkans, n'avait pas au Liban et dans les autres régions orientales de l'empire des visées aussi poussées que celle de la France et de l'Angleterre.

L'Autriche de Metternich avançait habilement les pions d'une grande politique orientale pour affirmer sa prépondérance au détriment de celle de la France à qui elle refusait le monopole de la protection des catholiques au Liban.[21] Dans son rapport au Ministre des Affaires Etrangères, le consul français Bourrée attire l'attention sur la concurrence faite par les autres pays européens, notamment l'Autriche; il écrit en 1841: 'Autrefois, en effet, nous régnions sans partage et on peut le dire sans souci, aujourd'hui, on nous discute, on nous pèse, on nous compare.'[22]

En plus de la protection qu'elle accordait aux melkites, l'Autriche aspirait à supplanter la France dans la protection des maronites. Quant à la Prusse, elle semblait se désintéresser de la politique orientale; du moins, elle n'y participait plus, depuis le début du dix-neuvième siècle, d'une manière active. Toutefois, ce désintéressement politique ne s'étendait pas au domaine scientifique et culturel car la science germanique s'initiait lentement aux problèmes de l'orientalisme et de l'actualité socio-politique du Proche-Orient.[23]

La Porte, tout comme les Etats européens, exploitait les dissensions entre les différentes communautés du Mont-Liban, et les opposait les unes aux autres pour prouver que les Libanais étaient incapables de se gouverner eux-mêmes, et qu'il était nécessaire de réduire l'autonomie du pays. L'autorité ottomane voulait convaincre les puissances européennes que seul un pacha ottoman serait capable de réduire l'anarchie et de mettre fin aux querelles intercommunautaires.[24]

La diplomatie française était consciente de la politique de dissension adoptée par la Porte mais n'intervenait pas efficacement pour la neutraliser car elle voulait ménager le Sultan en vue d'intérêts plus importants en Orient. D'un autre côté, la France voyait dans les querelles druzo-maronites un prétexte convenable pour assurer davantage son droit de protection aux maronites.[25]

Le conflit d'intérêts entre les puissances européennes et la Porte a eu des conséquences néfastes aussi bien sur l'évolution de l'idée nationale qui commençait à germer chez les différentes communautés pour libérer le pays de l'occupation égyptienne, que sur le statut politique de la Montagne qui a perdu son autonomie après l'abolition de l'émirat et son rattachement direct à l'administration ottomane.

L'Eveil d'une conscience nationale face à l'occupation égyptienne

Bien que l'antagonisme druzo-maronite ait été éveillé à l'époque de Bechir II Chehab et sous l'occupation égyptienne, la politique d'oppression pratiquée par Ibrahim Pacha tantôt contre les druzes et tantôt contre les maronites va pousser les deux partis à dépasser momentanément leurs querelles intérieures pour faire face, avec les autres communautés du pays, au despotisme du Pacha d'Egypte.

Une réunion préliminaire entre chefs druzes et maronites se tint dans une *khalwa* druze à Dayr el-Qamar le 27 mai 1840 à la suite de laquelle un appel à la guerre fut adressé à toutes les provinces libanaises, disant notamment: 'Nous avons décidé de faire la guerre à cette puissance trompeuse (l'Egypte de Mehemed Ali et Ibrahim Pacha), et d'assurer Son Altesse le grand prince notre gouverneur (l'émir Béchir) de notre entière soumission à ses ordres.'[26] Cette distinction entre l'autorité nationale d'une part et l'autorité étrangère d'autre part est à retenir.

Les chefs de la révolte nationaliste devaient riposter quelques jours plus tard aux menaces d'Ibrahim Pacha de 'détruire les insurgés et de réduire leurs maisons en ruines', en tenant, le 8 juin 1840, une grande réunion à Antélias dans la cour de l'église Saint Elie. Là, sur l'autel de l'église, druzes, chrétiens, chiites et sunnites habitant le Mont-Liban, prêtèrent serment d'avoir une seule voix et une seule opinion et signèrent un pacte de solidarité.

Ce même jour, les insurgés publièrent un manifeste dans lequel ils exposent leur griefs et leurs revendications, en appelant tous leur compatriotes à la lutte contre l'envahisseur.

Ces deux documents qui sont considérés comme les actes fondamentaux de l'insurrection de 1840, permettent d'enregistrer chez les différentes communautés libanaises, la volonté de dépasser les querelles intérieures pour libérer le pays de la conquête égyptienne. Ce pacte d'Antélias dont l'authenticité est contestée par certains historiens, serait le premier document écrit où des habitants non-chrétiens de la Montagne déclarent appartenir au Mont-Liban.[27]

Le texte du manifeste publié par les révolutionnaires mentionne, pour la première fois, le nom du 'Liban' tout court et présente les prémices d'une conscience nationale face au danger qui vient de l'extérieur. On y lit notamment:

> Ceux des nôtres qui sont déjà morts en luttant ont fait leur devoir. A partir d'aujourd'hui, il faut que nous évitions les discussions et les divisions. Faisons appel à nos sentiments de solidarité et de courage et agissons sans plus tarder. Ne craignez pas la puissance de nos ennemis car la tyrannie ne peut pas durer. Regardez plutôt les Grecs qui, à force de bravoure, ont obtenu avant nous leur complète liberté.[28]

Le soulèvement de 1840 ne peut être étudié uniquement dans ses dimensions libanaises car il fut, dans ses aspects extérieurs, un épisode de la Question d'Orient et de la guerre turco-égyptienne à laquelle l'Angleterre s'intéressa activement pour maintenir l'équilibre européen. Elle oeuvra activement pour signer le Traité de Londres (15 juillet 1840), qualifié de 'Waterloo de la diplomatie française', à cause du grand coup qu'il porta au prestige de la France.

Il est à noter que le clergé a joué un rôle actif dans l'insurrection nationale de 1840. Le patriarche maronite Youssef Hobeïche, ancien aumônier de l'émir Bechir II, prit fait et cause pour les insurgés et lança une excommunication contre ceux qui s'opposeraient à leur action: 'Nous ne permettons à aucune de nos ouailles, dit-il, de s'éloigner du but des populations insurgées . . . Tout homme qui oserait désobéir à ce présent ordre est excommunié de l'Eglise de Dieu et que la colère du Seigneur et ses vengeances tombent sur lui quel qu'il soit.'[29]

Le clergé européen s'est mis aussi de la partie. Le père Ryllo, un jésuite d'origine polonaise, a prêté secours aux insurgés en aidant à la distribution de secours autrichiens et de fusils anglais. Pour neutraliser son attitude hostile à sa politique, la France devait mobiliser les pères Lazaristes et dépêcher au Liban leur procureur général, le père Etienne, dans le but de faire de la propagande en sa faveur auprès des maronites.

Le Premier conflit druzo-maronite et la fin de l'émirat

L'intervention européenne au Liban ne s'est pas limitée au stade des manoeuvres diplomatiques. Un débarquement de troupes anglaises et autrichiennes a eu lieu, en août 1840, pour aider les troupes ottomanes à faire exécuter l'ultimatum adressé à Mohamad Ali afin d'évacuer le Liban.[30] Après le retrait des troupes égyptiennes, le Mont-Liban n'a pas retrouvé pour autant sa liberté. L'émir Bechir II fut destitué par un firman impérial et la Porte a nommé Bechir III gouverneur de l'émirat.

Par cet acte d'autorité, la Porte avait mis fin à la coutume immémoriale selon laquelle les notables de la Montagne, réunis en assemblée électorale, choisissaient l'émir gouverneur. En désignant unilatéralement Bechir III, la Porte avait réaffirmé la souveraineté turque sur la Montagne et réalisé un objectif auquel sa politique avait vainement tendu vers le passé.

Les luttes d'influences européennes eurent des conséquences néfastes, aussi bien sur l'entente intercommunautaire au Liban, que sur l'autonomie de la Montagne. D'un côté, les puissances européennes de l'époque encourageaient l'antagonisme communautaire pour créer des conditions propices à leur intervention dans les affaires de l'Empire ottoman. D'un autre côté, la Porte, craignant que le Mont-Liban n'échappe définitivement à son autorité, cherchait à réduire son autonomie, sinon à l'éliminer et le soumettre à son autorité directe.

Malheureusement, la flambée patriotique qui s'était manifestée contre l'occupant égyptien n'avait pas résisté après son retrait. Réanimé par la mauvaise gérance de Bechir III et encouragé par des agents extérieurs, l'antagonisme druzo-maronite est réapparu sur la scène politique qui se réclamait d'une nouvelle politique anglaise. Jusque-là, on avait remué toute la Montagne contre la domination égyptienne. A cette ancienne conduite était lié le nom de l'agent anglais M. Richard Wood, lui-même catholique, qui entretenait des relations très amicales avec les chrétiens du Liban et particulièrment avec le patriarcat maronite.

Le nouveau consul général, le colonel Rose, obéissait à de nouvelles directives qui visaient la division des populations libanaises. Il s'était rangé franchement du côté des druzes, et ses relations avec le patriarche maronite devaient prendre un caractère d'une violente hostilité.

Sur le plan du gouvernement de l'émirat, Bechir III manquait de fermeté. Sa faiblesse notoire et son impopularité l'empêchaient de surmonter les difficultés. Les antagonismes de clans, de religions et d'intérêts, contenus par la fermeté de son prédécesseur Bechir II, se déchaînèrent au grand jour. Les chefs féodaux druzes qui réclamaient la restitution de leur autorité, se sont légués contre l'émir. Ils étaient appuyés par les agents turcs qui leur avaient donné des armes en les incitant à attaquer les chrétiens et leur émir.[31] Au début, querelle purement politique, le conflit druzo-maronite dégénéra en guerre de religion.

La Porte trouva le moment propice pour mettre fin à la monarchie des Chehab et à l'autonomie de la Montagne. Le 15 janvier 1842, elle proclama la destitution de l'émir Bechir III et nomma un officier ottoman d'origine autrichienne, Omar Pacha, gouverneur du Mont-Liban.[32] Ce fut la première fois depuis 1516 que le Mont-Liban fut gouverné directement par l'autorité ottomane.

Les Anglais avaient porté un nouveau coup à l'influence française en Orient, en encourageant les Ottomans à destituer les Chehab, maronites et alliés de la France. Par l'abolition du régime de l'émirat qui a duré plus de trois siècles (1516–1842), le Mont-Liban a perdu son autonomie. Il est devenu le champ clos des luttes, d'intrigues et d'influences entre diverses puissances étrangères, se désormais, officiellement, hors de la compétence exclusive de la Porte.[33]

La Tutelle européene et le régime des deux *qa'imaqamiyya*

La France soupçonnait l'Autriche d'être derrière la nomination d'Omar Pacha qui était d'origine autrichienne. Les appréhensions françaises étaient exagérées car Metternich n'était pas favorable à un gouvernement ottoman direct du Mont-Liban, et considérait Omar Pacha comme un renégat à la solde de la Porte. En réalité, Metternich cherchait à garantir aux catholiques du Mont-Liban leur droit à l'autonomie. En 1840, lorsque le régime de Bechir II fut mis en cause, son ambassadeur auprès de la Sublime Porte négociait secrètement la possibilité de l'établissement d'une principauté chrétienne au Mont-Liban. Ce projet qui n'a pas vu le jour, à cause de l'évolution de la conjoncture régionale, est mentionné dans trois dépêches du comte de Pontois, ambassadeur de France auprès de la Porte.[34]

L'Autriche, ainsi que la France, l'Angleterre, la Russie et la Prusse avaient émis des réserves à l'égard du gouvernement direct d'Omar Pacha. Metternich appuyait le retour de la famille Chehab au pouvoir et oeuvrait auprès des partenaires européens de l'Autriche pour le rappel d'Omar Pacha. Mais pour la Porte, la destitution des Chehab était définitive. Son envoyé au Liban, le *sar'askar* Mustapha Pacha, faisait savoir à la population que 'la Porte avait déclaré que sa volonté immuable était de ne plus avoir un émir chrétien dans la Montagne, et que quiconque prononcerait le nom de la famille Chehab serait envoyé aux galères d'Acre'.[35] Devant ce refus catégorique, les représentants des cinq puissances à Constantinople devaient entamer des discussions pour l'élaboration d'un système de gouvernement qui satisferait les différentes parties en cause car les druzes, bien qu'hostiles au gouvernement d'Omar Pacha, refusaient le retour de la famille Chehab au gouvernement de l'émirat. Les druzes avaient l'appui des Anglais qui considéraient, à juste titre, que les Chehab étaient les alliés fidèles de la France.

L'hostilité totale de la population libanaise à un gouvernement ottoman direct de la Montagne était de nature à neutraliser les antagonismes intérieurs. Une nouvelle tentative d'union druzo-maronite eut lieu grâce à l'intermède d'Omar Pacha où des requêtes collectives rejetaient son gouvernement, contestant le principe même de sa désignation. Après une révolte des druzes dirigée par Chebli Aryan contre le gouvernement d'Omar Pacha, les notables maronites tinrent une grande réunion à Antélias pour discuter l'appui au soulèvement de leurs compatriotes. Ils décidèrent d'envoyer le cheikh Rushayd Dahdah, ancien secrétaire de Bechir II, qui fut mandaté par le patriarche maronite et la plupart des leaders chrétiens pour trouver un terrain d'entente avec les druzes, mesure qui assurerait le retour des Chehab au pouvoir.

Une grande réunion druzo-maronite a eu lieu à Mukhtara, le 19 novembre 1843. Les notables des deux parties discutaient l'élaboration d'un nouveau pacte druzo-maronite qui permettrait à l'émir Asaad Kaadan Chehab d'accéder au gouvernement de l'émirat, quand la Porte a déclaré, en accord avec les puissances européennes, la division de la Montagne en deux *qa'imaqamiyya*: un chrétien et un druze.

L'unité de la Montagne fut brisée par l'adoption du régime des deux *qa'imaqamiyya* car désormais les chrétiens et les druzes 'auraient chacun un chef distinct pris dans leur sein respectif, et nommé par le Pacha de Sidon auquel il sera soumis'.[36] Les deux *qa'imaqam*s étaient ainsi de véritables fonctionnaires turcs et non les chefs nationaux de deux communautés autonomes.

Désormais, et jusqu'à la fin de l'époque ottomane, les Libanais n'auront plus la possibilité de choisir leur gouverneur tel qu'ils le faisaient sous le régime de l'émirat. La guerre d'influence entre druzes et maronites avait réduit l'autonomie des uns et des autres. Il leur restait quand même un privilège: le *qa'imaqam* est choisi parmi les autochtones. Mais, à côté de ce privilège il y a un grand inconvénient: celui de l'institutionalisation du confessionnalisme dans le régime politique libanais. Alors que sous le régime de l'émirat, les émirs gouverneurs furent tour à tour druzes, sunnites et maronites, sans inconvénient quelconque, désormais la religion du gouverneur est fixée par un texte institutionnel. Il en sera de même sous le régime de la *mutasarrifiyya*.[37]

La Porte avait misé sur la division de l'émirat pour semer la discorde et affermir son autorité. Elle considérait que le système confessionnel des deux *qa'imaqamiyya* n'était, en fait, qu'une 'guerre civile organisée'.

En effet, le problème des régions mixtes a engagé un second conflit armé entre druzes et maronites en 1845, ce qui a donné l'occasion à la Porte d'intervenir de nouveau pour modifier le régime des *qa'imaqamiyya*. Les réformes de son envoyé Chekib Effendi firent du Wali de Sidon le gouverneur effectif de la Montagne. Chekib Effendi fit publier un statut administratif qui consacra la division du Liban en deux *qa'imaqamiyya*, en établissant dans chacun d'eux un conseil formé de membres représentant les différentes communautés qui composent sa population, afin d'assister le *qa'imaqam* dans l'administration. C'est au règlement de Chekib Effendi que remonte l'institutionalisation du confessionnalisme dans les conseils représentatifs libanais. Ce principe a été respecté pour le régime de la *mutasarrifiyya*, et reste toujours en vigueur dans la constitution actuelle du pays.[38]

Le Conflit de 1860 et le régime de la *mutasarrifiyya*

Les réformes de Chekib Effendi ont permis d'assurer à la Montagne 15 ans de répit. Au printemps de 1860, au moment où l'Europe croyait que le replâtrage des affaires du Liban avait réussi, les nouvelles d'un nouveau conflit entre chrétiens et druzes retentirent de nouveau. L'Europe fut indignée par les massacres qui causèrent des milliers de victimes.

Les représentants à Beyrouth de la France, l'Angleterre, l'Autriche, la Russie et la Prusse, formèrent avec Fouad Pacha, ministre des Affaires Etrangères et envoyé extraordinaire ottoman, une commission internationale, afin de procéder à une enquête sur l'origine et les causes des évènements et proposer une nouvelle organisation administrative de la Montagne.[39]

Après six mois de polémiques (24 septembre 1860–4 mai 1861), les membres de la commission décidèrent de poursuivre leurs travaux à Constantinople où les négociations définitives furent engagées sous la direction des ambassadeurs des cinq puissances.[40]

Les membres de la commission se sont rendus à l'évidence que la partition de la Montagne sur une base confessionnelle était à l'origine de la guerre civile. La France et l'Autriche ont préconisé le retour de l'unité du Mont-Liban sous un gouverneur chrétien maronite. La Russie a accepté le projet franco-autrichien avec hésitation, par égard pour ses protégés orthodoxes, alors que la Prusse a subordonné son assentiment à celui de la Porte. Mais le refus catégorique de l'Angleterre fit échouer le projet d'un gouverneur maronite; elle a été appuyée par la Porte qui insistait pour un gouverneur ottoman choisi en dehors de la Montagne.

Un accord fut scellé à Constantinople, par la signature du Protocole du 9 juin 1861 qui est considéré comme un compromis entre la thèse des chrétiens, soutenue par la France et l'Autriche, celle des Druzes, soutenue par l'Angleterre, et celle de la Porte. Aux chrétiens on a accordé l'unité de la Montagne et de son autonomie, aux Druzes l'exclusion des maronites de la fonction de gouverneur, et à la Porte le choix du gouverneur.

Le Protocole du 9 juin a été doublé, en annexe, d'un Statut Organique du Mont-Liban. Ces deux textes ont conféré au pays un statut de droit international dénommé '*Mutasarrifiyya* du Mont-Liban'. Le 6 septembre 1864, un nouveau texte, portant le même nom, est substitué au premier. Il a été conclu par les représentants des cinq puissances européennes signataires du premier protocole, qui furent d'accord pour donner certains avantages aux maronites.[41] C'est ce règlement qui a régi le Mont-Liban jusqu'à l'éclatement de la première guerre mondiale.

Le *Règlement Organique* réservait aux ambassadeurs des cinq états signataires le droit de contrôle sur la nomination du *mutasarrif*. Le Liban a été ainsi placé sous la tutelle collective de l'Europe. A la fin de la première guerre mondiale, la tutelle collective européenne a cessé en faveur de la France qui l'a exercée seule jusqu'en 1943 sous le régime du Mandat.

Conclusion

L'étude de l'évolution du système politique libanais au milieu du dix-neuvième siècle montre que ce petit pays a toujours suivi les méandres d'un courant qui cherche à travers des voies sinueuses une issue où il puisse s'écouler sans entraves extérieures. Connu, à travers son histoire, comme un refuge naturel des opprimés en Orient, le Liban a constitué un pays où diverses croyances religieuses avaient cherché et trouvé abri. Elles y ont longtemps vécu avec des traditions communes où l'appartenance politique primait souvent la différence de religion. Mais les querelles politiques, exploitées par les luttes d'influence étrangères, prirent un caractère confessionnel.

Le destin du Liban a été mêlé à celui des grandes puissances européennes dont les antagonismes se sont confrontés sur son petit territoire, mettant en péril l'unité et la liberté de son peuple. Mais le danger premier provient des dissensions intérieures qui permettent les ingérences de l'extérieur. Au dix-neuvième siècle, chrétiens et druzes ne voulaient plus d'émir qui ne fût des leurs. Leurs querelles eurent pour résultat la rupture de l'unité libanaise, l'adoption du régime des deux *qa'imaqamiyya* et la réduction de leur autonomie.

La division de la Montagne n'a pas assuré la stabilité à sa population. Elle a montré aux puissances européennes que 20 ans d'anarchie sous le régime des *qa'imaqamiyya* et deux guerres civiles entretenues et exploitées par l'étranger, n'ont pu venir à bout de l'entité libanaise. Cette entité avait atteint une vitalité telle que l'Europe dut intervenir, en 1861 et 1864, pour lui assurer un minimum d'existence et d'autonomie, sans pouvoir lui préserver le droit d'avoir un gouverneur autochtone.

La conclusion évidente qu'on tire des conflits communautaires du dix-neuvième siècle, c'est que ces conflits exposent l'existence du Liban, son unité et sa souveraineté à de graves menaces. Elle met aussi en évidence que toutes les crises confessionnelles ont connu des solutions à caractère confessionnel. Aux poussées fiévreuses communautaires n'ont jamais succédé des solutions purement libanaises, et les ingérences extérieures, loin d'assurer le succès d'une communauté sur l'autre, n'ont abouti qu'à la perte des deux parties antagonistes.

Le drame que vit le Liban depuis 13 ans ne fait que confirmer ce fait. Il est certain que l'instauration d'une paix stable dans le pays nécessite une réforme en profondeur de l'état, qui ne peut se faire sans l'éveil d'une conscience nationale où toutes les communautés religieuses mettraient en échec les ingérences extérieures. Ce n'est que dans la mesure où l'environnement aura cessé d'être hostile que ces communautés pourront entreprendre un dialogue réel en vue d'une solution nationale.

Notes

1. Joseph Hajjar, *L'Europe et les destinées du Proche-Orient (1815–1848)* (Paris, 1970), p. 515.

2. Edmond Rabbath, *La Formation historique du Liban politique et constitutionnel* (Beyrouth, 1973), p. 168.

3. Toufic Touma, *Paysans et institutions féodales chez les Druzes et les Maronites du Liban du XVIIème siècle à 1914*, 2 tomes (Beyrouth, 1972), t. I, pp. 47–50.

4. Henri Lammens, *La Syrie, précis historique*, 2 tomes (Beyrouth, 1939), t. II, p. 961.

5. Iliyya Hariq, *Al-tahawwul al-siyasi fi tarikh Lubnan al-hadith* (Beyrouth, 1982), p. 200.

6. Alphonse de Lamartine, *Voyage en Orient (1832–1833)*, 2 tomes (Paris, 1903), t. II, p. 461.

7. Lammens, *La Syrie*, t. II, p. 101; Touma, *Paysans et institutions*, pp. 78–83.

8. Philippe Hitti, *Lubnan fi al-tarikh* (Beyrouth, 1959), p. 528.

9. Hariq, *Al-tahawwul*, p. 94.

10. As'ad Rustum, *Al-mahfuzat al-malakiyya al-misriyya*, 5 tomes, 2ème éd. (Jounieh, 1987), t. III, pp. 312–344, nos 5225, 5259, 5268, 5296–9, 5305, 5310, 5312, 5317, 5321–2, 5336–7, 5370, 5502, 5507; t. IV, pp. 110–24, no. 5857, 5861, 5900, 5918, 5972, 6508, 6065.

11. Adel Ismaïl, *Histoire du Liban du XVIIème siècle à nos jours*, 4 tomes (Paris, 1958), t. IV, *Redressement et déclin du féodalisme libanais (1840–1861)*, p. 131.

12. Archives des Affaires Etrangères françaises (AAEF), Corr. Pol., Beyrouth, Reg. I, no. 12, Rapport du consul Bourée, 30 mai 1840.

13. Ismaïl, *Histoire du Liban*, p. 128.

14. AAEF, Corr. Pol., Beyrouth, Reg. II, no. 11, Dépêche de Bourrée à Guizot, 7 octobre 1841.

15. Ibid., dépêche du 22 juin 1841.

16. La sympathie dont avait fait preuve le consul Bourrée envers les insurgés libanais devait aboutir à son rappel à Paris; Hajjar, *L'Europe et ses destinées*, p. 517.

17. Colonel Churchill, *Mount Lebanon, a Ten Years Residence (1842–1852)* (London, 1853), pp. vii–ix.

18. Il est à noter qu'avant 1840 et leur appui aux druzes, les anglais n'avaient pas une grande influence politique au Liban.

19. AAEF, Corr. Pol., Beyrouth, Reg. I, nos 28 et 33, Rapports de Des Meloizes, 20 novembre 1840 et 18 décembre 1840; Reg. II, Rapport anonyme, fol. 56 bis.

20. Concernant les démêlées entre les missionaires biblistes et les maronites, voir AAEF, Corr. Pol., Beyrouth, Reg. II, no. 5, Rapport de Bourrée, 25 août 1841.

21. AAEF, Corr. Pol., Beyrouth, Reg. X, no. 104.

22. Ibid., Reg. II, fol. 184.

23. Hajjar, *L'Europe et ses destinées*, pp. 168 et seq.

24. Ismaïl, *Histoire du Liban*, p. 142.

25. Guizot, ministre des Affaires Etrangères françaises, avait déclaré dans un discours devant le Sénat, que les autorités ottomanes opposaient les druzes aux maronites en aidant tantôt les uns, tantôt les autres pour qu'ils se déciment mutuellement; cf. Ismaïl, *Histoire du Liban*, p. 11, nos 19 et 20.

26. Nagib Dahdah, *Evolution historique du Liban* (Beyrouth, 1968), p. 171.

27. La dénomination 'Mont Liban' était donnée seulement à la région nord de la Montagne, habitée par les maronites; le centre était connu par le 'Chouf' ou le 'Mont des Druzes'. Ce n'est que vers la fin du dix-huitième siècle que la dénomination de Mont liban désignait effectivement toute la Montagne.

28. Dahdah, *Evolution*, p. 178.

29. AAEF, Corr. Pol., Beyrouth, Reg. I, no. 41, Rapport de Bourrée, 17 juillet 1840.

30. L'armée d'expédition qui a débarqué à Jounieh comprenait 4.000 soldats turcs, 2.000 anglais et 500 autrichiens. Voir AAEF, Corr. Pol., Autriche, Reg. 428, fol. 255; ibid., Beyrouth, Reg I, no. 7, Lettre de Soleman Pacha (colonel Sèves) à Des Meloizes, 11 septembre 1840.

31. A. Laurent, *Relation historique des affaires de Syrie depuis 1840 jusqu'en 1842*, 2 tomes (Paris, 1846), t. I, pp. 279 et 345–8.

32. Omar Pacha, alias Michel Lattas, est né en Croatie en 1806. Converti à l'islam, il fut officier dans l'armée ottomane et devint gouverneur du Liban du 16 janvier au 6 décembre 1842.

33. Rabbath, *La Formation historique du Liban*, pp. 195–8.

34. AAEF, Corr. Pol., Beyrouth, Reg. 24, no. 51, Dépêche du comte de Pontois à Mr. Thiers, 24 juillet 1840; ibid., Dépêche du 27 novembre 1840.

35. Ibid., Rapport no. 65, rédigé par le consul Bourrée, 28 octobre 1842.

36. Ibid., Reg. IV, Rapport du consul Bourrée, 30 juillet 1844.

37. L'émirat du Liban fut gouverné par un émir maronite depuis l'adoption de

christianisme par les émirs Chehab, d'après le rite maronite, à la seconde moitié du dix-huitième siècle.

38. Sur la tradition ottomane dans l'aménagement des rapports avec les minorités, voir Antoine Messarra, 'Constitution libanaise et pacte national en droit constitutionnel comparé', dans 'XXème Conférence du Comité National allemand de droit comparé' (Bonn, 21–4 septembre 1983), 42 pp. polycopiées.

39. Les représentants des pays dans la commisson étaient: Béclard pour la France, Lord Dufferin pour l'Angleterre, Weckbecker pour l'Autriche, Relifues pour la Prusse et Novikov pour la Russie.

40. Pour les procès verbaux des réunions de la commission, voir le Baron de Testa, *Recueil des traités de la Porte ottomane avec les Puissances étrangères*, 6 tomes (Paris, 1863), t. 4, pp. 105 et seq.

41. Le Règlement Organique est reproduit dans ibid., t. 6, pp. 36 et seq.; le *Règlement Organique* de 1864 se trouve dans George Young, *Corps de droit ottoman*, 7 tomes (Oxford, 1906), t. 1, pp. 104 et seq.

3

Zahle and Dayr al-Qamar

Two Market Towns of Mount Lebanon during the Civil War of 1860

LEILA FAWAZ

Zahle and Dayr al-Qamar were two predominantly Christian towns that reacted rather differently to the civil war which in 1860 flared up in Mount Lebanon and Damascus. The two towns had been subjected to the same sets of economic, social, and political changes that had overtaken Greater Syria during Western economic penetration, and to some extent their differences were lessened by them. They showed comparable patterns of growth and of social change.

But they could also sometimes react very differently to particular events, as they did in the crisis of 1860, and those different reactions can be traced to different local traditions and economic foundations. They also provide evidence that forces other than sectarian identity were at work in this conflict. People continued to identify at least as strongly with their town as they did with their sect—if sectarianism seemed to increase in that time, it is partly because the population in the towns became so homogeneous in sectarian terms that sect and home town became indistinguishable.

The differences in the reactions of Zahle and Dayr al-Qamar to the civil war of 1860 also bring into question the popular notion that the Christians were the victims of the civil war. Some among them had provoked the Druzes and were unquestionably the aggressors at the onset of the war, a fact that was obscured by the overwhelming defeat of the Christians in all the warring districts and the emotions this aroused in Greater Syria and beyond.[1]

It is a fair assumption that most travellers to Dayr al-Qamar and Zahle in the first half of the nineteenth century would have been more likely to describe them as villages than as towns.[2] Yet even then their inhabitants were proud of them. The local chroniclers, song writers, and poets praised their beauty, achievements, and prosperity. Zahle

pride in particular was unmatched in Mount Lebanon. The town
inspired delirious admiration from poets and others for the splendour
of its location in a deep and narrow valley carved by the Birdawni river
and opening out on the Biqaʿ plains. Zahle lies on the banks of the
river on the eastern flank of Mount Lebanon about 3,000 feet above
sea-level.[3]

The inhabitants of Dayr al-Qamar were more reserved, but they too
sang their town's praises. For centuries it had received the attention of
the amirs of Mount Lebanon. The Maʿni Amir Fakhr al-Din was the
first to beautify the town with fountains, marble courts, mansions, and
a serai of Italian inspiration. Under the Shihabs, particularly Bashir
II, more buildings were constructed and the population grew and
prospered. In the words of the popular historian ʿIssa Iskander
al-Maʿluf (himself a native of Zahle), Dayr al-Qamar had become a
'paradise'.[4]

Both towns were regional centres. By the mid-nineteenth century,
Zahle had become Lebanon's largest commercial centre. Trade was a
natural outgrowth of its location on the western edge of the Biqaʿ,
which lies between the Lebanon and Anti-Lebanon ranges and the
Syria hinterland, that is between the grain-producing areas of the
Biqaʿ and Hawran and the livestock-breeding pastures of Mount
Lebanon. It was surrounded by vineyards, truck gardens, and
orchards, olive groves, and the mulberry trees needed to support the
cultivation of silk. It supported industries that depended on abundant
water: tanning, milling wheat (there were 13 flour mills there at the
beginning of the nineteenth century), cloth-dyeing, and arrack
distilleries.[5]

Dayr al-Qamar, in the heart of the Druze-dominated southern
districts of Mount Lebanon, had functioned since the seventeenth
century as a relay between Sidon, the mountainous hinterland,
Damascus, and the Syrian interior beyond. One of its major items of
trade was raw silk, which had been cultivated in the Mountain since
the seventeenth century and sold to France since the early eighteenth.
Dayr al-Qamar was a collection centre for it. From its markets, silk
was sold to middlemen working for entrepreneurs in Sidon and Beirut,
or to Syrian traders in Damascus, Aleppo, Homs, and Hama. It was
also itself known as a centre for the manufacture of silk cloth. The
town also held the local grain and livestock market. It had flour mills, a
soap factory, and other enterprises vaguely referred to by one traveller
as 'numerous branches of industry'. Small workshops employing about
ten workers multiplied in the mid-nineteenth century until the textile
industry of Dayr al-Qamar boasted 120 looms. The town was also a
centre for cotton weaving and it crafted objects of exceptional quality
that were said to rival even those of Damascus. The abaya robes, worn

by shaykhs, of cotton or silk woven with gold and silver were made there. By the middle of the nineteenth century, Dayr al-Qamar had established itself as the richest town in Mount Lebanon. Its leading citizens displayed their wealth in grand houses and elegant clothes.[6]

Dayr al-Qamar was also an administrative centre. The seat of power of the Ma'ni and Shihabi dynasties until Bashir II moved his seat of government to Bayt al-Din, it benefited from the proximity of the amirs and shaykhs who dominated the surrounding area. It was exempted from the taxes the rest of the Mountain had to pay. Its special status was also recognized under the *qa'imaqamiyyatan*. It was the only town to have its own Druze and Christian *wakil*s which protected it from the direct jurisdiction of the Abu Nakad shaykhs of the Manasif district in which it was located. It provided services, including money lending and tax collecting, to the amirs and shaykhs of the region.[7]

The rate at which Zahle's and Dayr al-Qamar's prosperity grew is reflected in their population figures. At the end of the eighteenth century, Zahle had less than a thousand inhabitants and 200 houses. At the beginning of the nineteenth century, Dayr al-Qamar had 4,000. Data for the first half of the nineteenth century are unreliable, but by the late 1850s the population had probably reached between 10,000 and 12,000 in Zahle,[8] and between 7,000 and 10,000 in Dayr al-Qamar[9]—which, if these estimates are at all accurate, means that Zahle started smaller than Dayr al-Qamar and grew faster. In any case, it is safe to say that the population of both towns had grown sharply since the beginning of the century.

Whatever the total population in the late 1850s, the Christian population in both towns had overtaken the Druze. In Zahle, most of the increase could be accounted for by emigration from the countryside—peasants and semi-nomads who left the Biqa', Ba'albek, and Hawran—most of whom were Greek Catholic or Greek Orthodox converts. The emigration therefore shifted the balance from an equal share of Greek Catholics and Druzes in the eighteenth century to an overwhelmingly Greek Catholic population in the nineteenth. In the case of Dayr al-Qamar, Greek Catholic and mostly Maronite Christians dominated the town in an otherwise Druze part of the country. Mishaqa's memoirs convey the impression that the town was mainly Christian. Colonel Rose, the British consul in Beirut in the 1840s, tells us that Bashir II deliberately increased the Christian population and that by 1843 it exceeded the Druze by five or six to one. Charles Henry Churchill, the British colonel who spent most of the 1840s and 1850s in Mount Lebanon and Beirut and wrote extensively about his stay there, tells us that all the landed property once owned by Druzes in the neighbourhood of Dayr al-Qamar had passed into Christian hands, and that the few Druzes who still lived in the town had lost all influence.[10]

As Zahle and Dayr al-Qamar grew, so did their differences. A good portion of the population of Zahle were merchants and entrepreneurs who traded with itinerant peddlers, exchanged goods with wholesalers and small buyers in other districts, speculated in grain, bought and sold land, and acted as tax farmers and advisers to the shaykhs of the Biqa' and the governors of Damascus. But in spite of these enterprises, theirs remained essentially an agricultural economy. The population included a substantial number of peasants who tilled the land in the valley and sheltered nomads on their way to or from the Biqa', the Hawran, and regions east. It therefore retained its rustic and agrarian population who earned their livelihood in grain, livestock, and land in Zahle and the Biqa' and Ba'albek areas.[11]

Zahle, at the edge of Mount Lebanon and open to the plains of Biqa' and the Syrian interior beyond, also nurtured a frontier mentality. People came to it partly for protection, which reinforced that mentality. It was exposed to political influences from both Mount Lebanon and Damascus, the centre of power for the Syrian interior. It had to be ready to defend itself from attack from the plains and the regions beyond. It was too far from the seat of power of the amirs of Lebanon to rely solely on them for defence, and this caused the population to develop a hardened, self-sufficient, aggressive attitude; yet they were not entirely without political acumen, for alliances had to be forged and competing centres of regional influence played off against each other. Zahle's *qabadayat* ('tough men') with their frontier mentality of self-reliance, their bravery, and their vigilante style of law and order, were the town's protection.[12]

Although Zahle was larger than many of its neighbours, it remained essentially a rural community. As a result, the Zahalni were at one and the same time open to strangers and provincial in attitude. As caravans passed through, they learned of worlds beyond: of the riches of Damascus and the diversity of Beirut's trade; of the power struggles between Ottoman governors in Damascus, shaykhs and amirs in the Mountain, and Ottoman governors and European consuls on the coast. The European missionaries, especially the Jesuits, in their midst opened them up to European influences. But though the outside world impinged upon their lives through hearsay, they only rarely, if at all, ventured into it. They were content to live and work in Zahle; they had no desire to leave.

This provinciality also included a sense of separateness from the rest of the Mountain. The continuous hostility between shaykhs and amirs encouraged them to maintain their distance from the Mountain; the administrative division of Mount Lebanon in the 1840s and 1850s into two districts added further to their aloofness. Nor did the instability of the Syrian steppe encourage any alliances there; on the contrary, nomad attacks from that direction left them constantly isolated and besieged.

This combination of isolation, strategic vulnerability, and superior attitude encouraged bellicosity. The Europeans complained that the Zahalni were insolent, abusive to strangers, and tyrannical. Churchill tells us that 3,000 of the townsmen bore arms. Even those who admired their bravery found them cruel and high-handed. They were also increasingly bigoted, as the town became the stronghold of Greek Catholic interests in the Mountain. Because Greek Catholicism was centred in Zahle, and the Greek Catholics were otherwise a minority in Mount Lebanon, sectarian interest also increased their zealotry. They fought Protestants and Druzes alike. When Christians were attacked by non-Christians, they came to the defence of the church, but when Christian sects became the aggressor, they were no less eager for battle. The enemy was apt to be defined in terms of religion—an attitude abetted by their particularly aggressive and powerful clergy who repeatedly urged their parishioners to take up arms against non-believers—but it was a religion very narrowly defined.[13]

Dayr al-Qamar was about the same size as Zahle, but considerably more urbane, though still provincial by Beiruti, not to mention Damascene or Cairene, standards. Its people too were involved in politics and government, thanks to members of the Ma'n and Shihab dynasties who lived in their midst with their retinues of advisers and followers. Politics and trade opened up their horizons as well, for a continuous stream of people came to town, and they traded with the interior, the coast, and beyond. A few even had relatives in other countries—the Mishaqas in Egypt, for example—with whom they established a lively trade. The Dayr al-Qamaris' relative sophistication was reflected in their crafts. They were skilled artisans and craftsmen, noted for the delicacy of their embroideries and other handiwork. They learned the intricacies of finance and at least small-scale industry easily. The town could produce as sophisticated and open-minded an observer as Mikha'il Mishaqa; it would seem unlikely that he could have been produced by Zahle as it then was. Mishaqa's family, like so many others, came to Dayr al-Qamar in the days of Bashir II to seek the amir's protection and to make a living serving the amirs and shaykhs, working as tax collectors, scribes, money-lenders, or goldsmiths.[14]

In contrast to the Zahalni frontier mentality, the Dayr al-Qamaris thrived on compromise and conciliation. Their location made the town a Christian enclave in the Druze heartland, where persuasion and not force was an asset. The town's tradition of compromise and

conciliation had been encouraged when the Shihabs made it an asylum
for political refugees. Some were fleeing the amirs or shaykhs in the
Mountain; some the governors on the Syrian coast or the interior;
some, especially the peasants, skirmishes in the countryside.[15]

Prosperity and a shift in the sectarian balance at a time of growing
Druze–Christian tension in Mount Lebanon toward the end of Bashir
II's reign changed all this. As the Dayr al-Qamaris became richer, they
began to show off like *nouveaux riches* and to attack outsiders as being
ill bred and arrogant. They too maintained a standing armed force,
which the British consul-general in 1841 said was 800 or 900 strong;
Churchill claimed it was more like 2,000 warriors ready to overrun
three times that number of Druzes. Abkarius called them 'strong'; the
British consul-general found them 'warlike'. They became more
aggressive, involving themselves in the affairs of the districts around
them to protect Christian interests against the Druzes. The Druzes in
the town itself grew uneasy.[16]

Some Dayr al-Qamaris, however, clung to their tradition of
tolerance and compromise. Their folk tales often revolved around
Maronites and Druzes joining forces to defeat oppressors at whose
hands both had suffered. Mishaqa took pains to explain that loyalty,
not religion, was the essence of mountain society; for, as he put it, the
custom among clansmen was not to judge followers by their religion,
but rather by their loyalty and devotion. Mishaqa's subordination of
religion to communal virtues was not exceptional; it was expressed by
others, notably Antun Dahir al-'Aqiqi, another chronicler of Lebanon
in the middle decades of the nineteenth century. To some extent these
attitudes were those of any society whose well-being and prosperity
depended on maintaining the security of its mutually dependent
constituent parts where business interests, and not ideology, dictated
attitudes, and where passions were controlled in the name of
self-interest.[17]

When war came, the differences became clear. The Zahalni met the
challenge aggressively, indeed provocatively. They were often divided
among themselves; but, easily taking offence, they faced the enemy
with determination, and were quick to fight. Adding fuel to fire, they
thrived on the skirmishes, disputes, and conflicts that resulted. The
Dayr al-Qamaris, on the other hand, at least most of the time, attracted
as little political controversy as possible and responded to hostility
rather than provoking it. Conciliatory qualities that made them strong
in peacetime made them appeasers in time of war. They were
sometimes so eager to ward off trouble that when it came they refused
to recognize it and failed to prepare adequately for it. Faced with a
hostile force, they either moved away or pretended it was not there,
bringing catastrophe on themselves in 1860.

As tensions built up, the Zahalni threw themselves in equal measure into alliances and quarrels. Sometimes they formed coalitions with the Shi'is of the plains around them; but more often than not they pitted against their neighbours, especially the Druzes with whom their relations deteriorated steadily from the days of Bashir II until the 1850s. Through it all, they increased their reputation for courage, bellicosity, and foolhardiness. They fought on the slightest provocation in the name of their town, their leaders, their sect, and their families. These were the limits of their loyalties and concerns.[18]

When the civil war began in the spring and early summer of 1860, it was not surprising to find the Zahalni in the forefront. As sporadic fighting turned into general conflict the 'Urqub and the region around Zahle became the theatres of battle. It is uncertain whether the war began there or not, but a battle certainly raged around Zahle on 31 May 1860, when the Zahalni rushed to fight the Druzes. The excuse was retaliation for Druze maltreatment of Christians from the 'Urqub district who had sought refuge in Zahle; they had been intercepted on the way and fired upon by the Druzes. Hundreds of Zahalni fought at 'Ayn Dara, where two battles ended in a Druze victory that pushed the Christian forces back into Zahle.[19]

The Dayr al-Qamaris by contrast reacted to the Druzes with ambivalence. Thanks to the aggressivity it had acquired in the last years of Bashir II's rule, Dayr al-Qamar had taken a leading part in the sectarian clashes of 1841. After that, however, there is no evidence that the townspeople provoked the Druzes as the Zahalni regularly did. They had learned the price to be paid for armed conflict. The Druzes had come back to settle scores with them, and fighting did not cease until the Ottoman authorities intervened. The nearby presence of an Ottoman garrison encouraged them to count on the government, and not only on themselves, for protection. The location of the town in the midst of Druze territory also entailed commercial and financial transactions between the town and countryside that were vital to their welfare. Anyone who did not want to deal with the Druzes simply left town. After the clashes of 1841, many of the Christians who could afford it sought the protection of European consuls and co-religionists in Beirut, but that was an option open mainly to merchants and other wealthy townspeople. For the majority, the only choice was to stay. As a result, many of those who could afford to were leaving; those who could not were moving from the surrounding countryside into the comparative safety of Dayr al-Qamar itself. By choice or by force, or a combination of both, Dayr al-Qamar lived in relative peace with its Druze neighbours until 1860.[20]

Even after the war broke out the Dayr al-Qamaris reacted with ambivalence, unlike the Maronite clergy elsewhere who were busily

recruiting followers in the Mountain and in Beirut. While the Zahalni
were seeking out the Druze enemy, the Dayr al-Qamaris responded to
Druze aggression but they did not provoke it. Mishaqa later described
the first Druze attack on 1 and 2 June 1860 as a minor affair involving
few losses, but the French consul-general presented it as a major
Druze offensive. Whichever it was, the townsmen withstood the attack
well and, uncharacteristically for Christians during that civil war,
suffered fewer casualties than the attackers. When they surrendered,
the town was looted and its outskirts were destroyed.[21]

The surrender of the Dayr al-Qamaris after so little resistance was
attributed by Churchill to lack of preparation and what he obviously
thought was misplaced trust in Druze professions of friendship and
Turkish promises of protection. He also accused them of refusing to
listen to warnings and calls to arms by Christians from other places,
rejecting their grounds that they wished to remain 'perfectly neutral'.
Even after the Druze attack was launched, only half of the townsmen
took part in the defence of the town. To Churchill, their passivity was
tantamount to treason, though it was consistent with the town's
tradition of moderation and tolerance; however, the rules of the game
had been broken: Druze pledges were not kept and Ottoman
protection did not materialize.[22]

After the initial skirmishes, the Zahalni began to prepare for a
major Druze attack. The Dayr al-Qamaris collected a circle of
influential Druze, Ottoman, and European representatives and asked
for protection. After the battles of 'Ayn Dara in early June, some of the
Zahalni fighters went to the aid of the Christian population in the
nearby village of Kfar Silwan; others engaged the Druzes in a series of
skirmishes in the plains around Zahle where many Zahalni owned
land. Around 14 June, a number of them attacked the enemy at its
local headquarters at Qabb-Ilyas in the Biqa' plains, but they were
disorganized and soon forced to retreat.[23]

As news of one Druze victory after another reached the Zahalni,
they increased their defences; sent out appeals for help to Christians in
the northern districts, where Taniyus Shahin, Yusuf Karam, and
others could muster large forces; recruited able-bodied men among the
refugees in town and others who came to help; dug trenches and built a
crenellated brick wall on the southern edge of town; erected barricades
in the narrow alleys and streets; filled warehouses with food and other
supplies; and hid their valuables. They were well supplied with
ammunition and horses, and could count on a force of some 4,000 to
7,000 fighters.[24]

By contrast, the preparations of the Dayr al-Qamaris consisted of
rounds of talks or leaving town. Unnerved by mounting hostilities,
those who had the means or the money used Druze and other

connections to find protection nearby or leave for Beirut. The overwhelming majority remained and continued to do nothing. When the Ottoman authorities (some sources report the Druzes) ordered a general disarmament, the Dayr al-Qamaris put up little resistance. Handing over their arms they hurried to the serai for refuge, taking their families and valuables with them.[25]

When the Druzes attacked Zahle on 18 June, the Zahalni demonstrated once again that they were brave but undisciplined. Joined by bedouins and Shi'is, the Druzes assaulted the town and rapidly took it. This event sealed the triumph of the Druzes and the total defeat of the Christians in the civil war. The Zahalni diminished their already poor odds by their intrigues among themselves. According to the anonymous author of *Kitab al-ahzan*, this undermined the effectiveness of their resistance. They did however fight with a bravery conspicuously absent from most other Christians in the war. The struggle they put up at least may have spared them the enormous human losses incurred elsewhere: figures for Zahle range from less than 100 to 700 people as compared with Hasbayya, Rashayya, Dayr al-Qamar, and other major Christian strongholds where losses were estimated to be much higher.[26]

As it became more and more obvious to the Dayr al-Qamaris that they were going to be attacked again, they turned to Divine Providence, the authorities, and their Druze contacts to prevent the worst, while offering no opposition whatsoever. They proclaimed their peaceful intentions rather than prepared for battle. They met with Ottoman officials and explained they had resisted all calls to join the battle by other Christian groups. By 20 June, their efforts to talk the Druzes out of attacking failed, but even then, Dayr al-Qamar still had what the Druze chronicler Abu Shaqra estimated to be some four thousand armed fighters, but none took up their arms. He may have been wrong: other sources report the Dayr al-Qamaris were by then already disarmed and an easy prey in the serai. But what is certain is that there was no resistance and there was a massacre. Estimates of the dead range from 900 to over 2,000, and the higher figures are the most often quoted. The town was sacked and levelled.[27]

After the civil war, both Zahle and Dayr al-Qamar were left in ruins. The population of Dayr al-Qamar had been so reduced that in October 1860, after many survivors had returned, there were still under 400 inhabitants: 182 men, 109 women, and 95 children. Zahle was little different, despite its fewer losses, because people had run away after the battle. Its morale, however, was better, because the Zahalni had put up a fight. General Beaufort d'Haupoul, commander-in-chief of the French expeditionary force to Syria in 1860–1, at least found it less dispirited and demoralized than Dayr al-Qamar, where conditions were worse and the people were dying of hunger.[28]

As the two towns began to recover, Zahalni aggressivity manifested itself once again, in small ways which worked to their advantage. When wood was needed to rebuild houses, the Zahalni obtained permission to cut trees from the woods of the Biqa‘ and went on cutting with so much energy that Fu’ad Pasha, the envoy of the Sublime Porte, complained they were exploiting the privilege by cutting wood as far away as Damascus. Such a complaint was not uncommon, but in the case of the Zahalni it is particularly easy to believe it was justified. By the spring of 1861, having enlisted the help of the Ottomans and Europeans, Zahle had begun to recover. Its population had grown to 6,174, and 2,207 houses had been rebuilt.[29]

Dayr al-Qamar’s recovery was slower. It had suffered losses in the civil war greater than almost any other place. Its leaders and richest citizens had moved away, and few returned—certainly fewer and more slowly than the inhabitants of Zahle did. Morale was low; at the slightest sign of danger people simply fled. Not until French troops were stationed there in the fall and winter of 1860–1 did the population begin to return to the town. By April 1861 there were 1,343 inhabitants, a great improvement over the few hundred of the preceding October. The French troops departed in early June 1861, and panic spread again. In the end, only a few hundred inhabitants actually fled, but the fact that so many talked of it is an indication that the town’s survival was still in doubt.[30]

The problems of reconstruction were immense: relief of the most needy was urgent; streets needed clearing; houses and other buildings had to be rebuilt. Money was short, but eventually problems of financing were at least partly solved. The town recovered within a year of its destruction. By April 1861 its shops had reopened and its industry was reviving.

A more serious, if less tangible, problem was that of morale. How to generate faith in the future was a question whose answer was indispensable both for the repopulation of the town and for future harmonious relations between its citizens and their Druze neighbours. Harmony among groups mattered everywhere in the Mountain, but all the more in mixed Druze and Christian districts.

Sectarian harmony was possible, although every sectarian outbreak made it more difficult. Even at the height of the conflict, the behaviour of the people in Zahle and Dayr al-Qamar suggests that concerns other than sectarianism could come first: sources speak of divisions among the Zahalni and betrayal among the Dayr al-Qamaris.

In the aftermath of civil strife and in the long term, however, more powerful positive factors were needed to ensure peace, given the bitterness of the struggles in the mid-century. Essential among these factors was the restoration of a central authority in the Mountain. Without it, the Lebanese would inevitably revert to building their local armies and fending for themselves once again. It was ironic that during the civil war Zahle, the town that had more readily taken the law into its own hands, came out of the conflict better off. The absence of an acknowledged central figure in Mount Lebanon since the end of Bashir II's rule had encouraged a vigilante mentality in the Mountain. It was imperative to restore that central authority before the energies of towns such as Zahle and Dayr al-Qamar could be encouraged to renew their economic growth. It was also imperative to develop institutions that would counteract the pull of sectarian loyalty.

A new settlement for Mount Lebanon had to be worked out. No outside power has ever been able to force a people to forgive and forget, but a climate of peace and trust can encourage them to. Ultimately, re-establishing that climate was the responsibility of the international commission that met in Beirut and Istanbul in 1860–1 to decide on a new administrative settlement for the Lebanon. It was to provide for an effective central authority and a balanced distribution of power and privileges among the groups of the Lebanon. The *Règlement Organique* was the result. Signed in 1861 by the International Commission and the Sublime Porte and revised in 1864, it made possible—at least for the remaining years of Ottoman rule—the stability required.[31]

After the reorganization of Lebanon, Zahle and Dayr al-Qamar prospered again. The population of both towns grew in the late nineteenth and early twentieth century.[32] Neither lost their character. Zahle continued to be a stronghold of Greek Catholic sentiment. Dayr al-Qamar may well have hardened its sectarian outlook, a process that had begun in the mid-nineteenth century, as the eruption of violence in 1841 intensified in 1860. In the first years of the twentieth century, a traveller noted that people in Lebanon still remembered the civil war, and that no Druze dared pass through Dayr al-Qamar.[33]

Although Lebanon's independence created a different political context altogether, in the recent past Dayr al-Qamar continues to produce hard-line politicians, reflecting perhaps the more general trend whereby attitudes acquired in the mid-nineteenth century were reinforced by developments under the French mandate and after independence.[34]

Notes

1. Research for this project has been made possible by grants from the Social Science Research Council and the American Philosophical Society. Lebanon here refers not to the modern nation, but is used in its nineteenth-century geographical sense of all Mount

Lebanon, the original Jabal Lubnan covering the northern districts and Jabal al-Duruz or southern districts. (See Kamal S. Salibi, *The Modern History of Lebanon*, London, 1966, pp. xii–xiii.)

2. Alixa Naff, 'A social history of Zahle, the principal market town in nineteenth-century Lebanon', 1972 PhD thesis, University of California, LA (Ann Arbor: University Microfilms, 1973), pp. 59–60; Henri Guys, *Beyrouth et le Liban: Relation d'un séjour de plusieurs années dans ce pays* (Paris, 1850), II, p. 33; Alphonse de Lamartine, *Voyage en Orient*, vol. VII of *Oeuvres complètes de M. de Lamartine* (Paris, 1840), p. 257.

3. I have relied on Alixa Naff's very informative study on Zahle for most of my information on that town.

4. 'Issa Iskander al-Ma'luf, 'Dayr al-Qamar 'ala 'ahd al-amir', extracts from an article in *al-Jinan* repr. in *al-Mashriq* (April, 1931), pp. 302–4; Isma'il Haqqi, *Lubnan: Mabahith 'ilmiyya wa ijtima'iyya*, ed. Fu'ad Ifram al-Bustani (Beirut, 1970), p. 198; *Murder, Mayhem, Pillage, and Plunder: the History of the Lebanon in the Eighteenth and Nineteenth Centuries*, trans. from *al-Jawab 'ala iqtirah al-ahbab* and compared with the Beirut manuscript by Wheeler McIntosh Thackston, Jr (Albany, NY, 1988). I am grateful to Wheeler Thackston for putting his book manuscript at my disposal.

5. Naff, 'Social history of Zahle', p. 25, *passim*; Antoine Abdel Nour, *Introduction à l'histoire urbaine de la Syrie Ottomane (XVIe–XVIIIe siècle)*, Publications de l'Université Libanaise, Section des Etudes Historiques, XXV (Beirut, 1982), pp. 349–50; I. M. Smilianskaya, 'The disintegration of feudal relations in Syria and Lebanon in the middle of the nineteenth century', trans. in *Economic History of the Middle East, 1800–1914: a Book of Readings*, ed. Charles Issawi (Chicago, Ill., 1966), pp. 227–47; Paul Saba, 'The creation of the Lebanese economy: economic growth in the nineteenth and early twentieth centuries', in Roger Owen ed., *Essays on the Crisis in Lebanon* (London, 1976), pp. 1–22.

6. Toufic Touma, *Paysans et institutions feodales chez les Druses et les Maronites du Liban du XVIIe siècle à 1914*, Publications de l'Université Libanaise, Section des Études Historiques, XXI (Beirut, 1972), II, p. 419; Abdel Nour, *Histoire urbaine*, pp. 360–1; Smilianskaya, 'Disintegration of feudal relations', pp. 227–47; *Murder, Mayhem*; *The Lebanon in Turmoil; Syria and the Powers in 1860: Book of the Marvels of the Time concerning the Massacres in the Arab Country by Iskander Ibn Yaq'ub Abkarius*, trans., annotated, and intro. by J. F. Scheltema (New Haven, Conn., 1920), pp. 101, 132 n. 98; Baron I. Taylor, *La Syrie, la Palestine et la Judée: Pèlerinage à Jerusalem et aux Lieux Saints* (Paris, 1860), p. 36; Edouard Blondel, *Deux ans en Syrie et en Palestine (1838–1839)* (Paris, 1840), p. 87; Roger Owen, *The Middle East in the World Economy 1800–1914* (London, 1981), p. 94; Saba, 'The creation of the Lebanese economy', pp. 1–22; Haqqi, *Lubnan*, p. 442; John Carne, *Syria, the Holy Land, Asia Minor, etc., Illustrated* (London: Fisher, 1836–8), p. 61. For silk see Boutros Labaki, Roger Owen, Charles Issawi.

7. Salibi, *Modern History of Lebanon*, pp. 66–7. Under the *qa'imaqamiyya*, in each of the mixed districts, a Druze and a Christian agent (sing.: *wakil*) were chosen by their communities and approved by the local *qa'imaqam*. Each was responsible to the latter for his own sect, and to take over for his own sect; he also had for the members judicial and tax-collecting functions that had formerly belonged to the shaykhly families of each district; Haqqi, *Lubnan*, pp. 359, 618; *The Lebanon in Turmoil*, pp. 53–4; *Murder, Mayhem*; Dominique Chevallier, *La Société du Mont Liban à l'époque de la révolution industrielle en Europe* (Paris, 1971), p. 95.

8. Naff, 'Social history of Zahle', pp. 52ff. Guys, *Beyrout*, II, p. 35, mentions 5,000 for what is probably either the 1820s or 1830s. During the 1830s and 1840s, estimates ranged from 5,000 to 12,000. Charles Henry Churchill, *Mount Lebanon: a Ten Years' Residence from 1842 to 1860* (New York, 1973), II, p. 217, estimated Zahle's population to be 6,000 in the 1840s. Abkarius, *The Lebanon in Turmoil*, gave Zahle about 8,000 people on p. 88 and only 5,000 on p. 94: the first estimate may refer to the later period in which Abkarius wrote (d.

1885); and the second to the number of inhabitants around 1860. Cyril Graham, 18 July 1860, *Parliamentary Papers*, no. 69, vol. LXIX, 1860, 'Further papers respecting disturbances in Syria' (henceforth cited as 'Further papers'), p. 42, referred to Zahle as the largest town in Mount Lebanon with a population of 10,000. General Beaufort placed the population before the civil war at about 7,000–8,000: France, Archives de Vincennes (henceforth cited as 'V.'), G4/1, Beaufort-Randon, 9 September 1860. The anonymous *Kitab al-ahzan fi tarikh waqi'at al-Sham wa-ma yalihuma bi-ma asaba al-Masihiyin min al-Duruz wal-Islam fi 9 tammuz 1860*, p. 29, mentions the figure 12,000. See also Chevallier, *La Société du Mont Liban*, pp. 61–2; Touma, *Paysans et Institutions*, I, p. 221; Abdel Nour, *Histoire urbaine*, p. 80. I am grateful to Axel Havemann, Fritz Steppat, Abdul Rahim Abou Hussein, and Fuad Debbas for providing me with copies of *Kitab al-ahzan* and other rare sources to which access is difficult because of conditions in Lebanon.

9. Writing of the first or second decade of the nineteenth century, Mishaqa (*Murder, Mayhem*) estimated 4,000 people. In 1822–3, Lamartine, *Voyage en Orient*, p. 220, reported 10,000–12,000, a figure which seems too high. Guys, *Beyrout*, I, p. 136, wrote that during the 1830s Dayr al-Qamar's population numbered 4,000 at most. I. M. Smilianskaya, *Al-harakat al-fallahiyya fi Lubnan*, trans. Adnan Jamus, ed. Salim Yusuf (Beirut, 1972), p. 16, mentions that a Russian doctor named Ravalovich gave the population as 10,000 around 1840; more realistic estimates for the same period are probably Abkarius, *Turmoil in Lebanon*, p. 98, who gives 7,000, and Charles Henry Churchill, *The Druzes and the Maronites under the Turkish Rule from 1840 to 1860* (London, 1862), p. 104, who gives nearly 8,000. In 1860, Cyril Graham, 'Further papers', 18 July 1860, p. 42, mentioned again the figure of 7,000. See also Chevallier, *La Société du Mont Liban*, pp. 61–2.

10. Naff, 'Social history of Zahle', pp. 53–4; GB, Public Record Office, Foreign Office Archives, London (henceforth cited as FO) 226/83, Rose-Stratford Canning, no. 24, 30 April 1843; Churchill, *Druzes and Maronites*, p. 104; V., G4/1, Beaufort-Randon, 9 September 1860; Guys, *Beyrout*, p. 36.

11. Naff, 'Social history of Zahle', chs 2 and 3.

12. This whole section is based on Naff, 'Social history of Zahle', ch. 2. For the understanding of the more general phenomena of local leadership and social relations in villages and small towns, I am also indebted to the works of Samir Khalaf, Fuad Khuri, Michael Gilsenan, and Janet Abu-Lughod.

13. Naff, 'Social history of Zahle', ch. 2; Churchill, *The Druzes and the Maronites*, p. 107; J. L. Porter, *Five Years in Damascus* (London, 1855), II, p. 279; *Lebanon in Turmoil*, p. 90 n. 117.

14. *Murder, Mayhem*; Taylor, *La Syrie*, p. 36; Ma'luf, 'Dayr al-Qamar 'ala 'ahd al-amir', p. 202; *The Lebanon in Turmoil*, p. 101; Edouard Blondel, *Deux ans en Syrie et en Palestine (1838–1939)* (Paris, 1840), p. 87.

15. *Murder, Mayhem*.

16. FO 226/83, Rose-Stratford Canning, no. 24, 30 April 1843; Churchill, *Druzes and Maronites*, pp. 105–7; *Strife in the Lebanon*, p. 74; *Lebanon in Turmoil*, p. 99; I. de Testa, *Recueil des traites de la Porte Ottomane avec les puissances étrangères*, III, p. 76, cited by Smilianskaya, *Al-harakat al-fallahiyya*, p. 90.

17. *Murder, Mayhem*; Antun Dahir al-Aqiqi, *Thawra wa fitna fi lubnan*, ed. Yusuf Ibrahim Yazbak (Damascus, 1938), p. 94.

18. Salibi, *Modern History of Lebanon*, pp. 50–1; Naff, 'Social history of Zahle', pp. 54–5, 269–70, 285; *Lebanon in Turmoil*, pp. 90–1; Abu Shaqra, Hussayn Ghadban Abu Shaqra and Yusuf Khattar Abu Shaqra, *Al-harakat fi Lubnan ila 'ahd al-mutassarrifiyya*, ed. Arif Abu Shaqra (Beirut, 1952), p. 120.

19. Salibi, *Modern History of Lebanon*, p. 90; Churchill, *Druzes and Maronites*, pp. 141–3; *Lebanon in the Last Years of Feudalism, 1840–1868: a Contemporary Account by Antun Dahir al-'Aqiqi and Other Documents*, trans. with notes and commentary by Malcolm H. Kerr

(Beirut, 1959), pp. 58, 60; France, Les Archives du Ministère des Affaires Étrangeres, Correspondence Politique et Consulaire, Beyrouth (henceforth cited as as A.E., CPC/B/), vol. 12, Bentivoglio-Thouvenel, no. 30, 30 June 1860; *The Lebanon in Turmoil*, pp. 91–2; Naff, 'Social history of Zahle', p. 362.

20. Salibi, *Modern History of Lebanon*, pp. 49ff.; Chevallier, *La Société du Mont Liban*, p. 162; FO 226/83, Rose-Stratford Canning, no. 24, 30 April 1843; Churchill, *Druzes and Maronites*, pp. 44–5. For Mishaka, *Murder, Mayhem*, the provocation came from the Druzes.

21. *Murder, Mayhem*; FO 195/655, Moore-Bulwer, no. 31, 3 June 1860; ibid., Moore-Bulwer, no. 32, 6 June 1860; A.E., CPC/B/12, Bentivoglio-Thouvenel, no. 18, 7 June 1860; ibid., Bentivoglio-Thouvenel, no. 19, 8 June 1860; ibid., Bentivoglio-Thouvenel, no. 29, 28 June 1860; 'Further papers', Graham's report, 18 July 1860.

22. Churchill, *Druzes and Maronites*, pp. 151–3. I am grateful to Michael Gilsenan and Albert Hourani for their comments on this point.

23. A.E., CPC/B/12, Bentivoglio-Thouvenel, no. 28, 27 June 1860; Churchill, *Druzes and Maronites*, pp. 182–3; *Lebanon in the Last Years of Feudalism*, p. 62; Abu Shaqra, *Al-harakat fi Lubnan*, p. 126; Salibi, *Modern History of Lebanon*, p. 102; Naff, 'Social history of Zahle', p. 364.

24. Abu Shaqra, *Al-harakat fi Lubnan*, p. 126; *Lebanon in Turmoil*, p. 94 n. 125; Churchill, *Druzes and Maronites*, p. 186; Salibi, *Modern History of Lebanon*, pp. 102–3; Naff, 'Social history of Zahle', pp. 363–4.

25. *Murder, Mayhem*; *Lebanon in Turmoil*, pp. 114–15; FO 195/655, enclosure in Moore-Bulwer, no. 42, 27 June 1860; Abu Shaqra, *Al-harakat fi Lubnan*, pp. 174–7.

26. *Kitab al-ahzan*, p. 28; Abu Shaqra, *Al-harakat fi Lubnan*, pp. 127–8; *Lebanon in Turmoil*, pp. 97–8; *Lebanon in the Last Years of Feudalism*, p. 63; 'Further papers', Brant-Bulwer, 26 June 1860; V., G4/1, Beaufort-Randon, 9 September 1860; Churchill, *Druzes and Maronites*, pp. 186–7; Naff, 'Social history of Zahle', pp. 365–6; Salibi, *Modern History of Lebanon*, pp. 103–4; Kamal Salibi, 'The 1860 upheaval in Damascus as seen by al-Sayyid Muhammad Abu'l Hasibi, notable and later *Naqib al-Ashraf* of the city', *Beginnings of Modernization in the Middle East*, ed. W. R. Polk and R. L. Chambers (Chicago, Ill., 1968), pp. 191–2; Chevallier, *La Société du Mont Liban*.

27. *Lebanon in Turmoil*, pp. 110ff.; FO 195/655, enclosure in Moore-Bulwer, no. 42, 27 June 1860; A.E., CPC/B/12, Bentivoglio-Thouvenel, no. 29, 28 June 1860; Abu Shaqra, *Al-harakat fi Lubnan*, p. 131; Churchill, *Druzes and Maronites*, pp. 189–90; 'Further papers', Graham's report, 18 July 1860; Salibi, *Modern History of Lebanon*, pp. 104–5.

28. V., G4/1, Beaufort-Randon, no. 17, 20 October 1860; ibid., Beaufort-Randon, 4 October 1860; ibid., Beaufort-Randon, 11 October 1860; ibid., Beaufort-Randon, no. 49, 26 April 1861.

29. V., G4/1, Beaufort-Randon, no. 48, 19 April 1861; ibid., Beaufort-Randon, 4 October 1860; FO 78/1626, 7e Séance du 30 Octobre 1860.

30. V., G4/2, D'Arricau-Beaufort, no. 192, 18 April 1861, and enclosures; V., D'Arricau-Beaufort, no. 221, 6 May 1861, and enclosure; V., G4/1, Beaufort-Randon, 11 October 1860; V., G4/2, D'Arricau-Beaufort, 1 June 1861; ibid., D'Arricau-Beaufort, 3 June 1861.

31. John P. Spagnolo, *France and Lebanon 1861–1914*, St Antony's Middle East Monographs no. 7 (London, 1977).

32. *A Handbook of Syria (including Palestine)* (London), p. 178, suggests this growth occurred at the turn of the century. Published probably in 1920, this report by British naval intelligence tells us that Zahle in 1885 had only one stone building (a church), but that by 1909 there were many large stone built houses. It also points out that although the last quarter of the nineteenth century witnessed heavy emigration from Lebanon, a number of towns like Zahle grew; clearly a sign not of overall increase, but of growth restricted to particular towns whose emigrants had returned. In Zahle, for example, one street was named

Brazil Street, after the country where many of the new house-owners had made their fortunes. Even the few towns that grew during that period only did so in relative terms: how large they were is hard to ascertain. Estimates range widely. For example, in the 1890s Vital Cuinet, *Syrie Liban et Palestine: géographie administrative statistique, descriptive et raisonnée* (Paris, 1896), p. 211, estimated that there were 16,674 people in Zahle, and 23,990 people in Dayr al-Qamar. But a French report during the French mandate, *La Syrie et le Liban en 1922* (Paris, 1922), p. 284, estimated that in 1913 Dayr al-Qamar had only 8,455 people; it gives no estimates for Zahle, but does provide one of 35,000 people for the whole district. Cuinet gives a larger estimate for Dayr al-Qamar than Zahle, but this is quite exceptional. The first world war dramatically changed the demographic picture, but like most pre-first world war sources, the British naval intelligence report quoted above, p. 176, makes Zahle the larger town—in fact, 'the only town of some size' in Mount Lebanon, and numbers the population at 14,000.

33. Lewis Gaston Leary, *Syria the Land of Lebanon* (New York, 1913), p. 17.

34. Roger Owen, 'The political economy of Grand Liban 1920–1970', in Owen ed., *Essays on the Crisis in Lebanon*, pp. 23–32; Albert Hourani, 'Ideologies of the Mountain and the city', ibid., pp. 33–41; A. Hourani, *Political Society in Lebanon: a Historical Introduction*, Centre for Lebanese Studies, Papers on Lebanon 1, pp. 1–16; Hourani, 'Lebanon: the development of a political society', and 'Lebanon from feudalism to nation-state', in Hourani, *The Emergence of the Modern Middle East* (London, 1981), pp. 124–48.

4

Ottoman Reform and Lebanese Patriotism

YOUSSEF M. CHOUEIRI

The decades which followed the withdrawal of Muhammad 'Ali's forces from geographical Syria witnessed a host of profound economic changes and political upheavals throughout the Ottoman empire. It was during this period that the Ottoman state launched a wide-ranging programme of reforms designed to halt its economic decline and reassert direct military and political authority over its territories. The Sublime Porte, having wrested effective control of the state policies from the sultan, became through its reforming ministers an active agent in creating the minimum prerequisites for an economic upsurge, particularly in the agricultural sector.

Public security was perceived as the most effective pre-condition for applying various reforms proclaimed in the *Hatt-i-Şerif* of 1839.[1] Consequently, rebellious areas were pacified, mountainous regions brought under tighter control, and bedouin harassments contained and repulsed. The results of these measures manifested themselves in a noticeable growth in population and an extension or intensification of agriculture. The drive for public security stemmed from two interrelated objectives: an earnest desire to secure an effective system of tax-collection and accumulate sufficient revenues allocated for financing the reforms; and an equally patriotic zeal to ward off direct European intervention or occupation. The long-term negative aspects of abolishing trade monopolies and lowering the tax levied on imported goods to 5 per cent, while exports were taxed at 12 per cent, as the provisions of the Anglo-Ottoman Trade Agreement of 1838 stipulated, were not fully digested.

These reforms coincided with, or were a vigorous response to, European military pressures, commercial expansion and financial penetration. This European expansionism, launched and sustained by newly invigorated capitalist, and largely industrial nation-states, precipitated the reorganization of a wide variety of forces and relations of production. It initiated a massive shift of trade from the hinterland to the coastal areas, whereby each region tended to specialize in one single cash crop, such as cotton, grain or silk. The introduction of British, French, Austrian and Russian steamships facilitated the penetration of Ottoman markets, and ensured a regular, cheaper and more efficient means of supplying the local consumers with luxury and manufactured goods. With the economic scales tipped in favour of manufactured goods, a constant trade deficit between Europe and the Ottoman territories became a sign of the new age.

The advent of European goods and capital reactivated or brought into being various groups of local intermediaries which acted as a link between European merchants and companies and the local producers or consumers. It was between 1840 and 1860 that Beirut became an important commercial, financial and diplomatic centre. Moreover, it linked for the first time the fortunes of Mount Lebanon, as a silk producer, to its own cycle of economic and political activities. Whereas the silk of Lebanon had formerly been sold in the markets of the Ottoman empire, it now bypassed these markets and became the monopoly of European, mainly French, merchants and creditors resident in Beirut. The cities of Europe gradually replaced Damascus, Cairo and Baghdad as the dynamic regenerator of Lebanese pro-duction and liquid assets. However, the lion's share of the whole enterprise was often pocketed by local traders, commercial agents and intermediaries. It is this new role of Beirut which eroded the isolation of the Mountain as an enclave of heretic and religious minorities, and turned it into a region ready to receive certain Ottoman reforms.

The departure of the discredited Amir Bashir II from Lebanon, in 1840, signified the end of an era. Having misjudged the true balance of power and allied himself with Ibrahim Pasha, Muhammad 'Ali's son, in return for keeping his ruthlessly nurtured privileges, he was formally stripped of his authority by the Ottoman sultan and sent into exile. The appointment of his successor, Bashir al-Qasim, as a salaried functionary of the Sublime Porte marked, in a tangible and far-reaching way, the beginning of the transformation of Lebanon's history beyond recognition. A council of 10 or 12 members drawn from the notables of the six main sects was to be set up for the purpose of overseeing, under the supervision of the new amir, the assessment and collection of the *miri*, or imperial revenues.

However, the forces unleashed by the successive developments and economic upheavals of the last decade made the constitution of such a council a sanguine gesture. The Druze tax-farmers,[2] who had fled their districts or were exiled as a result of their opposition to the policies of both Ibrahim Pasha and Amir Bashir II, resumed their agitation for the restoration of their traditional privileges, lands and authority over their largely Maronite tenants. In the meantime, the Maronite church launched a persistent campaign to reinstate the former amir as the chief tax-farmer for all of the Mountain. The role of its patriarch in consolidating the unity of the Maronite community assumed at the same time a crucial importance as the old order began to crumble. Both communities added to the complexity of the situation by articulating their grievances and demands against the background of the newly proclaimed Ottoman reforms. Moreover, these developments unfolded in the main in the mixed areas of central Lebanon. The demographic explosion of the Maronites lent these grievances an alarming tone of urgency. The British dragoman and political agent of both his government and the Sublime Porte, Richard Wood, frankly acknowledged that the restoration of 'feudal rights over the peasantry' was meeting stiff resistance:

> The peasantry said they would resist it and claimed the equal participation of rights granted to them by the *Hatti Scheriff* which promise made them take up arms to expel the enemy.[3]

As a matter of fact, the immediate application of the new reforms became the main focus of Wood's activities. He correctly observed that the weakening of the tax-farmers' hold over their tenants would greatly enhance the authority of the sultan, and make it easier for him to introduce further reforms. In a letter to the British ambassador at Istanbul, dated 12 May 1841, he stated:

> Both the Druse and Christian sheikhs of Mt Lebanon have insisted more than once to have the '*mukataa*s' (districts) restored to them in feudal tenure, the same as they were held by their ancestors. Their object is evidently to acquire a certain right over the peasants in order to despoil them of their produce by illegal extortions as they were in the habit of doing heretofore. The undersigned has desired His Excellency the Emir Beshir [al-Qasim] not to accede to a demand founded more on an assumed than a real right, particularly as it was contrary to the Provisions of the *Tanzimat Hairiye* . . .[4]

Thus it was in Mount Lebanon, a predominantly Maronite area, that the application of the reforms *tanzimat* began in earnest.

Bashir al-Qasim was overwhelmed by rapid changes, shifting alliances and constant civil strife. His futile attempts to bridge the gap between two warring camps revealed his tenuous position and hesitant character. By January 1842, he was stripped of his powers and sent to Istanbul. The active involvement of the Ottoman authorities in the internal reorganization of Mount Lebanon became more pronounced. 'Umar Pasha, the Ottoman emissary, set about dividing the Mountain into two separate districts: one Maronite in the north, and one Druze in the south. His actions were opposed by both the Maronite patriarch and the foremost Druze chieftain, Sa'id Junbulat. In the wake of the 1845 civil war Shakib Efendi, the Ottoman foreign minister, finally succeeded in setting up the two districts, which were placed under the direct authority of the governor of Sidon, who resided in Beirut. By that time the British were reverting to their time-honoured policy of aligning themselves with those they considered the natural leaders of the inhabitants—the Druze and Maronite tax-farmers. France, having backed what Wood called 'the enemy', tried to recapture its influence by extending political and material support to the Maronite church.

By enforcing the establishment of representative councils, presided over by the two Maronite and Druze *qa'imaqam*s in their respective districts, Shakib Efendi was finally endowing the Mountain with one of its first modern institutions. Moreover, in the mixed districts, in contrast to the overwhelming Maronite northern areas, Maronite and Druze agents, or *wakil*s, were chosen by their own co-religionists and empowered to defend their interests as tenants or share-croppers of Druze tax-farmers. The fiscal, judicial and administrative functions of the tax-farmers were severely restricted; both the members of the councils and the agents were Ottoman functionaries receiving a fixed salary, whereas the *wakil*s were invariably drawn from outside the ranks of the *muqata'ji*s. Writing in 1908, the Maronite lawyer and historian, Bulus Nujaym, attributed to the *Règlement* of Shakib Efendi the main responsibility for hastening the destruction of 'the feudal traditions' prevailing in the mixed areas. It was, in his opinion, in those districts which did not introduce the principle of electing representative agents that the agitation of the peasantry reached its most violent manifestation. This was the case in the 1858–9 peasant revolt in Kisrawan which elected Taniyus Shahin as *wakil 'am* or general agent, and demanded the strict application of Ottoman reforms pertaining to tax assessment and collection.[5]

By eroding the political and fiscal authority of the tax-farmers, these institutional and administrative innovations created a suitable framework for the development of commercial and financial trans-actions. The peasant-tenant was afforded the opportunity and the means to detach himself as far as possible from the direct and pervasive control of his tax-farmer. The money-lender, merchant and creditor, operating from their base in Beirut, stepped in as inter-mediaries between him and European capital, particularly in its French dimensions.

Between 1845 and 1861 a new Lebanon came into being. Its economic, social and political structures were entangled within the multiplex dynamism of Ottoman reform and European expansionism.

Its social divisions were redistributed creating new configurations within each community. The overwhelming majority of Maronites remained tillers and cultivators of terraces and fields which were dotted with mulberry trees. The introduction of steam-reeling factories, owned and operated by Europeans, offered them new temporary opportunities for employment and survival. Migration was another option which, along with the silk industry, acted as a safety valve against renewed tensions. The Greek Orthodox and Greek Catholics, concentrated in relatively prosperous towns and cities, gave Lebanon its wealthiest and most successful merchants, bankers and traders. The Druzes either migrated to the district of Hawran, or became reconciled to the new Ottoman scheme of things. However, social and economic divisions within each sect did not disappear. For the time being, different social forces performed relatively definite functions under new circumstances. It was not, as some scholars tend to emphasize, simply a matter of the persistence of primordial traditional norms pitted against forces of change. The whole society was jolted onto a different level, which entailed a reordering of its various elements. Thus, the principles of the Ottoman *tanzimat* and their immediate impact deserve more than a passing reference. Furthermore, the positive or negative role of the Maronite church in the history of the Mountain was an almost faithful reflection of the struggle against these reforms.

The *Hatt-i-Şerif* of 1839 envisaged the solution to the empire's problems in the creation of 'new institutions to give to the provinces composing the Ottoman Empire the benefit of a good administration'.[6] These new institutional and administrative measures were meant to have a rational basis, in harmony with the needs of a new age. They were supposed to increase the prosperity and strength of the state, replacing 'the irregular administration' with uniform and coherent institutions and policies. The *Hatt-i-Şerif* identified three main measures to be implemented as matters of immediate urgency:

1. The guarantees ensuring our subjects receive perfect security for life, honour, and fortune.
2. A regular method of assessing and levying taxes.
3. An equally regular method for the levying of troops and the duration of their service.

This regular system, based on property security, taxation uniformity, and modern military conscription, was marshalled against the abuses of the empire's tax-farmers. They were targeted as the main culprits who robbed the state of the necessary revenues allocated to meet the expenses of the new reforms. It is this 'fatal custom', with its 'venal concessions, known under the name of "Iltizam" ', that the imperial edict singled out for destruction. This was a condemnation of an economic and social system rather than a mere fulmination against the whims of a coterie of persons. It was a call for the elimination of an economic, 'civil and financial administration', which imposed its own additional dues, obligations and contractual rights.

The Maronite peasants were among the first to avail themselves of these official pronouncements and devices. However, with the exception of abolishing monopolies, these regular measures had already been applied by Muhammad 'Ali in the 1820s and 1830s. Hence, the innovative and revolutionary character of the *tanzimat* resided in anchoring the new institutions to wider principles of patriotism and loyalty to the state. Whereas Muhammad 'Ali spoke and acted as the sole repository of power in Egypt, the Ottoman reformist statesmen inculcated the notions of love of 'the fatherland' and devotion to 'the native land'. These notions and feelings, binding together the subjects of the sultan, were deemed 'the source of the most praiseworthy actions.'[7] The principle of patriotism was a totally new innovation in the Arab world; it was propagated and made an article of faith by Ottoman reformers, long before Christian Arab intellectuals ventured into this virgin territory. The *Hatt-i-Humayun* (imperial rescript) of 1956 reaffirmed and elaborated the same concepts. It once again referred to 'the cordial ties of patriotism', uniting all the subjects of the empire irrespective of religion or race.[8] After 1856, the notion of *hub al-watan* (*l'amour de la patrie*) began to gain currency in the intellectual and bureaucratic circles of the Arab world, particularly in geographical Syria, Egypt and Tunisia—three regions which witnessed the application of similar programmes of reforms.

It has been observed that the *tanzimat* contained, both in theory and practice, two contradictory and irreconcilable elements: they simultaneously affirmed the equality of all Ottoman subjects and called on the non-Muslim Ottomans to reorganize their communities along the old divisions of the discarded millet system. Such an undertaking defeated its own purposes and consolidated the separatist nationalism of the various communities.[9] Although this line of argument overlooks the way European powers interpreted the reforms as concessions to their agents, protégés, and the Christians of the empire in general, it is still useful as far as it unwittingly illuminates the separate trajectories of the 'Syrian' and 'Lebanese' patriotic movements.

By and large, Arab intellectuals, professionals, merchants and officers tended to adopt the principle of Ottomanism, coupled with an emphasis on their loyalty to what the *Hatt-i-Şerif* of 1839 called 'the native land'. Thus, Ottomanism and local patriotism coexisted and intersected as two facets of a single entity. This was, for example, the elaborate and deliberate political and cultural outlook of the Bustanis as they descended from the Mountain and settled in Beirut. Their secular Syrian patriotism was propounded with an equally secular Ottomanism, without having to depart from the broad outlines of the *tanzimat*. Syrian patriotism, as it developed in the second half of the nineteenth century, was a product of the same changes which swept the Ottoman empire. It had distinctly secular terms of reference that bypassed sectarian, religious or racial allegiances; it affirmed the integrity of the Ottoman territories, while demanding at the same time a recognition of its autonomous and particular status; its representatives proclaimed the necessity of economic self-sufficiency, and aspired to deal with Europe on an equal and independent basis.

By contrast, Lebanese patriotism was entwined, in its search for authentic historical and theoretical roots, in the fortunes of one particular sect—the Maronites. Its less strident counterpart unfolded within the institutions of Ottoman reform. The theoretical world of Lebanese-cum-Maronite patriotism was highly sectarian, extremely suspicious of the Ottomans, and openly soliciting direct European interference and protection. The Maronite church embodied this trend, and sought to control its ultimate outcome.

There is general agreement among scholars, of various political and ideological persuasions, about the enormous progressive influence exerted by the Maronite church to emancipate its flocks from the tyranny of their landlords. Its cultural and religious connections with Europe are equally stressed as the main factors which made it amenable to the world of capitalism and industrialization. [10] Another militant and enlightening role is assigned to the Maronite merchants and bankers. Precise dates and exact names are produced to back up the argument. The election of Bulus Mas'ad as patriarch in 1854 is invariably cited as the turning point of the church towards total identification with the cause of its downtrodden believers. Being of peasant origin, the new patriarch is automatically endowed with a populist ethos which prompted him to break the hegemony of the Khazin family, as the Maronite tax-farmers in Kisrawan. To what extent are these deductions reliable as interpretative devices?

The social origins of an ecclesiastic or lay leader are often a poor guide to his political views and economic preferences. If one does not take account of the institutional framework, the educational background, and the general conditions within which an individual operates, no adequate evaluation of political or other views is likely to emerge. Mas'ad received his education at the College of Propaganda in Rome, and was imbued with the teachings of the Vatican. That high seat of Catholicism is not known to have preached the espousal of

peasant revolts against landowners. Moreover, he was elected by the
same body of bishops which had raised to the highest office of the
church his two immediate predecessors, both drawn from tax-farming
families.[11]

The Maronite church itself was rapidly becoming the largest
landowner in the Mountain. Although it did not operate an openly
oppressive system in extracting the agricultural surplus from its
tenantry and share-croppers, the exploitation of its lands did not
diverge in its main thrust from the norms of tax-farming. Whereas the
traditional tax-farmers extracted their additional dues by coercion, the
church received its own by performing its various functions within a
world of religious superstitions and mounting social dislocations. The
church, furthermore, mounted a vigorous campaign against Ottoman
reforms, considering their implementation to be a blatant infringement
of its authority. In the 1840s, the Maronite clergy insisted on the
reinstatement of Bashir II as a single Christian governor of Mount
Lebanon. His main usefulness lay in his obvious animosity towards
Ottoman encroachments. It should be remembered that the reforming
zeal of Ibrahim Pasha, except in its negative aspects, hardly touched
the districts under the old prince of the Mountain. Another demand of
the church was its constant entreaty to be placed under the direct
protection of France. It represented one of those demands that France
was either reluctant to accept, or unable to fulfil.

By 1856 silk factories, under the control and management of
European capital and entrepreneurs, had become a permanent feature
in the densely populated, mixed districts of the Mountain. Maronite
monasteries, along with tax-farmers, cultivated mulberry trees and
supplied cocoons for the silk-reeling factories. The monks and priests
used their persuasive powers to convince reluctant fathers and
husbands of the benefits they would receive if they allowed their
daughters and wives to work in these factories as daily or seasonal
labourers. It may be safely assumed that the male family heads
unfailingly pocketed the meagre proceeds.

Capitalist and industrial relations were thus nipped in the bud.
Both the factory owners and their clerical suppliers were generally
satisfied with such lucrative operations. However, two socially
antagonistic strata were losing out: the traditional tax-farmers and
their tenants. The tax-farmers, whether Druze or Maronite, having
suffered in some instances the erosion of their fiscal and legal
prerogatives, began to accumulate debts to bankers and merchants
resident in Beirut. Maronite tenants faced the same vicious circle of
debts, fuelled by usurious rates and unscrupulous methods of
commercial transactions. The city creditors—distant and scattered—
escaped immediate blame. The financial and political difficulties of the

numerous members of the Khazin family were considerable, as they
attempted to unseat the presiding Maronite sub-governor (*qa'imaqam*)
and petition Ottoman officials and foreign consuls. Squabbling among
themselves, they evoked the loyalties of their tenants by unleashing
additional obligations and dues.[12] Before the situation exploded into
violent clashes, the Maronite church was preoccupied with far
weightier issues. The Ottoman reformist challenge persisted in making
inroads into its ecclesiastical privileges.

In 1856, the *Hatt-i-Şerif* proclaimed by Sultan 'Abdulmejid
tackled in a frank and deliberate manner the internal affairs of the
various churches and ecclesiastical institutions within the Ottoman
empire. The drive to create a regular system of administration had to
raise the question of the immunities and unaccountability enjoyed by
those who received religious endowments and by Christian ecclesi-
astics. The imperial edict, asserting the need 'to renew and enlarge still
more the new institutions', announced its intention of reforming the
material and spiritual affairs of non-Muslim subjects. It was now the
duty of these millets to set up commissions, under the supervision of
the Sublime Porte, and examine their 'actual immunities and
privileges'.

The Maronite church, having resisted but failed to disrupt the
appointment of Lebanese officials as Ottoman salaried functionaries,
found itself confronting yet another disturbing challenge. It stood to
lose its independence, immunity, and operational autonomy. The
Maronite patriarch, who never sought his formal investment from the
Ottoman sultan as was the custom of other church heads, stood to be
deprived of his freedom of action and become, along with his clergy,
an Ottoman functionary receiving a fixed salary. His 'ecclesiastical
dues' were to be subjected to close inspection, and the outcome
included the possibility of annulment. All the Ottoman Christian
hierarchies resisted these measures as they deemed them concrete
indications of a shift towards a secular government, anxious to
demarcate temporal and spiritual matters, while endeavouring to
extend to lay members a clear advantage over their clergy. Both the
Armenian and Greek Orthodox churches, for example, had to be
cajoled and coerced by Ottoman officials to bring their internal
structures into conformity with the central organs of the state.[13]

As both the French and British governments were committed to the
general policies of the Ottoman reformists, the Maronite church began
to sense its precarious position. Unable to confront the Ottomans
directly, it turned against those it considered their faithful allies: the
Druzes. Its desire to entice France into making a rescue mission hung
in the background as an inevitable course of action.

The eruption of the purely Maronite peasant revolt of Kisrawan in

1858 was both an unwelcome distraction and unexpected. However, the distraction was relatively contained within a year of its inception, while the grievances were channelled into wider horizons. Hence the moderate role played by the patriarch in his various mediating efforts: his apparent endeavours to place the church above two warring factions; and his gentle appeals for a compromise and a peaceful settlement. This almost direct involvement of the Maronite patriarch is often misinterpreted as a sympathetic attitude towards the peasantry. There is no concrete evidence to support such a contention. Taniyus Shahin, the radical leader of the revolt, was frowned upon as a rabble-rouser, a ruffian, and an agent of both the Ottomans and the British.[14] Yusuf Karam, a minor notable from the north was consequently encouraged to curb Shahin's influence and carry his career into obscurity. Once the rebellion was over, the Khazins were allowed to return to their district and repossess most of their property. The civil war which erupted in 1860, and then spilled over into Damascus, partly achieved its objectives. It magnified the plight of Ottoman Christians, amplified the Lebanese crisis, and provided the French with a valid case for military intervention.

It is at this juncture that the careers and political ambitions of both Yusuf Karam and 'Abd al-Qadir al-Jaza'iri (who saved thousands of Damascene Christians from the fury of the mob) become of direct relevance to the issues at hand.[15] Their complementary roles have so far been treated separately, though it is well known that a close personal and political relationship existed between them. They corresponded and exchanged views over a long period of time.[16] Moreover, Karam and the Algerian leader enjoyed the warm and active support of certain French religious and diplomatic circles. Yusuf Karam was being groomed as the future governor of a Christian Lebanon, while 'Abd al-Qadir al-Jaza'iri was promoted as a resplendent monarch of a Syrian or Arabian kingdom. It is also worth noting that the Damascene mob, unlike the indiscriminate Druzes of Lebanon, displayed a relative sophistication and precision in picking out its targets. Thus the Greek Catholic quarter of Damascus bore the brunt of the attack, while the Damascene Greek Orthodox escaped virtually unscathed. 'Abd al-Qadir al-Jaza'iri conveniently absented himself on the morning of the attack, and did not initiate his laudable deeds until the third day of the massacre.[17]

Although the riots had their obvious economic and financial causes, a condition which obtained in almost every Ottoman city, the whole Damascene massacre seemed designed to produce one single hero with an undisputed international reputation. Even the timing of the riots, erupting on 9 July 1860, after the Ottomans had managed to bring hostilities in Lebanon to an end, raises further questions which are still unanswered.

One further observation is in order. Lebanese merchants and bankers, who were in their overwhelming majority Greek Catholics and Orthodox, do not seem to have either instigated or welcomed the outbreak of the civil war. A Greek Catholic silk merchant, based in the town of Dayr al-Qamar, is reported to have acted as a mediator between Druzes and Christians. One merchant, As'ad Djawish, was in no doubt as to the guilty party: 'In fact, he puts a great deal of blame on the Maronite leaders, of whom he mentions the Patriarch Bulus Mas'ad, and the archbishops Butrus al-Bustani and Tubiya 'Awn . . .' [18]

The Ottoman authorities, using a combination of military pacification, prompt punishments and diplomatic agility, managed to disentangle the Lebanese and Damascene crises, and proceeded to lay down their own conditions for the forthcoming settlement. This settlement unfolded under the auspices of an international commission. Its decisions were hammered out, in Beirut and Istanbul, between the representatives of the European powers and Ottoman ministers. The inhabitants of Mount Lebanon were simply expected to obey the decisions made on their behalf by the representatives of their Ottoman sovereign. Accordingly, Lebanon was reconstituted into a single Ottoman district, or *mutasarrifiyya*, under the direct rule of an Ottoman non-Lebanese Christian, chosen by the sultan in consultation with the five European powers. The system of *iltizam* was formally abolished. An Administrative Council consisting of 12 members, with equal representation of the six major sects, was established. In 1864, the quota of representation changed slightly in favour of the Maronites who were awarded four representatives, while the Druzes had three, the Greek Orthodox two, the Greek Catholics one, and the Sunni and Shi'i communities one each. The numerical strength of the Maronites had by that time reached over 200,000, while the Sunnis numbered less than 8,000. Thus proportional representation was excluded in order to prevent the hegemony of one single sect to the detriment of the interests of less numerous ones. However, the Maronites enjoyed considerable influence in the local administration, the judiciary and the newly established gendarmerie.

Once again, Ottoman diplomacy had scored an obvious triumph. It was a triumph which made the Maronite church all the more determined to resist its consequences. Soon it found its instrument in the grievances of Yusuf Karam who had coveted the governorship of the Mountain, and in the opposition of the northern districts to a more regular system of taxation. With the depletion of the numbers of the Druzes, more of their property was taken over by Maronite farmers, or redistributed to former tenants by the new *mutasarrif*, Daud Pasha.

Some of the Druzes migrated to the Hawran region, while others entered into the new political and administrative order either reluctantly or out of conviction.

Daud Pasha, with the assistance of Ottoman military contingents and his newly formed gendarmerie, succeeded in bringing Karam's revolt to an end. By January 1867—the date of Karam's journey towards permanent exile—the Maronite patriarch, dreading the prospect of direct Ottoman occupation and having been increasingly exposed to judicious remonstrations of French diplomacy, succumbed without acknowledging the legitimacy of an Ottoman governor. [19] In refusing to entertain the introduction of Ottoman reforms, the Maronite church was embarking on a course of isolation and conservatism. Its ever-increasing acquisition of lands, owned by debt-ridden farmers and peasants, served to focus attention on its activities among the ranks of its own community. Consequently, French diplomats thought they were witnessing the emergence of a new Maronite 'middle class' bent on whittling away the authority of the church. [20] The landed properties of the church and their mismanagement assumed scandalous proportions which prompted the intervention of the Vatican. However, no tangible results were ever achieved. The French, who had their doubts about the competence of the new 'middle class', reverted to their reliance on the Maronite patriarch as the natural leader of his community. It was left to the Ottoman governor and members of his Administrative Council to foment various forms of protest against the temporal authority of the Maronite church. This state of affairs prevailed throughout the governorship of Muzaffar Pasha (1902–7). As the new patriarch, Ilyas al-Huwayyik (who was elected in 1899) fell increasingly under the conservative influence of his bishops and their landowning allies, who received their majority from Kisrawan, the political life of the Maronites was exposed to the new currents sweeping the Ottoman empire at large.

The relative prosperity which the Mountain witnessed between 1865 and 1900 led to an accelerating growth of population, which in turn increased the movement of emigration to the United States, Latin America and Africa. The silk industry, in its local and foreign branches, began to decline as it faced the competition of Japanese and Chinese producers. Having relied on French capital and markets for its survival and operation, it was suddenly denied its secure source and destination once the same French market found more efficient and better quality supplies. Thus, the historical arguments for annexing Beirut, the Biqa' Valley and other areas, to Mount Lebanon took on an immediate economic relevance. To someone like Jouplain (Nujaym), the very survival of the Maronites depended on the annexation and colonization of these territories. In propounding his case—for a reformed Maronite church, a new political system based on proportional representation, and the annexation of Beirut with its modern harbour—Lebanese patriotism, in its Maronite articulation, assumed the character of an expansionist revitalization of hitherto backward areas extending from the town of Ba'albek down to the north of Palestine.[21] Moreover, France, as the natural protector of the Maronites, was called upon to fulfil the wishes of its faithful clients. Jouplain, in his well-documented and polemical extensive history of Lebanon, covering the course of its development from its immemorial origins down to his own time, inaugurated the abrogation of the history of *the other*—the Muslim Arab.

At a time when the Ottoman state was leaving behind the *tanzimat* along with Sultan 'Abdulhamid, stepping into a new world of secular nationalism, or political independence, most Maronite intellectuals were either pleading for French military occupation or elaborating an exclusively Christian identity. Those who opposed these two trends clung to a particular attitude of Ottoman practice and diplomacy, oblivious of its recession before their own eyes. In a sense, the Administrative Council, and those associated with the institutions of the *mutasarrifiyya*, represented the continuity and rehabilitation of the vanishing age of the *tanzimat*. When the French finally invaded Lebanon in 1918, steam-reeling silk factories and the cultivation of mulberry trees had ceased to be the main economic activity of the Mountain. Hence, Beiruti merchants and bankers were diversifying their financial investments and seeking more lucrative markets outside the confines of Mount Lebanon.[22] France itself arrived with a claim on the entirety of geographical Syria. Even some of the most ardent former Lebanese francophiles shifted their position to accommodate one French authority presiding over one united geographical Syria.

The proclamation of an independent Arab government in Syria under the leadership of Faysal, in addition to armed and popular resistance which sprang up against permanent French presence, and the oscillation of Faysal between full independence and a milder French influence, convinced the French of the necessity of a viable Greater Lebanon. In the event, the Maronite patriarch received more than he had bargained for; while his brother, Sa'adallah al-Huwayyik, the Maronite councillor of the district of Batrun, along with six other members of the Administrative Council, hesitated between an emergent Arab Syrian movement, and the acceptance of a temporary French presence.

By 1920, the rapid succession of events imposed its own logic. The Administrative Council took the first option, albeit in its mildest versions. On 10 July 1920 the seven members issued a decree demanding an independent neutral Lebanon, closely allied with the newly proclaimed Syrian kingdom of Faysal I. The decree, which is invariably overlooked by official Lebanese historiography, outlined the following means as the best safeguards of the future of Mount Lebanon:

1. The complete and absolute independence of Mount Lebanon.
2. Its political neutrality, in the sense that it shall not have an army and it shall not be subject to any military intervention.
3. The restitution of the territory that was detached from it, which shall be effected through mutual agreement between it and the government of Syria.
4. The study of the economic conditions by a mixed commission whose decision shall be effective after it has been ratified by both the Lebanese and the Syrian parliaments.
5. The two parties shall co-operate in the move to have the Powers sanction and guarantee the four articles above mentioned.[23]

The seven members were arrested by the French authorities as they headed towards Damascus. They were promptly put on trial, accused of high treason, and sent into exile. The Administrative Council itself was dissolved as the last Ottoman institution of Mount Lebanon. [24]

In a final symbolic act of complete abrogation, the French high commissioner, General Gouraud, chose the pine forest of Beirut to declare before an assembled audience the creation of Greater Lebanon. It was in the same forest that in 1861 the Ottoman reformist statesman, Fu'ad Pasha, had announced to a large gathering the official establishment of the *mutasarrifiyya*.

Notes

1. The *Hatt-i-Şerif* of Gülhane issued by Sultan 'Abdulmejid (1839–61) upon his accession was the first open statement of intent to introduce fundamental reforms in the Ottoman state.[Ed.]

2. *Muqata'ji*s or *multazim*s as they were commonly known in other parts of the Ottoman empire.

3. A. B. Cunningham, *The Early Correspondence of Richard Wood 1831–1841* (London, 1966), p. 214. Letter to Lord Ponsonby, Beirut, 17 February 1841.

4. Ibid., p. 242.

5. M. Jouplain (Bulus Nujaym), *La Question du Liban*, 2nd edn (Juniya, 1961), pp. 324–5; Antun Dahir al-'Aqiqi, *Thawra wa fitna fi Lubnan* (Beirut, 1938), pp. 161–3.

6. For a full English translation of the *Hatti-i-Şerif* of Gülhane, to which references are being made here, see J. C. Hurewitz, *Diplomacy in the Near and Middle East: a Documentary Record 1535–1914*, vol. 1 (Princeton, NJ, 1956, 1958), pp. 113–16. For a French translation, see *British and Foreign State Papers 1842–1843*, vol. XXXI (London, 1858), pp. 1239–42.

7. J. C. Hurewitz, *Diplomacy*, p. 114.

8. *British and Foreign State Papers 1856–1857*, vol. XLVII (London, 1866), pp. 1363–8; J. C. Hurewitz, *Diplomacy*, pp. 149–53.

9. See for example R. H. Davison, *Reform in the Ottoman Empire 1856–1876* (New York, 1963, 1973), p. 132.

10. This school of thought finds its most coherent illustration in a work published by a Lebanese Shiʻi Marxist: Waddah Sharara, *Fi Usul Lubnan al-Taʼifi* (Beirut, 1975).

11. Yusuf Hubaysh (1823–45), and Yusuf al-Khazin (1845–54).

12. The origins and unfolding events of the revolt have been extensively studied. See for example D. Chevallier, 'Aux origines des troubles agraires libanais en 1858', *Annales* XIV (1959) 35–64; Y. Porath, 'The peasant revolt of 1858–1861 in Kisrawan', *Asian and African Studies* II (1966) 77–157.

13. R. M. Davison, *Reform in the Ottoman Empire*, ch. 4.

14. Kamal Salibi, *The Modern History of Lebanon* (London, 1965), p. 86; Dominique Chevallier, *La Société du Mont Liban* (Paris, 1971), p. 289 n. 3.

15. For a direct account of ʻAbd al-Qadir's intervention on behalf of the Christians of Damascus during the massacre of 1860, see Col. Charles Churchill, *The Druzes and the Maronites under the Turkish Rule from 1840 to 1860* (London, 1862), pp. 212–17.

16. The texts of a number of letters exchanged between Karam and al-Jazaʼiri were published by two Maronite authors. Istifan al-Bishʻalani, *Lubnan wa Yusuf Karam* (Beirut, 1924), pp. 569–73; Simʻan al-Khazin, *Yusuf Bey Karam fi al-Manfa* (Tripoli, 1950), pp. 346–56.

17. Linda Schatkowski Schiller, *Families in Politics, Damascene Factions and Estates of the 18th and 19th Centuries* (Stuttgart, 1985), pp. 88–9.

18. Fritz Steppat, 'Some Arabic manuscript sources on the Syrian crisis of 1860', in J. Berque and D. Chevallier eds, *Les Arabes par leurs archives (XVIe–XXe siècles)* (Paris, 1976).

19. Henri Jalabert, *Un montagnard contre le pouvoir: Liban 1866* (Beirut, 1975), pp. 42 and 215.

20. Adel Ismail ed., *Documents diplomatiques et consulairs relatifs à l'histoire du Liban*, vol. 18 (Beirut, 1979), pp. 332–4; Joseph Hajjar, *Le Vatican—la France et le catholicisme oriental (1878–1914)* (Paris, 1979), pp. 477–8.

21. M. Jouplain, *La Question du Liban*, pp. 466–534. See in particular his argument for settling Maronite peasant colonies on what he considered depopulated or neglected areas outside Mount Lebanon (pp. 529–30).

22. Roger Owen, *The Middle East in the World Economy, 1800–1914* (London and New York, 1981, 1987), p. 253.

23. Walter L. Browne ed., *The Political History of Lebanon, 1920–1950. Documents on Politics and Political Parties under French Mandate, 1920–1936*, vol. I (Salisbury, NC, 1976), pp. 17–18.

24. Yusuf Muzhir, *Tarikh Lubnan al-ʻam* (Beirut, 1955), pp. 920–8.

5

The Administrative Council
of Mount Lebanon

ENGIN DENIZ AKARLI

In 1861, when the *mutasarrifiyya* regime was first established in Mount Lebanon, the Lebanese were a people divided against themselves.[1] Except for the Maronite church, there was not a single group of leaders or organization which could speak for a significant number of them. As for the church, its generally sectarian stance on local issues and heavy reliance on France in external relations seriously impaired its ability to speak for the entire people of the Mountain.

By the end of the first world war, however, a political leadership representing the interests of different regions, sects and dominant social classes had formed in Lebanon. The Administrative Council of the *mutasarrifiyya* had come to provide the institutional framework within which the Lebanese leadership endeavoured to consolidate their conflicting material and moral interests according to preconceived norms and procedures. As it was an established electoral system that brought the councillors to power, their right to speak for the Lebanese was hardly challenged either internally or externally. This paper narrates this evolution of the Administrative Council from its unimpressive origins to an institution of respected political leadership.

Composition and duties of the council

The organizational framework of the new regime established in Mount Lebanon in 1861 was defined in an international agreement called the *Règlement et protocole relatifs à la réorganisation du Mont Liban*. The *Règlement*, which went through a major revision in 1864, stipulated the formation of an Administrative Council to provide counsel to the governor (1864: art. 3).[2]

The council would be composed of 12 members: four Maronites, three Druzes, two Greek Orthodox, one Greek Catholic, one Shi'i (*mutawali*), and one Sunni Muslim. The constituencies of the councillors were also specified. Batrun and Kisrawan would each send one councillor to the council, and they would both be Maronite. The three councillors from Jezzin were to be Maronite, Druze and Sunni Muslim; and the four from Matn Maronite, Druze, Shi'i and Greek Orthodox. The only Greek Catholic member of the council was to be elected by the town of Zahle, which was depicted as a constituency in itself (1864: art. 2).

This arrangement concerning the composition of the council was based on rough estimates of the distribution of the population and landownership. The population and land counts completed in 1868 necessitated revisions in the composition of the council; henceforth, the Sunni councillor was elected from Shuf and the Shi'i councillor from Kisrawan.[3]

The Maronites were not proportionally represented in the council. While they constituted 57.5 per cent of the total population and paid 51.2 per cent of the land tax,[4] they had only four votes in the council. There were, however, clauses in the 1864 *Règlement* and a number of administrative measures which ameliorated the representation of the Maronites. According to the 1864 *Règlement*, each village community, as a whole, irrespective of its denominational composition, would elect a village shaykh for itself, and the village shaykhs of each administrative district would elect the councillors from that district. Although not explicitly stated so in the *Règlement*, in practice the village shaykhs were elected from among the dominant denomination in each village.[5] Consequently, the Maronites, who constituted the majority of the population in Batrun, Kisrawan, Matn and Jezzin, and 30 per cent of Shuf's population, found themselves in a strong position to influence the outcome of the elections, irrespective of the denominational specifications for running in the elections. In Jezzin for instance, where three councillors were elected, each from a different religious group, all candidates had to win the support of the Maronite village shaykhs, who were clearly in the majority. Aside from necessitating political alliances that crossed denominational lines, participation of the communities in the election of the shaykhs and the councillors helped the Maronites to accept the new regime more willingly.

An additional measure towards the same end was taken by Daud Pasha, the first governor of the *mutasarrifiyya* (1861–8). He introduced the post of deputy chairman to the council and appointed a Maronite to it. Such a position did not exist in the *Règlement*, which designated the governor as the natural chairman of the council. Nevertheless, Daud's deputy in the council participated in its meetings and ran it in the governor's absence. This practice set a precedent for successive governors. The deputy chairman, invariably a Maronite, became a regular member of the council with a right to vote.[6] In time, as the council's power and prestige increased, so the deputy chairmanship of the council became the most coveted position in the *mutasarrifiyya* administration.[7]

At first the council had a basically consultative function. According to the *Règlement*, its duties were to 'apportion taxation, supervise the administration of revenue and of expenditure and give an advisory opinion on questions submitted to it by the governor' (1864: art. 2). In addition, the governor was obliged to consult the council, if under unusual circumstances he deemed it appropriate to call in the regular Ottoman troops stationed in the neighbouring provinces (art. 14). These duties did not add up to much, and they were not even backed by specific sanctions, except for the council's right to veto by majority vote any tax increases proposed by the governor.[8]

In an effort to generate indigenous support for the new regime, however, Daud Pasha and his successor Franco Qusa Pasha (1868–73) encouraged the participation of the council in the government more closely than was stipulated in the *Règlement*. The settlement of internal disputes of minor diplomatic significance was left to the council. The governors also sought the co-operation of the council in a number of sensitive issues, such as the well-known resistance of Yusuf Karam.[9] It was the council's power of veto over tax increases that eventually brought it to the forefront of Lebanese politics.

The council's weapon: its right to veto tax increases

The *Règlement* set a maximum limit of 3.5 million piastres to the taxes imposed on the people of the Mountain. The tax revenue was to be devoted primarily to administrative costs and public works in the Mountain. If the expenditures necessary for the proper administration of the Mountain exceeded the revenue from taxation, the Imperial Treasury would provide the difference so long as the Sublime Porte approved the extra expenditure (1864: art. 15).

A codicil, which was incorporated into the *Règlement* at the last minute in 1861 and remained in effect thereafter, stipulated that taxation could be raised above the predetermined sum if the governor, the Sublime Porte and the Administrative Council agreed on its necessity. The codicil thus gave the council the right to veto tax increases, and this right proved to be its most effective weapon against the governors.

Soon after the establishment of the *mutasarrifiyya*, its expenditures began to lag behind its revenue, due to the expansion of the governmental apparatus and the implementation of projects to improve public security and transportation, as well as to a modest economic revival and consequent price increases.[10] At first, the Ottoman central government met the *mutasarrifiyya*'s budgetary deficits with substantial subsidies. At the time of Rustam Pasha's governorship (1873–83), however, the grave deterioration of Ottoman finances precluded such help. Unable to subsidize the *mutasarrifiyya*, the Porte kept pressuring Rustam to balance his budget. Rustam's efforts to raise the fixed level of taxation or to introduce fees on certain governmental services were nullified by the opposition of the council.

At this stage, the council, especially its Maronite members, had a tendency to view Ottoman financial aid to the Mountain as an obligation of the central government under the international conventions which ratified the *Règlement*. From the Porte's point of view, however, the subsidy was a benevolent measure directed towards the removal of internal tension and the foundation of peaceful order and effective administration in the Mountain. Once order was established, its financial burden was meant to be shouldered by the Lebanese themselves.

Perhaps it was natural for the Lebanese, as represented by the council, to want to minimize their tax burden whatever the cost and complications for the Ottoman government. But the council's insistence on holding the Porte responsible for the payment of the *mutasarrifiyya*'s budgetary deficits made little sense in the face of Ottoman financial insolvency. Besides, interpreted literally, the international conventions, on which the council based its argument, obliged the Porte only to spend the revenue from extra taxation in the Mountain itself, and not to underwrite the budgetary deficits of its government. Under the circumstances, the council's attitude raised the likelihood of having to make do with poorer public services.

Unable to raise additional revenue at a sufficient rate and pressured by the Porte to balance his budget, Rustam made rigorous cuts in salaries, reduced the size of the local security force, and cut down on other public expenditures as well. He also resorted to forceful measures to collect the regular tax arrears accumulated since their final waiver in 1872. His policy helped to decrease the annual budgetary deficit, but it also widened the gulf between him and the council on all issues. He ignored the council altogether, hardly ever referring any significant issue to it for consultation.[11] By the end of Rustam's term, the council had solidly established its power to block administrative decisions on financial issues, but it had not yet demonstrated a capacity to offer solutions to the problems that adversely affected the regime which was its *raison d'être*.

Early in Wasa's governorship (1882–92), the Porte dispatched a significant sum to the *mutasarrifiyya* to help restore relations between the new governor and the council, but on the absolute condition that the *mutasarrifiyya* never again incurred a deficit. In the following years, the Porte no longer provided financial assistance to the *mutasarrifiyya*, except for occasional and insignificant amounts. Istanbul's determined position and other developments (discussed below) compelled the council to reach a reconciliation with the governor over the creation of new revenue sources in order to avoid the impairment of governmental and other public services in the Mountain.[12]

The solution to the problem was the development of a hitherto insignificant item in the *mutasarrifiyya*'s budget. This was the so-called *muhmalat* account, or the fees charged for the financing of specific public services and projects by the decision of the council and under its exclusive control. Franco Pasha had been the first governor to initiate the *muhmalat* account but on a very modest scale. Rustam's efforts to enlarge it had been only partially successful. But during Wasa's governorship, the account developed into a distinct budget, which afterwards became both larger and more varied. It was kept separate from the regular accounts of the *mutasarrifiyya* and, unlike the *mutasarrifiyya*, was not subject to inspection by the Ministry of Finance in Istanbul. The imposition of the *muhmalat* dues as well as the use of the funds thus raised were determined exclusively by the Administrative Council.

The growing importance of the *muhmalat* budget did not altogether dispel the tension between the governors and the council over taxation. Whenever the finances of the *mutasarrifiyya* were strained, the council would tend to insist on the Porte's financial assistance for a solution while the governor would be inclined to raise the level of taxation fixed by the *Règlement*. Ultimately, if the sides agreed, they would create a new *muhmalat* item or raise the rates of the old ones. As the monetary funds under the council's direct authority thereby increased, so did its effective power and importance in Lebanese politics.

By the end of Wasa's term, the council had already become the chief governmental agency responsible for the construction of public works, especially bridges and roads. It planned public construction projects, organized taxation from the people who would theoretically benefit from those projects, and saw to their implementation. These politically difficult tasks put the councillors at the centre of public attention. This outcome cannot be understood properly without reference to Wasa's efforts to make the councillors co-operate with him. In order to attract the councillors to his side, Wasa became involved in their elections, and thereby in the internal politics of the Mountain, more deeply than any of his predecessors.

Elections and politics in the Mountain

According to the *Règlement*, the councillors were to be elected for a
term of six years (by the village shaykhs, as described above).
Re-election was possible. New elections were held for one-third of the
councillorships in rotation every two years (art. 10).

In the earlier years of the *mutasarrifiyya*, the stipulations of the
Règlement were applied quite informally. In Daud's days, the
councillors were appointed only after consultation with the religious
leaders and notables of each district.[13] Recourse to the village
shaykhs' opinion began in Franco's days, and then for only three
councillors from Batrun, Kura and Jezzin.[14] In these elections, the
shaykhs were asked to appear on a specified day in the district seat to
express their choice orally before an election committee composed of
the district head and judges.[15] Rustam Pasha introduced the 'secret
ballot'. On the announced day of the elections, the shaykhs wrote
down their choices on a piece of paper and cast it into an election box
before the election committee. They voted as they wished, but were
required to undersign the ballots and stamp them with their official
seals.[16]

To the best of our knowledge the elections, whether by consensus
or the oral vote, and the undersigned ballot, did not lead to a
significant rise in the political tension in the Mountain until Wasa's
time.[17] Political ambitions were directed towards acquiring administrative and judicial positions[18] rather than the relatively unimportant
councillorships. The local notables and religious leaders almost
dominated the elections through their influence over the village
shaykhs, who were mostly semi-literate and had little experience of
nation-wide politics.[19] The Maronite clergy were particularly effective in influencing the opinion of the shaykhs. The Maronite church
remained a powerful organization. It enjoyed the diplomatic and
financial support of the French; had an intelligentsia of its own;
controlled large tracts of arable land and other sources of livelihood;
and wielded religious authority over the majority of the population.[20]

Daud Pasha realized that he had to make the new regime acceptable
to the Maronite clergy for it to strike roots in the Mountain. He
encouraged the Maronite clergy to play an active role in the
administration in at least three ways that are pertinent here. First, he
appointed to the Maronite judgeships people who belonged to the
clergy or were backed by them. Second, he kept the most powerful
Druze notables away from governmental posts and even physically
away from the Mountain. Finally, he left the selection of the councillors
to the clergy and notables. Daud's successor Franco, who had a much
closer relationship with the leading Maronite clergy, continued the

policies of Daud.[21] The first two governors' conciliatory attitude towards the Maronites in general and the Maronite church in particular facilitated the establishment of the *mutasarrifiyya* on firmer ground than would have been possible otherwise.

The third governor, Rustam, turned his attention to the accommodation of the powerful Druze notables. He also brought pressure on the Maronite patriarch and bishops to make them acknowledge Ottoman suzerainty formally and clearly. This was a demand which the Maronite church, with French backing, considered an impingement upon its autonomy. Rustam also began to replace high-ranking judicial and administrative officials, who were known for their affinity to the Maronite church and the French consulate, with a cadre whom he held to be professionally better qualified to serve the interests of the *mutasarrifiyya*.[22] In turn the French consul and the Maronite clergy launched a campaign against Rustam.[23]

The conflict that erupted between the governor and the council over financial issues was partly a consequence of this campaign. The Maronite clergy, orchestrated by the influential Bishop Yusuf Dibs, maintained that the governor wanted to increase their tax burden unlawfully. Their activity affected the councillors, especially the ones who came from the predominantly Maronite districts, where the clergy wielded a strong influence on the electors.[24] Rustam did not interfere with the electors, but he rebuked the councillors and treated them haughtily, thereby only deepening the cleavage.[25] He believed that his opponents in the council were being used by the Maronite bishops and the French consulate in order to force him to observe a policy that catered to the partisan interests of the church and the consulate.[26] Hamdi Pasha, the governor of Damascus, agreed with Rustam;[27] so did Rustam's successor, Wasa.

Soon after his arrival in the Mountain, Wasa became convinced that certain councillors had exceeded the bounds defined in the *Règlement* by interfering with political and diplomatic affairs. To please the circles they served and so that 'unbefitting' people could be employed in government jobs, these councillors had even opposed projects beneficial to their own country. Wasa enquired from the Porte whether dismissing these councillors was possible.[28] The Porte's response was strictly to prohibit this. On the basis of the legal opinion reached by the Council of State, the grand vizier forced Wasa to observe the rights of the council stipulated in the *Règlement*. He also reminded Wasa that as the chairman of the council the governor was in a position to prevent the councillors from exceeding the bounds of their rights and duties. Even if a councillor persisted in ignoring warnings, in deference to foreign interests, a categorical decision was impermissible. Each case was to be handled individually, with reference to the damage done to the interests of the state and in accordance with the laws.[29]

Upon this response, Wasa turned his attention to the elections as the only means to alter the composition of the council. New elections were due for four of the councillors in the spring of 1885. Wasa hoped for the replacement of the two whom he believed to be backed by the Maronite church and the French consulate. A month before the elections, he began to prepare the Porte for possible reactions against his election policy. He argued that

> since the councillors were elected for an uninterrupted term of six years into a body that collectively represented the population [of the Mountain], their word bore some influence on the simple folk. Consequently, the election of the councillors from among those who adhered to a specific circle [with foreign linkages] would be inexpedient from the government's point of view.

If the Maronite church and the French consulate got their own partisans into the council, this would entail the expansion of foreign influence and 'thus disgrace the government and adversely affect its interests'. Wasa asked the Porte not to heed petitions which the opponents of his government would surely lodge, should their candidates lose.[30] When the elections were finally held, the results turned out to be to Wasa's full satisfaction. All the candidates whom he favoured won the elections by an absolute or near-absolute majority.[31] In later reports, he was to boast that in 1885 'he had smoothly managed to get elected councillors who shun adherence to foreign interests'— thereby confessing that he had designed the outcome beforehand.[32] In 1885, Wasa had caught the French consulate and the Maronite church unawares, preventing them from launching an effective campaign against the election results. At the next elections, however, due in the spring of 1887, the governor was to face more sustained oppostion.

To use Wasa's own classification, the 'partisans of the government' and the 'partisans of the French' found themselves involved in intense competition during the 1887 elections. These elections were again for four councillors: two Druzes from Shuf and Jezzin, one Greek Catholic from Zahle and one Maronite from Batrun. The Druze candidates supported by the government were certain to win the elections without serious challenge. Competition therefore concentrated in Zahle, and especially in Batrun where close to 85 per cent of the population was Maronite. In Zahle the candidate supported by the government partisans won the votes of 28 electors out of a total of 41. In Batrun, too, Wasa's favourite, Kan'an al-Zahir, defeated the church's candidate 'Assaf Baytar.[33]

Both results were immediately contested. Concerning Batrun, it was argued that ten villages had not been represented in the elections as the shaykhs had been absent because of last-minute dismissals or other reasons. No time had been allowed to replace them. Besides, local administrative officials had been personally involved in propaganda for the candidates supported by the government. Furthermore, contrary to customary procedure, the administration had made the shaykhs vote in small groups by subdistricts and on separate days, instead of the same day.[34] A group of protesters marched from consulate to consulate in the streets of Beirut to demonstrate their dissatisfaction with the election results. They then came to Ba'abda to file complaints with the governor himself. Wasa sent them to the council, which conducted an investigation and decided that the election had been fairly held and that there were no legal grounds for contesting the outcome.[35]

Upon this decision, a new wave of protest erupted, with people marching in the streets and to Wasa's house in Beirut objecting to the council's decision. According to their own account, there were 500 of them, including village shaykhs and notables. According to Wasa, they were a 'lowly' group of 70 or 80 composed of peasants, workers, beggars and the like who resided in the vicinity of Bishop Freifer's residence in Batrun. Wasa not only refused to talk to them but, according to the protesters, he pulled a gun to disperse them. He also ordered the arrest and trial of five people who were alleged to be the ringleaders. The suspects were tried and found guilty: three of them were sentenced to a year imprisonment and the other two were fined. The decision was upheld by the Appeal Court, and Wasa made sure that the council sanctioned the final decision.[36]

The French consul turned the case into a diplomatic issue, which lingered on for several months, much to the distaste of the French ambassador in Istanbul, who favoured the cultivation of good relations with the Ottoman government in order to serve French interests around the empire, not just in Lebanon and Syria.[37] Wasa took advantage of the ambassador's position to consolidate his authority in the Mountain and his influence over the council. He arranged with the Porte the release of the imprisoned by means of an imperial amnesty on the anniversary of the sultan's accession, provided that the French consul in Beirut acknowledged the legality of the elections. The French embassy in Istanbul went along with the arrangement and peace was made between the governor and the French consul.[38] This was an achievement which impressed upon the Lebanese Wasa's ability to influence the elections. The candidates supported by the governor had little difficulty winning the elections in 1889 and 1891.[39]

From the beginning, Wasa had set about bringing together a group of councillors who would co-operate with him. He believed the influence of the Maronite clergy over the councillors and their electors had to be broken. To this end he influenced the elections with the assistance of administrative personnel who were willing to help him. His predecessor Rustam had already made significant changes in the administrative and judicial personnel to weaken the influence of the Maronite clergy in government offices. Wasa pursued a similar policy and strengthened the position of the administrative officials who had replaced the protégés of the Maronite church. They in turn helped the governor procure agreeable results in the council elections. They blocked the campaigns of candidates supported by the Maronite clergy, and even used their authority openly in favour of alternative candidates. In doing so, they pitted themselves against the Maronite church and invested their future in the institutions of the *mutasarrifiyya*. This group constituted the core of Wasa's 'government party'.

The Maronite church continued to play a major role in all aspects of Lebanese politics, from mass demonstrations to diplomatic crises. Its weight certainly entered the calculations of everybody from the village shaykhs to government officials and the governor. Nevertheless, by the end of Wasa's term the church's power had declined, in the sense that it had to act within a more complicated system with firmer institutions, and bargain harder to perpetuate its interests against other circles of interest.

The councillors found themselves interposed between the church and government 'parties'. Unlike the clergy, they were not directly linked to outside powers. Unlike the administrative and judicial officials, they were in principle elected and not appointed, and they could not be summarily dismissed. Under Wasa, councillors who wanted to be elected had to reconsider their political affiliations and alliances, and cultivate good relations with the governor and his assistants. But that was only a necessary and not a sufficient condition for success. The councillors had to retain some popularity to be worthy of support. Since such popularity would not arise if the councillors severed their relations with the church completely, they were not expected to do so. On the contrary, the council was encouraged to act as a buffer between the church and the administration, as illustrated by the role it played in the anti-government demonstrations of 1887 described above. This position of the council between the church and government parties, and the principally autonomous constitutional status of the council, were conditions which enhanced its importance in Lebanese politics.

Wasa's conciliatory attitude towards the council was yet another factor. He was always ready to come to terms with the councillors.[40] He bore no grudges against former opponents and was willing to make concessions to the council both as an institution and as a group of individuals. The development of the *muhmalat* budget is the best case in point. Each fee and due proposed by the governor and accepted by the council enhanced the council's authority and the councillors' prestige in Lebanese society. Being in direct charge of monetary matters provided the less conscientious councillors with opportunities for self-enrichment.[41] But any councillor was in a good position to defend or promote regional interest, to distribute benefits, and to pursue the affairs of others in government offices, including the council itself, which now actively participated in important governmental decisions. Given sufficient tact when dealing with older centres of power in Mount Lebanon, a councillor could turn himself into a political boss in his own right.[42] But in the early 1890s, the council had yet to prove itself as a stable institution, capable of acting in reasonable harmony.

Upon Wasa's death in 1892, an imperial decree authorized the council to take charge of the administration until the Porte appointed a new governor. The council failed to live up to the responsibility. Divided against itself, with all the Maronite councillors and one of the Druze councillors on one side and the remaining councillors on the other, the council became bogged down in petty quarrels for over two months. Twice the Porte ordered the governor of Beirut to act as a peacemaker between the two sides but to no avail.[43] Meanwhile, the church party procured 1,200 signatures for a petition which called for precautions to assure full freedom in the elections. The petition claimed that since the village shaykhs were subordinates of the governor, he could at times dismiss them, thus retaining an indirect influence on the council.[44]

In response to such complaints, two amendments were made to the *Règlement* by way of the protocol for the appointment of Na'um Pasha as the governor of Mount Lebanon in 1892. One of these amendments obliged the governor to respect the guarantees allowed to the judiciary and to base the dismissal of judges on investigations that should be carried out by the council. This amendment not only enhanced the constitutional authority of the council, but also provided protection to electors against administrative fiat, since the village shaykhs were justices of the peace as well as electors and village heads. The 1892 protocol also underlined the necessity of compliance with the duties of the council and the need to secure the freedom of the elections.[45] The grand vizier's instructions to the new governor confirmed the same points and warned against the recurrence of political tension over the elections.[46]

Na'um Pasha (1892–1902) observed the form rather than the spirit of his instructions. From the beginning, he made it clear that he was unwilling to encourage the enhancement of the council's authority and influence.[47] A convenient convergence of local and international interests enabled if not urged Na'um to restrict the council to routine tasks.

Na'um was the son-in-law of Franco Qusa, who had helped resolve the feud between the Khazins, once the lords of Kisrawan, and the Maronite church. The Khazins supported Na'um. Yuhanna Hajj, the Maronite patriarch who owed his position to the support of a socially conservative group of bishops and priests—who were mostly from Kisrawan and favoured moderation in relationships with political authority—also backed the governor. Na'um, in turn, was readily willing to co-operate with the church. He was also able to enlist the support of the powerful Druze leader Mustafa Arslan. This formidable local alliance was unhampered by the usual contradictions between the major international guarantors of the regime in Mount Lebanon, for Na'um's governorship coincided with a period both of consensus of interest among these powers over Ottoman affairs and of relative tranquility in Ottoman politics. Under the circumstances, Na'um and his local advocates smoothly pushed the key administrative officials who had supported Wasa as well as the councillors into oblivion.[48]

The socio-political stability that marked Na'um's ten-year term fostered a conformist attitude in Lebanese politics for all its underlying tensions. Councillors, bureaucrats, notables, and the newly rich adhered to similar manners and catered to similar values of social distinction, irrespective of their denominational, political and class differences. In this sense, the period witnessed the rise of an enduring social elite that helped define a distinct Lebanese identity.[49]

One group within this elite had reasons to become increasingly wary of the *rapprochement* between the traditionally influential families and the church, because it implied the eclipse of the council. They were the younger public figures in Mount Lebanon who had built their power bases in Wasa's days, as a direct consequence of the enhanced importance of the council and the council elections. They now realized that success in the system depended more on connection to well-established circles than an ability in grass-roots politics. Defence of the rights of the council as the representative of the Lebanese people served as a rallying point for this group. They began to form an anti-Qusa faction which, in their criticism of the establishment, contained liberal overtones. They seem to have had an influence in thwarting the efforts to prolong Na'um's tenure or to appoint his brother-in-law Yusuf Qusa in his place.[50] Instead, an obscure Ottoman general of Polish background, Muzaffar Pasha, was chosen to replace Na'um.

The council as the representative of the people

Muzaffar Pasha (1902–7), whether by choice or necessity, sided with the anti-Qusa faction, thereby pitting himself against powerful vested interests. Under the circumstances, he kept falling back on the council to provide weight to his major administrative decisions.[51] Simultaneously, he took measures to make the council more representative of regional interests. These measures included the introduction of the completely secret ballot and more impartial supervision in both stages of the elections.[52]

How effectively the new election procedures were applied in different parts of the Mountain is difficult to tell, but there is evidence which suggests that the election became better organized, freer and more competitive. In at least two districts, namely Kisrawan and Matn, secular alliances clearly outweighed sectarian differences, and the councillors tended to consider themselves as the 'representatives of the people' with increasing assertiveness and self-confidence.[53] Muzaffar frequently disagreed with some or even the majority of the councillors, but he did respect the duties of the council and encouraged it to initiate financial projects of its own.[54] The council once more moved to the centre of Lebanese politics.

Accusations of corruption against the council and the governor mounted simultaneously. As Muzaffar's term approached its end, his opponents intensified their charges and campaigned for the appointment of Yusuf Qusa to his place. A number of the councillors, led by Muzaffar's long-time deputy Habib Sa'ad, openly opposed the idea. But when Muzaffar died in 1907, Yusuf was speedily appointed as the new governor.[55]

Yusuf Pasha (1907–12) returned to power men employed by Na'um, and began to put pressure on the council. On the advice of his advocates, he suspended Shadid 'Aql, a Maronite councillor from Matn associated with the anti-Qusa faction, on charges of bribery (April 1909). Shadid did not have an unsullied reputation as a politician, but the legal flimsiness of the charges brought against him, and the prolongation of his case due to administrative evasions, justify his belief that he had been persecuted in an effort to subdue the council. Shadid himself was not vindicated until early 1910,[56] but the tide of events changed in favour of the defenders of the council's autonomy soon after the July 1908 *coup d'état* in Istanbul. Yusuf felt obliged to appoint Salim Ammun as his deputy in concession to the liberalist demands of a group of councillors and politicians. For about a year the 'liberal' councillors dominated the government of Mount Lebanon.[57] Some of their deeds, however, could hardly be called liberal.

Their conduct in the elections held in Kura and Kisrawan early in
1909 is a case in point. In Kura, the elections were to take place in
August 1908 to replace the deceased Jirjus al-ʿAzar, a close friend of
the Qusas. His son Fuʾad was the strongest candidate. The liberals
wanted to contest him, but they needed time to work on the electors in
favour of their candidate Jirji Tamer. They managed to postpone the
elections. Fuʾad's supporters responded by accusing Jirji of bribery
and machinations. The council at first agreed to investigate the
complaints but later retracted its decision. The elections were finally
held in February 1909 amid ongoing protests by Fuʾad's supporters,
which ended in bloody clashes with the security forces. Fuʾad was
arrested as an instigator and the council declared Jirji as the winner of
the election.[58]

In the Kisrawan elections of March 1909, the incumbent Shiʿi
Muhammad Muhsin ran against al-Hajj ʿAli Kazim. Muhammad was a
humble person in comparison with his rival, but he enjoyed the
support of his Maronite colleague Jirjus Zuain. Jirjus was the most
impetuous of the 'liberal' councillors and in a position to bring
significant pressure on the Maronite electors as well as the administrative officials in Kisrawan. He used his means unabashedly to effect
Muhammad's re-election. ʿAli Kazim appealed against the outcome to
Istanbul, claiming that election regulations had been violated and
accusing the council of covering up for Jirjus. At this point, Yusuf
opted to defend the council against the charges, despite the strength of
ʿAli's case.[59]

Under the control of the liberals and aided by the circumstances,
the council had effectively curtailed the powers of the governor. A
reaction was building against the liberals, however, among Ottoman
statesmen, European diplomats and, most importantly, among the
Lebanese themselves. Riding on this reaction, Yusuf once again found
himself in a position to contest the council's autonomy. The tension
that began to build between the two sides by mid-1909 finally erupted
in a showdown of force in early 1910. Jirjus kicked the doors of
Yusuf's office open for Yusuf's refusal to talk to 'a representative of
the Lebanese people', only to find himself in gaol.[60] Yusuf turned the
incident into an excuse to demand from the Porte permission to
dismiss the entire council.[61]

When the Porte refused his request on the grounds that it was
unlawful and unprecedented, petitions condemning the misconduct of
the councillors, and signed by individuals from different districts and
groups, began to pour into Istanbul. These petitions accused the
councillors of the violation of election procedures in force, the abuse of
financial duties and the mismanagement of public funds for self-
enrichment. Councillors were said to represent their own interests

alone, and their dismissal was necessary in order to make possible the free and lawful election of honest representatives who would serve the development of Mount Lebanon.[62] Yusuf must have been instrumental in the preparation of these petitions, but it is doubtful that he could have instigated them without substantial support from the Lebanese themselves. Even if the accusations of corruption were exaggerated, the liberal councillors' partisanship seems to have evoked sufficient popular resistance to enable their opponents to launch an effective campaign against them.

In defence of their position, the liberal councillors went round the consulates in Beirut accusing the governor and his advisers of oppression. Their arguments imply that they wanted the governor to seek the council's approval not only on financial issues but also on all important administrative decisions, including the application of Ottoman laws in Mount Lebanon and even the appointment of senior officials. The consuls were unmoved by these claims and by implication sided with the governor.[63]

Their attitude was not unbiased. If the consuls had agreed to the council's demand for greater powers, they would have complicated the interests of their own governments. There were a number of agreements between the Ottoman and European governments which the majority of the Lebanese political leadership, for all their differences, considered as constraints to the economic development of the Mountain. A powerful council was as likely to rule against these agreements as against other disliked Ottoman legislation. A development in this direction would have jeopardized the interests of the French above all, for they were the greatest beneficiaries of the agreements. The French might still have gone along with the demands of the liberal councillors had they trusted the ability of the Maronite church to influence the outcome of the council elections. But the complexity which the socio-political conditions and political alliances had acquired in Mount Lebanon deprived the French of that assurance. Consequently, they preferred to side with the governor over whose appointment they and their British and Russian allies had greater control.[64]

The consuls' support strengthened Yusuf's hand against the liberal councillors. He intensified the pressure on them in a number of ways, which included reviving complaints concerning the spring 1909 elections and reiterating his request that the council be dismissed. It did not escape Istanbul that those complaints implicated the governor as much as the concerned councillors.[65] He was advised to be cautious; not to alienate the people of his governorate; to tolerate protests and complaints which did not manifestly breach the law; and to try to win an enduring respect by compassion, understanding and equitable justice.[66] Without the Porte's approval, the legitimacy of Yusuf's policy was called into question, despite the support of the consuls. Yusuf gave way. The council had demonstrated that without its co-operation the governors could no longer rule Mount Lebanon.

Yusuf's term ended in June 1912, and appointment of a new governor was delayed for over six months. During this period, the council ran the Mountain—and smoothly too,[67] in marked contrast to the interregnum after Wasa's death. The councillors, with the liberals still in the majority among them, had evidently learned how to reconcile their differences and appease opponents in order to augment the support and respect they enjoyed from the public. The elimination of the controversial Shadid 'Aql and Jirjus Zuain from among their ranks may also have helped. Besides, the position long advocated by some councillors, that the council was the representative of the Lebanese people and therefore deserved a more active position in the Mountain's administration, was gaining popularity within the Lebanese political and intellectual elite.[68]

The pressure the Lebanese put on the Porte and on the guarantor powers to augment the authority of the council was reflected in the 1912 protocol for the appointment of the new governor.[69] The protocol re-emphasized the rights and autonomy of the council and included stipulations to broaden its electoral base. It also alleviated some of the constraints on the Mountain's economy which resulted from the agreements between the Ottoman and European governments and which had been steadily opposed by the council. According to the stipulations of the protocol concerning the elections, a representative of every hundred taxpayers would join the village shaykhs as the electors of the councillors.[70] The protocol also stipulated that a fifth Maronite councillor, to be elected from the town of Dayr al-Qamar, would join the council as its thirteenth member, while the Druze councillor of Jezzin would henceforth be elected from the Shuf.

When the new governor Ohannes Pasha arrived in Mount Lebanon in January 1913, he decided, in consultation with the council and the Porte, to apply the new election procedures gradually, as the terms of the incumbent councillors came to an end.[71] Consequently, the councillors who had administered the Mountain on their own for six months remained in office—with the addition of Dayr al-Qamar's representative.[72] Ohannes, following advice given him in Istanbul,[73] appointed a fitting person, Habib Sa'ad—a veteran advocate of the cause of the council but a cautious politican—as his deputy to the council.

Ohannes co-operated closely with him and governed the Mountain with the council's now indispensable assistance. To be sure, relations between the council and the governor were sometimes strained, but the differences were ultimately reconciled on the basis of mutual respect and concessions.[74] If this partnership helped individual councillors buttress their power bases, they in turn combined to make the council the representative of the complex network of political alliances which crossed the regional, sectarian and class boundaries in the Mountain. The council was no longer a source of political tension but an arena for its resolution.[75] As such, it acquired a position akin to that of an assembly, at the hub of Mount Lebanon's governmental structure. To many, and above all to the councillors themselves, it appeared that Lebanon was only one step from becoming an independent state and that the council spearheaded the development in that direction.

The fundamental constituents of such a state were already there.[76] Over the fifty-odd years of the *mutasarrifiyya* regime, an indigenous governmental apparatus with well-established administrative, judicial and fiscal institutions and traditions, a centralized law-enforcement agency, effective networks of communications and public services, and an indigenous cadre of experienced personnel to man these institutions had been formed in Mount Lebanon. Since the beginning, however, a basic organizational feature of this apparatus had been a strong governor appointed by forces external to Mount Lebanon. It had been the responsibility of the governors first to set up the system and then to keep it operational by balancing all internal and external forces.

So long as the people of the Mountain lacked widely accepted norms and established institutions to resolve their disputes, an external governor equipped with broad powers served as the nexus of the political set-up. He was often compelled to side with one or other of the discordant groups in Mount Lebanon, but he remained the ultimate arbitrator and co-ordinator of interests well into Yusuf Qusa's governorship. The council assisted the governor in his task of arbitration to the extent that the governor acknowledged the interests of the council—by necessity or by choice, depending on the circumstances. By Ohannes's time, however, the council had reached a position to be able to lead the Lebanese polity, should the external conditions allow. It had grown into an established institution, with procedures and norms of its own; autonomy on fiscal issues; a significant weight in administrative decisions; and a structure as well as tradition that allowed it to claim to be the true representative of indigenous Lebanese interests.

It was the same council which 'spoke for Lebanon', and took care of the Mountain's administration by popular will after the with-drawal of the Ottomans from Syria in October 1918 until the proclamation of the State of Greater Lebanon under French mandate in September 1920.[77] And during the mandate days, it was the rich and hard-earned experience of the *mutasarrifiyya*'s Administrative Council that informed Lebanese politicians in their quest for effective political union within new boundaries, as well as in their continuing struggle for independence.

Notes

1. For the foundation of the *mutasarrifiyya* regime see J. P. Spagnolo, *France and Ottoman Lebanon, 1861–1914* (London, 1977); Toufic Touma, *Paysans et institutions féodales chez les Druzes et les Maronites du Liban du XVIIe siècle à 1914*, 2 vols (Beirut, 1971), I, pp. 289–333 and *passim*; Ahmad Tarbayn, *Lubnan mundhu 'ahd al-mutasarrifiyya ila bidayat al-intidab, 1861–1920* (Cairo, 1968); L. Khater, *'Ahd al-mutasarrifiyya fi Lubnan, 1861–1918* (Beirut, 1973); and E. D. Akarli, *Cebel-i Lübnân'da Mutasarriflık Düzeni, 1861–1915* (Bosphorus University doçentship thesis, Istanbul, 1981).

2. For the texts of the 1861 and 1864 versions of the *Règlement* see G. Noradounghian, *Recueil d'actes internationaux de l'empire ottoman*, 4 vols (Paris, 1902), III, pp. 144–50 and 223–8 respectively. Also see *Sâlnâme-i Cebel-i Lübnân, 1307*, 4th year (Bitiddîn, 1307 (1889–90)); and Prime Ministry Archives in Istanbul, 'Gelen-Giden' (henceforth 'GG'), no. 1013, pp. 23–7 and 30–5.

For the Ottoman documents from the Prime Ministry Archives used in this paper see E. D. Akarli, 'Ottoman documents concerning the governorate of Mount Lebanon, 1861–1918', in *Studies on Turkish–Arab Relations: Annual 1986* (Istanbul, 1987), pp. 13–19. (The Gregorian equivalents of the *hijri* or *mâlî* dates that appear on Ottoman documents are indicated in parentheses.)

3. See GG 1016: 4 L 1322 (Dec. 1904). Cf. 'Yıldız Esas Evrakı' (henceforth 'YEE'): 35/439/122/105, defter 1, pp. 58–9; 'Bâb-ı 'Alî Evrak Odası, Cebel-i Lübnân, Mümtâze' (henceforth, 'BEO-MTZ-CL'): 6/229 (the elections of 1911); As'ad Rustum, *Lubnan fi 'ahd al-mutasarrifiyya* (Beirut, 1973), p. 171; and Yusuf al-Hakim, *Bairut wa lubnan fi 'ahd al-'Uthman* (Beirut, 1980), p. 66.

4. See *Sâlnâme 1307* p. 100, and Isma'il Haqqi ed., *Lubnan: mabahith 'ilmiyya wa ijtima'iyya*, 2nd edn (Beirut, 1970), facing p. 644.

5. For the village shaykhs, who also functioned as justices of the peace, see E. D. Akarli, 'Judiciary organization in Ottoman Lebanon as a mechanism of social consolidation, 1861–1918', Abdeljelil Temimi ed., *Les Provinces arabes et leurs sources documentaires à l'époque ottomane* (Tunis, 1984), pp. 59–72.

In the town of Zahle, a different system evolved in time to elect the electors: in principle one delegate (elector) was elected by each 50 tax-paying male residents and these delegates elected the councillor. (Touma, *Paysans*, I, p. 308 n. 20; GG 1013: p. 169; and Rustum, *Lubnan*, pp. 124 and 173.)

6. Rustum, *Lubnan*, pp. 167–8; BEO-MTZ-CL: 1/21, 16 Ca 1323 (July 1903).

7. Walid 'Awad, *Ashab al-fakhama: ru'asa lubnan* (Beirut, 1877), p. 75.

8. This right of veto stemmed from a 'codicil' to the 1861 *Règlement* as discussed later in the text. For the codicil and its reaffirmation see GG 1013: pp. 28 and 35.

9. For the relations between Daud and Franco Pashas and the council see Rustum, *Lubnan*, pp. 40–150, esp. 64–72, 76, and 124–7; and Tarbayn, *Lubnan*, pp. 241–3.

10. For detailed information on financial issues discussed here see E. D. Akarli, 'Taxation in Ottoman Lebanon, 1861–1915', forthcoming in the *Abhath* of the American University of Beirut.

11. GG 1013: pp. 73–4, 20 Z 1293 (Jan. 1877); GG 1016: 17 Z 1299 (Oct. 1882); Spagnolo, *France*, p. 154, and Rustum, *Lubnan*, pp. 174–5 and 191.

12. On these issues and what follows on the so-called *muhmalat* budget see Akarli, 'Taxation'.

13. Rustum, *Lubnan*, pp. 125 and 174.

14. Ibid., p. 125. Rustum says four, adding the December 1871 elections in Zahle. But the information he provides himself makes clear that Zahle's councillor was elected by consensus among the town's notable personages (*wujaha*).

15. Ibid., p. 125.

16. Ibid., pp. 168–71 and 174.

17. The information provided by Rustum suggests that there was some tension involved in the selection of Zahle's councillor in 1871, and in the 1879 Jezzin elections (pp. 124f. and 171f.)

18. Rustum, *Lubnan*, pp. 177–8; and Samir Khalaf, *Persistence and Change in 19th Century Lebanon* (Beirut, 1979), pp. 109–10.

19. Rustum, *Lubnan*, pp. 172–4; and the reports of Hamdi Pasha in YEE: 18/417/3/40, 9 M 300 and M 300 (Nov. 1882). (Hamdi Pasha was the governor of Damascus and Beirut at the time.)

20. Hamdi Pasha's two reports mention in note 19; and also by Hamdi Pasha: YEE: 30/2198/51/78. Inspector Riza Pasha's report: YEE: 14/244/126/7. Governor Wasa Pasha's retrospective evaluations: YEE: 35/439/122/105, defter 1, pp. 49–50, 29 L 305 (July 1888); defter 1, p. 61, 1 Za 306 (June 1889); defter 2, p. 30, 25 R 305 (Jan. 1888). Also see YEE: 35/429/122/104, varak 27, 30/2 and 24. Cf. Spagnolo, *France*, pp. 155 and 160–1; and W. Kawtharani, *Al-ittijahat al-ijtima'iyya al- siyasiyya fi jabal lubnan wa-al-mashriq al-'arabi, 1860–1920* (Beirut, 1976), pp. 80ff.

21. Akarli, *Cebel*, pp. 61–6, 158–9, and 167–8; Spagnolo, *France*, pp. 61–3 and 114; and Khater, *'Ahd*, pp. 36–7.

22. Akarli, *Cebel*, pp. 66–72 and 168–9; Spagnolo, *France*, pp. 154–68.

23. Tarbayn, *Lubnan*, pp. 339–56; Khater, *'Ahd*, pp. 66–137.

24. Hamdi Pasha's report: YEE 18/417/3/40, 9 M 300 (Nov. 1882), p. 3; Rustam Pasha's report: YEE: 18/515/127/44, 6 Ra 300 (Jan 1883).

25. Wasa Pasha implies that Rustam did interfere with the elections: YEE: 35/439/122/105, defter 1, pp. 11–12, 7 C 302 (March 1885). Shakir al-Khuri (quoted in Rustum, *Lubnan*, p. 172) implies the same. Hamdi Pasha asserts that the allegations are 'nonsensical' (see note 24). This allegation does not appear among the complaints expressed in the numerous petitions against Rustam (see Khater, *'Ahd*, pp. 71–115).

26. Rustam Pasha's report: YEE: 18/515/127/44, 6 Ra 1300 (Jan. 1883).

27. Hamdi Pasha's reports mentioned in notes 19 and 20.

28. YEE: 35/429/122/104, varak 1, 12 Şubat 1299 (Feb. 1884).

29. Ibid.

30. YEE: 35/439/122/105, defter 2, pp. 11–12, 7 C 302 (March 1885), and pp. 7–8, 4 Şubat 1300 (Feb. 1885).

31. YEE: 35/439/122/105, defter 2, p. 13, 6 B 302 (April 1885), and p. 19, 21 Z 302 (Oct. 1885).

32. YEE: 35/439/122/105, defter 1, p. 22, 26 C 304 (March 1887). Cf. defter 1, p. 16, 7 Z 303 (Sept. 1886).

33. Same place, same documents as in note 32, and defter 1, pp. 22–3, 11 B 304 (April 1887).

34. From a petition to the Porte signed by 300 people: YEE 35/429/122/104, varak 54/2 (March 1887).

35. YEE: 35/439/122/105, defter 1, pp. 23–4, 23 B 304 (April 1887), from Wasa to the Porte.

36. For the protesters' view see the petition mentioned in note 34; and for Wasa's interpretation, note 35.

37. For the French policy concerning the Ottoman state at this juncture see Spagnolo, *France*, pp. 181–2; for the Ottoman policy concerning France see E. D. Akarli, 'Problems in

Ottoman politics under 'Abdulhamid II, 1876–1909', Ph.D. thesis, Princeton University, 1976, pp. 44–55.

38. YEE: 35/439/122/105, defter 1, pp. 24–36 and 38–9, B–Z 1304 (March–Aug. 1877); and YEE: 35/429/122/104, varak 39–43 and 53–69 and their annexes, B 1304–M 1305 (March–Sept. 1887).

39. YEE: 35/439/122/105, defter 1, pp. 58–9, 2 Ş 306 (April 1889), and defter 2, p. 35, 1 Ş 306 (April 1889) for the 1889 elections. Detailed information on the 1891 elections does not exist in Wasa's papers. I assume they did not cause trouble to the governor, but why and how remain to be established. We know that at this stage he had reached a compromise with at least some of the bishops and the new Patriarch Yuhanna Hajj (Akarli, *Cebel*, pp. 169–74, and Spagnolo, *France*, p. 184). This is a development that very likely eased the tension in the elections.

40. Cf. YEE: 35/439/122/105, defter 2, p. 13, 6 B 302 (April 1885); defter 2, p. 19, 21 Z 302 (Oct. 1885); and defter 1, p. 10, 21 Z 302.

41. Allegations of self-enrichment abound in journalistic accounts. The sources of these accounts are often the political rivals of the accused; consequently they should be viewed with reservations. For the possible ways fraud could be committed see the minutes of the committee established to investigate the allegations against councillor Shadid 'Aql: BEO-MTZ-CL: 5/207, documents 90–173, and the petitions of complaint mentioned in note 62 below.

42. Shadid 'Aql of Matn and Kan'an Zahir of Batrun are good examples.

43. GG 1013: p. 111, 29 M 310 (Aug. 1892); and GG 1016: same date.

44. GG 1013: pp. 93–4, 5 Tem. 308 (July 1892).

45. GG 1013: pp. 105–6, 15 Aug. 1892. Cf. Spagnolo, *France*, p. 192.

46. GG 1013: p. 111: 29 M 310 (Aug. 1892).

47. Bishara K. al-Khuri, *Haqa'iq Lubnaniyya*, 3 vols (Beirut, 1961), I, pp. 23–45, esp. 23 and 28–9; and Spagnolo, *France*, pp. 194ff. Both al-Khuri and Spagnolo say that Na'um dispelled the council. Antoine Khair repeats the same (*Le Moutaçarrifat du Mont-Liban* (Beirut, 1973), p. 92). This is contradicted by Ottoman evidence: see BEO MTZ-CL: 1/21; GG 1019: 17 Şubat 1325 (March 1910), and 9 and 14 Şubat 1328 (Feb. 1913).

48. Akarli, *Cebel*, pp. 90–1 and 172–5; Spagnolo, *France*, pp. 186–9, 193–202; al-Khuri, *Haqa'iq*, pp. 24ff.; and Khater, *'Ahd*, p. 154. On diplomatic conditions: Akarli, 'Problems', pp. 23–76, 136; and W. Shorrock, *French Imperialism in the Middle East* (Madison, Wis., 1976), pp. 138–48. Important documents on church–governor relations: GG 1016: 8 Z 309 (July 1892); 3 S 310 (July 1892); 16 S 311 (Aug. 1893); 16 Ca 1311 (Nov. 1893); 27 Za 312 (Aug. 1894); 8 Şubat 1314 (Feb. 1899); and BEO-MTZ-CL: 3/118 and 3/144.

49. Habib Sa'ad's career inspires me to argue so ('Awad, *Ashab*, pp. 57–115), and so do the impressions of Bishara al-Khuri's father on him (*Haqa'iq*, I, esp. pp. 23–49).

50. See the file on Shadid 'Aql: BEO-MTZ-CL:5/207, esp. documents nos 16 and 31; and Spagnolo, *France*, p. 218.

51. Based on 'Abdallah al-Mallah, *Mutasarrifiyya jabal lubnan fi 'ahd Muzaffar Pasha, 1902–1907* (Beirut, 1985), pp. 243–58, 263–77, 176–8; BEO-MTZ-CL: 3/134; GG 1016: 16 Za 323 (Jan. 1906); YEE: 5/2195/83/2, 3 Za 320 (Jan. 1903); Spagnolo, *France*, pp. 225–9; and Khater, *'Ahd*, p. 171.

52. For details see Mallah, *Mutasarrifiyya*, pp. 129–34; and Spagnolo, *France*, p. 224.

53. Mallah, *Mutasarrifiyya*, pp. 304–15; and Spagnolo, *France*, pp. 230–5. Also see BEO-MTZ-CL: 5/207, the file on Shadid 'Aql.

54. See the sources mentioned in note 51, and Spagnolo, *France*, p. 259.

55. Spagnolo, *France*, pp. 235–6; GG 1013: pp. 160–1 (July 1907); and for the campaign against the Qusas, BEO-MTZ-CL: 5/207, esp. nos 16 and 31.

56. The file on Shadid 'Aql, BEO-MTZ-CL: 5/207. Cf. GG 1019: 4 Kan. sani. 325 (Jan. 1910).

The Administrative Council

57. Spagnolo, *France*, pp. 249–50, 259; Khater, *'Ahd*, pp. 177–81; and 'Awad, *Ashab*, pp. 79–83.

58. BEO-MTZ-CL: 6/230. Cf. Khater, *'Ahd*, p. 180.

59. BEO-MTZ-CL: 6/229.

60. BEO-MTZ-CL: 6/233–1 and –2. Cf Khater, *'Ahd*, 181–4. For the earlier tension see GG 1019: *passim*, and BEO-MTZ-CL: 6/241.

61. GG 1019: 4 Şub. 325 (Feb. 1910). Cf. BEO-MTZ-CL: 6/230, no. 44.

62. BEO-MTZ-CL: 6/230, no. 15, petition from groups (24 April 1910); nos 45–50, several petitions but the same text by about 900 people from different districts (1–10 April 1910); nos 16–17, 23–6, another petition signed by many people (24–30 April 1910). A group of people from Kisrawan sent additional petitions in defence of 'Azar's rights: nos 20, 27, 32 (28 March 1910), and 29, 34, 35, 36 (28 March 1910). Tamer, whose election 'Azar opposed, had somewhat distanced himself from the 'liberals' as evidenced by no. 41 in the file.

63. BEO-MTZ-CL: 6/230, nos 38, 39, 41, 42, and 44 (May 1910); and GG 1019: 8 Mayis–28 Haz. 1326 (May–July 1910). The councillors who defended this position were Sa'adallah al-Huwayyik (Maronite, Batrun), Khalil 'Aql (Maronite, Matn), Mahmud Junbulat (Druze, Jezzin), Muhammad Sabra (Druze, Matn), Ilyas Shuwayri (Greek Orthodox, Matn), Yusuf Baridi (Greek Catholic, Zahle), and Muhammad Muhsin (Shi'i, Kisrawan). Jirjus Zuain (Maronite, Kisrawan) was in custody. Jirji Tamer (Greek orthodox, Kura), the Sunni councillor of Jezzin, the Druze councillor of Shuf (Fu'ad 'Abd al-Malak), the Maronite councillor of Jezzin, and the deputy chairman Maronite Qabalan Abi al-Lami' (who had replaced Salim Ammun in April 1909) did not participate in the demonstrations of the former group.

64. For considerations of the guarantor powers and the complications of their Lebanese policy see Spagnolo, *France*, pp. 220–1, 234–6, and esp. 255–63. Also see Akarli, *Cebel*, pp. 90–4; and Shorrock, *French*.

65. BEO-MTZ-CL: 6/230, no. 44; and GG 1019: 28 Haz.–7 Teş. ev. 326 (July–Oct. 1910).

66. He was cautioned twice: on 2 March 1910 (GG 1019), and again on 23 Feb. 1911 (23 S 329 in GG 1019). The remarks above are from the latter document. Cf. BEO-MTZ-CL: 6/229, no. 12 (Jan. 1911), and 6/230, no. 44.

67. GG 1019: 2 Tem.–8 Kan. ev. 328 (July–Dec. 1912). Sa'adallah al-Huwayyik was the acting deputy chairman through most of this period. Cf. Khater, *'Ahd*, p. 187.

68. Even the petitioners complaining of the councillors in April 1910 argued in terms of the council's representativeness. See note 62 above. Also see the petitions by Shadid or his lawyers and supporters in BEO-MTZ-CL: 5/207, esp. nos 34, 73 and 171–2. On this point also see Khater, *'Ahd*, pp. 186–7; Mallah, *Mutasarrifiyya*, pp. 43–72; 'Awad, *Ashab*, p. 84; and Spagnolo, *France*, pp. 274–80. Yusuf Pasha himself complains about this development: BEO-MTZ-CL: 6/230, no. 42, 23 Nis. 326 (May 1910); cf. no. 41.

69. Spagnolo, *France*, pp. 275ff. For the Ottoman position and the final text: GG 1013: pp. 163–9.

70. The idea was explicitly inspired by the procedures that had applied in Zahle for a long time. See note 5 above.

71. The stipulations of the protocol were deemed non-retroactive, but some members of the 'Imad family in Shuf opposed the application of this principle to the Druze member from Jezzin (Mahmud Junbulat) whose constituency had been shifted to Shuf. See GG 1019: 5–14 Şub. 328 (Feb. 1913).

72. Daud Ammun was elected to the post. Elections were also held in Kura, where Niqula Ghasan replaced Jirji Tamer. See Y. Hakim, *Bairut*, pp. 67–8; but Hakim's assertion about the renewal of all elections (p. 65) is contradicted by Ottoman sources.

73. The advice was from Salim Malhama Pasha. See Khater, *'Ahd*, p. 193; and 'Awad, *Ashab*, p. 85.

74. Hakim, *Bairut*, pp. 76–7, and *passim*; 'Awad, *Ashab*, p. 86; and Khater, *'Ahd*, p. 194–5.

75. Based mainly on Hakim's treatment of the relations between Ohannes and the council under Habib's leadership (*Bairut, passim*).

76. For a detailed treatment of the following argument see Akarli, *Cebel*.

77. Ottoman martial authorities had dismissed the council during the first world war and sent most of its members to exile in Anatoli. After the war they returned to Lebanon and resumed their posts. (See e.g. Hakim, *Bairut*, pp. 148ff.)

6

Franco-British Rivalry in the Middle East and its Operation in the Lebanese Problem

JOHN P. SPAGNOLO

In nature there are neither rewards nor punishments—
there are consequences.

Robert Green Ingersoll, *Lectures and Essays*

The history of Lebanon's recurring problem has been one of discord and civil war generated not only from within by socio-economic and religious friction but also, to a corresponding measure, from without by regional tensions and international intrusions. This problem, or more precisely the problem of Mount Lebanon, the area in the Ottoman empire to which it was geographically confined during the nineteenth century, became a source of contention between France and Britain as a result of the Syrian wars of the 1830s and the ensuing Levant Crisis of 1840–1.

The two European powers were in danger of clashing over the promotion of their interests with the Ottoman government and in Muhammad 'Ali's Egypt, who were themselves regional protagonists for domination of the economically and strategically important eastern mediterranean lands, of which the Mountain formed a part. Inevitably, therefore, France and Britain came to be similarly deployed in the fractious confrontations of the Maronite and Druze communities of Lebanon. Thereafter, the opposition of French and British interests in the Middle East remained a major aspect of the Lebanese problem for just over a century.

This imbroglio took the form of a persistent sub-plot in a broader encounter of power, politics and society between Europe and the Ottoman empire. Though at times promising a satisfactory resolution, the Lebanese problem continued as an aspect of the twentieth-century encounter of the Middle East with a world of modernizing changes, regional complications and international tensions. The Lebanese experience has now become an example of the long-term unsettling effects of the 'bitter embrace' in which Europeans held the Middle East, indiscriminately stimulating both disruption and development in the diverse regional administrations and religious and linguistic communities under Ottoman hegemony.[1]

Looking at a general and a particular consequence, Europeans provoked changes that ultimately caused the dissolution of the government of the pluralistic Ottoman empire, while threatening the Lebanese political system on which, in many ways, it remained modelled. Directly by intervention, or more often indirectly by economic and social influence, Europe precipitated the realignment of traditional relationships of power, interest and status. Consequently, a varied combination of political, economic and social factors, of endogenous or foreign inspiration, were set in motion in different parts of the Ottoman empire, and among its many peoples, producing correspondingly diverging results. The period of the Syrian wars, for example, in which the interests of France, Britain and Mount Lebanon were involved, illustrates the extent to which reform policies, mixtures of so-called 'traditional' and 'modern' inspiration, which were adopted by Muhammad 'Ali Pasha and Sultan Mahmud II, had led them to pursue conflicting ends. To close a circle of consequences, the opposing combination of foreign and regional interventions in the conflict in turn exacerbated the breakdown in Mount Lebanon of the traditional hierarchy of communal status and jurisdictional compromises that had governed the relations between Maronites and Druzes—relations that were already for some time endangered by the incongruous effects of a combination of European-influenced and indigenous socio-economic changes favouring one community over the other.[2]

What Europe and European influence could tear apart, however, they could also help to join in very different unions. Thus, whether remaining within the Ottoman empire, or leaving it, political structures were modernized and new states formed to govern the societies and territorial administrations to whose realignment Europe had helped give impetus. The British and the French, in their own imperialist dispositions and conquests around the Middle East during the nineteenth and twentieth centuries, contributed to this shuffle by carving and reorganizing a number of countries or other administrative configurations out of the Ottoman empire. In contrast, however, it may be argued that, in their management of the Lebanese problem, it was specifically the politics of their imperial rivalry that contributed to distancing the government and society of Lebanon from regional currents of integration. The argument may also be made that they helped sustain, when they did not help determine, a sectarian-based and pluralistic system of governing relationships that have distinguished the situation of Lebanon from the differently constructed and more centralized governments taking root in its Ottoman surroundings, and later, by extension, its Arab environment. Taken together, French and British intrusions, directly or indirectly, reinforced those asymmetries that have mapped out for the modern history of Lebanon an equivocal course of conflict and consensus.

The pattern of Franco-British relations in the Middle East

The operation of Franco-British relations in the affairs of Lebanon was a function of the involvement of the two powers in the Eastern Question. The Question was raised by the uncertain fate of the Porte's imperial hegemony threatened by heightened tensions in the varied social composition and administrative organization of the Ottoman empire, the effects of which were reflected in Lebanon. The last of the great Islamic empires had in its heyday inherited, improved upon, and gained sustenance from a traditional—though partial and conditional—Muslim recognition of regional interests and social pluralism, as was the case with the sectarian and regionally concentrated Maronite and Druze communities of Mount Lebanon. In Lebanon, as elsewhere, the various elements of the Ottoman mosaic of semi-autonomous communal organizations and regional administrations maintained a delicately balanced coexistence over which the Ottoman Porte exercised a centralizing influence that often amounted to little more than a loose hegemony. The success of the Porte, therefore, in holding this empire together over the centuries had depended on its regulation of centripetal and centrifugal socio-economic and religious forces that, depending on prevailing local circumstances, tended to bring different communities together or drive them apart. The Ottomans presided over not only a balance of regional administrations, but also a balance of communal interests. Consequently, when the great European powers included the affairs of the weakened Ottoman empire in their foreign policy calculations, they were, by the nature of things, forced to address themselves both to the whole and to its parts, to the centre and to the periphery. Of course, in dealing with the prevailing structural tensions in the Ottoman dominions, they tried to contrive differently apportioned accommodations, favouring the inner core or parts of its outer layers, as best suited their current interests in upholding or undermining the situation of the Ottomans, or in steering a course between the two alternatives.

Even before the Eastern Question became an integral aspect of
nineteenth-century international relations, the French had, in the
formulation of their Ottoman policy, developed a patterned response
that took into consideration, at least as far as it affected their interest in
the Lebanese situation, the tension between the general and the
particular. From the time of the wars of Francis I and the Hapsburgs,
early in the sixteenth century, the French welcomed the involvement
of the Ottoman empire in the European balance of power against their
common enemy. They perceived it in their interest to court the
friendship of the Porte, even though they were betraying an obligation
they believed themselves to have inherited from the Crusades, of
warring against Islam for the sake of Christendom and its Holy Places.
They were generally content, however, to find absolution for this
failing in the pursuit of a much-vaunted Protectorate of the Catholics
in the Ottoman dominions—the informal link through which French
interests were first tied to those of the Maronite and other Catholic
Uniate sects of Lebanon. Thus, during their initial involvement with
the interplay of institutions and peoples that made up the Ottoman
mosaic, France's general attitude was to maintain good political
relations with the Porte and to develop a substantial interest in the
commerce of the empire. The application of its influence to the pursuit
of regional interests, in this instance a Christian policy for Lebanon,
took on a real, but secondary importance.[3]

For over two and a half centuries the French generally preserved
the continuity of a policy that, figuratively, assigned greater value to
the whole than to the sum of its parts. At times, they found it hard to
respect the merits of this forced equation; particularly after the
reversal of fortunes that gave a modernizing Europe the advantage
over the Islamic world and cast doubt on the viability of the Ottoman
empire. They also doubted its advantages after the end of the
eighteenth century when the European wars sparked by the French
Revolution spilled over into the mediterranean. French strategies of
conflict and conquest were difficult to reconcile with good relations at
the Porte, particularly after Britain's domination of the mediterranean
in the 1790s positioned it between France and the Ottoman empire
strategically and economically. Bonaparte's pugnacious imagination,
briefly fired in 1798–9 by the potential economic and strategic
importance of Egypt, even forced a short war with the Porte. It is
interesting to note, however, that despite the many gyrations of war
and diplomacy, then and during the rest of the Revolutionary and
Napoleonic periods, the general pattern of French priorities in the
eastern mediterranean and the logic of good relations with the Porte
remained. Unrealistic as it may seem in retrospect, even Bonaparte, at
the outset of his ill-fated expedition to Egypt, said his objective was to

serve the interests of the Ottomans by reforming their wayward province—strengthening the whole, as it were, from one of its parts. Later, as emperor, Napoleon felt he could no longer deny the importance of the Straits and the heart of the Ottoman empire.[4]

France's diminished status in the hierarchy of European powers at the conclusion of the Napoleonic Wars produced commensurable effects on the continuity of French policy in the Middle East—with lasting repercussions on the affairs of Lebanon. The change began to chip away at the latitude the French enjoyed in making those accommodations between their 'greater' and 'lesser' interests that were such an important feature of the Eastern Question. Defeat imposed constraints on both the character of French expectations in the Middle East and the prospects for their realization, constraints that were now also defined by France's relative situation to Britain. The British, having taken pains to cripple Bonaparte's Egyptian expedition, accorded him the backhanded compliment of investing the Middle East with a geopolitical importance that they, above all others, would later hold to be axiomatic. Having stolen the march on France, they were able to follow up this advantage with political influence at the Porte, and a broadly based economic presence in the Middle East—assets against which the French were forced, thereafter, to measure themselves.

Gradually, the consequences of the unequal contest that followed made itself felt in Lebanon, the only part of the eastern mediterranean that could be considered to be within the reach of French influence. In the long term, particularly after the collapse of the Ottoman empire, the declining role of France in the Middle East relative to that of Britain proved to be a major obstacle in Franco–British relations, one that the two powers were never able to overcome for long, even when they were able to develop better relations elsewhere and over other matters. At the end, during the second world war, the various constraints on both Vichy France and the Free French were so severe that they could no longer maintain any influence in Lebanon. The critical legacy for the Lebanese was the manner in which Franco-British rivalry played itself out on the eastern mediterranean stage.

The operation of Franco-British rivalry in shaping the Lebanese problem

During the nineteenth century, the general opposition of the disproportioned influence of the two powers, in a weakened Ottoman empire, was contained within the framework of the ever-persistent Eastern Question. Both in terms of conception and composition, traditional Ottoman pluralism was being eroded by winds of change blowing from the differently informed modernizing societies of Europe, carrying generalized and specific notions of socially and economically restructured, centralized and unitarian states.

The particular nature of the Ottoman-governed mosaic of regions and societies, with a built-in potential for polarizations, was becoming susceptible to changes that could, in different and separate ways, both affect the central administration of the empire, and its various parts. On the one hand, therefore, change acted on the whole, as when the Porte undertook military modernizations or bureaucratic reforms aiming to strengthen its authority, and to integrate the different sectors of the empire by organizational means or by force. On the other hand, the same factors could also act on the parts, as when change brought to different segments of the empire sufficient organizational or communal cohesion to carry them to a separate existence outside the pluralistic system with which they had previously been conditionally associated. This proved to be the case with the Balkan independence movements involving the great powers of Europe, and particularly Russia and Austria, in the affairs of the Porte.

In these circumstances, it is not surprising that the British and the French were both preoccupied in the eastern mediterranean with the fate of the Asiatic and African provinces of the Ottoman empire, geographically situated in an economically and strategically important arc: at one end of this arc lay the Straits route to the Black Sea; at the other the Suez route to India; while in the centre the affairs of Lebanon were unfolding. During the greater part of the nineteenth century, the advantages the British enjoyed inclined them towards the preservation of the status quo in the Ottoman empire. The Porte was able to benefit from their espousal of its rights to the control of the Straits and the shorter land and sea routes to India, if not always under its direct administration, then at least within its hegemony. However, the French were interested in exploring what benefits could be gained from their connections with centres of change that could offer a counterweight to Ottoman authority in the very regions Britain had come to prize. Through their contacts with the Maronites, and other smaller Christian communities in the Lebanon, the French were associated with a region of increased activity where education, demographic change and commerce were leading to a redistribution of power in the Mountain's traditional sectarian mosaic. Maronite clerics, merchants, and even peasants were in different ways challenging the established socio-economic order of land-based notables, and distancing themselves from their conditional participation in a pluralistic system still favourable to the dominant Druzes.[5] French interests in Lebanon, though, seemed not so promising as in Egypt.

The order of priorities governing French policy in the eastern mediterranean is better illustrated by the relations the French developed with Muhammad 'Ali Pasha's strengthened and increasingly autonomous province. The advice and support they gave Egypt linked them to a centralizing government that threatened to surpass, if not supplant, comparable efforts by the Porte. Not only did the relationship promise to offset some of Britain's advantages in the eastern mediterranean, but aspects of its political and economic character were analogous to those France had previously enjoyed in the Ottoman empire. Furthermore, even though Egypt's centripetal organization threatened the traditional autonomous status of the Christians, the greater degree of religious egalitarianism practised by Muhammad 'Ali's government fulfilled aspects of France's Christian policy by freeing them from some of the restrictions under which they had traditionally lived in the Islamic world. Also, France had contacts with forces in the Lebanon and Egypt which threatened to undermine Ottoman pluralism; these forces were not difficult to combine because the two regions supported each other in an informal alliance, and there was a good understanding between the Mountain's Amir Bashir and Egypt's Muhammad 'Ali. The complication set in when, after the First Syrian War of 1831–3, the Egyptian administration slowly super-imposed the authority of one region over the other. Then, Egypt's military measures and centralizing control endangered the privileged collective autonomy that was of more obvious benefit to France's Maronite allies as a counterweight to their traditional subordination to a Muslim socio-political order. Consequently, when the second Syrian war broke out between the Porte and Muhammad 'Ali in 1839, expediency allied the Maronites and the similarly affected Druzes in a rebellion against Egyptian domination.[6]

The French were embarrassed to find themselves on both sides of a contradiction in this conflict—tugging, figuratively, at both ends of their own dilemma. Nevertheless, in the brief period before Britain and the Concert of Europe acted to help the Porte expel the Egyptian forces from Lebanon and its Syrian environs, the French demonstrated a marked degree of continuity in giving preference to their 'greater' interest in Egypt over their 'lesser' one in Lebanon. While Paris could not avoid entertaining divided counsels at the highest levels on the question of helping the Maronites, in the last analysis it denied them the kind of direct assistance that counts. It seems reasonable to assume that the consequences of the dominant French policy at this time would have been either to force the Maronites to identify more closely with their socio-economic environment, or to force them to test their communal determination in a costly campaign of opposition to Muhammad 'Ali's European-inspired military establishment, and to his

more centralized administrative system. In the event, the British
helped the Lebanese revolt with their own forces to steal once again
the march on France, particularly when they forged links with the
Druzes so also constraining French influence in Mount Lebanon. The
Levant Crisis of 1840–1 left the French in such disarray that in their
eyes the Maronites, with whom they had belatedly patched up
relations, assumed the importance of a fall-back position whose
interests they could now little afford to ignore.

The operation of Franco-British rivalry remained a decisive aspect
of the Lebanese problem even after the withdrawal of Muhammad 'Ali
and the removal of his ally, Amir Bashir. Their departure released
pent-up socio-economic and religious tensions caused by the Mountain's progress along diverging paths of change or modernization, in
some cases of a clerical character, that separated Maronites and
Druzes, and exposed Lebanon to further external intervention. The
Porte, at the other pole of centralizing activity to Eygpt, and on whose
behalf Britain had fought Muhammad 'Ali, could be forgiven the
assumption that the Pasha's retreat was meant to be to its advantage.
In 1841–2, during an initial period of the interregnum in the
government of the Mountain, the Ottomans, following the logic of
their own reform policies, attempted to administer it directly. Once
again, however, after the Levant Crisis, as before it, Lebanon briefly
skirted the challenge of incorporation into a modernizing entity greater
than itself. Had history permitted this to happen, it is conceivable the
Mountain would have seen the political significance of its sectarian
composition much diluted, and its political fortunes more closely
bound up with its regional environment. Alternatively, the Maronites
and one or more sects in Lebanon would have had to gamble on the
protracted costs and uncertain outcome of attempting to forge an
independent nation-state, such as the more numerous and better-
equipped nationalist classes in the Balkans were in the process of
carving out of the Ottoman empire. In the event, measures aimed at
bringing Lebanon directly into the orbit of Ottoman government,
whatever might have been their long-term consequences, were
stillborn: undermined by another revolt of Maronites and Druzes,
jealous guardians of their privileged autonomy, who on this occasion,
however, also received the combined support of their foreign mentors.

France and Britain did as much as anyone to divorce the course of
Lebanese history from that of its neighbours when they made it a
corollary of their relationship in the Mountain to secure the arena of
their rivalry against unsolicited third-party interventions. The French,
who could not at the time afford the distraction of any 'greater' interest
in the eastern mediterranean, had little reason to countenance undue
Ottoman intervention in their threatened sphere of influence. They

were determined to make it up to the Maronites for the neglect that had brought their protégés close to defection. The British, for their part, would only bestir themselves to preserve the Porte's hegemony in Lebanon, not to impose its centralizations. They preferred to let their friendship with the Druzes work to contain France and its Maronite allies within Britain's conception of what was a sufficient Ottoman presence. As a result, France and Britain, acting within the framework of the Eastern Question and the Concert of Europe, saw to it that the Porte took its place in the management of the Lebanese problem as *tertius inter pares* while they pursued their rival interests. The subsequent division of the Mountain into two separate administrations, the Dual *qa'imaqamiyya* (*qa'imaqamiyyatan*), the one Maronite and the other Druze-dominated, should have been convenient for the safeguard of their respective interests, but it was not so. Neither administration was able to cope with the socio-economic tensions that were being generated in Mount Lebanon. The two powers had neutralized each other and the Porte sufficiently to allow considerable scope for educational, social and economic change in the Mountain's plural society. They had, by the same token, however, also helped deprive it of any government strong enough to deal with inter-communal tensions accompanying the incongruous effects of change for which they had made way.

If France and Britain added to the causes of the conflict that broke out between Druzes and Maronites in 1860, they also helped in its settlement. Within the context of the Porte's hegemony and under the aegis of the Concert of Europe, as well as in the presence of a French army, they oversaw the establishment of an autonomous *mutasar-rifiyya* for a reunified Mount Lebanon endowed with a political system that would prove adaptable to its sectarian society. This seemingly sudden and uncharacteristic agreement was, nevertheless, also the product of their rivalry—but of a rivalry muted by significant changes in the relationship of the two powers that had antedated the disturbances of 1860. Soon after the conclusion of the Second Syrian War and the weakening of Egypt, the French had refocused their policy in the Eastern Question to give priority to their situation at the Porte, a task made easier when the *entente cordiale* of the 1840s improved their relations with Britain. The 'corrosive' relations between the French and British representatives involved in the affairs of the Mountain persisted,[7] but the importance of Lebanon to France had diminished. The changes taking place there, even if of socio-economic advantage to the Maronite community, brought problems causing many Maronite clerical and secular leaders—more clerical than secular at this stage—to look to France for support, but they only received perfunctory hearings. The French gained greater advantage in the 'larger' arena of the Middle East when Napoleon III joined Britain in the Crimean War to defend the Ottoman empire from further Russian interpositions. Not since the Revolution had France been so well placed to look after its political and economic interests at the Porte; to share influence with Britain on a more equal footing; and to look at the affairs of Lebanon with a more detached gaze.

In the early 1840s the Maronites had, largely by default, made inroads into France's 'greater' eastern mediterranean interests. By the early 1860s the Second Empire, more concerned with managing venturesome European initiatives, along with imperial interventions elsewhere than the Ottoman empire, was mindful of the constraints the British imposed on its actions in Lebanon through the protection of its Druze allies. The compromises resulting from this accommodating stand-off gave the Mountain a constitutional settlement that, in time, proved to be a hallmark, albeit controversial, of the Lebanese system of government. The Porte and the European powers together sponsored an autonomous Lebanese administration with secular powers, whose composition reconciled the demographic imperatives of representation by numbers (to favour the Maronites), with representation by sects (to safeguard the interests of the Druzes and other religious communities in Lebanon's pluralistic society).[8] If earlier in the century the rival interests of France and Britain had conspired to shield the Mountain from Egypt's influence, and then immediately thereafter from that of the Porte, they now, with converse effect, did so to prevent the Maronite community from striking out along its own clerically mapped-out road to greater autonomy. French willingness to live with these constraints was demonstrated in the mid-1860s when they agreed to see a controlled measure of Ottoman force used against the Maronites to impose the secular settlement. The French in this period were again well enough situated at the Porte to subordinate the particular to the general in the apportioning of their priorities. Despite divided counsels, their military intervention in Lebanon after the civil war was not used to the unalloyed advantage of Maronite ambitions. For a time, combining France's traditional commitment to the Catholic Protectorate with a Napoleonic twist reminiscent of Bonaparte's proclaimed intent to reform the Ottomans from Egypt, the French justified the Lebanese experiment in sectarian government as being an example for the edification of the Porte in the administration of Muslim–Christian relations in the Ottoman empire.[9]

The flexibility of France's Lebanese policy was short lived. The conditions governing its management of the Lebanese problem were irreversibly changed when the Second Empire collapsed in 1870 before the German onslaught. Thereafter, for a period of 75 years, up to 1945, the preoccupation of the French with Germany produced a circuitous chain of consequences that both rekindled Franco-British rivalry and complicated the affairs of Lebanon. France's European preoccupation left it at a permanent strategic and geopolitical disadvantage in the eastern mediterranean upon which the British naturally, if at times unintentionally, capitalized. In the prevailing age of imperialism, when their rivalry was translated into a contest for empire, the French were unable, or unwilling, to spare such margins of power as were necessary to match the imperial stakes raised by the better placed British. This was doubly unfortunate for the French who remained handicapped throughout the closing half century of Ottoman history and the first world war, a critical time for aspiring heirs to Ottoman hegemony in the eastern mediterranean.

During this period the Porte succumbed to erosion from without, and to revolution and nationalist movements from within, so that the countervailing forces of change and modernization at the centre and the periphery of the Ottoman dominions finally resolved themselves at its expense. The full sweep of these changes began to unfold to the greater advantage of the British than the French from the time of the Bulgarian massacres and during the Russo-Turkish War of 1877–8. The spectre of the collapse of the Ottoman empire, and therefore of the bulwark shielding Britain's traditional 'greater' interests in the region, seemed to present itself more substantially with these upheavals than had previously been the case. The British responded by arranging for the occupation of Cyprus; and in 1882 they also occupied Egypt, where the strategically situated Suez Canal was rapidly becoming Britain's major interest in the eastern mediterranean. By the turn of the century, and particularly after the 1904 Entente, even the French would have had to acknowledge that the British were in control of a fall-back position from which they could contemplate the final demise of the Ottoman empire with a certain equanimity. This was a contingency that the French, by contrast, remained ill-prepared to face.

In the 1870s the only likely alternative to France's 'greater' Ottoman interest remained its much 'lesser' presence in Lebanon which the French were now determined to preserve at all costs. Understandably, the readiness the Second Empire had shown to sacrifice the interests of its Maronite clients for the sake of an experiment in the secular government of a sectarian society quickly became a casualty of the Franco-Prussian War. France adopted a much less adventurous Ottoman policy in which the Third Republic concentrated on retaining its influence in the management of the Eastern Question, and defending its time-honoured Protectorate of the Catholics from both Ottoman encroachments and the predatory claims of Italy and Austria. When it became axiomatic, after 1870, for France, even in its secular republican incarnation, to uphold scrupulously the privileges of its Christian allies as a measure of French influence in the region, the French naturally shifted their priorities towards the Maronites in Lebanon. The advantages they gained from this change however were modest, as France's reliance on its Catholic policy to sustain a political presence in the Mountain's plural society only fuelled Franco-British tensions. The disparities of power left the French wringing meagre returns from a Catholic policy on whose deficiencies and limited appeal the British were ever ready to dwell. A stand off between the two rival powers in the Mountain, however, had the advantage of serving the status quo, the minimum requirement for France's general holding policy.

During a period of accelerating change, therefore, Britain and France were again of like mind in preserving not only the arena of their rivalry but also the political interests of their clients and, therefore, the autonomy of the Mountain from Ottoman encroachments. When they constrained the administration of the Lebanese *mutasarrifiyya* to march, more or less, to its own drum, they reinforced the asymmetries between its development and that of its regional environment. On different occasions between the mid-1870s to the eve of the first world war, they helped distance Lebanon from a succession of political changes, constitutional, autocratic and revolutionary, experienced by the Ottomans. However, if the Mountain's administration lost its externally imposed experimental objectives, and was denied the facility of adapting to its regional environment, it did gain the experience of internal sectarian political accommodations, administrative compromises and representative practices that became the distinctive feature of the political culture of the nineteenth-century *mutasarrifiyya* and of its twentieth-century successor. The preservation of the administrative autonomy of Lebanon, useful as it was to France's holding policy, did not of itself, however, resolve the problem the French faced in managing the effects on the Lebanese of the faster pace of socio-economic and political changes at the turn of the century.

The French once again fashioned their own dilemmas when, by the end of the nineteenth century, they translated their political interest in the Ottoman empire into an even 'greater' economic one, and raised new problems in the allocation of their priorities. The extent of French investments in the Ottoman empire, rivalling on the eve of the first world war those they made in Russia, depended to a large degree on maintaining the viability of the Porte as a source of authority for a revenue-bearing administration.[10] Accordingly, the French had to tread warily when they affected the interests of the Lebanese, particularly the interests of their more economically active clients, who found it advantageous to participate in the economic life of their region from the vantage point of their privileged *mutasarrifiyya* in a manner that ran counter to French interests. The Lebanese, for example, resented the constraints imposed on their commerce by Ottoman monopolies from which French capital profited, and the regulation of their outlets for trade to the advantage of the French. The French had to be equally wary of the dangers to their Ottoman policy of the political ferment among their Christian clients whose social, economic and educational changes, encouraged by their European contacts, induced aspirations for secular advantages and greater autonomy. In their negotiations with the Porte on the Lebanese problem, therefore, the French were little inclined to complicate matters by favouring new departures that undermined their clerical policy, or turned them into conduits for reforms of the Mountain's constitution that implied a further loosening of Ottoman hegemony.[11]

France's difficulties in offsetting its 'greater' and 'lesser' interests in the eastern mediterranean under the watchful eyes of the British were not the only developments shaping the Lebanese problem. After the British took Cyprus and Egypt, there was also the serious imbalance the French faced in securing their share of the Ottoman inheritance. The British occupation of these two Ottoman provinces, important in the history of imperialism for helping to trigger the 'scramble' for Africa, was also a notable spur to French interest in the Arab East, the partition of which by the allied rivals after the first world war added new dimensions to the Lebanese problem. Despite a compensatory concession of Tunisia to France at the Congress of Berlin in 1878, the settlement granting Cyprus to Britain after the Russo-Turkish War exposed French weaknesses in the eastern mediterranean to a degree that they felt they could not ignore. The imbalance was confirmed in 1882 when they felt themselves unable to accompany Britain in its intervention in the Egyptian question. Already, in the intervening years, French fears that Britain was better positioned to wrest a legacy from the demise of the Porte heightened the sense of urgency in their links with the Maronites reminiscent of the early 1840s after the Levant Crisis. A specially prepared contingency proposal even suggested that Mount Lebanon was the 'fortress' from which, in the event of the Porte's collapse, French forces could be expected to uphold France's claim to its rightful share of the Ottoman legacy against all rivals.[12] This claim, also, was to become the justification for a sphere of influence vaguely defined geographically as 'Syria'. It extended from the emerging commercial centres of the Ottoman coastal province of Beirut across the Mountain into the two Syrian provinces of Damascus and Aleppo.

When the French perceived themselves forced to focus, more intently than ever, on Syria as the potential site for a strategic fall-back

position in the eastern mediterranean, they inserted, between the
'lesser' Lebanese and the 'greater' Ottoman concerns with which they
were already having problems, a new 'intermediate' level of difficulties. Thereafter, the last two regularly threatened to come unstuck
when France, in order to consolidate its presence in Syria, encouraged
substantial economic investments in Beirut, and in the improvement of
the city's links with the commerce of the Syrian hinterland. These
investments, though, either failed to turn a profit, or proved to be of
marginal interest to French investors in the Porte's wider dominions.[13]
The French found it even more difficult, however, to manage their
'lesser' and 'intermediate' interests in the sphere of influence they
hoped to cultivate. The winds of change blowing around the eastern
mediterranean produced different and overlapping effects on the
various, similarly overlapping, Arab social and political constituencies
in the region, whether Syrian and Lebanese, Muslim and Christian, or
traditional and secular. Beirut and the other urban centres of the
region were contained in the centralizing government of the Porte, but
the viability of the Ottoman empire remained an open question,
particularly after the 1908 revolution and the Balkan wars of 1912–13.
The fluidity of the political situation in Beirut and the Mountain, and
a degree of effervescence in the spirit of the times could bring about
lateral friction between the various constituencies, but it also
facilitated lateral accommodations and interaction, such as had already
occurred in their commercial relations.[14] Whatever the underlying
direction of the prevailing political aspirations—decentralization,
greater autonomy, or at this stage the much less likely objective of
independence—the Mountain was becoming less isolated from the
political activity of its regional environment, particularly from
neighbouring Beirut. While the French could count on substantial
loyalty from their Maronite and Uniate clients, Syrian political activity
was in Muslim and Orthodox Christian constituencies: Muslims were
naturally alarmed by the oppressive aspects of French colonial policies
in North Africa; Orthodox Christians were, by definition, largely
indifferent to France's Catholic policy; while both were more than a
little suspicious of the French imperial presence. Consequently, if
signs of political ferment cast a shadow on the future of Ottoman
hegemony in Syria, it also cast doubt on France's ability to hold on to
its influence in Mount Lebanon, let alone expand it to realize a Syrian
inheritance separate from British constraints.

The fragility of French claims to the Lebanon and Syria became the
most serious problem for Franco-British relations in the Middle East,
despite the fact that Germany's threatening pre-eminence in the ranks
of the great powers brought the two veteran empires together in the
1904 Entente, and that in 1912 the British conceded France's

publicized claim to a zone of influence in Lebanon and Syria.[15] On the eve of the first world war, a warning sign of trouble to come was Britain's growing dependence on its Veiled Protectorate in Egypt to sustain its presence in the eastern mediterranean after it found itself in the unaccustomed position of sharing influence at the Porte with Germany as a lesser among equals. The defence-conscious British, naturally, developed an interest in the north-eastern approaches to their strategic base through Syria. For the French this was a worrisome form of sub-imperialist threat, not without parallels with the adversity they had experienced over Fashoda. French fears were compounded by the example of Britain's informal government of Egypt which enabled the British to carry influence in Syria uncluttered by anything as restrictive as France's Catholic policy or its North African colonial reputation.

Egypt's reawakening interest in its Arab identity, and its multifaceted links to the Syrian Arabs, offered the British some useful indicators of the prevailing direction of political activity in their rival's back yard. Altogether, France's predetermined reliance for influence in Beirut and the Syrian provinces on a policy that was, at best, only moderately successful among the Lebanese again exposed deficiencies, on which the British capitalized with even greater effect in the larger region to which the French aspired. Not surprisingly, the French blamed Britain for what they considered its persistent exploitations of their weaknesses; while the British thought that France had only itself to blame. The Entente notwithstanding, a contest of views repeating the same flaws, became, by the eve of the first world war, the single most important irritant, after the basic imbalance in their respective imperial circumstances, which carried Franco-British rivalry to its twentieth-century climax.

The concluding phase in the opposition of the two powers that helped shape the Lebanese problem after the first world war underlined the greater facility with which Britain and France assigned the division of sacrifices on the Western Front and in the Middle East than that with which they were able to reconcile their differences in victory. Soon after the outbreak of hostilities between the Ottoman empire and the Entente powers, the French, fully committed on the Western Front, had not concealed their suspicion that Britain, in planning its various offensives against the Porte, would be tempted to pre-empt their eastern mediterranean interests, particularly when the British took up the cause of the Hashemite Arab Revolt. France was initially encouraged by their assurances in the Sykes–Picot Agreement, on the partition of the Arab provinces of the Ottoman empire, of an equitable division of the spoils; but, by the end of the war, execution of the document, already more often breached than observed, seemed altogether threatened by Britain's pervasive military presence in the Middle East. More than ever preoccupied with Europe, France's physical and material contribution to the balance of power in the eastern mediterranean was of almost negligible proportions, while the British remained the beneficiaries of the strategic emplacement of their base in Egypt. Consequently, when the war incapacitated the Porte and made the age-old determinants of the Eastern Question void, regenerating them, phoenix-like, in newer Middle Eastern problems, Britain was already there before the French, exercising the law of possession. Britain substituted a 'greater' Arab interest in its management of the Lebanese problem to its earlier Ottoman interest.[16]

France's ultimate contribution to the determination of the Lebanese problem also dates from the destruction of the Ottoman empire. The hegemony of the Porte over Syria and the Mountain, as elsewhere, had become a necessary condition, politically and economically, to French influence in the eastern mediterranean after 1870, to the extent that (paraphrasing Voltaire), had it not been in existence, it would have had to be invented. In the closing years of the nineteenth century, France's exercise of a pattern of accommodations in the Ottoman empire between centre and periphery had lent—if at times only illusory—credibility to its participation as a major player in the management of the Eastern Question alongside Britain. Naturally, at the conclusion of the first world war the French would have liked the resurrection of their traditional 'greater' Ottoman interests in some general form that would restore value, if not profitability, to their sizeable pre-war investments in the former Muslim empire. However, the post-war management of the peace with the Ottomans, and with their Turkish successors, over which Britain and France were frequently bitterly at odds, did not permit such a solution. Understandably, when the French were forced to acknowledge the bankruptcy of their 'greater' Ottoman interest, they placed heavier demands on their residual ones; the Levant then witnessed a brief replay, on a more reduced and by now much-distorted scale, of the dilemmas in France's traditional eastern mediterranean policy where Syria took the place of the Ottoman empire, but Lebanon remained the 'fortress' of last resort.[17]

The political and social geography of the twentieth-century Lebanese state, and the initial stage of its independent existence, were conditioned by even deeper rifts in Franco-British relations. These last, and ultimately near bellicose, confrontations became inevitable after Britain's Arab interest was first superimposed over France's remaining zone of influence. France, with its eyes firmly fixed on Europe, was ill-prepared to assume authority in Lebanon and Syria when Britain, with help from the Hashemite-led Arab Revolt, occupied the region. In the wake of the retreating Ottoman forces, the British and the Hashemites made way for the recasting of Syrian and Lebanese political constituencies favourable to Arab activity into a Syrian Arab nationalist movement aspiring to an independence that was even more inimical to French interests than previously.[18] Their actions once more opened the way for lateral political activity, suggesting a higher degree of integration of the Mountain with its Syrian social and geographical environment. France was able to deny this option to the Lebanese when it obtained from Britain its minimum demands of assistance in occupying Beirut, the Levant coast and Mount Lebanon. French perceptions, though, that their alliance with Britain in victory had done little to enhance their influence in the eastern mediterranean, were confirmed soon enough. While Britain helped the French to the Levant coast, it did not feel obligated to provide the same advantages for them elsewhere. Moreover, after Britain had helped itself to northern Iraq, Palestine and Transjordan from the conquests of the first world war, the French were left to conquer anew, or negotiate for what they had believed would be their share of an agreed Ottoman inheritance: namely, Ottoman Cilicia, Damascus and other parts of the Syrian interior. By the summer of 1920, not only were the French in a precipitate and hopeless retreat before an onslaught of Turkish nationalists in Cilicia, but they had also become the disparaged conquerors of a Syrian Arab nationalist government. Not surprisingly, French imperialists once again saw themselves to be on the defensive in the Middle East. They left little room for divided counsels on the importance of France's 'lesser' interest and its minimal requirements for security against the perceived threat of a British-inspired Arab reaction. Consequently, one of the most important externally determined causes of the inclusion of parts of Syria in a Greater Lebanese 'fortress', comprising the Mountain and Beirut, resulted from the last stand of French imperialism against the generally inexorable regression of French influence in the eastern mediterranean dating from the French Revolution.

The intrusion, albeit in the two distinctive stages traced above, of Franco-British relations in the Middle East into the management of the Lebanese problem after the first world war once more contributed to a deflection of the course of Lebanese history from that of its regional environment. The distinctive pluralistic form of Lebanese government, initially designed to deal with the relations of the Maronite and Druze communities, was now subjected, under the authority of a French mandated Greater Lebanon, to further complications. Mount Lebanon's system of political accommodations, administrative compromises and representative practices had to adapt

to large Sunni and Shi'i Muslim communities who, at the outset, were
opposed to being separated from their former lateral Syrian contacts.
In the event, the Lebanese system proved more effective and durable
than the French mandate. During the 1920s and the 1930s the political
and economic relations the system encouraged were more successful in
furthering the integration of the various sectarian communities
juxtaposed in the newly enlarged state, than France was successful in
imposing itself upon them. The French had gone a long way in
fulfilling the territorial ambitions of their Maronite clients with an
enlarged Lebanon, but they were no more able than before to deflect
the effects of the progressive winds of change on the country's
pluralistic society. The rising expectations of the Lebanese enabled
them to see through the thinly veiled imperialism of the mandatory
administration that was obstructing their road to independence.

The way to independence for the Lebanese was cleared when
Franco-British relations reached their nadir in the second world war.
Until then the French administration of Lebanon continued to be
measured against precedents set by the British, whose imperial
experiences, at least in Egypt and Iraq, allowed them in the 1920s and
1930s to be more sensitive to the aspirations of the Arabs; the British
were also in a better geopolitical position to grant Arabs, if not all the
substance of independence, then more of its illusions. The French
were also unable to escape Britain's persistent exploitation of the
deficiencies of their Catholic policy, linking their secular republic to an
unchanging tradition of dependence on the Maronites. They could not
fully appreciate the extent to which the Christian communities,
including many Maronites, and the Muslim communities were
interacting in opposition to mandatory political and economic policies
more favourable to French interests than to those of the Lebanese. At
the end, of course, when Germany occupied France, the French were
helpless to prevent the British from taking advantage, for the last time,
of the extreme distortions in their relationship. During the second
world war, after Vichy Frenchmen in the Levant had given vent to
their long-simmering enmity towards Britain in the eastern mediterranean, and while the Free French, who had helped liberate Lebanon
and Syria, were at the mercy of British assistance, in November 1943
Britain took the unusual step of issuing the French with an ultimatum:
the French were forced to take steps that would lead them to recognize
the independence of Lebanon, and by 1945 abandon their last and
'lesser' Middle East interest in Lebanon and Syria for the benefit of
what Britain then hoped would be its 'greater' Arab interest.[19]

The British, who were the first to place the affairs of Mount
Lebanon on the international agenda in the 1840s, when they alarmed
France with their rival interest in the Mountain, were also the last of

the two powers to influence the management of the Lebanese problem. Content to assume that the wartime Free French administration of liberated Lebanon was guilty of political shortsightedness and general inefficiency, Britain took a direct hand in Lebanese politics. Reaping from the harvest of intercommunal relations that had reconciled the various Lebanese sects to coexistence in a single entity, the British sponsored the political activity that enabled prominent Christian and Muslim leaders to launch Lebanon into independence. To this end, Britain witnessed, in the National Pact of 1943, the fine-tuning of compromises necessary to improve the political and administrative government of Lebanon's pluralistic society. At the conclusion of the second world war, the British, who had first become involved in Lebanon because of its turmoil, left it at peace. The French who had first had to deal with Lebanon as part of the Ottoman empire, marched out under the watchful eyes of their rivals and left it independent.[20]

The legacy of the Franco-British management of the Lebanese problem, however, remained equivocal. In a century full of turmoil and change, their management was distinguished by the way their wide-ranging differences in the Middle East had offset each other's influence in Lebanon to keep the course of Lebanese history marching to a different drum to that of its socio-political environment. Also, in a century of violent imperial encounters with Third World revolutions, the two powers had seen each other out of Lebanon without forcing a liberation struggle which, in many other states, has put unresolved social tensions to the test, and collapsed unsupported political compromises.[21] The French and British legacy to Lebanon was not the result of neglect, neither of the rivals could afford to neglect so sensitive a region; nor was it a Machiavellian design, to which neither could aspire without being forestalled by the other; rather, it was the consequence of the adoption of expedients whose effects were to sustain a degree of continuity in the course of Lebanese history upon whose merits the Lebanese have yet to decide.[22]

Franco-British rivalry: source of conflict or consensus?

There are historiographical pitfalls in formulating an interpretation of the recent history of any country in the shadow of civil war, and particularly with the war that broke out in Lebanon in 1975 with tragic consequences. The tangled skein of events has claimed attention in its own right, such as that which Thucydides accorded the civil war of the Greeks. The scope of the conflict he witnessed, and its significance to his world, seemed so much greater than the sum of its antecedent parts, that he dismissed the importance of causation.[23]

In contemplating the relation of today's Lebanon to the Lebanon of the past, similar misgivings apply to the importance of the Franco-British management of the Lebanese problem. Any discussion of whether the intervention of the two powers will go down in history as a factor contributing to the Lebanese conflict or to its consensual resolution depends on the outcome of the intervening, and as yet inconclusive, civil war. In the marriage of the historian and the past, the past should be constant and the historian a scientist, but in the absence of such an ideal, of course, the reality of the relationship is more complex. Impressions of the past, intertwined with perceptions of the present and conceptions of the future produce hybrid histories, the legitimacy of which can only be established with hindsight. Hence the difficulty of assessing Europe's legacy on the Lebanese socio-political system, when it is to be assumed that the shape of the order that will proceed from the civil war will colour impressions of the order that preceded it. Some future historiography will have to show how the consequences of Franco-British intervention came to be seen as part of the cause of, or part of the solution to, the Lebanese imbroglio. Some future historian will have to show how, in the last analysis, they furthered the evolution of a modern Lebanese body politic, or delayed revolutionary changes.

Be that as it may, it seems fair to say that the equivocal legacy of the international relations of Lebanon owes much to the manner in which the histories of the Eastern Question and of the Lebanese problem were meshed and then unmeshed. Initially a certain symmetry existed between the two. Important aspects of the Eastern Question were construed in terms of European relations with an Ottoman empire composed of a mosaic of peoples and regions. Similarly, the international politics of Lebanon derived from the interaction of Europe with the sectarian and regional mosaic of Mount Lebanon and its environs. By the twentieth century, however, symmetry had given way to contrast. In the case of the Ottoman empire, Europe, in different ways, by example or through imperialism, helped undermine the coexistence of its parts, or altogether detach them, most notably in the Balkans and in North Africa. With the dissolution of the Ottoman empire, the emergence of Turkey and the separation of the Arab world, national states, nationalist aspirations or, at least, the centralization of socio-political life became the order of the day. In the case of Lebanon, however, the contrary happened when the basic features of an Ottoman pluralism of peoples and regions was carried over to modern times. By the twentieth century, external challenges to the sectarian socio-political order in Lebanon had been warded off, the coexistence of its parts organized, and then the application of the system geographically and demographically extended.

In the century or so during which France and Britain helped manage the Lebanese problem, they encouraged a contradiction such that the course of change in Lebanon followed a different direction from that of its neighbours. Whether it is compared with Muhammad 'Ali's centralization, the Porte's Ottomanism, the aspirations of Arab nationalists, or France's own imperial government, Lebanon took the anomalous course, not conforming to the prevailing models for change and integration in the eastern mediterranean provoked by the European nation-state. It has, however, become one of the ironies of history that the instigators of change have had second thoughts on the course of their own development. Europeans, after two tormenting, prolonged and costly wars, beginning with what the Indian historian Pannikar described as Europe's 1914–18 civil war,[24] have discovered the merits of a pluralistic community of peoples, regions and institutions. Now the Lebanese, too, are no longer being spared the bitter cost of resolving for themselves the problem of choosing a course to follow through the winds of change blowing around the eastern mediterranean. The options before them include merging into some entity larger and more centralized than the one they now share, or welding the country into a nation-state. These options, however, once more risk taking Lebanon along anomalous paths of change. It is no less ironic that the shape of the European community, unlike the nation-state, is akin to the Ottoman tradition of communal and religious pluralism, of Islamic inspiration, that was unintentionally preserved for the Lebanese in the twentieth century by the operation of Franco-British rivalry in the Middle East.

Notes

1. I should like to thank the Centre for Lebanese Studies, Oxford, for the opportunity to focus on this particular aspect of Franco-British relations in this conference paper, and for exercising editorial patience with my revisions. I should also like to acknowledge the assistance of the Social Sciences and Humanities Research Council of Canada in funding a broader study of which this is a part.

See L. Carl Brown, *International Politics and the Middle East* (Princeton, NJ, 1984), p. 18, for the apt use of the phrase 'bitter embrace' in a stimulating discussion of the politics of Western penetration in the Middle East.

2. See Samir Khalaf, *Persistence and Change in 19th Century Lebanon: a Sociological Essay* (Beirut, 1979), ch. 1, for the need of greater nuance in our theoretical understanding of change; also Iliya F. Harik, *Politics and Change in a Traditional Society: Lebanon, 1711–1845* (Princeton, NJ, 1968), ch. 5, and William R. Polk, *The Opening of South Lebanon: 1788–1840* (Cambridge, 1963), particularly ch. 8, for discussions of 'mix' in the sources of change among the Maronites, and on the changing relationship of the Maronite and Druze communities.

3. For discussions of the pattern, and the tensions in the apportionment of French interests

in the Ottoman empire during this period see A. H. Hourani, *Syria and Lebanon: a Political Essay* (London, 1946), pp. 147–50; F. Charles-Roux, *France et chrétiens d'Orient* (Paris, 1939); and André Bruneau, *Traditions et politique de la France au Levant* (Paris, 1932).

4. Vernon J. Puryear, *Napoleon and the Dardanelles* (Berkeley, Calif., 1951). Charles-Roux, *France et chrétiens*, pp. 24–5, claiming the Fourth Crusade's occupation of Byzantium for France, provides an early example of the apportionment of French priorities in the eastern mediterranean, disappointing to the crusaders stranded in the Holy Land!

5. For studies of these socio-economic changes see Dominique Chevallier, *La Société du Mont Liban à l'époque de la révolution industrielle en Europe* (Paris, 1971); and Toufic Touma, *Paysans et institutions féodales chez les Druzes et les Maronites du Liban du XVIIe siècle à 1914*, vol. 2, pt III (Beirut, 1971–2).

6. For discussions of the background, course and consequences of the second Syrian war in Mount Lebanon see Caesar E. Farah, 'The Lebanese insurgence of 1840 and the powers', in *The Journal of Asian History* 1 (1967) 105–32, and his 'The Quadruple Alliance and proposed Ottoman reforms in Syria, 1839–1841', in *International Journal of Turkish Studies* 2 (1981) 101–30; also Alfred Schlicht, 'The role of foreign powers in the history of Lebanon and Syria from 1799 to 1861', in *Journal of Asian History* 14 (1980) 97–126; Khalaf, *Persistence and Change*, chs 4–5; and A. J. Abraham, *Lebanon at Mid-Century: Maronite–Druze Relations in Lebanon 1840–1860* (Washington, 1981), ch. 5.

7. An apt description borrowed from John Marlowe, *Perfidious Albion: the Origins of Anglo-French Rivalry in the Levant* (London, 1971), p. 296, in his discussion of the relationship of the two powers on a wider stage.

8. See Albert Hourani's seminal essay, 'Lebanon: the development of a political society', in Leonard Binder ed., *Politics in Lebanon* (New York, 1966), pp. 22–3; and J. P. Spagnolo, 'Constitutional change in Mount Lebanon: 1861–1864', in *Middle Eastern Studies* 7 (1971) 25–48.

9. See John P. Spagnolo, *France and Ottoman Lebanon 1861–1914* (London, 1977), chs 2, 4 and 5.

10. Jacques Thobie, *Intérêts et impérialisme français dans l'empire Ottoman, 1895–1914* (Paris, 1977), pp. 720–4.

11. Spagnolo, *France and Ottoman Lebanon*, ch. 11.

12. Capitaine Louis de Torcy, 'Rapport sur une mission en Syrie' of 1 August 1880 in the series *Mémoires et documents: Turquie*, V. 123 , item 38, in the archives of the French Ministry of Foreign Affairs, Paris.

13. J. P. Spagnolo, 'French influence in Syria prior to World War I: the functional weakness of imperialism', in *The Middle East Journal* (1969) 53–5.

14. Leila Tarazi Fawaz, *Merchants and Migrants in Nineteenth Century Beirut* (Cambridge, Mass., 1983), ch. 8.

15. On Franco-British differences in the region prior to the first world war see William I. Shorrock, *French Imperialism in the Middle East: the Failure of Policy in Syria and Lebanon, 1900–1914* (Madison, Wis., 1976), ch. 9; and Rashid Ismail Khalidi, *British Policy Towards Syria and Palestine 1906–1914* (London, 1980).

16. For a discussion of Franco-British relations in the regeneration of the Eastern Question in terms of 'New wine, old bottles' see Brown, *International Politics*, pp. 117–22; on the France's initial dependence on the Sykes–Picot Agreement see Jan Karl Tanenbaum, 'France and the Arab Middle East 1914–1920', in *Transactions of the American Philosophical Society* 68 (1978); for a summary of French military views of their situation on the ground during and immediately after the war see General C. R. du Hays *Les Armées françaises au Levant 1919–1939*, vol. I (Château de Vincennes, 1978), pp. 3–5.

17. For the post-war tensions in Franco-British relations during this period see Christopher M. Andrew and A. S. Kanya-Forstner, *France Overseas: the Great War and the*

Climax of French Imperial Expansion (London, 1981) chs 7–9; and Meir Zamir, *The Formation of Modern Lebanon* (London, 1985), ch. 2.

18. Philip S. Khoury, *Syria and the French Mandate: the Politics of Arab Nationalism, 1920–1945* (Princeton, NJ, 1987), ch. 1.

19. For the British war cabinet's determination to force the French to make the ultimate concessions see the minutes of 12 November 1943 in PRO/CAB 65/36/WM153 (43), and those of 30 and 31 May 1945 in PRO/CAB 65/53/CM2 (45) and 4 (45).

20. See Wm Roger Louis, *The British Empire in the Middle East, 1945–1951* (Oxford, 1984), pt 3, ch. 3, who points out that Lebanon and Syria were the 'first states to achieve independence from the European colonial system as a result of the Second World War'.

21. Hourani ('Lebanon', p. 28), writing in the early 1960s, noted that the 'events of 1943–1946 were child's play compared to the struggles through which other nations have won their independence', and went on to suggest that 'already in 1946 a prescient observer could have seen that the process was not yet over . . .'

22. Cf. A. B. Gaunson, *The Anglo-French Clash in Lebanon and Syria, 1940–45* (London, 1987), p. 191, who concludes that in the light of the final departure of both powers from the Middle East 'only the curious borders remain as a monument to Anglo-French power in the Middle East'.

23. Thucydides, *The Peloponnesian War*, trans. Rex Warner (Harmondsworth, 1954), p. 13.

24. K. M. Pannikar, *Asia and Western Dominance* (London, 1953), p. 197.

7

La Perception du Grand-Liban chez les maronites dans la période du mandat

FADIA KIWAN

The breakdown of consensus in Lebanon in 1975 and the conflicts which followed it have renewed the polemic surrounding the entity of Lebanon itself. The Maronites were the most fervent partisans of Grand Liban; the present conflict centres on them, one side accusing, the other defending. It is therefore useful to examine the history of their community during the mandate. From 1920 to 1943, with the gradual transfer of power to the Lebanese, the Maronites became divided among themselves as they took part in a wider game of alliances of government and opposition, inevitably with political personalities from the other communities.

In its relations with the Maronites, France took account of two considerations: it wished to negotiate with the Syrian nationalists and it wished to become closer to the other religious communities. Thus Grand Liban and the Maronites were always at risk of being used as barter. For their part, the Maronite leaders considered themselves to be the founders of Grand Liban and displayed an excessive attachment to it as well as a tendency to exercise hegemony over the new state.

To safeguard the entity of Lebanon, the Maronites sought French guarantees and made alliances with Lebanese Muslims. However, the successive crises from 1926 to 1943, often caused by the intrigues of the Maronites and their personal ambitions in the desperate struggle for power, each rocked the foundations of the entity of Lebanon. In the 1930s there was a split between Emile Eddé and Bishara al-Khuri without there being any divergence in the fundamental options they were offering. From 1932, Eddé followed a policy of alliance with the Sunni leaders in order to incorporate them into the defence of the territorial integrity of Grand Liban with French support.

From 1936, however, a current of opinion emerged calling for integral independence and for the strengthening of links with Arab countries; the 1940s proved favourable for an English breakthrough in the region in opposition to the French presence.

Through the particular combination of circumstances, the Maronites linked themselves to those Muslims hostile to the French presence and, paradoxically, wrenched Lebanese independence from the French.

The authors of the Pact of 1943 shared among themselves the apparatus of state and its institutions, but the nation that was to be formed remained unformed, the nation that is currently the only possible safeguard of the entity of Grand Liban. But this nation has to involve all the communities and the leaders of the communities have no reason to wish to form it.

La dernière rupture du consensus au Liban en 1975, et les conflits aigus qui s'y déroulent depuis, ont renouvelé la polémique autour de l'entité libanaise elle-même. Et des thèses partitionnistes et unionistes, ayant—au début de ce siècle—fait couler beaucoup d'encre, et ayant décliné depuis 1943, émergent à nouveau et se revitalisent en recevant une nouvelle impulsion dans les difficultés rencontrées par l'état libanais depuis 1943, dans ce que certains appellent 'l'échec du projet d'Etat', ou 'le malentendu historique', ou encore 'le Pacte national manqué'.

Nécessité s'impose donc d'interroger l'histoire. Mais laquelle? Celle diffusée par les artisans de 1943 ne cadre plus avec les événements et les crises ultérieures de l'état libanais indépendant. Il faut surtout faire une nouvelle lecture de l'histoire pour saisir le cheminement du Liban vers l'indépendance, avec toutes les secousses et les tensions qui ont accompagné ce cheminement. Cela seul nous permettrait de comprendre l'échec de l'entreprise nationale et surtout la résurgence des thèses unionistes et partitionnistes. Le conflit libanais actuel ayant cristallisé sur la communauté maronite, que les uns accusent et les autres défendent, il s'avère de première importance de suivre l'itinéraire de cette même communauté durant la période du mandat. Il est entendu que pareille rétrospection inclut, de fait, les rapports intercommunautaires aussi bien qu'intracommunautaires, de même que les rapports des uns et des autres avec l'autorité mandataire, avec les différentes grandes puissances, et avec les pays voisins, les maronites ayant été 'accusés' à l'époque d'avoir déployé tous leurs efforts en vue de la création du Grand-Liban. L'analyse de la période du mandat sera donc articulée autour de ce thème central: 'le Grand-Liban'; comment était-il perçu; comment devait-il être organisé sur le plan interne, c'est-à-dire au niveau du rapport entre ses différentes communautés, et sur le plan externe, c'est-à-dire au niveau de ses rapports avec son voisinage et avec la société internationale?

L'idée du Grand-Liban avant le 1er septembre 1920

Depuis la deuxième moitié du dix-neuvième siècle, plusieurs tendances s'étaient dessinées au sein de la vie intellectuelle de l'Orient contrôlé par les ottomans. On notait particulièrement un réveil de la conscience arabe chez beaucoup de jeunes étudiants en Europe et un renforcement de la tendance autonomiste chez les Libanais avec l'instauration du régime de la *mutasarrifiyya* qui en donnait une nouvelle consécration. Mais l'autonomie libanaise de 1861 était estropiée par l'amputation des régions à potentiel économique important, sur une initiative du délégué ottoman à la commission internationale, Fouad Pacha, qui avait su profiter des dissensions européennes—ce qui rendait l'entité libanaise ainsi diminuée particulièrement vulnérable sur tous les plans. Au début du vingtième siècle et avec les prémisses de l'effondrement de l'Empire ottoman, plusieurs courants d'idées vont apparaître à propos de l'avenir du Liban.

Parmi ces courants, un des premiers appelait à un 'Grand-Liban intégralement indépendant, dans ses frontières naturelles et histor- iques, et sous la garantie des grandes puissances'. Il fut représenté surtout par le parti de l'Alliance libanaise fondée en 1909 par des Libanais résidents en Egypte.[1]

Un second courant appelait à la formation d'un Liban indépendant, ayant recouvré ses frontières historiques et sous la protection de la France.[2] Ce courant, très répandu dans les milieux chrétiens, surtout maronites, plonge ses racines dans une histoire assez lointaine de ces derniers, étant donné leurs liens historiques avec la France. Ce courant va réclamer dans un premier temps—janvier 1919—l'autonomie administrative et judiciaire, ainsi que l'extension du territoire libanais, avec l'aide de la France. Cette autonomie devait évoluer pour aboutir à l'indépendance. Mais en mai 1919, ce courant va se radicaliser et réclamer tout simplement l'indépendance politique.[3]

Un troisième courant réclamait le rattachement du Liban à la Grande-Syrie 'qui constitue à elle seule une unité géographique, historique et économique, et qui est impossible à démembrer'. Les liens avec la Syrie seraient de type fédératif ou confédératif, organisés et supervisés par la France qui serait l'autorité mandataire dans les deux pays. Ce courant était surtout représenté par le Comité central syrien, dont les figures les plus illustres étaient Chukri Ghanem et Georges Samné, propriétaires de *Correspondance d'Orient* à Paris.

Un quatrième courant réclamait uniquement l'autonomie du Mont-Liban dans le cadre d'un royaume arabe sous l'égide du roi Fayçal. Ce courant était constitué par des nationalistes arabes au Liban, recrutés surtout dans les milieux musulmans. Quelques chrétiens, même maronites, y participaient, d'autant que le gouverne- ment de Fayçal à Damas allait faire une place à des chrétiens pour les convaincre de se rallier à son projet.[4] Les troisième et quatrième courants sont antagonistes, bien qu'ils se réclament du même territoire de Grande-Syrie. Cela revient à la divergence fondamentale sur la nature du régime politique à établir.[5]

Un cinquième courant, beaucoup moins représentatif, réclamait que le Liban soit considéré comme un département français, ou encore, la constitution d'un protectorat modelé sur celui des croisés, avec un émir maronite pour la gestion des Affaires Intérieures, et cela sous l'égide de la France. Ferdinand Tyan était l'un de ses représentants.[6]

Enfin, un dernier courant reflétait des sentiments de crainte dans certains milieux maronites et exaltait l'idée d'un foyer de chrétiens. Ce courant d'idées ne s'est pas autonomisé au début de ce siècle parce qu'il correspondait paradoxalement aux voeux des partisans de l'unité de la Grande-Syrie et à ceux des partisans de l'émir Fayçal, ces derniers ayant de part et d'autre fait une place plus ou moins autonome au Petit-Liban dans un état plus grand.

En réalité, vu les contradictions, convergences et divergences des différents courants d'idées, on peut tenir compte de la représentativité des différents courants pour simplifier ces données et parler de deux courants antagonistes principaux : celui qui réclamait la reconstitution du Grand-Liban indépendant sous protection française et celui qui réclamait son rattachement à la Grande-Syrie de Fayçal. Ces deux courants reflétaient plus ou moins un double clivage:

1. Chrétiens et musulmans, bien que tous les chrétiens ne soient pas dans un camp ni tous les musulmans dans l'autre.
2. Régime démocratique de type occidental/royaume arabo-musulman.

Avec la tenue de la conférence de la Paix à Paris en 1919, une de ces tendances va progressivement prédominer et va orienter les décisions de ladite conférence. Il s'agit de celle qui réclamait l'indépendance du Liban, dans ses frontières naturelles et sous la protection de la France. Elle était représentée par les trois délégations libanaises successives à la conférence. Celles-ci, quoique composées de délégués de plusieurs communautés, étaient largement dominées par les maronites et exprimaient leurs désirs et aspirations.

Daoud Ammoun, chef de la première délégation à Paris, déclara à la presse: 'Nous le savons, il ne nous est pas possible de nous développer économiquement et d'organiser notre liberté sans le concours d'une grande Puissance, car nous manquons de techniciens au courant des rouages de la voie moderne et de la civilisation occidentale'.

Le patriarche Elias Hoyek, chef de la deuxième délégation, précisa à la presse les trois objectifs de la délégation: 'l'indépendance absolue du Liban, la restitution des limites naturelles et historiques, et le renforcement de ses relations avec la France'.

La troisième délégation à la conférence de Paix se trouva obligée de protester contre une décision transmise à Paris de la part du Congrès syrien, qui, à Damas, venait de proclamer Fayçal roi de Syrie et qui déclarait prendre en considération 'tous les désirs patriotiques des Libanais relatifs à l'administration de leur contrée, dans ses limites d'avant guerre, à condition que le Liban se tienne à l'écart de toute influence étrangère'. Elle fut néanmoins rassurée par le président du Conseil et ministre des Affaires Etrangères, Alexandre Millerand, qui était un ami d'Emile Eddé, membre de ladite délégation.

Globalement, les négociations de Paris s'étaient déroulées conformément aux grands lignes fixées par le Conseil administratif du Mont-Liban.

La proclamation du Grand-Liban le 1er septembre 1920

Cette proclamation du général Gouraud consacrait le triomphe de la tendance indépendantiste francophile sur les autres, et notamment sur celle qui se prévalait d'un émirat arabo-musulman sous le règne de Fayçal ou d'un état syrien de type fédératif, dans le cadre duquel le Mont-Liban bénéficierait d'un brin d'autonomie. Cette proclamation va constituer un tournant historique dans la vie politique des Libanais: d'une part, elle consacrait une alliance islamo-chrétienne (souhaitée et recherchée quoique précaire), exprimée symboliquement par la présence du patriarche maronite et du *mufti* des musulmans, aux côtés du général Gouraud et en présence des chefs religieux des autres communautés; et d'autre part, le discours prononcé par Gouraud à cette occasion présentait la formation du Grand-Liban comme une victoire marquée contre la Syrie, sinon contre les partisans de la Grande-Syrie.

'Il y a cinq semaines, dit-il, les petits soldats de France . . . donnaient l'essor à tous vos espoirs, en faisant s'évanouir en une matinée de combat, la puissance néfaste qui prétendait vous asservir', faisant manifestement allusion à l'éphémère royaume arabe de Syrie de Fayçal. Et il achève en mettant l'accent sur le rôle de la France dans la protection du Liban:

> Les soldats français sont les parrains de votre indépendance. Et vous n'oublierez pas que le sang généreux de la France a coulé pour elle comme pour tant d'autres . . . C'est pourquoi, vous avez choisi son drapeau, qui est celui de la liberté, pour le symbole de la vôtre, en y ajoutant votre cèdre: Vive le Grand-Liban! Vive la France! A jamais unis.

En ces termes, Gouraud pensait sceller l'union des deux états. Cependant, ce tournant ne signifiait pas que le problème était réglé. Bien au contraire, les relations intracommunautaires, intercommunautaires avec la France et l'Angleterre et avec les pays voisins, vont provoquer des secousses au sein de cette construction et vont maintenir sa précarité jusqu'au-delà de l'indépendance, opérée dans une fuite en avant jusqu'à ce que le pays eût volé en éclat.

L'instauration du Grand-Liban va susciter deux séries de réserves: de la part de certains milieux maronites méfiants quant à la composition multicommunautaire élargie en 1920,[7] et de la part des partisans du rattachement à la Syrie.[8] Et si les premiers se contentèrent d'une attitude de méfiance et de scepticisme, se contractant avec le temps et perdant du terrain devant les promesses de protection prodiguées par la France, les seconds passèrent à une véritable opposition, assez violente dans quelques unes de ses manifestations, protestant contre cette nouvelle entité et demandant le rattachement à la Syrie, ou, dans le pire des cas, 'la décentralisation par rapport à l'Etat du Liban'.

La vie politique sous le mandat

Le courant maronite partisan du Grand-Liban sous protection française va prendre une part très active au gouvernement du pays durant la période du mandat. Mais la période allant de 1920 à 1943 va se caractériser par la revendication croissante d'une plus grande autonomie, d'une plus grande institutionalisation et d'une gestion libanaise autochtone des affaires de l'état. Le passage progressif du pouvoir aux Libanais va diviser rapidement les maronites entre eux et va les pousser à rechercher la collaboration de personnalités politiques parmi les autres communautés religieuses. Cette période est marquée par la restriction du champ politique à des cercles très réduits, concentrés autour de quelques personnalités qui regroupaient autour d'elles des clientèles personnelles et non organisées. Les politiciens se recrutaient surtout parmi les avocats, médecins, ingénieurs, journalistes, hommes de lettres, commerçants et grands propriétaires terriens.

L'intelligentsia maronite était de formation française, partagée entre des études faites directement en France et des études faites dans des établissements français au Liban; elle puisait dans la culture française son ethos et ses modèles de référence. Les orthodoxes et les sunnites s'orientaient plutôt vers les études en langue anglaise— chose qui était favorisée par la présence des missions évangéliques et celle de l'Université américaine de Beyrouth.

Les personnalités politiques les plus représentatives des aspirations des maronites à l'époque étaient celles qui avaient plus ou moins directement participé à la conférence de la Paix à Paris: Habib Pacha Saad, président du Conseil d'administration, Daoud Ammoun, Emile Eddé, respectivement chef et membre de la délégation libanaise à la conférence de la Paix, et enfin le patriarche maronite Elias Hoyek, étroitement associé aux efforts libanais pour l'édification du Grand-Liban. Un peu plus tard, Bechara el-Khouri se fera remarquer aussi à l'occasion de sa prise en charge du premier poste de secrétaire général du gouvernement, que les autorités françaises venaient de lui attribuer, le 5 février 1920, manifestement sur une recommandation du Père Catan, directeur de l'école des Jésuites où Khouri avait fait ses études.[9]

En janvier 1921, le Parti du progrès est fondé, 'pour le Liban avec la France', réunissant parmi ses fondateurs le Marquis M. de Freige, Selim Asfar, Emile Arab, Emile Kachou, Emile Eddé, Naoum Bakhous, Alfred Naccache, Chukri Kurdahi, Michel Chiha, Bechara el-Khouri, Alphonse Zeineh et Youssef Gemayel. Ce parti se fixe pour objectif la sauvegarde de l'indépendance politique du Grand-Liban avec le mandat français et la défense des traditions nationales et des libertés religieuses ainsi que la représentation parlementaire dans le cadre d'un régime fondé sur les compétences et les mérites . . . On remarque que les deux antagonistes des deux décennies suivantes se réunissaient autour des mêmes objectifs politiques au début du mandat.

Cependant, malgré l'absence de divergences profondes dans les options fondamentales, la période du mandat va rapidement être marquée par des tensions très violentes et une grande instabilité gouvernementale. Et le champ politique va témoigner aussi rapidement d'une polarisation en deux camps: celui de Emile Eddé et celui de Bechara el-Khouri. La raison principale qui avait provoqué ce clivage était que les maronites se trouvaient appelés à participer à un jeu plus élargi d'alliances de gouvernement et d'opposition, inévitablement avec des personnalités politiques appartenant aux autres communautés religieuses et face à une politique mandataire qui obéissait à son tour à un rapport de forces intérieur français et à la loi de la concurrence avec les autres grandes puissances, surtout la Grande-Bretagne. Le Parti du progrès va donc bientôt tomber dans l'oubli et ses membres vont s'éparpiller dans les différents groupements politiques qui vont se former, opposés les uns aux autres, et les clivages vont perdre leur couleur communautaire pour prendre le contour des ambitions, querelles et rancunes des uns et des autres.

Mais en marge des groupements politiques qui vont participer activement au processus de prise de décision, il y avait dans les milieux chrétiens, même maronites, des cercles d'intellectuels assez réduits qui se prévalaient d'autres options politiques. Parmi eux, on peut citer Youssef el-Saouda, partisan d'un Grand-Liban intégralement indépendant et fondateur d'une formation de scouts, al-Sabbaka, en 1925.[10] Plus tard, en 1938, Saouda sera co-fondateur du Parti du Pacte national. Il faut signaler aussi le nom de Amin Rihani qui développait dans ses écrits des options nationalistes syriennes panarabes. Rachid Nakhlé pour sa part, prendra l'initiative de réunir 'un congrès national en août 1933, pour réclamer de substituer au mandat un traité à conclure entre la France d'une part, et la Syrie et le Liban d'autre part, sur la base de l'autonomie libanaise dans l'Unité Syrienne'.[11]

Le courant maronite francophile

Mais les points de vue des partisans du mandat parmi les maronites bénéficiaient des plus grands échos parmi la population maronite, surtout que cette orientation politique était avalisée par Bkerké; l'analyse de cette période se limitera donc à leurs prises de positions, déclarations et alliances.

Ce qui mérite d'abord d'être noté, c'est que les relations entre les autorités mandataires et les dirigeants maronites n'étaient pas aussi sereines que le laisse entendre la pérennité des relations entre les maronites et la France. De son côté, la France avait des considérations multiples concernant ses intérêts au Levant et sa politique sera toujours aliénée par deux soucis:

1. Celui de négocier avec les nationalistes syriens, ceux de Fayçal d'abord et les gouvernants syriens successifs après, surtout avec le Bloc national syrien. A ce niveau, le Liban se trouvera souvent menacé d'être une monnaie d'échange dans les négociations.[12] Cela poussait les dirigeants maronites à entreprendre des contacts acharnés avec des instances officielles et officieuses en France pour appuyer la thèse du maintien du Grand-Liban dans ses frontières naturelles et historiques et de son accès à l'indépendance.
2. Celui de donner des assurances aux autres communautés religieuses libanaises et de leur prouver qu'elles ne s'alignaient pas sur les maronites. Cela va pousser les autorités mandataires à jeter du lest aux musulmans et aux orthodoxes[13] et à donner satisfaction à quelques unes de leurs revendications, surtout concernant les postes gouvernementaux et administratifs à pourvoir.[14] Cette politique du haut commissariat qui visait à se rapprocher des groupes initialement hostiles à la présence française, ou bien méfiants, ne fit que développer les ressentiments, le chantage et l'opportunisme dans toutes les communautés, y compris chez les maronites.

En même temps, les hauts-commissaires successifs essayaient d'encourager dans le camp maronite plusieurs centres de décisions, plusieurs pôles d'attraction pour pouvoir traiter avec des dirigeants plus conciliants, moins exigeants, plus dociles même.[15] Cela ne pouvait qu'exacerber le conflit intracommunautaire, et augmenter les sollicitations tactiques de toutes parts.

De leur côté, les dirigeants maronites se considéraient comme étant les fondateurs du Grand-Liban et estimaient, par conséquent, qu'il revenait à eux d'en protéger les assises et d'en guider le destin. La communauté avait déployé des efforts inégalés pour le Liban. Elle trouvait légitime que les maronites soient établis aux postes de commandement. Avec le gouverneur français, c'était le président du Conseil des ministres qui était maronite. Quatre personnalités maronites allaient se succéder: Auguste P. Adib, Bechara el-Khouri, Habib Pacha Saad et Emile Eddé. La politique des trois premiers gouvernements était essentiellement gestionnaire, alors que le pays était accablé par les problèmes économiques et sociaux, par les réseaux de clientèles établis au sein de l'administration publique et par les secousses provoquées de temps à autre par les groupes hostiles à l'état du Grand-Liban, qui connut une nouvelle consécration par la constitution dont il fut doté en 1926. Cette constitution avait eu pour rôle de confirmer une nouvelle fois ses frontières naturelles et historiques et de lui donner des garanties institutionnelles.[16]

Les options fondamentales des maronites pour la sauvegarde de l'intégrité territoriale

Les maronites voyaient ainsi s'exaucer leur voeu le plus cher. Mais ils savaient que l'essentiel restait à faire: puisqu'il ne suffisait pas de proclamer l'indépendance, il fallait bien la sauvegarder. Pour les maronites, la lutte pour la sauvegarde de l'indépendance se déroulait sur deux plans:

1. *Interne*: il s'agissait de créer et de consolider un large consensus intercommunautaire autour de l'entité libanaise.
2. *Externe*: il s'avérait indispensable de poursuivre les contacts et les pressions pour faire avorter les projets des unionistes syriens. Ces projets vont continuer d'alimenter les négociations franco-syriennes pendant toute la période du mandat.

Etant donné la permanence du danger d'assimilation à la Syrie, les maronites vont faire un choix historique: réclamer les liens les plus étroits avec la France pour la ranger de leur côté. Le chef de file de cette tendance sera le président Emile Eddé. Pour les fondateurs du Grand-Liban, seule une garantie française appuyée sur de grandes traditions dans les relations des maronites avec la France pouvait faire échapper le Liban à ce danger. Le Liban devait être un foyer indépendant pour les maronites mais non pas nécessairement un

foyer maronite. En optant pour le Grand-Liban largement multicommunautaire, les maronites faisaient délibérément cette concession: un
Liban foyer des chrétiens mais non pas chrétien, d'autant plus qu'il
n'existe pas dans les milieux maronites une idéologie d'état
théocratique. Il s'agissait plutôt d'un état démocratique où les citoyens
maronites seraient des citoyens à part entière et où les libertés de
croyance, de pensée, d'association et d'action seraient garanties à tous.

D'autre part, les maronites savaient qu'ils ne représentaient pas
tous les chrétiens du Liban, et encore moins ceux du Levant.[17]
Toutefois, les tendances autonomistes des maronites étaient les plus
exacerbées parmi les chrétiens du Levant, alimentées par les souvenirs
des conflits et des persécutions. En fait, les maronites avaient été parmi
les plus affectés par la situation économique sous le régime de la
mutasarrifiyya dans la deuxième moitié du dix-neuvième siècle et au
début du vingtième siècle. Ils avaient d'ailleurs connu de grands
mouvements d'émigration et avaient été affectés par la famine au début
du vingtième siècle. Ils avaient réalisé que le Mont-Liban n'avait
aucune viabilité et qu'il ne leur donnait qu'une illusion d'autonomie.
C'est pourquoi leur choix du Grand-Liban était unique, inévitable et
définitif; et la satisfaction qu'il devait assurer à leurs aspirations leur
imposait de pratiquer une politique d'ouverture par rapport à leurs
concitoyens, chrétiens et musulmans. Mais il est entendu que les
circonstances qui avaient amené la reconstitution du Grand-Liban,
donnaient aux maronites une occasion—qu'ils croyaient légitime—
d'exercer une hégémonie sur l'Etat libanais. Ils étaient presque les
seuls à l'époque à avoir perçu le Liban comme leur patrie définitive,
et ils pensaient que par conséquent, ils y étaient attachés plus que tout
le monde et qu'ils y avaient le plus de droits.

Parallèlement, le Grand-Liban continuait à être contesté par des
groupes assez représentatifs des communautés musulmanes, et ce
négativisme avait pour effet de durcir les positions des maronites et de
renforcer leur attachement au Grand-Liban.

Deux options vont donc marquer la politique des maronites dans la
période du mandat:

1. La réclamation de garanties françaises.
2. L'attraction des musulmans libanais.

Mais ces constantes vont se heurter à une tactique de la part des
unionistes libano-syriens, qui cherchaient à diviser les chrétiens
maronites et à les appuyer les uns contre les autres pour faciliter le
rattachement de tout le Liban à la Syrie. Deux personnalités
musulmanes participaient au pouvoir, d'autres à l'opposition. Et en
même temps, on entretenait dans les milieux musulmans libanais une
appréhension du Grand-Liban et des désirs d'unité syrienne.

Une tentative de réforme des appareils d'état
et de resserrement des liens entre centre et périphérie

Après les quelques cabinets ministériels de simple gestion et devant le malaise général du pays, un nouveau cabinet est formé par Emile Eddé le 12 octobre 1929 et présente un programme de réformes le 17 décembre 1929, qui est approuvé au parlement par une majorité de 30 voix contre 6. Ce programme prévoyait des réformes dans tous les domaines et notamment dans l'organisation de la justice, dans l'enseignement public et les services administratifs. Il prévoyait une nouvelle organisation administrative, simplifiée, plus centralisée et reconstituant des unités administratives multicommunautaires pour intégrer les régions rattachées au Liban en 1920, et les amener à tisser des liens plus étroits avec le reste du pays. Il prévoyait aussi une compression du personnel administratif, incompétent et improductif. Une fois approuvé à la chambre, le programme Eddé est mis à exécution, et une épuration est opérée dans l'enseignement et la magistrature visant de nombreux éléments incapables, hérités de l'époque ottomane. 'C'est lui qui donnera au Liban son organisation administrative actuelle.'[18] Mais bien vite une grande agitation va se manifester, surtout dans les milieux musulmans, réunissant les mécontents de toutes parts, et cultivée par les adversaires chrétiens de Eddé. Le cabinet finira par succomber 'sous la coalition des intérêts particuliers lésés, des rancunes personnelles, imprudemment éveillées et d'une opposition confessionnelle habilement exploitée . . . ', comme le précisera Ponsot dans une note au ministère des Affaires Etrangères. En fait, les licenciements de fonctionnaires nécessités par la compression du budget de l'état provoquaient un mécontentement 'parmi les personnes licenciées ainsi que parmi leurs patrons politiques qui les avaient placées et dont ils servaient les intérêts'.[19]

Le parlement libanais, qui avait initialement acclamé et approuvé le programme Eddé et qui lui avait accordé le droit de procéder par décret lois qui seraient ultérieurement ratifiées par le parlement, va voter une motion qui retirera sa confiance au cabinet Eddé, sans indiquer de motif ou faire allusion aux réformes. Revêtue de 25 signatures, cette motion sera approuvée le 20 mars par 27 députés sur 39 présents. Le prétexte de l'opposition était la suppression d'un certain nombre d'écoles officielles, ce qui frappait plus directement les intérêts des communautés musulmanes. Mais sur les 27 députés qui retiraient leur confiance au gouvernement, 17 étaient chrétiens et 10 seulement étaient musulmans. Et sur les 17 chrétiens, on comptait bien 11 maronites.[20] En réalité, la campagne contre les réformes avait pour cible le chef du cabinet lui-même et elle était fomentée par ses adversaires maronites qui avaient réussi à exploiter les sentiments de frustration des milieux musulmans. De fait, ces derniers refusèrent toute collaboration avec Eddé. Pourtant, pour marquer leur attachement au chef du cabinet, Ponsot et le président Debbas étaient favorables à ce qu'il forme lui-même un autre gouvernement. Mais Eddé se retira et le ministère qui lui succéda déclara vouloir respecter le programme de M. Eddé[21] sans que cela ne soulève un quelconque mécontentement . . .

En fait, les réformes susmentionnées visaient à moderniser, rationaliser et rendre plus efficaces les services de l'administration publique. Elles ont buté contre un système de clientèle bien établi puisque conjugué avec des préjugés et des ressentiments confessionnels.

En réalité, à chaque fois qu'une crise, de quelque ordre qu'elle soit, venait secouer le champ politique intérieur, c'était le Grand-Liban qui subissait une secousse et qui se trouvait menacé et c'est ainsi que la crise confessionnelle occasionnée par la tentative de réforme ranimait les craintes et les méfiances.

L'appui au candidat musulman de Tripoli aux présidentielles

L'année 1932 va témoigner elle aussi d'une forte tension, et c'est l'année du recensement après celui de 1922. Les chiffres de 1932 montraient une nette progression des populations musulmanes. Les chrétiens n'étaient plus que très légèrement majoritaires.[22] En cette même année, le pays devait connaître une autre échéance: l'expiration du mandat présidentiel, et l'ouverture de la campagne électorale avec une vive concurrence entre Eddé et Khouri. Cheikh Mohamad Jisr, président de la Chambre, se déclara candidat à la présidence. Et de Tripoli et de Dannieh arrivaient les télégrammes d'appui à Jisr, exprimant

> les voeux les plus ardents des différentes communautés de la région, de voir à la tête de la République libanaise leur très aimé et très vénéré Cheikh Mohamad Jisr . . . pour son mérite personnel et son dévouement à la France et au Liban, avec reconnaissance profonde et anticipée au cher peuple français.[23]

Le Cheikh Jisr était effectivement un partisan du mandat mais les autorités françaises voulaient maintenir une prépondérance des chrétiens au Liban.[24] En même temps, Ponsot oeuvrait pour écarter à la fois Jisr et Eddé. C'était le seul moyen dc satisfaire les nationalistes syriens et de maintenir les constantes de la politique française au Levant. Eddé se rendait compte des intentions de Ponsot et une occasion lui était donnée pour redresser le profil que ses adversaires avaient dessiné de lui chez les musulmans lors de la crise de 1929–1930. Eddé devait aussi profiter de cette occasion pour renforcer l'allégeance des citoyens de Tripoli et de Dannieh à l'état libanais. Ces régions subissaient à l'époque beaucoup de pressions en vue de les rattacher à la Syrie. Et les responsables français multipliaient les promesses de garantie de l'intégrité territoriale du Liban, en même temps qu'ils promettaient aux Syriens un accès à la mer.

Dans son militantisme pour le Grand-Liban, Emile Eddé, comme tous les autres dirigeants maronites, savait qu'il devait compter sur les alliances avec des dirigeants des autres communautés et c'est sur ce terrain que ses adversaires avaient essayé de le combattre. Ce sont ces mêmes adversaires qui lui donnaient ainsi l'occasion de se réhabiliter aux yeux des musulmans. Eddé va appuyer ouvertement la candidature de Cheikh Jisr. Plusieurs députés maronites en feront de même et Cheikh Youssef el-Khazen se proposera d'accompagner Cheikh Jisr chez le haut-commissaire Ponsot pour le convaincre d'accepter cette candidature.

Eddé réussit ainsi à regagner des sympathies qu'il avait maladroitement perdues quelques années plus tôt. Mais Ponsot ne se pliera pas devant le fait accompli. Il va suspendre la vie constitutionnelle et proroger le mandat de Debbas.[25]

Emile Eddé avait réussi là un coup de maître, et il était lui-même gagnant à long terme puisque l'appui à la candidature d'un musulman de Tripoli était un coup porté aux unionistes syriens, car l'accès d'un musulman tripolitain à la présidence pouvait désolidariser les tripolitains de leurs alliés traditionnels, les unionistes syriens. Plus tard, lors de son mandat présidentiel en 1936, Eddé appuyera la candidature de Kheir el-Din el-Ahdab, également tripolitain, à la présidence du Conseil. L'opposition se hâta alors d'appuyer celle d'un sunnite, l'émir Khaled Chehab, à la présidence de la Chambre et insista pour que les élections à la Chambre aient lieu en premier: si l'émir devait être élu, le président Eddé ne pourrait plus appuyer la candidature de Kheir el-Din el-Ahdab et leur alliance tomberait à l'eau. Effectivement, l'émir Khaled fut élu président de la Chambre mais cela ne fit pas changer d'avis le président de la république: il appela Kheir el-Din el-Ahdab—comme prévu—pour former le gouvernement, et il inaugura ainsi une règle coutumière qui fera que la présidence du Conseil était attribuée aux sunnites. Pour Eddé, ce n'était pas une question de comptabilité mathématique, mais une forme de participation au pouvoir qui dissiperait craintes et ressentiments; le plus important était plutôt l'allégeance au Liban plutôt qu'à la chrétienté.

Ces événements et le genre de rapports politiques qu'ils supposent sont assez de preuves du non fondé des thèses qu'on lui prêta, surtout dans les milieux sionistes, à propos de son appui à la réduction territoriale du Liban.[26] De même, son acharnement à lutter pour le Grand-Liban depuis sa participation à la délégation libanaise à la conférence de la Paix en 1919 jusqu'à sa démission de la présidence de la république en 1941, rompt nettement avec le contenu du mémorandum, qu'on lui attribue à tort et qui aurait été adressé au sous-secrétaire d'état au Quai d'Orsay en 1932, relatif au détachement de Tripoli et du Liban-Sud.

Le traité franco-libanais ou la consécration de la garantie de l'intégrité territoriale

Une des grandes coordonnées de la politique des maronites pour sauvegarder l'intégrité territoriale du Liban était le projet de traité avec la France que le président Eddé essaiera de mettre à exécution en 1936. Dans les milieux maronites, on croyait fermement qu'un traité d'amitié et d'alliance avec la France aurait pour effet le plus immédiat de protéger les frontières du Liban de 1920.

En fait, à partir de 1930, le projet d'un traité franco-syrien et d'un autre franco-libanais circulait sans difficulté dans les milieux politiques.

Même les unionistes syriens avaient changé de position—ou de tactique—à ce sujet et ils préconisaient ce traité à condition qu'il prépare les deux pays à la souveraineté nationale. Ils revendiquaient l'unité territoriale de la Syrie en acceptant en même temps l'unité territoriale du Grand-Liban dans les limites de 1920. En faisant allusion à cette nouvelle attitude, le patriarche Arida critiquera les unionistes libanais tout en réaffirmant la nécessité que le Liban conserve ses frontières de 1920: 'Pourquoi les congressistes du Sahel ont-ils refusé l'indépendance libanaise quand les syriens eux-mêmes demandèrent l'indépendance complète pour eux-mêmes et pour le Liban?'[27]

Le patriarche Arida rappellera le 13 mars 1936 que le Bloc national syrien avait accepté l'indépendance du Liban dans ses frontières actuelles.

En fait, le Congrès national musulman qui se tiendra le 23 octobre 1936, tout en rappelant l'attachement des musulmans à l'unité syrienne du point de vue politique et économique, réclamait l'insertion dans le traité franco-libanais d'un article prévoyant la décentralisation administrative entre les départements et assurant l'égalité entre les diverses communautés. Les protestations sont déjà nuancées et ne touchent pas au mandat ou aux bases du Grand-Liban.

En 1936, les négociations sont entreprises entre le gouvernement libanais et les autorités françaises au sujet du traité, et l'on déclarait au Liban que 'le Liban ne pouvait se contenter d'une situation inférieure au statut conventionnel, procuré par le traité que demande la Syrie'.

Pour renforcer l'attitude du gouvernement libanais, un congrès se tient à Bkerké—le 6 février 1936—et les évêques et prélats de la communauté maronite adressent une lettre au haut-commissaire, insistant sur cinq points, dont l'intégrité territoriale en premier:

1. Le maintien de l'entité libanaise.
2. L'indépendance effective du Liban et la souveraineté, sans préjudice pour la consolidation de ses rapports fraternels avec la Syrie soeur, sur le plan notamment de la coopération économique et sociale.
3. Une nouvelle constitution qui garantirait les libertés publiques.
4. La conclusion d'un traité avec la France parce que le Liban ne saurait se contenter d'une situation inférieure au statut conventionnel, procuré par le traité que demande la Syrie.
5. L'entrée du Liban à la Société des Nations.

Cette prise de position des prélats maronites donne lieu à une assemblée de quartiers musulmans, au nom de laquelle le *mufti* de la république affirme trois principes:

1. Souveraineté nationale.
2. Indépendance pléniaire.
3. Unité syrienne par voie de référendum.

Pourtant, le traité allait fixer définitivement la pérennité du Liban et anéantir à jamais l'espoir d'en détacher les fractions annexées.

Le Congrès du Sahel, tenu en octobre 1936, publiera un manifeste réclamant:

1. L'unité syrienne au nom des musulmans, comme étape préliminaire à l'unité arabe.
2. Eu égard à la difficulté de réaliser, dans les circonstances actuelles, l'unité avec la Syrie, les musulmans décident d'adhérer au principe des négociations avec la France en vue d'un traité franco-libanais qui devra préparer la voie à la réalisation de l'unité politique, économique et sociale avec la Syrie. A cette fin, ils font appel à tous les chrétiens du Liban, partisans de l'unité, pour qu'ils apportent leur contribution à cette oeuvre capitale.
3. Une répartition équitable des emplois publics et une décentralisation régionale des services de l'état.
4. Une protestation contre la délégation aux négociations.

En réalité, le président Eddé avait pressé la France de commencer les négociations avec le Liban pour la signature du traité, comme elle l'avait fait avec la Syrie. Ce traité devait consacrer l'intégrité territoriale, l'indépendance politique sous garantie d'une grande puissance et la coexistence et la collaboration entre les différentes communautés. Les querelles reprenaient au moment de la formation de la délégation libanaise. Et en fin de compte, Bechara el-Khouri allait accompagner le président Eddé à titre de chef de délégation parlementaire.

Eddé déclarera à l'occasion de la signature du traité que 'l'essentiel des intérêts de nos deux pays est commun, et notre entente naturelle' et 'l'amitié et l'alliance franco-libanaises qui remontent à plusieurs siècles dans le passé, ne pourront que se consolider et se perpétuer à l'avenir . . . '

Le traité est ratifié par la Chambre libanaise à l'unanimité et dans un discours à la Chambre, Bechara el-Khouri considérait le traité comme un acte qui 'consacre votre souveraineté et votre indépendance . . . Ce traité constitue le code de notre alliance et de notre amitié avec la France', et, plus loin: 'c'est le couronnement de notre passé et la garantie de notre avenir.'

Le traité bénéficiait donc d'un large consensus dans les milieux politiques maronites. Aux yeux des maronites, le traité apportait la garantie de la France pour le statut du Liban et de ses frontières. Et la présence de l'armée française sur son territoire pour 25 ans—clause inclue dans le traité—était un gage supplémentaire de sécurité.

Du côté français, le traité devait être un engagement ou une reconnaissance définitive du territoire du Grand-Liban, ce qui exclurait tout engagement vis-à-vis de l'Etat d'Israël concernant l'éventuel détachement et l'annexion du sud.[28]

En fait, le Liban ne se trouvait plus seulement menacé d'assimilation par la Syrie, mais il était surtout menacé d'être amputé du Liban-Sud au profit d'un foyer national juif que le mouvement sioniste tentait d'implanter en Palestine. Le traité franco-libanais devait constituer un soutien pour l'état du Grand-Liban face à tous ces risques.

Faisant suite au traité, le président Eddé donnera des garanties au haut-commissaire de la République française relatives aux droits civils et politiques des ressortissants libanais sans distinction aucune et, de même, des assurances relatives à un plan de réforme visant à octroyer aux municipalités des attributions plus étendues. Ces assurances visaient vraisemblablement à rassurer les musulmans libanais.[29]

La période des négociations franco-libanaises témoignait d'un minimum de consensus entre les Libanais et surtout de convergence des différents pôles d'attraction maronites. Le patriarcat maronite,

Eddé et Khouri s'alignaient sur les mêmes positions, mais bientôt des changements vont survenir dans le camp chrétien.

En effet, le 2 janvier 1936 le patriarche maronite Arida adressera un mémorandum au haut-commissaire dénonçant la détérioration de la situation dans le pays et le monopole accordé à la Régie française des Tabacs.[30] A la même époque, le patriarche avait eu un échange de lettres avec des dirigeants damascains. Il avait eu également des contacts avec Rome et il avait commencé à réclamer plus de liberté et moins de monopole des compagnies étrangères. De même, il protestait contre la situation d'infériorité dans laquelle étaient placés les fonctionnaires libanais par rapport aux français. Dans les milieux chrétiens bien informés, on soupçonnait déjà une influence britannique et une influence directe sur le patriarche exercée par Youssef el-Saouda qui était partisan d'un Liban intégralement indépendant, à la fois par rapport à la Syrie et à la France. Les autorités françaises étaient contrariées par l'attitude de Bkerké, et entretenaient par contre de très bonnes relations avec Monseigneur Moubarak, un pro-mandataire, ainsi qu'avec Monseigneur Salibi, prélat orthodoxe qui se rapprochait des français et exprimait son appui au mandat.[31]

Le tandem Eddé-Ahdab proteste contre le détachement de Tripoli

Ce qui est remarquable c'est que sous le mandat Eddé des dirigeants musulmans de Tripoli seront associés aux efforts des maronites pour lutter contre le détachement de leur ville du Liban et son rattachement à la Syrie. C'est ainsi que le président Eddé et son président du Conseil, Kheir el-Din el-Ahdab, vont envoyer ensemble une lettre à Léon Blum protestant contre les visées syriennes sur Tripoli et le Akkar.[32] Le ministère français des Affaires Etrangères s'étonnera et les rassurera en affirmant que le problème était déjà réglé par les traités franco-syrien et franco-libanais. Et Ahdab reviendra à la charge le 11 juin 1937 en envoyant une autre lettre au ministre français des Affaires Etrangères, réaffirmant l'unité du Liban.

Le glissement à distance de Arida et de Khouri à partir de 1936–1937

Un vent nouveau soufflait sur la région et les nationalistes syriens se rapprochaient de certains dirigeants libanais, dont Bechara el-Khouri et le patriarche Arida.[33]

Certains nationalistes arabes libanais exprimaient de leur côté des vues nettement plus modérées concernant les frontières. Amin Rihani, connu pour sa position unioniste, fait remarquer 'qu'il n'est pas opportun d'insister pour le moment sur la question des frontières . . . le premier devoir qui s'impose, soit aux Syriens, soit aux Libanais, est d'obtenir la réalisation de leurs aspirations politiques.'[34] Le rapport de Meyrier du 7 août 1936 à son ministre des Affaires Etrangères exprime une appréhension des rapprochements syro-libanais.

> Le Liban libre et indépendant, c'est-à-dire libéré des troupes françaises, c'est dans les quelques années qui suivront la conclusion du traité, l'annexion pure et simple au Royaume arabe de la seule terre où dans le Proche-Orient, les chrétiens peuvent encore respirer librement. Il est à coup sûr regrettable que des maronites chrétiens et probablement Libanais sincères s'emploient à réaliser pareille tâche . . . Il nous incombera de les neutraliser. Mais ce sera peut-être difficile dans un parlement où des préoccupations particulières ou partisanes émoussent le sens de l'intérêt national . . .'[35]

Et dans un rapport ultérieur, Meyrier précisera que 'les Chiites comptent quatre députés au Parlement libanais, et qu'ils ont affirmé au président Eddé qu'ils restaient indéfectiblement attachés à l'intégrité du Liban dans ses frontières actuelles'.[36]

En fait, les contacts entre le patriarche Arida et Bechara el-Khouri avec Damas s'intensifiaient et n'étaient plus un secret pour personne. Le haut-commissaire De Martel fera un rapport sur ces nouvelles données en faisant remarquer que les partisans de Khouri—'que l'échec de leur chef à l'élection présidentielle jette nécessairement dans l'opposition'—adoptaient les principes des nationalistes musulmans et s'unissaient au patriarche maronite pour assumer le rôle de défenseurs des libertés nationales dans un pays où les questions d'intérêt personnel l'emportent sur les intérêts d'ordre général:

> Il ne faut pas s'étonner que B. Khoury—écrira De Martel—candidat des chrétiens, adopte les thèses favorables aux aspirations musulmanes, alors que le président Eddé, qui doit son succès au vote musulman, reste fidèle à la tradition, et se souvienne que les Libanais n'ont bénéficié depuis un siècle d'un régime spécial qu'en qualité de minoritaires protégés par la France . . . Pour B. Khoury comme pour le patriarche maronite, il s'agit évidemment de raisons matérielles beaucoup plus que d'idées . . . '[37]

Mais à cette époque, Khouri entretenait de bons rapports avec les autorités mandataires qui lui manifestaient de l'intérêt et prenaient en considération ses points de vue, apparemment pour l'éloigner des unionistes. En août 1937 il formula le souhait d'aller en France et il effectua une visite à Paris en août–septembre où il engagea des contacts avec les responsables français. Après sa visite, le ministre français des Affaires Etrangères écrira à De Martel que Khouri lui avait affirmé qu'il partageait les positions du président Eddé sur deux points, c'est à dire l'unité du Liban et la position vis-à-vis de la cause libanaise, et l'amitié avec la France, mais qu'ils divergeaient sur un point: le gouvernement de Eddé était monocratique alors que Khouri serait favorable au renforcement des institutions constitutionnelles. Khouri aurait même demandé l'appui des autorités mandataires. Les autorités mandataires vont par la suite effectuer des contacts intensifiés[38] pour rapprocher les deux blocs antagonistes, et pour atténuer les divergences entre eux. Et les deux blocs se présenteront ensemble aux élections dans des listes d'union qui gagneront d'ailleurs dans toutes les régions.

Mais les fuites ne disparaîtront pas et les ponts lancés par le groupe de Khouri et le patriarche maronite avec Damas seront maintenus. Des contacts seront intensifiés avec l'Italie.[39] Le déclenchement de la guerre mondiale déplacera les centres d'intérêt et suspendra les démarches en attendant de voir le cours que prendront les événements, et le nouveau rapport de forces des grandes puissances.

La conjoncture des années 1940 sera tout à fait favorable à une percée anglaise en Syrie et au Liban, opérée par l'entremise du général Spears, ministre délégué du gouvernement britannique en Syrie et au Liban. Cette même conjoncture placera la puissance mandataire dans une position très affaiblie, à cause de sa situation dans la seconde guerre mondiale. Occupée, divisée, la France était manifestement en perte de vitesse dans les pays du Levant.

Ce nouveau rapport de forces va déterminer des changements de position au Liban et plus particulièrment parmi les chrétiens maronites. Et alors que le président Eddé s'apprêtait à démissionner avec son chef de cabinet, face à la politique à la fois plus faible et plus raide des autorités mandataires en difficulté, Bechara el-Khouri glissait vers l'adoption de la carte anglaise, depuis l'occupation des pays du Levant par les forces alliées.

Cette période va témoigner aussi de l'apparition dans le champ politique de plusieurs partis politiques qui vont prendre une part active à la mobilisation de l'opinion à propos de l'entité libanaise et des rapports libano-syriens, sans être encore très influents sur le processus de prise de décision; parmi ces partis, le Parti national social syrien d'Antoun Saadé, les Chemises blanches de Toufik Awad, les Phalanges libanaises de Pierre Gemeyel, les Najjadés de Adnan el-Hakim. Des manifestations sont organisées par les uns et les autres, prenant l'allure d'une provocation confessionnelle.[40]

D'autre part, un nouveau courant d'opinion se développe et trouve des échos dans certains milieux musulmans et chrétiens, appelant à renforcer la collaboration entre les communautés au Liban et à une plus grande ouverture et collaboration avec les pays arabes. On trouvait parmi les adeptes de ce courant:

1. Des hommes d'affaires chrétiens ayant déjà des projets économiques et financiers dans les pays arabes, tels que Henry Pharaon et Michel Chiha,[41] artisan de la constitution de 1926, favorables à l'ouverture économique sur le monde arabe et dénonçant déjà les visées sionistes au Liban.
2. Des notables musulmans encouragés par le rôle économique grandissant de la ville de Beyrouth.
3. Des nationalistes arabes ou libanais qui avaient choisi la tactique de la modération pour faire partir les français.
4. Des chrétiens cultivant un nationalisme quelque peu chauvin.

Toujours est-il que les germes de la 'philosophie du Pacte national' apparaissent déjà dans les années 1938–1940. Ils pointent déjà dans les éditoriaux sous la plume de personnes comme Michel Chiha et Charles Helou. Ils caractérisent aussi la constitution du Parti du Pacte national, fondé le 6 septembre 1938 par Youssef el-Saouda, Habib Kayrouz, Rafik Boueiz, Zouheir Osseiran, César Gemayel, Toufik Awad, Omar Fakhouri, ainsi que d'autres, et qui appelle au renforcement des liens entre les communautés et les régions, à l'indépendance intégrale et au renforcement des liens avec les pays arabes dans le sens d'une alliance.

Les slogans de coexistence, de collaboration, et d'ouverture arabe sont donc diffusés par plusieurs milieux, pour des raisons différentes et parfois contradictoires. Toutefois, ce courant d'opinion ira en s'amplifiant et préparera le terrain aux décisions du congrès de Bkerké en 1941 et en 1943 à l'élaboration du Pacte national par Bechara el-Khouri et Riyad el-Solh.

En 1942, Bechara el-Khouri se rendra en Egypte avec Jamil Mardam Bey, y rencontrera Nahhas Pacha et discutera avec lui d'une formule de fédération arabe alignée sur les Anglais.[42] A cette époque, les unionistes musulmans libanais se rapprochaient des chrétiens qui s'éloignaient de la France et les encourageaient à s'aligner sur l'axe anti-mandataire en leur promettant des garanties.

La conjoncture aidant, une vague de nationalisme submergea les maronites de l'opposition et les détacha de la France, leur protectrice traditionnelle, et ils s'empressèrent de contracter un compromis avec les musulmans libanais traditionnellement favorables à l'unité syrienne et hostile à la présence française. Il est entendu que ce revirement de l'opinion publique chrétienne témoignait d'une tendance indépendantiste authentique chez les uns, quoique simpliste et ignorante des considérations stratégiques, et de beaucoup d'opportunisme chez d'autres.

Le Liban allait avoir accès à l'indépendance en 1943, mais une indépendance paradoxalement arrachée à la France, avec l'appui des nationalistes syriens et des anglais, alors qu'initialement la France soutenait, bon gré mal gré, l'état du Grand-Liban contre les visées d'annexion syriennes et les engagements anglais vis-à-vis des sionistes, depuis la déclaration de Balfour.

Qu'allait prévoir le Pacte national pour sauvegarder l'entité libanaise? Un consensus intercommunautaire précaire et des alliances avec ceux qui menaçaient directement cette entité. Les chrétiens maronites ont-ils creusé leur propre tombe? Seront-ils acculés à se replier dans un réduit isolé et menacé, qu'ils avaient eux-mêmes fait éclater en faveur d'un état démocratique moderne, plus grand que leur montagne rocheuse?

Le choix du Grand-Liban semble avoir été une nécessité inéluctable pour les maronites afin de réaliser leurs grandes aspirations. Mais si la conjoncture internationale ne lui permettait plus de s'appuyer sur la protection et la garantie d'une grande puissance pour se maintenir, il fallait lui trouver d'autres garanties, à savoir un plus large consensus intercommunautaire, un programme de développement économique et social qui atténuerait les écarts entre les différentes régions, particulièrement entre le Mont-Liban et les régions rattachées en 1920, et, enfin, un minimum de culture politique qui aurait resserré les liens de tous les Libanais avec leur état. Le développement de certains secteurs économiques à l'époque du mandat avait déjà permis de tisser des liens plus étroits entre les citoyens du nouvel état. D'un autre côté, le processus de différenciation fonctionnelle impliqué par les efforts de rationalisation dans les activités économiques pouvait, lui aussi, soutenir une plus grande intégration nationale.

Mais ces facteurs ne sont pas suffisants, et si les artisans du Pacte de 1943 ont réussi à départager entre eux les appareils de l'état et les institutions, la formation d'une nation est demeurée le maillon perdu, dans un état profondément pénétré par les influences extérieures et dans un Proche-Orient qui constitue depuis 1948 un foyer de tension et de conflits régionaux et internationaux. En fait, seule la nation pourrait sauvegarder les assises du Grand-Liban. Mais une nation doit nécessairement être transcommunautaire, et les dirigeants communautaires n'ont aucune raison de vouloir la former.

Les maronites avaient vraisemblablement au départ un projet d'état démocratique moderne, mais leur politique n'était pas à la hauteur du projet. Toutefois, il ne faut pas isoler leurs comportements politiques du fonctionnement de l'ensemble du système politique local, et des comportements perceptibles des autres communautés religieuses du Liban.

Notes

1. Yusuf al-Sauda, *Fi sabil al-istiqlal* (Beyrouth, 1967), p. 94.

2. L'idéal du Grand-Liban est attribué à Bulus Noujaim qui aurait appelé à la 'reconstitution du Liban de la grande époque', dans *La question du Liban*, Etude d'histoire diplomatique et de droit international, publié en 1908 sous le pseudonyme de M. Jouplain (2ème éd. Jounieh, 1961). Voir M. Buheiry, 'Bulus Noujaim and the Grand Liban ideal 1908–1919', in Marwan R. Buheiry (sous la dir. de), *Intellectual Life in the Arab East* (Beyrouth, 1981).

3. Déclaration de D. Ammoun au quotidien français *le Temps* en janvier 1919, cité dans al-Sauda, *Fi sabil al-istiqlal*, p. 168; Document No. 22, 13 février 1911 et 23 janvier 1919 dans Georges A. Karam (sous la dir. de), *Qadiyyat Lubnan 1918–1920* (Beyrouth, 1985), pp. 60–2; Proclamation de l'indépendance libanaise par le Conseil Administratif, le 20 mai 1919.

4. En 1920, plusieurs chrétiens faisaient partie du congrès syrien: Georges Harfouche, Rachid Naffah, Wadih Abou Rizk, Youssef Nammour, Toufik Moufarrege. D'autre part, le gouvernement fayçalien proclamera le maintien du Mont-Liban et le rétablissement de son autonomie en conformité avec le règlement de 1865. Il nomme Habib Pacha Saad gouverneur de la Montagne et ce dernier prête serment de fidélité et de dévouement au roi Hussein du Hedjaz. Voir E. Rabbath, *La Formation historique du Liban politique et constitutionnel* (Beyrouth, 1973), p. 271.

5. Ibid., p. 279.

6. Buheiry, 'Bulus Nujaim', p. 81.

7. Parmi les chrétiens sceptiques vis-à-vis du Grand-Liban, Chebl Dammous écrit le 1er septembre 1920 les vers suivants:

الا وبالا عليكم غير ميمون   أبناء مارون هلا كان سعيكم

فتهجرون مقام الذل والهون   ظنتم كبر لبنان يشرفكم

تكبير لبنان تصغير لمارون   تالله ما قدركم الا الصغير في

Al-Nahar du 19 août 1987. Chebl Dammous est le chef de la commission parlementaire qui est chargé d'élaborer la constitution en 1926. Il est grec catholique.

8. Parmi les partisans de la seconde tendance, nous pouvons signaler les résolutions des Congrès du Littoral (*Mu'tamar al-Sahil*) qui regroupaient à chaque fois des personnalités assez représentatives des communautés musulmanes sous la présidence de Salim Ali Salam (16 novembre 1933, 19 mars 1936) et le Congrès national musulman en octobre 1936.

9. Bishara al-Khuri, *Haqa'iq lubnaniyya*, 3 tomes (Beyrouth, 1960, 1961), pp. 100–1.

10. Les scouts de Saouda se recrutaient en bon nombre parmi les jeunes écoliers et villageois de la Montagne, comme l'attestent certains documents répertoriés par Dr I. Khalifé dans les archives personnelles de Saouda.

11. Rabbath, *La Formation historique du Liban*, p. 398.

12. Picot a assuré à une délégation maronite, lors de sa visite à Beyrouth le 10 mai 1919, que 'puisque la France va obtenir le droit du mandat sur toute la Syrie, les intérêts des chrétiens libanais seront sauvegardés, c'est pourquoi il n'y a pas de nécessité pour détacher le Liban de l'ensemble de la Syrie'. Mais le patriarche maronite et le Conseil administratif s'opposèrent à cette position française et le 20 mai 1919, le Conseil administratif du Mont-Liban contredit son communiqué de décembre 1918 et réclame l'indépendance intégrale du Liban, dans ses frontières historiques et naturelles, sans aucune allusion au mandat français.

13. En réponse à l'intention exprimée par le général Sarrail, haut-commissaire au Liban en 1924, de nommer un gouverneur local, plusieurs députés libanais essayèrent de le dissuader en prétextant que le pays n'était pas encore assez mûr pour cela, de peur qu'un maronite ne soit nommé. Même dans les rangs maronites, le même conseil était prodigué par Habib Pacha Saad, devant les chances de l'élection d'Emile Eddé, président du Conseil représentatif à cette époque. Voir M. Zamir, 'Emile Eddé and the territorial integrity of Lebanon', *Middle Eastern Studies* (May 1978) 208–9.

14. La nomination de Charles Debbas comme premier chef de l'état libanais, alors que les deux candidats qui se disputaient les postes étaient Eddé et Khouri. D. Ayoub Tabet et Petro Trad sont eux aussi des chrétiens non maronites (le premier est un maronite converti au protestantisme et le second est orthodoxe).

15. Khouri est nommé secrétaire général du gouvernement le 5 février 1920 et le général Gouraud lui fait une seule demande: ne pas suivre le politique de Habib Pacha Saad, son parent, parce qu'elle ne leur plaît pas; Khuri, *Haqa'iq lubnaniyya*, p. 101.

16. La constitution libanaise est promulguée par le haut-commissaire De Jouvenal le 23 mai 1926. 'La République libanaise se trouvait dotée aussi d'un statut organique, d'un président national, d'un sénat, d'un drapeau, de tout ce qui constitue l'outillage politique d'un Etat indépendant. Elle trouve aussi une confirmation de l'intégrité et de l'inaliénabilité du territoire libanais.' Massoud Daher, *L'Histoire socio-politique de la République libanaise sous mandat français, 1926–1943*, 2 tomes (Paris, 1980), p. 180.

17. La communauté grecque orthodoxe déployée dans plusieurs pays arabes a toujours manifesté en son sein des aspirations nationalistes arabes, parfois aussi syriennes. La communauté grecque catholique se déploie, elle aussi, au-delà des frontières libanaises.

18. N. Dahdah, *Evolution historique du Liban*, 3ème éd. (Beyrouth, 1967).

19. Note de Ponsot au ministère des Affaires Etrangères; cité dans Daher, *L'Histoire socio-politique*, p. 243.

20. Ibid., p. 141.

21. Les grandes lignes de son programme de réforme portaient sur: (1) Le rajeunissement des cadres et l'augmentation des traitements des magistrats, en même temps qu'une simplification des méthodes et qu'une écomomie des dépenses improductives. (2) Le décret relatif à la réorganisation de la juridiction libanaise: 23 magistrats sont licenciés par suppression d'emploi. (3) Le décret portant sur la réorganisation de la juridiction mixte. (4) Le décret portant sur la réduction administrative: les *muhafazat* sont portées à 5 et ils visent à resserrer les liens entre le centre et la périphérie et à encourager l'intensification des rapports intercommunautaires. En effet, les *muhafazat* évitent volontairement de se superposer à la répartition confessionnelle. Les *qadas* sont portés à 14 et les *nahiyas* sont supprimées, avec licenciement de 17 *mudirs* par suppression d'emploi. v. Le décret portant sur la réorganisation des écoles officielles qui entraînait la fermeture de 5 écoles et le licenciement de 210 instituteurs. vi. Le décret portant sur la réduction des emplois au ministère de Santé Public qui occasionne le licenciement de 67 fonctionnaires dans les hôpitaux de Beyrouth, Saida et Zahlé.

22. Recensement de 1922: 326.000 chrétiens dont 178.000 maronites; 226.000 musulmans dont 122.000 sunnites; 38.000 druzes. Recensement de 1932: 431.000 chrétiens dont 241.000 maronites; 348.000 musulmans dont 192.000 sunnites; 56.000 druzes. A.E. Syrie-Liban (1930–1940), No. 497, 22 janvier 1932, pp. 102–4.

23. 'Formant la moitié de la population de la République libanaise, nous aspirons à la haute magistrature parce que Liban d'aujourd'hui n'est plus celui d'avant guerre, foyer chrétien . . .'

24. Daher, *Histoire socio-politique*, p. 286.

25. Le patriarche maronite, dans une lettre de Bkerké le 10 mai 1932, remercia Ponsot: 'Nous tenons à remercier votre excellence du beau geste par lequel vous venez de suspendre à titre temporaire l'organisation et le fonctionnement du pouvoir exécutif et législatif au Liban.' Daher, *Histoire socio-politique*, p. 298.

26. Zamir, 'Emile Eddé', p. 233: 'According to Amin Sa'id—in his book—several of the Maronite leaders including the Patriarch Huwayyik and Emile Eddé knew of the plan of recognizing the Syrian rights to a sea port—and Eddé supported it and promised to try and convince his own people to accept it.'

27. Daher, *Histoire socio-politique*, p. 411. Le quotidien libanais *le Jour* rappellera le lendemain que les Syriens nationalistes n'avaient pas demandé la réunion du Liban à la Syrie.

28. Le mémorandum de l'organisation sioniste au conseil suprême de la conférence de la Paix le 3 février 1919 délimite les frontières de la Palestine dans une annexe qui stipule: 'Starting in the north at a point on the Mediterranean Sea in the vicinity of Sidon and following the watersheds of the foothills of the Lebanon as far as Jisr El Karaon, thence to El Bire . . . following the dividing line between the two basins of the Wadi El Korn and the Wadi El Teim . . . ' Voir Antoine Hokayem et Marie-Claude Bittar, *L'Empire ottoman, les arabes et les grandes puissances, 1914–1920* (Beyrouth, 1981), p. 114.

> The boundaries outlined above are what we consider essential for the necessary economic foundation of the country. Palestine must have its natural outlets to the seas and the control of its rivers and their headwaters . . . Some international arrangement must be made whereby the riperian rights of the people dwelling south of the Litani river may be fully protected. Properly cared for, these headwaters can be made to serve in the development of the Lebanon as well as of Palestine. (Ibid., p. 117.)

Les autorités françaises, suite à la déclaration Balfour du 2 novembre 1917, avaient publié un communiqué stipulant que le 9 février 1918, Mr. Sokolor représentant des organisations sionistes avait été reçu par Mr. Stéphan Pichon qui a été heureux de lui confirmer que l'entente est complète entre les deux gouvernements français et britannique en ce qui concerne un établissement juif en Palestine. (A.E. Guerre (1914–1918), t. 120C, fol. 144.)

29. Echange de lettres No. 6 et 6 bis avec le haut-commissaire français dans Rabbath, *La Formation historique*, p. 416.

30. Le patriarche était lié à Khalil Maatouk, un homme d'affaires libanais, directement affecté par le monopole du tabac. Texte du mémorandum dans A.E. Syrie-Liban (1930–1940), No. 515, 21 janvier 1936, pp. 27–64.

31. A.E. Syrie-Liban (1930–1940), No. 516, 16 octobre 1936, p. 80.

32. A.E. Syrie-Liban (1930–1940), No. 502 (R.V.), 10 février 1937, p. 177.

33. Dans un rapport de Meyrier au ministre des Affaires Etrangères, il est fait allusion à une collaboration entre le Bloc national syrien (Fakhri Baroudi et Lutfi Haffar à Bhamdoun) et le groupe de Khouri. A.E. Syrie-Liban (1930–1940), No. 501, 7 août 1936, pp. 164–5.

34. Le quotidien *al-Nahar* du 5 août 1936.

35. Ibid.

36. Ibid., 21 août 1936, pp. 182–3.

37. Rapport de haut-commissaire De Martel, ibid., 28 février 1936, pp. 15–16.

38. A.E. Syrie-Liban (1930–1940), No. 503/504, septembre 1937, pp. 164–5.

39. Le patriarche Arida fait un déclaration au quotidien *Tribuna* très favorables aux Italiens et réclamant l'indépendance avec les guaranties de toute l'Europe, dont la France et l'Italie. A.E. Syrie-Liban (1930–1940), No. 517, 9 juin 1937, p. 4. Lors de sa visite à Rome, le patriarche Arida est accompagné par Monseigneur Chedid (un italophile) et par Youssef el-Saouda, auteur probable du livre vert du patriarche, en contact avec le consul d'Italie, et membre des plus agissants de l'opposition politique depuis l'insuccès de son chef de file, Bechara el-Khoury, aux présidentielles de 1936. A.E. Syrie-Liban (1930–1940), No. 516, 13 avril 1937, pp. 184–5. Arida adressera aussi au quotidien *Messagero* une lettre, le 17 février 1938, dans laquelle il loue l'Italie et ses réalisations. A.E. Syrie-Liban (1930–1940), No. 518, le 17 février 1938, p. 45. Il fait aussi une déclaration contre le communisme. Ibid., pp. 72–83.

40. Un décret No. 1474/EC, en date du 9 novembre 1937, du président Eddé, suspend les

activités des parties à 'allure militaire'. Il touche directement les Chemises blanches, les Phalanges et les Najjadés. A.E. Syrie-Liban (1930–1940), Nos 203–4, p. 230.

41. Michel Chiha est un financier, de rite Latin, parent par alliance de Bechara el-Khouri.

42. A.E. Londres C.N.F. (Syrie-Liban), No. 61, p. 250.

8

The Attitude of the Arab Nationalists towards Greater Lebanon during the 1930s

RAGHID SOLH

Introduction

The Lebanese Syrian unionists began to change their attitude to the idea of a Greater Lebanon during the 1930s. This has been seen as marking the beginning of a process in which they lost interest in their unionist aims. Some have attributed this change of attitude to specific characteristics of the movement, in the sense that its leaders were ready to reconsider their attitude towards Greater Lebanon in accordance 'with the benefits emanating from the government'. The mass base of the Syrian unionist movement was held to be 'emotional', 'disorganized' and 'politically impotent'.[1] Consequently, the dominant power in Lebanon was able to lead the unionists away from their original objectives.

However, these and similar interpretations appear to have overlooked not only the extent of this change but also some of the factors that instigated it. This is partly because many of the undercurrents which affected the Syrian unionist movement remained largely unknown to outsiders.

The same applies to the role of the Arab nationalist parties during the 1930s, two of which gained prominence by establishing branches in a number of Arab countries apart from Lebanon: 'Usbat al-'amal al-qawmi (the League of National Action, LNA) and al-Hizb al-qawmi al-'arabi (the Arab Nationalist Party, ANP).

This paper will focus on the Arab Nationalist Party since its existence has only become public knowledge during the past few years. In fact, this organization was apparently never given a specific name. Sometimes it was referred to as Jama'at al-kitab al-ahmar (Group of the Red Book), and at other times the Arab Nationalist Party—the title used here since it is more indicative of the organization's aims. Another reason for focusing on the ANP is the availability of hitherto unpublished material and private papers which shed light on the role it played during the 1930s.

Political trends in Greater Lebanon

When General Gouraud proclaimed the independence of the Lebanese state on 1 September 1920, two main political tendencies were apparent: Kiyanism and Syrian unionism.

The Kiyanists were characterized by their loyalty to the idea of an independent 'Greater Lebanon'. In this they differed from the Lebanese autonomists who wanted a smaller (i.e. Mount) Lebanon with a clear Maronite majority. The Kiyanists began to pursue their objectives before the collapse of the Ottoman empire. With the end of the first world war and during the Peace Conference of 1919, they became more persistent and outspoken about their aims. Daud Ammun, the president of the Administrative Council of Mount Lebanon, appeared on 13 February 1919 before the Supreme Council of the Allies to demand the independence of Lebanon and the extension of its territories to its 'historical' and 'natural' frontiers. On 25 October of that year the Maronite Patriarch Ilyas al-Huwayyik raised similar demands in a memorandum submitted to the council.

The call for the extension of Lebanon's territories was based on three considerations. First, the Coast and the four *qada*s (the disputed territories) had in the past been part of Lebanon, which was dismembered by the Ottomans. Secondly, as Ammun put it,

> the territories within the said frontiers are necessary to our existence. Without them, neither commerce nor agriculture is possible for us and our population is bound to migrate. The mere closing of our frontiers by administrative measures would drive us, as has happened during the War, to actual starvation.[2]

Thirdly, the inclusion of the new territories within Lebanon would comply with the principle of self-determination, since the vast majority of the people living in these territories had petitioned the French government for the territories to become Lebanese.

The petition for self-determination was, however, considered highly contentious. Some members of the King–Crane Commission raised serious doubts about the validity of these petitions, and specifically the claim that the mainstream of the population outside Mount Lebanon was eager to join a Greater Lebanon.[3] It would be more correct to say that the 'mainstream' of Kiyanism was in geographical terms the Mountain and in confessional terms the Maronite community, though under the French mandate it enjoyed support outside these boundaries.

The Kiyanists were aware of the vulnerability of Lebanon, even after the extension of its territories. They continued to view city politics with some doubts if not disdain:[4] hence their vigilant attitude towards the non-Kiyanist Lebanese and their quest for French protection against their neighbour's designs. Though they appreciated French culture and France's past support for the Mountain, their main reason for maintaining their relations with France was to secure the full independence of *al-kiyan* (political entity) from Syrian unionism, pan-Islamism, Arab nationalism or any other similar schemes.

The Syrian unionists, the other main political tendency, were characterized by their adherence to the line adopted by the General Syrian Congress of 8 March 1920, regarding the Lebanese question. After proclaiming the Hashemite Amir Faysal as the monarch and Syria as an Arab kingdom to be ruled according to the principles of decentralization, the congress declared: 'The wishes of the Lebanese in administering their province Lebanon, with its frontiers which existed before the War, will be accommodated, provided that it remains free from any foreign influence.'[5] Though its mainstay was the Coast and among the Muslims, Syrian unionism also had a considerable following in other areas.

However, there were differences among the Syrian unionists which influenced their interpretation of the Faysalite formula. Though the vast majority of the Syrian unionist leaders belonged to the notability, one may distinguish between two main groups: the independent Syrian unionists such as 'Abdel Hamid Karami, Salim 'Ali Salam, the Beyhums (Omar, Muhammad Jamil, Amin, Ahmad Mukhtar), Sa'id Ammun and Yusef Istfan, and those Syrian unionists who joined the Arab nationalist societies such as al-Fatat, al-'Ahd and al-Istiqlal. The latter group included the Arslans ('Adel, Amin), the Solhs (Rida, Riyad, 'Afif), the Haidars (Muhammad Rustum, Sobhi, Ibrahim, Yusef), the Tali's (Rashid, Sa'id), As'ad Daghir, Tewfiq al-Bisar and Ahmad al-Manasfi, 'Arif Na'mani etc. This group was apparently more optimistic with regard to reconciling Syrian unionism and Lebanese particularism, and became actively involved in promoting the idea of Syrian unionism among some of the leading figures in Mount Lebanon. A case worth citing here is the attempt during the 1920s to establish contact and co-operation between the Lebanese Administrative Council and the Faysal government in Damascus. Though this second group was at times critical of Faysal's policies, it nonetheless identified with the Arab government of Damascus. Thus, after Maysalun, many of them had to flee the country, and they settled in other Arab capitals (e.g. As'ad Daghir) or were integrated into the ruling elites in neighbouring Arab countries (e.g. Muhammad Rustum Haidar and Al-Manasfi in Iraq, and Rashid Tali' in Transjordan).[6] To ensure their permanent exile, the French authorities in Beirut passed the death sentence on such figures as 'Adel Arslan, Rashid Tali' and Riyad Solh, while others had their property confiscated.[7]

It should be noted that the purging of organized Arab nationalist parties of their Lebanese members had begun as early as 1916 when the Ottoman authorities executed a number of activists. These two successive blows made the organized Arab nationalist groups in Lebanon almost ineffectual for a number of years and left the initiative in the hands of the independent Syrian unionist leaders, even though some of them also suffered after the collapse of the Faysalite government. Some of them received prison sentences upon their return to Beirut because of their involvement with the General Syrian Congress.[8] Unable to identify with the idea of a Greater Lebanon, they decided to boycott it and not accept senior government positions. They insisted that they were Syrians and refused to be counted in any census or to accept Lebanese identity cards.[9]

The attitude adopted by the independent Syrian unionists and the weakening of the Arab nationalists enabled the French mandatory authorities to restructure the Lebanese political landscape. This was based on the view outlined by Aristide Brian, the French foreign minister, in a letter sent to Gouraud to the effect that

> this Christian country should fully absorb our culture and depend on us and should without ulterior motives represent our long-standing influence in the Orient. Under no condition should this Christian element be swamped by the Muslim Arabs surrounding it and which outnumber it vastly. Under the mandatory system, Lebanon should be equal to Syria in spite of its smaller size.[10]

In line with this policy, a Kiyanist elite was placed in power. Leading figures of this new elite included Emile Eddé, August Bachus, Bishara al-Khuri, Charles Debbas, Ayub Tabet, all of whom had been active in pre-first world war Kiyanist organizations such as Jam'iyyat Beirut al-lubnaniyya (the Lebanese Society of Beirut, LSB).[11] In effect, the French did not 'neutralize the apparatus of the state in relationship' to the Syrian unionists,[12] but instead tried to neutralize and marginalize them in relation to the state.

The promulgation of the Lebanese Representative Council on 18 March 1922 posed a problem as it provided a channel through which those Syrian unionists willing to join the political process could pursue their aims. There were nevertheless sufficient safeguards to offset this possibility. To begin with, the prerogatives of the council were relatively limited and were at times ignored by the high commissioner who tended to rule by decree.[13] Secondly, to quote Gouraud, the 'Council was not permitted to initiate any legislative measure which would weaken the independence of Lebanon and surreptitiously prepare the ground for its dismemberment'.[14] Thirdly, the appointment of one-third of the parliament by presidential decree was introduced in 1927. Fourthly, the mandatory authorities tended to exert direct pressure on the 'extreme' Syrian unionists or Arab nationalists to withdraw from the elections—in 1922, for instance, Muhammad Jamil Beyhum, an Arab nationalist who tried to enter the parliamentary elections, was forced to withdraw. Finally, the authorities also tended to interfere in the elections, to the point that the Representative Council was a 'council merely so in name'.[15]

The French policy of excluding them from the political process alienated the mainstream among the Lebanese Syrian unionists, an attitude which became more pronounced after the failure of the 1925–6 Syrian revolt. Having been excluded from the political process, these activists began to search for alternative political structures as a means of pursuing their objectives. Such unionist leaders as Omar Beyhum, 'Abdel Hamid Karami, Riyad Solh (who had meanwhile returned from exile), Ahmad al-Da'uq, 'Abdullah al-Yafi and Sobhi Haidar decided to organize a Conference of the Coast. The proceedings and the resolutions of this conference shed light on the attitude of established Syrian unionist leaders regarding the Lebanese question.[16]

The first Conference of the Coast was given impetus by the election of the Syrian constituent assembly in June 1928. This assembly, which came under the control of the Syrian National Bloc, embarked on the drafting of the Syrian constitution as a prelude for a Franco-Syrian treaty. Since this implied the definition of Syrian frontiers, the Lebanese Syrian unionist leaders decided to hold a conference to express their views regarding this issue. The title of this conference denoted the centrality of the Coast and the predominance of its leaders in debates over the disputed territories. But there were also delegations from the Biqa', Jabal 'Amil and even from Latakia and Wadi al-Taym attending the conference. That it was chaired by Karami symbolized the leading role of Tripoli in the Syrian unionist movement. The conference did not claim to represent the Muslims. Rather, it purported to represent the disputed territories 'which were being denied the right of self-determination and whose inhabitants were united by bonds which did not distinguish between sectarian affiliations'.[17] That Damascus was chosen as a site for the conference was a further indication of the attachment of the Lebanese Syrian unionists to the Syrian capital. It was significant that of the 47 Lebanese participants, only two had attended the General Syrian

Congress in 1920, and only one of these two had played a leading role in the Arab nationalist societies active during the Faysalite period.

The conference issued its resolutions on 23 July 1928, demanding the return of the disputed territories to Syria. These resolutions were addressed to the Syrian constituent assembly which was called upon to seek the unity of Syrian lands. However, no strategy was suggested for realizing this aim; instead, satisfaction was expressed about the policies the Syrian National Bloc pursued.

A new generation of Arab nationalists

More or less during the same period in which the idea for the Conference of the Coast was born, a younger group of Lebanese Syrian unionists with strong Arab nationalist orientations emerged in Beirut. They launched al-Nadi al-ahli, which came to be located in 'Ayn al-Mreiseh and which, in order to escape the attention of the authorities, was licensed as a sports club. The list of members included Khayir Eddine Beyhum, Muhi Eddine Nusuli and Habib Abi Shahla, each of whom was in turn elected president of the club. Though 'Abdullah al-Yafi, 'Adel Solh and Sa'id Taqi Eddine were also members, the core group of this club consisted of Kazem and Taqi Eddine Solh, Muhammad 'Ali Hamadeh, Husain Sej'an and Anis al-Sagheer. The club extended its activities beyond the confines of Beirut by inviting literary and political figures from Syria and Egypt to take part in its programme. It appears that these particular contacts as well as the political background of some club members and the number of Christians involved in these activities led the mandatory authorities to dissolve al-Nadi al-ahli in 1929.[18]

Though they lost al-Nadi al-ahli, the members of the core group remained united by friendship, the experience of working together and the similarity of their political views. They showed a particular interest in the Egyptian nationalist movement led by Sa'ad Zaghloul's Wafd Party as well as the Indian nationalist movement led by Mahatma Gandhi's Congress Party.[19] These two parties were deemed to have successfully dealt with the sectarian differences among their respective populations and to have succeeded in engaging the masses in successive confrontations with the dominant foreign power.[20] In 1931, they attempted to emulate the Indian boycott of foreign interests by organizing a six-month boycott of the Tramway and Electricity Company in Beirut which was controlled by a Franco-Belgian consortium.

This boycott was also endorsed by Hizb al-istiqlal al-jamhuri (the Republican Independence Party, RIP), which in fact served as a temporary alternative to al-Nadi al-ahli. The party, which began its activities in 1931, brought together a number of professionals with different religious affiliations such as Du'aibis al-Murr (head of the Lawyers Association), 'Aziz al-Hashem, Sami Arslan, William 'Usaily, Maurice Gemayel, 'Adel Solh, Nasri Ma'louf and Muhammad 'Ali Hamadeh. The RIP called for the full independence of Lebanon and for the preservation of economic unity with its neighbouring countries. It also endorsed the concept of the arabism of Lebanon but without associating it with any specific unitary scheme.[21]

The position of al-Nadi al-ahli as regards Arab nationalist and Syrian unionist politics was further delineated in 1933. In November of that year another Conference of the Coast was convened in Beirut, chaired by Salim 'Ali Salam. It reiterated the demand for Syrian unity and chose an executive committee to pursue its objectives. However, those who later formed the Arab Nationalist Party did not participate in this conference. They had instead been involved in establishing the League of National Action (LNA), which was launched in August 1933, only a few weeks before the conference.

The LNA called for the unity of the Arab lands and rejected local chauvinism.[22] While recognizing the differences existing between Arab territories it nevertheless managed to retain a position from which it could appreciate the particularities of the Lebanese situation. Some members of al-Nadi al-ahli attended the founding meeting of the LNA but discovered that they disagreed with the League over certain issues, specifically concerning the Syrian National Bloc. Thus the idea of forming a new party was revived. Such deliberations brought al Nadi al-ahli into contact with another group in Lebanon, which was composed of intellectuals and academics from the American University of Beirut such as Constantine Zurayk and Fu'ad Mufarrej who were contemplating similar ideas. The discussions eventually came to include similarly oriented groups in Palestine and Syria, and by 1935 the Arab Nationalist Party (ANP) was launched.[23]

Beirut was chosen as the headquarters of the ANP where its covenant, *Kitab al-qawmiyya al-'arabiyya: haqa'iq wa-idahat wa-manahib*, was published. The covenant included a number of clauses which had special implications for Lebanon. In defining Arab nationalism, it emphasized a 'national' rather than a 'religious' state which, it was envisioned, would encourage religious tolerance and unreserved respect for a person's religious convictions. Another significant feature in the covenant was the definition of Arabs as those who spoke Arabic, lived in Arab lands and had no group affiliations preventing them from being integrated within an Arab nation.[24]

The ANP was—to use Duverger's typology—an exterior party which originated outside the parliamentary institutions of the Arab

East. Similar to al-Fatat of an earlier period, it adhered to a policy of strict confidentiality which was adopted in order to evade the security measures taken by the French authorities against the 'extremist' Arab nationalist organizations. Secrecy also helped the ANP to infiltrate and influence other groups and organizations of that period, though its secretive nature did not imply that it was anti-parliamentarian. Its members were carefully selected by the party's command for their deep commitment to Arab nationalism; their readiness to abide by ANP principles; their moral qualities; and their physical fitness to carry out risky tasks.

The ANP was able to establish footholds in some urban centres of the Arab East. Its command kept records of 240 members, which included detailed data on 59 of them,[25] all from urban areas: 17 from Damascus, 13 from Sidon, 8 from Beirut, and the remainder from such centres as Baghdad, Mosul, Kuwait, Homs, Hama, Jerusalem and Gaza. Of the 59 members for which data on employment are available, 19 were mobile in the sense that their occupations at times entailed relocation. This included Lebanese, Syrian and Palestinian teachers working in Iraq, and students at the American University of Beirut and immigrants in the United States. The ANP records also detail the nationality of 178 members: 56 were from Iraq; 52 were Lebanese; 49 were Syrian; 16 were Palestinian; 4 were from Kuwait; and 1 was from Transjordan. The membership record futhermore indicates the age group of some 66 of the 240 members. The youngest was born in 1914 and the oldest in 1896, which by 1936 meant an age span of 22 to 41 years, though the majority were in their thirties at the time. Arab Nationalist Party members appeared on average to be a generation younger than the earlier Arab nationalists of the Faysalite period, most of whom had been born during the 1880s.[26]

The records also provide information on another 48 of the 240 members. Of these, 11 were schoolteachers; 9 were employees; 8 were lawyers; 6 were landowners; 6 were physicians; 5 were merchants; and 3 were students. Few if any came from a working-class or peasant background. From their names and based on my personal knowledge it may be deduced that the majority of the ANP members were Muslims and that only 8 per cent were Christians. Nevertheless, the relatively high percentage of Lebanese may be taken as an indication of the ANP's emphasis on cross-sectarian policies, of its interest in reconciling Arab nationalist thinking with Lebanese particularism.

The events of 1936 served to foster a more pronounced cross-sectarian strand in Lebanese politics. They were to a large extent related to changes taking place in France as well as in the neighbouring Arab countries. The Popular Front in France was becoming more assertive and was pressuring the French government to adopt a more liberal line in its dealings with the nationalists in Syria and Lebanon.[27] This pressure as well as international and regional political considerations led the French authorities to restore gradually constitutional life in Lebanon. The first step in this direction was the election of Emile Eddé in January 1936 as president of Lebanon. Some Syrian unionist leaders preferred Eddé's political rival, the Constitutionalist Bishara al-Khuri. But others such as Omar Beyhum and Salim 'Ali Salam supported Eddé, influenced as they were by his promise to work towards closer co-operation with Damascus regarding independence from France and for greater equality between Christians and Muslims in the sharing of political power. Eddé also maintained cordial relations with such Syrian unionist leaders as Riyad Solh on whose behalf he intervened, asking the French to let him return from exile in April 1928.[28]

Differentiation within the Syrian unionist movement

Apart from the restoration of constitutional life in Lebanon, developments in Syria led to treaty negotiations between the new French Popular Front government led by Leon Blum and the Syrian National Bloc, which in turn made an impact on the Lebanese Syrian unionists. The circumstances surrounding the treaty negotiations alarmed some of the leading members of the executive committee of the 1933 Conference of the Coast such as Salim 'Ali Salam. These members feared that by attempting to secure the goodwill of the Maronite Patriarch Antoine Arida and some of the Kiyanist critics of French policies in Lebanon, the Syrian National Bloc would go as far as to keep silent on the issue of the disputed territories or even abandon the idea altogether. To pre-empt such a possibility, the executive committee with the support of 'Abdel Hamid Karami called for a new Conference of the Coast to be held on 10 March 1936 in Beirut.[29]

Salim 'Ali Salam, in whose house this conference was convened, was elected chairman and Salah Beyhum was given the post of secretary. As in the previous Conferences of the Coast, the participants here were predominantly, though not exclusively, from the Muslim communities and the coastal areas. Of the 30 members, 6 were Christian and 7 came from the Lebanese interior. To lend the conference more credibility, the organizers attempted to include representatives from the major Lebanese groups which for various confessional, ideological and social reasons were challenging the status quo. The list of participants as well as the debates among them indicated that, like the Faysalite movement of an earlier period, there were differences between the independent

Syrian unionists and those who were members of the different Arab nationalist organizations.

The main exponents of the independent Syrian unionists were Salam and Karami. Both were in agreement that the 1936 Conference of the Coast was in fact the continuation of the two previous conferences of 1928 and 1933; hence their belief that in this forum they should reiterate and confirm the previously proclaimed Syrian unionist objectives. However, one difference did emerge between the two leaders. Whereas Karami, together with the Tripolitan leader 'Abdel Latif al-Bisar, had opted for 'full Syrian unity', Salam, followed by some Beiruti members such as Muhammad Jamil Beyhum and Hasan al-Qadi, had adopted a more lenient attitude towards the inhabitants of Mount Lebanon by suggesting a return to the resolution of the 1928 conference. This implied that it would be left to Mount Lebanon to decide whether or not it wished to join the Syrian unity. This divergence in views suggested a growing distinction between the attitude of the Beirutis and the Tripolitans towards Greater Lebanon. To appreciate these differences, a number of factors should be kept in mind.

Compared with Tripoli, Beirut had for some decades been more involved in cross-sectarian economic and political transactions. Beiruti notables such as the Beyhums, the Da'uqs and the Salams—i.e. families who were involved in commerce—tended to be more secularized than the notables of Tripoli, such as the Karamis or the Jisrs, whose status was predicated on their religious background. Consequently, the Christian 'colouring' of Greater lebanon tended to cause more consternation in Tripoli. Furthermore, the rapid growth of Beirut as a Levantine port was accompanied by the dwindling importance of Tripoli as a commercial centre, in particular in its commercial relations with the interior. This development, not surprisingly, shaped the attitude of the Tripolitans and the Beirutis towards Greater Lebanon. The French attempted to reduce this alienation by according Shaykh Muhammad al-Jisr a senior post in the government. While this appears to have had a positive impact on al-Jisr's constituency in Tripoli, its effect on rival clans like the Karamis and the Bisars was not necessarily the same. Interestingly, though Sidon had also suffered from the rising importance of Beirut, it appears that the Sidonians were better able to accommodate Beiruti politics.

The differences which emerged between the Syrian unionists of Beirut and those of Tripoli were only alluded to during the debate of the 1936 Conference of the Coast. However, when it came to the actual resolutions, Tripoli's stand prevailed and the participants called for the full unity and freedom of Syria. The resolutions were presented in a memorandum addressed to the French government through the high commissioner in Beirut. The signatories expressed their confidence that France would adhere to the principle of self-determination, and that it would fulfil the demands of the disputed territories with regard to full independence and Syrian unity.

The members of the Arab nationalist organizations who attended the 1936 conference, namely 'Ali Nasser Eddine (LNA) as well as Kazem Solh, Shawqi Dandashi and Shafiq Lutfi (ANP), were reluctant to endorse this resolution. Solh, Lutfi and 'Adel Ossairan (a Shi'a notable from Sidon) refused to add their names. The following day, Solh published a long article in the Beirut press outlining his views on the main issues dealt with during the conference. He argued that the concern was with the fate of the nation as a whole and the future of Arab nationalism, which should override preoccupation with specific areas (i.e. the disputed territories) or certain religious communities. Hence his criticism of the proceedings of the 1936 Conference of the Coast. By calling on France to bring about the unification of Syria, the conference had in effect implicitly recognized the mandate system. The conference also failed to recognize or even acknowledge the positive shift in the attitude of many Kiyanist leaders as well as public opinion towards the independence of Lebanon from French rule. This failure would push the Kiyanists to reinforce their alliance with France, thus leaving Mount Lebanon a fertile ground for French anti-Arab activities. Solh also stressed that the Lebanese Arab nationalists should concern themselves with Lebanon as a whole rather than focus their attention only on the issue of the disputed territories. These nationalists should be working towards freeing Lebanon from French domination and towards arabizing it by winning the Kiyanists over. The only means of achieving this would be to initiate free dialogue with the genuine representatives of Kiyanism rather than dealing with segregated forums.[30]

The initial reactions to Solh's point of view were far from favourable. The sponsors of the conference began to express doubts over the motives behind his stand. The Syrian National Bloc (SNB) in Damascus, which meanwhile was changing its attitude towards Greater Lebanon and the issue of the disputed territories, appeared to be dissatisfied both with the conference and with Kazem Solh's viewpoint. In fact, the SNB appeared keen to consolidate an understanding with Patriarch Arida as well as with the Constitutionalist Bloc led by Bishara al-Khuri. Accordingly, the SNB dispatched a conciliatory delegation to Arida on 13 March 1936, a step which in effect disassociated the SNB from the conference. But at the same time the SNB made a point of expressing its disapproval of Kazem Solh's attitude towards the issues raised during the conference.

Thus, it appears that though the SNB was prepared to grant certain concessions over the issue of the disputed territories, it attempted at the same time to use this as a bargaining chip in its negotiations with the French. Had the SNB permitted the Lebanese Arab nationalists to take the initiative in becoming more flexible over the issue of Greater Lebanon and the disputed territories, then its position during negotiations with the French would have been weakened. This attitude led Solh to rush to Damascus where he held long discussions with some of the SNB leaders with the aim of convincing them of the position he had taken.[31]

The ANP endorsed the views adopted by some of its members during the conference and thus attempted to win over the anti-mandate leaders and public opinion. It was encouraged by a particular event—the Islamic Meeting, which took place in the house of Omar Beyhum on 24 October 1936. Riyad Solh suggested that, hence-forward, the opponents of French rule should organize their conferences on a national rather than a confessional basis. He proposed a Syro-Lebanese confederation as a compromise, bringing together Kiyanists and Syrian unionists to work for the independence of Lebanon from French rule. Riyad's proposition explains his decision to absent and distance himself from the 1936 Conference of the Coast, a decision which came about after consultations with ANP members. His close relations with leading ANP members in Lebanon contrib-uted to the party's influence and helped it to mobilize public opinion further.

Another encouraging sign in this respect was the positive response to Riyad's propositions from such leaders as Salim 'Ali Salam, Omar Beyhum, Ahmad 'Arif al-Zein and Ahmad Rida. Of equal importance was the absence of the Tripolitan leaders such as Karami and Bisar from the 1936 conference on the grounds that Bisar was unwilling to discuss the issue of Tripoli. This stand further deepened the gap between the Tripolitans on the one hand and, on the other, those in Beirut and the south.[32]

The ANP consolidated its gains within the Syrian unionist constituency by penetrating al-Najjadeh, a paramilitary organization which had emerged from a Muslim boy scout movement. Four ANP members—Jamil Mikkawi, Husain Sej'an, Anis al-Sagheer and 'Abdullah Dabbus—joined the command of al-Najjadeh and each became president.[33] The ANP attempted to reorient this organization in the direction of a national anti-mandatory policy. During the same period, the ANP also attempted to extend its contacts with Maronite intellectuals. This culminated in the establishment of an informal discussion group involving ANP members such as Taqi Eddine Solh and Salim Idriss and such Maronite intellectuals as Yusef al-Sawda,

'Aziz al-Hashem, Ra'if Abi Lama' and As'ad 'Aql. This discussion group eventually became the Committee for the Lebanese National Pact.[34]

The shift in attitude on the part of some of the anti-mandate leaders and their constituencies was partly influenced by the optimistic interpretations of events taking place during 1937. The perceptible thaw in Franco-SNB relations, as well as Eddé's initiative in appointing Khair Eddine Ahdab as prime minister of Lebanon in January 1937, was regarded as a step forward in fulfilling the aims of the Muslim leaders. Though Ahdab had been a member of parliament since 1934 and was by 1937 a confirmed Eddéist, the fact that he was a Muslim and had once co-published an Arab nationalist daily (*al-'Ahd al-jadeed*) was of some significance to the Syrian unionists.

The Arab nationalists and the Lebanese political process

Pressure on opponents of the status quo began to be lifted and, perhaps more importantly, preparations for the restoration of constitutional life began to be initiated. However, by the summer of 1937 it became apparent to the anti-mandate leaders that their expectations would not be fulfilled. The French foreign minister instructed the high commissioner De Martel in September of that year to adopt all possible measures to prevent the Arab nationalists or the 'extremists' among them from entering parliament. The best means for achieving this end was perceived to be the forging of an alliance between the two main Kiyanist parties, the Constitutionalists and the Eddéists.[35] De Martel accordingly pressured the two parties into an electoral coalition while at the same time attempting to prevent the Syrian unionists from participating in the elections planned for October 1937.[36] This French pressure was successful in Tripoli where Karami decided to withdraw from the electoral race with the explanation that he did not trust the authorities' promise of neutrality. In Beirut, Riyad Solh and Omar Beyhum decided to put the proffered neutrality to the test by participating in the elections with the full support of Salim 'Ali Salam. These decisions, in effect, served to widen further the gap between Karami in Tripoli and Riyad, Beyhum and Salam in Beirut with regard to the issue of Greater Lebanon. The election results confirmed Karami's suspicions since French intervention led to the defeat of the anti-mandate leaders.[37] But it also served the interests of the French since they could now justifiably point out that freedom of choice did not apply to Arab nationalist and Syrian unionist constituencies. Unmoved by these claims, De Martel wrote to the French foreign minister that 'the most notable result of this national consultation is the defeat of all Moslem and unitary irredentism, even though Riyad Solh had tried to rally the voters by proclaiming himself a partisan of a Lebanese state impregnated by an Arab spirit.'[38]

The ANP members, who had supported the Beyhum–Solh list, were disillusioned by the events of 1937. They had made an effort to change their negative attitude towards the Lebanese state and had adopted a gradualist approach towards Arab unity. Furthermore, they had been willing to pursue their objectives through the Lebanese political process. Instead of recognizing this, the mandatory authorities had overlooked the 'democratization' of the Arab nationalist tendency in Lebanon. More importantly, the Kiyanist parties had not only ignored this change in attitude but had even joined hands to form an anti-Arab nationalist electoral coalition.

However, this situation did not prevail due to changes in France's policy which in turn had been instigated by a number of interrelated factors: the rising tension in Europe; the disintegration of the Popular Front government in France; and the increasing agitation of a French lobby against the treaty systems in Syria and Lebanon. These factors combined to pressure the mandatory authorities into suspending constitutional life and initiating a policy of depoliticizing Lebanon.[39] Such a policy alienated not only the Arab nationalists, but also the Constitutionalists and a number of other leading Kiyanists. It had the effect of reviving the prospects of co-operation between the Arab nationalists and the disaffected Kiyanist leaders, specifically those from the Constitutionalist Party. Furthermore, this French policy served to reduce the anti-Kiyanist feelings which had spread among Syrian unionists as a result of the 1937 election.

The pressure exerted by the French encouraged the ANP in 1938 to move its headquarters away from Beirut. This led ANP members to take advantage of their presence in neighbouring Arab states and to familiarize public opinion there with the intricacies of the Lebanese question. Thus, for example, the command of the ANP stated in its annual report for the year 1938–9 that 'the criteria we use in Lebanon to assess other parties are different from those we apply in Syria, Palestine or Iraq. The command therefore suggests a more flexible approach to these groups in this country.'[40] This entails conciliation between, on the one hand, the sponsors of a Lebanese entity independent of Syria and the other Arab countries and, on the other hand, those who demand the partial or total integration of Lebanon within a greater Arab entity. Such conciliation could be achieved by concentrating on furthering the nationalist movement and on encouraging a positively oriented government. The ANP believes that the fulfilment of these two objectives would eventually bring Lebanon closer to the rest of the Arab world as well as lead the Lebanese to espouse the idea of arabism.

The attitude expressed by the ANP in this annual report is all the more significant if we remember that the party was an active participant in Arab politics during this period, even though the existence of this organization continued to remain a well-kept secret. For example, the ANP played an important role in steering the LNA in the direction of the objectives it was pursuing. For a period it also controlled al-Nadi al-'arabi and al-Maktab al-qawmi al-'arabi in Damascus.[41] Furthermore, the ANP exerted a considerable influence over Lajnat al-difa' 'an filastin fi suriyya (the Committee for the Defence of Palestine in Syria), which had taken the initiative in organizing the Pan-Arab Bludan Conference in 1937.[42] It also controlled Nadi al-muthanna, a cultural club in Iraq, as well as a number of youth organizations there. One may say that the ANP reached the height of its influence if not power when three of its members, Yunis Sab'awi, Mussa al-Shahbandar and Muhammad Salman Hassan were given ministerial posts in the government of Rashid 'Ali in 1941.[43] The ANP also had active branches in Palestine and Kuwait and was even able to secure the support of some recruits in Saudi Arabia and North Africa. All these activities enabled the ANP to achieve a measure of influence over Arab public opinion, specifically with regard to understanding the particular conditions in Lebanon compared with the other Arab countries.

Concluding remarks

The Arab nationalist tendency during the 1930s, as embodied in organized political parties such as the ANP with its cross-sectarian outlook, contributed to the process of reconciliation among the Lebanese through sustained political action in Lebanon as well as in neighbouring Arab countries. The ANP did not abandon its Arab nationalist goals, but sought to achieve them through a gradualist approach and by working within the political system in Lebanon.

However, the role of the ANP was inhibited by two interrelated factors. The first was the restrictive measures introduced by the mandatory authorities which aimed at keeping the Arab nationalists, in particular the leading activists among them, outside the political process. This policy limited the possibility of the democratization of Arab nationalist political tendencies. The second factor was that these repressive policies encouraged the ANP to remain a clandestine as well as a close organization instead of openly challenging the mandatory authorities and establishing itself as a mass party among the poorer classes in urban centres and rural areas of Lebanon.

Notes

1. N. W. Atiyah, 'The attitude of the Lebanese Sunnis towards the State of Lebanon', Ph.D. thesis (unpublished), University of London, 1937, pp. 102–54.

2. FO 371/35183, 9/11/1943, pp. 132–8; see also Y. Mizhir, *Tarikh lubnan al-'amm*, vol. II (n.d.), pp. 889–98.

3. H. N. Howard, *The King–Crane Commission* (Beirut, 1963), p. 146.

4. A. Hourani, *The Emergence of the Modern Middle East* (London, 1981), p. 175.

5. A. Kadri, *Mudhakkirat 'an al-thawra al-'arabiyya al-kubra* (Damascus, 1956), p. 184.

6. The battle of Maysalun, which lies outside Damascus, took place on 24 July 1920 when the French defeated King Faysal's Syrian forces. For a full account of this episode, see Sati' al-Husri, *Yawm Maysalun* (Beirut, n.d.)

7. Q. Qal'aji, *Jil al-fida* (Beirut, n.d.), pp. 407–8; see also M. I. Darwazah, *Hawl al-haraka al-'arabiyya al-wahida* (Sidon, 1950), pp. 30, 77–8.

8. L. Meo, 'The separation of Lebanon from Greater Syria', Ph.D. thesis (unpublished), Indiana University, 1961, p. 78; see also Y. Mizhir, *Tarikh lubnan al-'amm*, pp. 934–5.

9. H. Hallaq, *Dirasat fi tarikh lubnan al-mus'aser* (Beirut, 1985), p. 111.

10. MAE, Arabie 1918–1929, Télégramme du 17 mars 1921, serie E, vol. 12, pp. 115–17, quoted in A. Mahafza, *Mawqif faransa wa-almaniya wa-italiya min al-wihda al-'arabiyya 1919–1945* (Beirut, 1985), p. 107.

11. B. Khuri, *Haqa'iq lubnaniyya*, vol. I (Beirut, 1960), p. 70.

12. C. Geertz ed., *Old Societies and New States* (New York, 1967), p. 128.

13. Y. Mishir, *Tarikh lubnan al-'amm*, p. 992.

14. H. Abu Fadil, *al-Barlaman* (Beirut, 1985), p. 23.

15. FO 371/7847, Cairo to London, 21/6/1922, p. 61; see also M. I. Beyhum, *al-'Ahd al-mukhadram fi suriya wa lubnan* (Beirut, n.d.), pp. 129–42; H. Abu Fadil, *al-Barlaman*, p. 30.

16. For the resolution and list of participants of the 1928 Conference of the Coast, see H. Hallaq, *Mu'tamar al-sahil wa-al-aqdiya al-arba'* (Beirut, 1985), pp. 43–70, 175–81.

17. Ibid., p. 166.

18. Members of the first executive committee of al-Nadi al-ahli included Khair Eddine Beyhum (president), 'Abdel-Qader Bakdash (director), Muhammad 'Ezz Eddine (deputy director), Yusef Lababidi (treasurer), Husain Sej'an, Omar al-Qaisi, Kazem Solh, Ahmad al-'Araisi, Muhammad 'Ali al-Zambi, Ihsan Makhzoumi (members), in K. Solh, Private Papers; also Al-Safir, 13/6/1987; Al-Shira' 9/5/1983: interview with Muhammad 'Ali Hamadeh.

19. K. Solh, Private Papers, Letter to Gandhi, 5/11/1931.

20. Ibid., Letter to Muhammad al-Majzoub, April 1931.

21. A. Solh, *Hizb al-istiqlal al-jamhuri* (Beirut, 1970), pp. 13, 21, 109–10.

22. D. Qarqut, *Tatawur al-haraka al-wataniyya fi suriyya: 1920–1939* (Beirut, 1975), p. 179.

23. Interview with Taqi Eddine Solh, London 6/11/1980; with Wasif Kamal, Paris, 17/3/1981.

24. K. Solh, Private Papers, The Constitution of the ANP.

25. Ibid., Membership Record of the Party (ANP).

26. For relevant data on Arab nationalists during the Faysalite period, see C. E. Dawn, *From Ottomanism to Arabism* (Chicago, 1973), pp. 174–9.

27. FO 371/20065, Damascus to London, 16/3/1936.

28. Personal conversation with Sa'eb Salam, 16/11/1984; interview with Taqi Eddine Solh, London 6/11/1980.

29. H. Hallaq, *Mu'tamar al-sahil wa-al-aqdiyah al-arba'*. See pp. 43–70 for the resolutions and participants' list of the 1936 Conference of the Coast.

30. K. Solh, *Mushkilat al-infisal wa-al-ittisal*, pamphlet published in Beirut in 1937.

31. Interview with Taqi Eddine Solh, London 6/11/1980.

32. *Al-Nahar* 25/10/1936.

33. K. Solh, Private Papers, Directives from the Command of the ANP, 28/1/1939; see also Al-Shira', interview with Muhammad 'Ali Hamadeh.

34. K. Solh, Private Papers, Letter to the Head of the SNB, July 1936; see also B. al-Jisr, *Mithaq 1943* (Beirut, 1978), pp. 84–6.

35. MAE, Syrie-Liban 1930–1940, vol. 503, 20/9/1937, p. 164; see also EMAT (AH) 7N4190, doss. 1, 20/9/1937.

36. B. Khuri, *Haqa'iq lubnaniyya*, p. 225.

37. Interview with Malek Salam, London 12/4/1983.

38. MAE, Syrie-Liban 1930-1940, vol. 503, 26/10/1937, p. 20.

39. G. Puaux, *Deux années au Levant. Souvenirs de Syrie et du Liban 1939–1940* (Paris, 1952), pp. 56–65, 225–6.

40. K. Solh, Private Papers, Minutes of the Meetings of the Command on 11, 12, 13/8/1938.

41. Ibid., Letter from Said Fattah al-Imam, Head of the Arab Club, to Colonel Portales; see also Minutes of the Council of Deputies, October 1938.

42. F. Mufarrij, *al-Mu'tamar al-'arabi al-qawmi fi Bludan* (Damascus, 1937).

43. S. H. Longrigg, *Iraq 1900–1950* (Beirut 1968), p. 295; see also M. Buheiry ed., *Intellectual Life in the Arab East* (Beirut, 1981), p. 166.

9

L'Economie politique du Liban indépendant, 1943–1975

BOUTROS LABAKI

The structure and functions of the Lebanese economy have their origin in the evolution of the regional economic role of Beirut during the nineteenth and early twentieth centuries.

From being the principal port of the Ottoman Levant in the nineteenth century, it became under the French mandate the economic capital of the 'States of the Levant'. This role as tertiary staging post (between the industrialized countries and the diverse regions of the Arab hinterland) was accompanied by a limited development of internal production of goods, the vicissitudes of the silk industry apart.

From the end of the nineteenth century, the importance of the economic role of Lebanese emigrants also became apparent.

In a similar context, what was the economic significance of the political independence of Lebanon from 1943 onwards?

This political independence was translated into the economic domain by a number of measures: monetary and financial links with France were broken by the agreement of 1948 and free trade was re-established; the traditional links and monetary union with Syria were broken off and 'common interests' abolished in 1950; regional Lebanese economic activity was redeployed towards the other Arab countries, in the framework of a series of inter-Arab economic agreements on the initiative of the League of Arab States; the process of internal redistribution of wealth across the state was systematized and accelerated (equipment for different regions, allocation of public-service jobs according to a system of quotas, etc.) This redistribution which had begun under the mandate was in fact a socio-economic extension of the 1943 National Pact, one of the bases of which was the apportionment of public powers among the leaders of the diverse Lebanese communities.

These economic measures reflected the political orientations agreed by the Lebanese leaders before independence: a distancing from France; no Syrian and/or Arab unity; 'Arab face' of Lebanon; internal distribution of power and wealth.

In the framework of these political measures, several regional factors favoured the economic growth of Lebanon: the war in Palestine in 1948; end of economic links with Syria in 1950; the political, economic and social upheavals of Egypt, Syria and Iraq in the 1950s and 1960s; the increase in production and revenues from oil in the Arab countries.

These factors favoured growth and the 'tertiarization' of Lebanese domestic and national products. This growth was largely oriented towards the needs of external markets, exporting services, goods and a qualified labour force to the Gulf countries.

This was followed by the social distribution of revenues, which gradually became more even, as did the level of development in the Lebanese regions.

The political economy of independent Lebanon (1943–75) is thus characterized by strong growth, extraverted and unbalanced, but having at the same time the mechanisms to correct the imbalance. It is in this context of tensions and balance that there has been the explosion of wars from 1975.

Introduction

Un bilan de l'économie politique du Liban pour la période 1943 à 1975 ne saurait être inutile pour évaluer les aspects économiques des causes et conséquences des guerres qui se déroulent au Liban depuis 1975 au double plan interne et externe. Loin de vouloir contribuer à la qualification des conflits qui se déroulent sur le sol libanais depuis 1975, de guerre civile, par ses causes, ses acteurs et ses enjeux, comme c'est encore souvent le cas après 12 ans de guerre, l'objectif de cette communication est de décrire et d'analyser les grandes lignes de la structure et des fonctions économiques du Liban entre 1943 et 1975, afin de pouvoir dégager leurs éventuels liens avec les guerres qui se répandent au Liban depuis 1975.

La formation économique au Liban (1800–1943)

L'économie libanaise telle qu'elle se caractérisait au moment de l'indépendance politique en 1943 s'est formée à partir du dix-neuvième siècle autour du rôle de relais tertiaire de la ville de Beyrouth, entre les pays industrialisés et diverses régions de l'hinterland arabe. En effet, de premier port de la côte orientale de la Méditerranée, qu'elle devint au début du dix-neuvième siècle, un siècle plus tard, Beyrouth passe au rang de troisième port de l'Empire ottoman après Istambul et Izmir. Ce rôle s'articule autour d'activités de transport maritime et terrestre, de commerce international, de crédit, d'assurances, de services éducatifs, sanitaires, touristiques, techniques, scientifiques, etc. Les activités se sont progressivement fixées dans la capitale, devenue entre 1920 et 1943 la métropole économique des 'Etats du Levant sous mandat français'. Ce type d'évolution économique implique un développement limité des activités produisant des biens, mis à part la sériciculture d'exportation jusqu'à la crise de 1929. De même, l'émigration libanaise qui démarre dans la seconde moitié du dix-neuvième siècle, commence à jouer un rôle économique majeur à partir de la fin de celui-ci.

L'ensemble des activités tertiaires, de même que les flux monétaires en provenance de la diaspora, connurent un net ralentissement avec la crise économique de 1929 et la seconde guerre mondiale—alors que les activités agro-pastorales et industrielles tournées vers les marchés libanais et syrien connaissent une relative expansion au cours de ces périodes, du fait du dégagement relatif de l'économie libanaise du marché mondial, dû à la crise et à la guerre mondiale.

C'est dans ce contexte, où s'était déjà formée une importante classe d'hommes d'affaires, qu'intervient l'indépendance politique en 1943. Ces hommes d'affaires n'étaient d'ailleurs pas absents de ce processus: le rôle de Michel Chiha et d'Henry Pharaon dans le groupe dirigeant du mouvement d'indépendance illustre bien ce fait.

Nous allons, dans ce qui suit, essayer de dégager les grandes lignes de la signification économique de l'indépendance politique, à partir d'un certain nombre de faits depuis 1943.

La signification économique de l'indépendance politique

A l'indépendance et surtout après la fin de la seconde guerre mondiale, un grand nombre d'hommes d'affaires libanais avaient accumulé de solides fortunes, du fait des dépenses des troupes alliées et des difficultés d'approvisionnement au cours de la guerre en produits importés. Ce groupe a joué un rôle moteur dans la croissance économique des décades ultérieures. La résultante des options économiques des milieux d'affaires allaient dans le sens du libéralisme économique interne et externe, option tout à fait normale dans un pays dont l'économie avait une fonction prédominante de relais tertiaire régional. D'un autre côté, le fait que l'indépendance politique ait été obtenue dans le cadre d'un consensus intercommunautaire interne de partage des pouvoirs, ne manquera pas de se refléter au niveau du développement économique et social.

L'indépendance politique est suivie d'une série de développements au niveau de l'économie que nous rappelons ici à grands traits:

La rupture des liens monétaires et financiers avec la France
De par les accords monétaires et financiers franco-libanais de février 1948, négociés et signés par Hamid Frangieh, le Liban sortait de la zone franc et s'orientait vers la liberté des changes, des mouvements de capitaux, de la gestion de ces finances publiques. Il pouvait ainsi mieux exercer ses fonctions de relais tertiaire et avec moins d'entraves.

La rupture des unions douanière et monétaire avec la Syrie en 1950 et la séparation de certains services publics (chemins de fer, Régie des Tabacs, douanes, Institut d'Emission, etc.)
Cette rupture permit à l'état libanais d'exercer à fond l'option

libre-échangiste dans le domaine du commerce extérieur, ainsi que la liberté des changes et des mouvements des capitaux. De même, elle lui permettait de mener une politique monétaire et financière orthodoxe: budgets excédentaires ou équilibrés, monnaie forte. Tout cela dans le but de ne pas entraver le rôle de relais commercial, financier et tertiaire du pays. Ce rôle fut renforcé dans les années 1950 par la législation sur le secret bancaire.

Le redéploiement économique vers les autres pays arabes

L'ensemble des développements précités, et ceux inhérents à d'autres pays arabes, facilitèrent le déploiement économique des hommes d'affaires libanais, vers ces pays (Irak, Pays du Golfe, Jordanie, Libye, etc.) et cela dans le cadre d'une série d'accords bilatéraux et multilatéraux sous les auspices de la Ligue des Etats arabes (accords de transit, de paiements, de transport, de commerce, etc.)

L'accélération de la mise en place et de l'action de mécanismes de redistribution des richesses entre couches sociales, communautés religieuses et régions

Ce processus mis en place par le mandat français s'amplifia, se diversifia et s'accéléra sous le régime de l'indépendance. En effet, la logique du Pacte national de 1943 impliquait parallèlement à la répartition du pouvoir entre les diverses communautés libanaises une certaine répartition des richesses, dans le but de renforcer la cohésion sociale et l'unité nationale.

C'est de là que provient la redistribution croissante du revenu national à travers l'expansion de l'enseignement public des équipements publics réalisés dans les diverses régions. De même, la répartition des emplois publics entre les différentes communautés suivant le système des quotas visait à privilégier les plus défavorisées.

A cela, il faut ajouter que la règle du quota communautaire dans l'emploi public s'étendit à des catégories croissantes d'emplois, le secteur public s'élargissant dans divers domaines (énergie, eaux, transport, communications, éducation, santé, services sociaux, etc.) en plus de la croissance quantitative et qualitative du secteur public traditionnel.

Ces quatre développements dans le domaine économique allaient parfaitement dans la logique du Pacte national dont ils étaient grosso-modo le reflet économique: éloignement de la France; pas d'union grand-syrienne et/ou arabe; 'visage arabe' du Liban; répartition interne des pouvoirs et de la richesse.

Après ce bref exposé des grandes lignes de la politique économique du Liban, il est nécessaire de rappeler à grands traits les facteurs régionaux qui favorisèrent la croissance économique du Liban.

Facteurs régionaux qui favorisèrent la croissance économique du Liban

Sous ce titre s'imposent les faits suivants:

La première guerre de Palestine 1948/9 amena au Liban un flux de réfugiés constitué d'une minorité de détenteurs de capitaux et de compétences et d'une majorité de main-d'oeuvre non qualifiée mais à bon marché, vu qu'elle recevait de l'aide des Nations Unies. Ceci, tout en ne favorisant pas l'emploi des Libanais dans les régions voisines des concentrations de réfugiés palestiniens vu la concurrence sur le marché du travail, eut des avantages certains pour les milieux d'affaires et l'activité économique en général.

La série des coups d'état et des changements politiques, économiques et sociaux qui eurent l'Egypte, la Syrie et l'Irak pour théâtres respectifs au cours des années 1960 et 1970 amena au Liban des capitaux de ces pays, de même que des compétences humaines dans les domaines économiques et techniques. Ceci renforça le potentiel économique libanais.

La croissance de l'extraction et des revenus pétroliers dans une série de pays arabes ouvrit des marchés croissants pour les activités tertiaires libanaises (commerce, transport, banques, tourisme, enseignement, services sanitaires, services techniques, etc.), de même que pour les produits de l'agriculture, de l'élevage et de l'industrie. Cette croissance offrit des emplois lucratifs pour diverses catégories de salariés libanais dans ces pays, et des opportunités intéressantes pour les investissements et les entreprises libanaises qui commencèrent à s'y installer en nombre croissant. L'ensemble de ces phénomènes s'accéléra dans les dernières années qui précédèrent la guerre au Liban.

La guerre de juin 1967, de par la fermeture du Canal de Suez qu'elle provoque jusqu'en 1975, canalisa une partie des flux d'importation des pays arabes vers le port de Beyrouth, de même qu'elle rendit certains produits libanais plus compétitifs que ceux des pays industrialisés sur certains marchés arabes vu la hausse des coûts de transport conséquente à la fermeture du Canal.

Après avoir passé en revue les politiques économiques internes et les facteurs économiques régionaux qui favorisèrent la croissance de l'économie libanaise, il est important de suivre les caractéristiques de cette croissance.

Les caractéristiques de la croissance économique du Liban indépendant

Nous allons suivre ici le rythme de cette croissance, son contenu sectoriel, ses moteurs, et ses effets sociaux et régionaux.

Une croissance rapide

Le produit national brut du Liban, en Livres libanaises courantes, a plus que quadruplé entre 1950 et 1970. Cette croissance s'accéléra au cours des années 1960. Entre 1970 et 1975, le produit augmenta de plus de 50 pour cent (cf. annexe).

Une croissance 'tertiairisée'

La part du tertiaire dans le revenu national augmente de 63 pour cent en 1950 à environ 70 pour cent en 1975.

Une croissance extravertie

La croissance économique est essentiellement mue par les besoins des marchés extérieurs, c'est-à-dire régionaux. Cela paraît évident au plan des services (transports terrestres et aériens orientés vers le Machrek arabe, tourisme et estivage arabes, part de dépôts arabes dans les banques libanaises, part des étudiants arabes dans les universités libanaises, rôle régional des entreprises libanaises de services techniques, etc.) Dans le domaine industriel, le volume des exportations est multiplié par 18 entre 1964 et 1973, alors que celui de la production est multiplié par 2,5. Dans le domaine agricole, les branches qui ont le plus progressé sont les grandes productions d'exportation: pommiculture, agrumiculture, aviculture, etc.

Dans l'ensemble, le rapport du volume des exportations de biens à celui du produit national passe de 9,68 pour cent en 1950 à 23,6 pour cent en 1974, illustrant bien la tendance à l'extraversion croissante de l'économie libanaise, même si l'on ne tient pas compte de l'exportation des services.

Un autre aspect important de cette extraversion est l'exportation croissante de population active et son rôle: le rythme annuel de cette émigration, qui était de 3.000 en moyenne entre 1945 et 1969, passe à 8.566 entre 1960 et 1970, pour culminer à près de 10.000 entre 1970 et 1974. La part des remises des émigrés passe de 5,38 pour cent du produit national en 1951 à 30 pour cent environ en 1974. Cette extraversion fragilise l'économie, comme le montrent les retombées actuelles de la guerre du Golfe sur la Livre libanaise.

Une croissance dont l'inégale répartition des fruits tend à se résorber

Les indicateurs quantitatifs dont nous disposons sur la période allant de 1943 à nos jours semblent converger en général sur le fait que les disparités sociales et économiques entre les Libanais ont tendance à diminuer quels que soient les groupes auxquels ils appartiennent (catégories de revenus, régions et confessions).

Dans cette partie, nous analyserons successivement les données disponibles pour les trois approches précitées.

Evolution de la répartition des Libanais d'après les différentes catégories de revenus. La première estimation dont nous disposons sur la répartition des Libanais d'après les catégories de revenus a été effectuée par le professeur Elias Ghannagé. Nous la reproduisons dans Tableau 1.

Tableau 1   *Essai de répartition de la population libanaise suivant les catégories de revenus en 1953*

Catégories de revenus	Groupes socio-professionnels correspondants	Pourcentage de la population	Pourcentage du revenu national
inférieure	ouvriers de l'industrie et de l'agriculture	78	20
moyenne	fonctionaires de l'état, des banques, du commerce, agriculteurs, artisans, petits et moyens	20	80
supérieure	banquiers, commerçants, industriels	2	

Source: Elias Ghannagé, 'La Redistribution des revenus au Liban', in *L'Economie libanaise et le progrès social* (Beyrouth, 1955)

La Mission IRFED a effectué une seconde estimation de cette même distribution en 1960 (voir Tableau 2).

Enfin, la dernière estimation disponible de la distribution sociale des revenus au Liban provient de l'enquête effectuée par Yves Schmeil et concerne les années 1973 et 1974, avec l'aide des étudiants de l'Institut des Sciences de l'Université libanaise et de l'Institut politique de l'Université Saint-Joseph. Nous en reproduisons les résultats dans Tableau 3.

Nous avons ramené les chiffres de revenus de 1973 à 1974 à des prix de 1960, afin de pouvoir les comparer à ceux de la Mission IRFED et ceci en utilisant un indice des prix à la consommation, et en calculant la moyenne de la catégorie de revenus (voir Tableau 4).

En comparant les données des Tableaux 2 et 4, on constate les phénomènes suivants:

Tableau 2   *Distribution sociale des revenus en 1960*

Catégorie de revenus	Moyenne du revenu familial annuel de la catégorie en Livres libanaises	Pourcentage de la catégorie dans l'ensemble de la population	Pourcentage de la catégorie dans le revenu national
miséreux	1.000	8,8	1,5
pauvres	2.000	41,2	16,3
moyens	3.500	32,0	22,2
aisés	11.000	14,0	28,0
riches	40.000	4	32

Source: Ministère du Plan, *Mission IRFED–Liban 1960–61* (Beyrouth), p. 93

Tableau 3   *Distribution sociale des revenus en 1973 et 1974*

Catégorie de revenus	moins de 3.000 LL/an	de 3.000 à 6.000 LL/an	de 6.000 à 12.000 LL/an	plus de 12.000 LL/an
Pourcentage de la catégorie dans l'ensemble de la population				
en 1973	23,5	28,1	25,9	22,2
en 1974	20,2	36,7	23,4	19,5

Source: Yves Schmeil: 'Sociologie du système politique libanais' (Grenoble 1976), p. 22

1. Une tendance à l'accroissement du volume des catégories moyennes du revenu entre 1960, 1973 et 1974.
2. Une tendance à l'accroissement du volume des catégories élevées du revenu entre 1960 et 1973, avec une contraction du volume de ces catégories entre 1973 et 1974.

Les causes des évolutions constatées entre 1973 et 1974 pourraient être les suivantes: élévation générale du niveau des revenus due à la hausse du prix du pétrole; accélération de l'inflation; hausse du salaire minimum et de l'ensemble de l'échelle des salaires du secteur privé et public en 1974.

Quant aux évolutions constatées entre 1960 et 1973, elles semblent normales dans un pays qui a connu le type de croissance économique décrit plus haut, qui s'est traduite par une hausse générale des revenus due à un ensemble de changements locaux et régionaux.

Tableau 4   *Distribution sociale des revenus en 1973-1974 déflatés aux prix de 1960*

1973		1974	
Moyenne de la catégorie en Livres libanaises	Pourcentage de la catégorie par rapport à la population totale	Moyenne de la catégorie en Livres libanaises	Pourcentage de la catégorie par rapport à la population totale
− 2.000	23,5	− 1.850	20,2
3.000	28,1	2.750	36,7
6.150	25,9	5.500	23,4
+ 8.000	22,2	+ 7.350	19,5

Source: Ghannagé, 'La Redistribution des revenus au Liban', Indices des prix à la consommation, recoupement des données de la Direction centrale de la statistique du ministère de l'Economie Nationale et de la Commission de la planification

Evolution des niveaux de vie dans les divers muhafazat *(provinces du Liban) entre 1960 et 1970.* La Mission IRFED a effectué en 1960 une enquête sur les niveaux de vie ruraux. Cette enquête a été reprise dix ans plus tard en 1970 par le directeur de ladite mission, à la demande du directeur du Ministère du Plan. Les résultats se trouvent dans Tableau 5.

Tableau 5   *Evolution des niveaux de vie dans les différents muhafazat rurales au Liban*

Région	Indice synthétique du niveau de vie en 1960	Indice synthétique du niveau de vie en 1970	Pourcentage de l'élévation de l'indice entre 1960 et 1970
Centrale	2,24	2,59	15,6
Nord	2,13	2,52	40,0
Sud	1,53	2,20	43,8
Bekaa	1,47	2,00	36,1
Liban rural	1,69	2,23	32,0

Source: Raymond Delpart, 'Liban. L'évolution du niveau de vie en milieu rural 1960–1970', Ministère du Plan, Doc Ronéoté, Beyrouth, 1970, p. 9

L'indice synthétique utilisé est une moyenne de plusieurs indices (sanitaire, économique et technique, domestique, résidentiel, habitat, scolaire, culturel, familial, social).

De ce tableau nous pouvons déduire que les régions périphériques du Liban (qui sont à majorité musulmane) sont celles qui ont le plus avancé. En particulier le Liban-Sud, à 70 pour cent musulman, a connu une hausse de niveau de vie de près de 44 pour cent entre

Tableau 6   *Evolution de la composition confessionnelle de quelques professions*

	En début de période étudiée		En fin de période étudiée	
Profession	*% Musul-mans*	*% Chrétiens*	*% Musul-mans*	*% Chrétiens*
Ensemble des fonctionnaires de l'Etat	1943 41,3	1943 58,7	1978 47,32	1978 52,68
Candidats aux fonctions publiques de la 3ème catégorie (niveau licence)	1963 56,0	1963 48,0	1974 64,0	1974 35,0
Propriétaires de sociétés commerciales (S.A.L.–S.A.R.L.)	1966 22,0	1966 78,0	1981 24,5	1981 75,5
Industriels	1950 33,0	1950 67,0	1978/9 32,4	1978/9 67,6
Banquiers	1950 0,0	1950 100,0	1980 29,0	1980 71,0
Propriétaires de compagnies de transport	1966 28,0	1966 72,0	1981 27,4	1981 72,6
Assureurs et agents d'assurances	1948 9,0	1948 91,0	1981 24,0	1981 76,0
Avocats	1948 13,5	1948 86,5	1974(Bey) 29,0	1974(Bey) 71,0
Ingénieurs	1948 12,0	1948 88,0	1977 42,2	1977 57,8
Médecins	1948 13,4	1948 86,6	1974 81,84	1974 68,15

Source: Université libanaise, Institut des sciences sociales, Travaux du séminaire de sociologie du développement 1981–1982 (Rabiyeh, Liban)

1960 et 1970. Le Liban-Nord, à 40 pour cent musulman, a progressé de 40 pour cent, et la Bekaa, à plus de 60 pour cent musulmane, a progressé de 36 pour cent. Le Liban central, à 70 pour cent chrétien, a progressé de 15,6 pour cent. Donc, malgré les différences importantes de niveau de vie allant jusqu'à 22 pour cent entre les diverses régions rurales du Liban en 1970, il faut noter que ces différences allaient jusqu'à 35 pour cent en 1960. L'ensemble du monde rural libanais aurait connu un accroissement de niveau de vie de 32 pour cent entre 1960 et 1970.

Ce type d'évolution semble être dû à la conjonction de plusieurs facteurs dont l'émigration rurale vers l'extérieur et vers les villes; à l'envoi et l'investissement des remises d'émigrés en milieu rural, et enfin à la politique active que mena l'état libanais dans le domaine de l'équipement dans les régions rurales à cette époque (routes, adduction d'eau, électrification, téléphones, bonification des terres, puits artésiens, équipement scolaire, sanitaire, culturel, social).

Evolution de la composition confessionnelle de quelques professions depuis l'indépendance. Nous essayons de décrire dans le tableau qui suit l'évolution de la composition confessionnelle d'une série de professions appartenant pour leur majorité aux élites économiques, administratives et aux professions libérales (Tableau 6).

Nous constatons à travers les données de ce tableau que les professions, dont l'accession nécessite l'acquisition d'un niveau d'enseignement supérieur (fonctionnaire d'état de troisième catégorie, profession libérale non-commerciale, avocats, médecins, ingénieurs) sont des professions dans lesquelles le rapprochement entre les participations des différentes confessions à la profession s'est accéléré au cours des trois à quatre dernières décennies. Le rapprochement équivalent pour les professions qui demandent un certain capital afin d'être exercées était lent avant 1975 (commerce moderne, industrie, banques, grandes sociétés de transport, assurances). Après 1975, le rapprochement s'est accéléré principalement dans le domaine des banques et des assurances. Cela semble être dû au 'boom' pétrolier et aux ressources financières importantes qui en ont résulté pour des pays comme le Liban, c'est-à-dire des pays dont l'économie est étroitement liée à celle des producteurs arabes du pétrole.

Les données statistiques concernant les professions industrielles et commerciales ne sont pas précises depuis 1975, mis à part les professions de la banque et de l'assurance.

Il convient ici d'ajouter quelques données sur les progrès du niveau d'instruction dans les différentes communautés que nous pourrons approcher à partir des données des Tableaux 7 et 8.

On mesure les progrès réalisés en comparant ces données à celles du

Tableau 7   *Religion et niveaux d'instruction (Liban 1974) en pourcentage de la population*

Niveau d'instruction Religion	Analphabètes complets	Partiellement analphabète	Niveau primaire	Niveau secondaire	Niveau universitaire
Musulmans	*14,2*	*18,6*	*32,9*	*27*	*9,1*
Chrétiens	*10,9*	*16,9*	*29*	*31*	*10*

Source: Schmeil, *Sociologie*, p.41

Tableau 8   *Proportion des illettrés dans les diverses communautés en 1932*

Communauté	Chiite	Sunnite	Maronite	Grecque catholique	Grecque orthodoxe	Druze
Pourcentage des illettrés	83	66	48	39	53	53

Source: L'Orient du 24 janvier 1938

Tableau 8 (pour 1932). Le niveau d'analphabétisme a été réduit jusqu'à 20 pour cent à 25 pour cent de celui de 1932, aussi bien pour les communautés chrétiennes que musulmanes. Pour les premières, le taux d'analphabètes passe de 46,6 pour cent en 1932 à 10,9 pour cent en 1974; pour les seconds, le taux passe de 67 pour cent en 1932 à 14,2

Tableau 9   *Répartition des écoles privées suivant les communautés de 1944/5 à 1977/8*

	1944–45		1977–78	
	Nombre	*%*	*Nombre*	*%*
Ecoles privées chrétiennes	*748*	*77,5*	*350*	*61,7*
Ecoles privées musulmanes	*206*	*21,3*	*217*	*38,3*

Source: Recueil des statistiques de la Syrie et du Liban 1945-46-47, t. 3 (Beyrouth, 1947); Centre de Recherches et de Développement Pédagogique

Boutros Labaki

pour cent en 1974. Du coup, les différences entre les taux d'analphabétisme entre les communautés ont été singulièrement réduits, de même que ceux pour les autres niveaux d'instruction.

Les Tableaux 9, 10 et 11 illustrent cette réalité pour les écoles privées et les universités.

On voit le chemin parcouru depuis un siècle, et la contribution de l'Université libanaise dans ce domaine. Le rôle rééquilibrant de cette université a dû s'accélérer depuis, avec l'ouverture de branches en province et celle de facultés techniques après 1975.

Tableau 10   *Composition confessionnelle des diplômés du Syrian Protestant College entre 1871 et 1882*

Communauté

	Grecque orthodoxe	Maronite	Latine	Grecque catholique	Protestant	Druze	Chiite	Sunnite	Total
Nombres de diplômés	9	15	3	10	10	3	0	1	51
%	17,6	29,4	5,9	19,6	19,6	5,9	0	1,9	100

Sources: Asad Rustum, '*Lubnan fi 'ahd al-mutasarrifiyya*' (Beyrouth, 1968), pp. 244–7

Ces phénomènes sont dûs, en plus de l'action redistributive multiforme de l'état, à l'action des associations communautaires s'occupant d'enseignement, de services sociaux, de développement communautaire et autres, de même qu'aux effets de l'émigration interne et externe des régions périphériques.

L'économie politique du Liban indépendant (1943–75) et les guerres qui s'y déroulent depuis 1975

Nous avons pu brièvement montrer que le Liban a connu depuis l'indépendance une croissance rapide, extravertie donc fragile, une croissance qui a connu des grands déséquilibres sectoriels, régionaux et sociaux. Mais la structure économique, la société civile et le système politique récèlent des mécanismes de rééquilibrage qui ont permis à ces déséquilibres de se résorber et d'être nettement moins aigus que lors de l'indépendance.

Tableau 11   *Structure confessionnelle de la population universitaire libanaise en 1972–1973*

Université	Effectifs des étudiants	Effectifs des étudiants chrétiens	En % de chrétiens par université	Effectifs des étudiants musulmans	En % des musulmans par université
AUB	2.303	1.267	55,01	1.036	44,99
BUC	501	275	54,89	226	45,11
MEC	100	87	87	13	13
Haigazian	303	242	79,86	61	20,14
UL	12.340	4.936	40	7.404	60
UAB	2.708	270	9,97	2.438	90,03
St Esprit	333	333	100	—	—
Sagesse	233	233	100	—	—
ALBA	209	105	50,23	104	49,77
USJ	3.257	2.605	79,98	652	20,02
ESL	548	356	64,96	192	35,04
CEM	338	202	59,76	136	40,24
TOTAL	23.173	10.911	47,08	12.262	52,92

Sources: Statistiques du Centre de Recherches et de Développement Pédagogique, et R.B. Bells, *Christians in the Arab East* (Athens, 1973) p. 124. Compilées par Salim Nasr

Cependant, ces déséquilibres et ces rééquilibrages ont doublement contribué à amplifier l'action des facteurs régionaux qui ont fait éclater les guerres au Liban depuis 1975 dans le tissu social libanais, en particulier par l'effet bien connu dans les sciences sociales de la 'dépravation relative'.

Annexe   *Produit national brut en livres et en pourcentages*

Secteurs	1961		1964		1967		1970		1973		1977		1980	
Agriculture	369	18,5	381	11,9	426	11,15	445	9,15	664	9,35	700	8,54	1.284	9,17
Industrie Energie Construction	322	16	658	20,5	781	20,45	992	20,4	1.476	20,85	1.795	21,89	2.860	20,43
Services Commerce Finances Communications Administrations	1.313	65,5	2.161	67,5	2.613	68,4	3.429	70,5	4.963	69,8	5.705	69,57	9.856	70,4
TOTAL	2.004	100	3.200	100	3.820	100	4.866	100	7.103	100	8.200	100	14.000	100

Source: 'Le Commerce', 15 Mars 1982

10

Urban Networks and Political Conflict in Lebanon

SAMIR KHALAF AND GUILAIN DENOEUX

This paper focuses on informal networks[1] in an effort to shed some light on the timing, scope, and forms of political mobilization among Lebanon's major urban communities. It also hopes to demonstrate that an emphasis on networks can provide a perspective from which one may better understand the intensity and ferocity of urban violence in Lebanon since 1975.

Urban networks in Lebanon prior to the war

Lebanon's eventful urban history has been elucidated elsewhere.[2] Here we intend only to highlight some of this history's striking features, in particular those which have a bearing on political mobilization.

One salient attribute, which Lebanon shares with other developing countries, is that 'urbanization' as a physical phenomenon has not been accompanied by any significant development of 'urbanism' as a way of life. Repeated studies carried out before the outbreak of civil hostilities showed that traditional ties and loyalties remained very strong in several of the rapidly urbanizing regions.[3] Indeed, informal networks based on kinship, communal and confessional attachments quite often seemed to be strengthened by urban residence.

In Beirut, throughout the period under consideration, the persistence of a high degree of parochialism manifested itself at several levels. Most of the voluntary and welfare associations were either confessional, communal, or familial in character. Lebanese shied away from impersonal, formal, large-scale associations. Whenever these appeared, they rapidly became attached to, and identified with, a traditional leader, or a sectarian or familial community. Quarters also often had an identity of their own, and, for many Lebanese, identification with the quarter became a meaningful and significant reference point. The individuality of many neighbourhoods in fact was so pronounced that Beirut often seemed more like a mosaic of distinctive communities existing side by side than a 'melting pot' of urban masses.

In Lebanon, as no doubt elsewhere, the resilience of traditional attachments provided a sense of identity, security, and intimacy. It helped maintain a relatively high level of cohesion, unity, and solidarity in an otherwise highly individualistic, fragmented, and competitive society. To some extent, this may also account for the low level of social disorganization and deviant behaviour in a society that was undergoing rapid socio-economic change.[4]

In short, confessional and communal organizations, family associations, urban quarters, and political patronage all seemed to be effective, at least at the local level, in holding society together. In a country where central authority was weak and where the government was regarded with suspicion and mistrust, such informal networks operated as the main channels of political mediation, participation, and integration. They also were instrumental in enabling large segments of the urban population to cope with a difficult environment, one characterized by material scarcity and latent or manifest insecurity.

It is understandable, under the circumstances, why many observers stressed the 'functionality' of urban networks, both for Lebanon as a whole and for its political system in particular. Yet, long before the outbreak of civil hostilities, it was clear that informal networks, and the traditional ties and loyalties sustaining them, also had dysfunctional, disabling, and even perverse consequences. A cursory inventory of such attributes, albeit self-evident by now, is worthwhile nonetheless.

At the most general level, the vitality of traditional ties and loyalties tended to thwart the development of a sense of civility and public-mindedness.[5] Thus, the Lebanese often remained more concerned with the interests of their own community than with those of the country. Disquieting also was the fact that virtually all networks had a confessional character: co-religionists often resided in the same quarters, and associations and patron–client clusters brought together only co-religionists. Thus, conflicts between groups or patrons could easily degenerate, as Lebanon's political history so richly demonstrates, into nasty and bloody sectarian strife.

It is however the debilitating features of the patronage system in pre-civil war Lebanon that should be underscored, particularly since they contrast so singularly with scholarly assumptions about the 'integrative' and 'functional' nature of clientelist relationships.

It should be borne in mind that, in relatively institutionalized polities, urban patrons are often agents of the central bureaucracy.

When they are not, they often work under the auspices of the central authority, since it is this authority that makes and unmakes patrons. By contrast, in post-independence Lebanon, an urban patron could best carve out a place for himself by being recognized as a leader by the street, not through endearment to some central authority. In urban areas, particularly in the capital, the patronage arena was competitive; a *za'im*'s (leader; pl. *zu'ama*) position was always precarious, and dependent upon the regular renewal of popular support.[6] One understands why, in such a context, Lebanese patrons recurrently displayed a tendency towards 'a somewhat demagogical exploitation of popular prejudices and moods, particularly of the religious and communal kinds, since those are the most intense and widespread'.[7] Indeed, there existed strict limits on how far urban patrons could go in opposing the tide of opinion in their community.[8] In the late 1950s for example, leaders, such as Sami al-Solh, who failed to identify with Nasserism at a time when it was becoming the ideology of the street, irremediably lost their influence in the community. Conversely, Najah Wakim, a virtual unknown, was able in the elections of 1972 to defeat one of the entrenched veterans of the Greek Orthodox community (Naseem Majdalani) because he courted such populist ideologies. In the end, it is only by invoking the slogans of Nasserism and pan-Arabism that many patrons were able to maintain control over their clienteles.[9]

A strong central authority also provides a sense of purpose, permanence and continuity, and tends to smooth or even prevent internecine strife between patrons. In Lebanon, by contrast, independent patron-warlords were concerned only with the short-sighted search for immediate political advantage, regardless of the long-term impact such strategies would have on the political system. In institutionalized polities, one may expect state officials, patrons and brokers to belong to the same institutional structure preventing them from working at cross-purposes to one another. In post-1958 Lebanon, by contrast, state-sponsored patrons, the other more autonomous patrons, and the *qabadayat* (on which more below) appeared as three largely distinct actors who, more often than not, through shifting coalitions worked to undercut each other's power. They were competing to extend the bases of their clientage.[10]

Furthermore, the effectiveness of Lebanese clientelism as a system of political control rested on the ability of the major *zu'ama* to reach some minimal consensus. This consensus was guaranteed mostly by informal procedures and tacit agreements, and could survive only as long as the major actors in the system wanted it to. By the early 1970s, this intra-elite consensus was rapidly falling apart. In the wake of its final collapse, in 1975, the political system disintegrated.

Most important perhaps, the Lebanese experience suggests that, in analysing any clientelist structure, special attention should be paid to those individuals—such as the *cacique* (chief) in Mexico[11] or the *qabaday* in Lebanon—who act as brokers between patrons and clients. These individuals' strategic position enables them to influence the effectiveness of clientelism as a system of political control. In normal times, they are the crucial transmission belt without which orders, goods and services cannot be passed down from the patrons to the client populations. It is through such vectors that popular support for the patrons is mustered and organized.

In unstable situations, however, these brokers may also reveal themselves to be weak links in the chains of clientelism.[12] Thus in Lebanon, when the state finally collapsed in 1975–6, 'the qabadays were able to strike out against the za'ims and establish themselves as independent leaders in their own right.'[13] Furthermore, this new-found independence took place in a context characterized by the increasing resort to pseudo-ideological slogans, as *qabadayat* began to redefine their role using the borrowed languages of Nasserism, Islam, populism, or Marxism.[14]

Informal networks and phases of mobilization

If informal networks constitute the most important mediating structures between the individual and the political system, then the possible relationships between types of informal networks and the timing, form and intensity of political mobilization have to be explored systematically. The following is an attempt to do so for each of the major urban communities in Lebanon (i.e. Maronites, Sunnis, and Shi'is) in the late 1960s and early 1970s. Needless to say, the protrayal here is much too sketchy and brief, and awaits fuller and more probing analysis and documentation.

The Maronite community

The Maronite community is a particularly appropriate starting-point for such an inquiry, since it initiated its mobilization relatively early.

By the late 1960s and early 1970s, members of the Maronite community had available to them three primary types of mediating structures: political parties, the Maronite church, and the community's system of private schools. Also, it is fairly safe to argue that only in the Maronite community did one find agencies of political representation presenting some of the features of political parties, for example the Phalangist (Kata'ib) Party, the National Bloc, the National Liberal Party. These parties, in fact, were all largely sustained by personalistic, kinship, and confessional loyalties.

Focusing on the Phalangists, the party which played the most prominent role in the civil war, is particularly instructive. Starting as a youth and sport organization in the 1930s, the Phalangists slowly evolved into a highly organized mass party. Membership picked up in the late 1950s, in the wake of the 1958 civil war. Yet, the 'party' really never ceased to represent what was simply 'a more sophisticated base for confessional politics, particularly in the capital city of Beirut'.[15] Its programme remained vague and simplistic, and its appeal was limited by and large to the Christian, particularly Maronite, population. The Phalangists, in fact, operated along the same lines as the traditional leaders it aimed to displace within the Christian community; that is, interceding with public officials on behalf of the clients, dispensing favours, solving personal problems. But to these traditional features, the party added the organization, the 'rationality', and the nation-wide basis that is characteristic of more formal associations. It came to function as a highly organized and efficient notable, 'offering services (*khadamat*) on a supra-family, supra-za'im, supra-regional basis, in other words, on a true communal basis, thus increasing tremendously the cohesion of the community'.[16]

The growing importance of the Phalangists in the Christian community is not too difficult to account for, given the socio-economic and political transformations the Christians (the Maronite community in particular) were facing at the time. If one regards the emergence of family associations, clubs, youth organizations, welfare, and voluntary associations as symptoms of, and reactions to, some of the dissociative forces inherent in rapid socio-economic change (urbanization in particular), then it is apparent that the Christians must have faced the dislocations associated with such processes comparatively early.[17] The many manifestations of gaps and differentials in socio-economic standards and levels of living also support such tendencies.

Against such a background, the civil war of 1958, burgeoning Arab nationalism and revolutionary ideologies, the inflow of capital and petro-dollars from the Gulf and the proliferation of Palestinian resistance movements began to threaten the hegemony and security of the Christian community. The Maronites, in earlier similar episodes, had proved more receptive and vulnerable to such dislocations and threats to their communal solidarity than other Christian communities. Indeed, they themselves have at times exaggerated such threats to reinforce their communal solidarity. It should be recalled, in this context, that prior to 1958 the Phalangists had consistently failed in all national elections to win a parliamentary seat. It was not until the by-election in Jezzin, in 1959 that a party member (Basile 'Abbud) was elected. Subsequently however, after the election of 1960, the party was consistently represented in parliament: six of its seven candidates were elected in 1960; four of its nine candidates in 1964; and all of its nine candidates in 1968.[18]

Even more important than the above, perhaps, in maintaining a particularly high degree of homogeneity and cohesion within the Maronite community, were the church and the educational system. The church—highly organized, centralized and efficient, and endowed with considerable resources (landholding), as well as a nation-wide network of religious institutions—helped mend dissensions within the community. It also provided access to goods, services and jobs, and acted as a representative and spokesman for the community both within and outside Lebanon. Most important of all, the church functioned as the 'collective memory' of the community,[19] continually reinforcing that community's sense of identity. The educational system also carefully preserved the prevailing Maronite world view, socializing successive generations in it.

The Sunni community

A very different image is presented by the Sunni community. No political party, at least not one with a predominantly sectarian base, ever emerged from within that community. The one exception, perhaps, al-Najjadeh, never managed to extend its constituency or appeal beyond its comparatively constricted membership. Patronage continued to be dispensed on a purely patron–client, personal, and tightly circumscribed basis, despite the resort to the pseudo-ideological rhetoric of Nasserism, Ba'thism, and pan-Arabism by leaders such as Sa'eb Salam, Rashid Karami, or Ma'ruf Sa'ad. Even the Maqasid, the major charitable institution and welfare association in the community, was closely identified with Sa'eb Salam for much of the period under consideration. Therefore, it did not so much reinforce sectarian cohesion as generate loyalty to a particular leader.

Thus, the mediating structures available to the Sunni community could not promote communal cohesion to the same degree as those mediating structures available to the Maronite community. A series of factors acted together to contribute to the fragmentation of the community. Most prominent among them were the absence of anything even remotely similar to a political party; the fact that patronage was dispensed through a multitude of competing patron–client clusters, often with a limited geographical basis; the lack of organization, resources, and efficiency within the religious establishment, as well as its submission to the traditional leaders of the community.

To make matters worse, it was becoming increasingly clear that patron–client arrangements in the Sunni community were under considerable stress. First, the elite of the community and its masses were slowly, but irremediably, drifting apart, as the elite became more attached to the Lebanese formation (from which it derived considerable material and symbolic benefits), while the masses were becoming more receptive to the slogans of pan-Arabism and Nasserism (which both crystallized latent class aspirations and grievances, and acted as a catalyst of communal feelings).[20] During and in the aftermath of the 1958 crisis, traditional Sunni leaders such as Sa'eb Salam and Rashid Karami were able to check popular aspirations and redirect them to their own personal advantage.[21] In the long term, however, the ideological rhetoric of such patrons only exacerbated the radicalism of the client populations. Lower-class grievances persisted, and became, over the years, more precisely formulated. The lower-class Sunni population became increasingly aware that its leadership was paying only lip service to its grievances in fields such as employment, social services, and education.[22]

Secondly, the traditional class was also becoming alienated from 'increasing sections of the status-starved, disillusioned, morally enraged, often remorselessly idealistic Muslim intelligentsia and the rapidly proliferating student population'.[23] Finally, more than a decade of Shihabism had exacerbated the problem, increasing the fragmentation and the centrifugal tendencies within the community, in part because the Deuxième Bureau had endeavoured to undercut the power base of many traditional leaders (the *qabadayat* were among the main beneficiaries of this).

The Shi'i community

The case of the Shi'i community presents yet another picture. What is most noticeable in this instance is the paucity and weakness of 'mediating structures' capable of integrating the increasing number of dispossessed and uprooted Shi'i migrants who came to the capital throughout the 1960s and up to the outbreak of the civil war.

The story of the migration of the Lebanese southern Shi'is is well known and has been told elsewhere.[24] What has to be emphasized is the fact that patron–client networks in Beirut proved unable to absorb the constant flow of Shi'i rural migrants. This is, doubtless, due to these migrants' comparatively recent presence in the capital, and, more significantly, to some of the basic provisions of the electoral law which links voting privileges not to residence but to one's place of origin. While Maronites and Sunnis had settled and were registered in their respective communities for several generations, the Shi'is did not experience any massive population shifts into Beirut until the 1960s. Hence, they remained marginal in more than an existential sense. They had to eke out a precarious existence in the 'misery belts' of

Beirut's peri-urban fringes, but could not, by virtue of the electoral laws, mobilize their collective protest or vent their grievances through their numerical voting prowess. No *za'im*, under such circumstances, would perform any services for a constituency that was in no position to reciprocate through its vote.[25]

As a result, the original Shi'i immigrants and subsequent descendants were not integrated into the clientelist system of the capital. The gradual increase in the rate of formation of family associations among Shi'is throughout the 1960s[26] seems to indicate not only a need, but also some success in devising strategies to compensate for the social, economic, and psychological tensions associated with rapid socio-economic change. From a communal viewpoint, however, far from from reinforcing the community's unity and cohesion, family associations could only contribute to its fragmentation.

The dispersion of the Shi'is in Beirut—let alone between Beirut, the Biqa' and southern Lebanon—also thwarted the development of residential solidarities. As for the religious institutions of the community, they were in no position to reinforce substantially its cohesion and political effectiveness. The Shi'i clergy was weak, materially deprived, fearful and under the reactionary influence of the traditional Shi'i leaders. Fouad Ajami has provided a vivid description of the Shi'i clerics' inability to come to terms with the modern world, and of their obscurantism and servility to those in positions of power and authority.[27] He also has correctly pointed out the suspicion and contempt with which they were regarded by many of their co-religionists, particularly by the most modernized segments of the community and by those (often the same) most bent on improving the lot of the Shi'is in Lebanon. Thus, in sharp contrast to the role of the Maronite church, the Shi'i clergy was in fact more a source of division and a subject of derision than a catalyst of communal solidarity and cohesion. Finally, the only communal institution, the Shi'i Higher Council, was created relatively recently, in 1969, under the influence of Musa al-Sadr and with the help of the state, but against the will of the traditional notables. The council, however, was not able to play any significant role before the outbreak of the civil war. This, presumably, was caused by its late emergence, the opposition it met from the traditional Shi'i *zu'ama*, and its somewhat dubious status due to its having been promoted by the state with a view to undercutting the community's traditional leaders (particularly Kamel al-As'ad).

In this context, the relaxation of the ties of the Shi'i migrants with their former lords, their socio-economic marginalization, the disruption of their former way of life, and their second-rate status as Lebanese citizens, all resulted in their becoming, to borrow from Karl Deutsch, 'available for new patterns of mobilization and behavior'.[28]

From informal networks to political mobilization

A focus on the kinds of informal networks available to each of the major urban communities sheds some light on the timing and forms of their political mobilization. Seen from this perspective, it is not coincidental that the Maronite community was the first to mobilize. While the church and the educational system constantly reinforced the community's cohesion, sense of purpose and unity, its political parties enabled it to act efficiently in the political arena. Indeed, the Maronites had been the most 'party-conscious'[29] community in Lebanon. This may have been because of its ever-present fear of being overwhelmed by the Muslim majority, and its resulting desire to compensate for its numerical inferiority by organization, as Binder has suggested.[30] Or, as Hottinger has argued, it may simply reflect the relatively more 'modern' character of the Maronite community as a whole.[31]

Whatever the case, it is undeniable that the presence of the Phalangist Party, and, to a lesser extent, of the PNL (Parti National Liberal) of Chamoun, was crucial in strengthening the politico-military efficiency of the Maronite community as soon as the war broke out. Nor were political parties the only military actors. Reminiscent of the mobilizing role they had played in earlier episodes of political violence, particularly during the peasant uprisings of the early and mid-nineteenth century, clerics were more than just covertly active in inciting and organizing armed struggle. Then, as now, they became directly involved in recruiting; in providing financial and material support; and in offering shelter and refuge in times of public distress.

More importantly, they gave moral and spiritual legitimization to acts of violence. No sooner had the fighting broken out in 1975 than the Maronite monastic orders, under the leadership of Sharbel Kassis, stepped promptly into the fray.

This is not to say that the Maronite community has been factionless and united. Deep divisions, sustained by regional and personal hostilities, continue to splinter the community and generate intermittent clashes between its recalcitrant warlords. The community has, nonetheless, always been able to secure at least a minimal degree of co-ordination between its various wings—as reflected, for instance, in the formation of the quadripartite Lebanese Front in the early stages of the war: the 'Front', in effect, emerged as the undisputed spokesman of the Maronite community.

By contrast, the multiplicity of non-institutionalized, locally circumscribed, personalistic patron–client networks in the Sunni community seem to have had the effect, over time, of eroding that community's *'asabiyya*[32] and its ability to exert a major influence on the course of events. In fact, the absence of any other significant mediating structure within that community had exposed it to the risks of fragmentation if clientelist networks were to break down. This is indeed what happened in West Beirut in 1975–6.[33] What this early episode of the civil war illustrates, among other things, is the precarious character of strategies of political control that rely too heavily, or even exclusively, on patron–client arrangements. Under stress, such arrangements may break down. When they do, it becomes difficult to control the spread of violence. This has double implications: when communal leaders are organized, they can mobilize violence; when they are fragmented and weak, they cannot curb it. Politics in the community is likely to take an anarchic turn, with multipolar, fragmented, polycentric expression. These, indeed, have been some of the most prominent features of political mobilization in the Sunni community throughout much of the civil war.

Turning to the Shi'i community, the acute lack of appropriate mediating structures does, in our opinion, account for much of the form that the political mobilization of the Shi'is has assumed. It tells us, for example, why the community was an important recruiting ground for leftist (particularly communist) parties advocating a radical change of the Lebanese socio-political order.

After 1968, the alienation of the Shi'is from the mainstream of Lebanese political life grew in intensity, as the state proved unable to prevent Israeli raids in the South. The southern Shi'is who settled in Beirut's 'misery belt' came to the capital with an acute sense of grievance towards a political system which had failed to protect them against foreign depredation. Southern Shi'is turned out to have a radicalizing and disintegrative effect on the capital's politics, clearly more so than had been anticipated by the majority of scholars and political observers. Not absorbed by the clientelist system, they organized themselves along lines that were at considerable variance with the predominant forms of the capital's political game. They opted for a more ideological, radical, anti-system and mass-based mode of political action, turning predominantly to leftist movements, and, in parallel, to Imam Sadr's communally based movement of the deprived.[34]

The fall, in February 1984, of West Beirut to the Shi'is (allied with the Druzes) was the culmination of a long process. This process can be traced back, to a large extent, to the inability of the clientelist structures of the capital to deal with the pressures involved with absorbing, from the early 1960s onward, an ever-growing number of dispossessed and bitter Shi'i migrants.

Finally, it is clear that Lebanon's experience for the last 12 years illustrates once again the peculiar logic of communalism. For example, the mobilization of the Maronite community along purely sectarian lines should be seen as one of the factors which prompted the shift of the main basis of mobilization of the Shi'i community from secular leftist parties to a communal movement, around 1978. The early years of the war had shown how vulnerable the Shi'i community was (for example the expulsion of Shi'i residents from al-Qarantina in 1976), when Maronites insisted on treating Shi'is not as members of secular-leftist parties, but as Shi'is. The experience of the Shi'i community at that time was only one among many similar subsequent incidents illustrating the fact that, when a community mobilizes along communal lines, other communities may be forced to do so over time. As Salamé has noted,

Shi'i populism was seriously crippled by many limitations. Shi'i youth were widely dispersed among a multitude of political parties, ranging from the rightist Phalanges to the Communist Party, and including a Sunni-dominated group such as the Murabitun . . . In Beirut, Musa al-Sadr's moderate and pro-Syrian views could hardly attract followers when Phalangist militias were destroying large Shi'i neighbourhoods (such as al-Naba'a) or when Syria was restraining the Leftist–Palestinian coalition.[35]

In the process, class-consciousness, much like other secular loyalties, became 'shrouded or swept away by the politico-confessional consciousness, constantly sustained by the fact that the Other across the green line consistently defined himself as a Christian'.[36]

In a similar vein, Maronite and Shi'i mobilization along sectarian lines pushed the Sunnis to act likewise. Thus, since the early 1980s, one of the most important trends in Lebanon has been the growth of Sunni fundamentalism, and a parallel growth of Sunni–Shi'i antagonism.[37]

In many ways, the political history of Lebanon appears to have degenerated, once again, into a history of communal conflict. Each of the warring factions is now indefatigably immersed in constructing and sustaining its own 'ideology of enmity'.[38] By 'demonizing'[39] the 'others' and attributing to them all sorts of despicable features, groups are rationalizing and absolving some of the guilt associated with acts of violence. Even relatively depoliticized and non-militant communities (such as the Greek Orthodox, Catholics and, to a lesser extent, Sunnis) have had to take measures—largely through conventions, retreats, and the formation of special collective bodies or councils—to reawaken interest in the distinctive attributes of their own communal history. By so doing, they hope to reassert their damaged or diminished stature in the political arena.

Perhaps the most significant phenomenon has been the intensity of the political mobilization of the Maronite community from the early 1970s. This, it has been suggested, ought to be linked to the Maronite community's ability to preserve its unity and sense of identity, not only at a time of rapid socio-economic change, but also as both the Sunni and Shi'i populations were drifting away from their traditional leaderships. In fact, such mobilization is but one of many examples in which a community, known for its strong sense of identity and its inner cohesion, reacts violently in what it perceives to be a defensive or pre-emptive move, against real or imagined threats to its way of life by hostile forces. The Palestinians, and the alliances they formed at the time with Lebanese Muslim organizations, crystallized the Maronites' latent fears of falling prey to the 'Muslim sea' around them. In this as in other similar instances, a high degree of internal solidarity and deeply felt attachment to traditions provided the community with the interests, the ideology, and the resources necessary to collective action.

Thus, communal attachments and the networks based on them may not so much dampen radicalism as exacerbate it. Instead of acting as a buffer against militancy, as has been recently argued, they may provide individuals and groups with both the determination and the resources to enter the political arena.

Informal networks during the civil war

It is not difficult to understand why informal networks have been strengthened by 12 years of intense, ferocious, and protracted conflict. With the collapse of the state and of its institutions, kinship, neighbourhood, and sectarian affiliations became ever more important. First, they became the only channels left to secure access to food, shelter, security, employment, fuel, water, electricity, and other vital necessities. Furthermore, they came to provide much needed psychological and moral support at a time when the public world had become cruel and unpredictable.

Within such a political milieu, it is instructive to determine which type of networks, and the various forms of solidarity they embody, have been most strengthened by the war.

Patronage

Patronage, as a mediating structure between the individual and the larger social, political and economic environment, has been weakened by the war. The war, in fact, provoked the collapse of the clientelist system in Sunni West Beirut. Paradoxically, however, it is perhaps among the Sunnis that some powerful *zu'ama* have been most able to resist the erosion of their power,[40] and to withstand (but for how long?) the challenge posed by the emergence of a younger and more radical leadership.

More generally, three facts stand out. First, there has been a narrowing of the geographical basis on which clientelistic relationships exert themselves. Second, by the same token it has become more difficult to determine the extent to which the nascent groups and organizations are based on clientelism—as opposed to other sources of solidarity, such as ideology, religion, or charisma. In other words, clientelism has now become more intertwined with a variety of other loyalties. Third, to the extent that one can identify clientelist relationships, these are clearly of an anti-system, radical type. Many militias and paramilitary organizations resemble clientelist networks in which individuals fight in exchange for access to the spoils of war. In both the Sunni and the Shi'i communities—but particularly in the former, which is now fragmented into a myriad of religiously oriented organizations—small groups are proliferating. The leaders of these groups have been recruited among religious preachers, thugs, *qabadayat*, and other members of the lower classes. Unlike the brand of notables which dominated Lebanese politics up to the mid-1970s, these new leaders 'sprout from among the masses themselves', come 'from a modest or poor socioeconomic background', live 'in modest houses in modest neighbourhoods', are 'in tune with the public mood', and are 'articulate in expressing the demands and desires of the people'.[41] They behave quite often like traditional patrons by dispensing goods and services and offering protection. However, to say the least, they demonstrate little propensity for the politics of compromise and bargaining of pre-civil war Lebanon. In fact, they have brought the prejudices of the street to the heart of the political process. Instead of controlling popular excesses, they constantly justify and exacerbate them by wrapping such excesses in the garb of old traditions and ideologies. As violence becomes institutionalized, and thus further accentuates mass radicalization, more opportunities arise for this new brand of 'patrons' to promote their leadership claims by demonstrating their ideological 'purity'.

Neighbourhood solidarities

Middle Eastern history offers repeated examples of a collapse of the central power leading to a strengthening of neighbourhood affiliations and to quarters sealing themselves off from the outside world.[42] In such situations, the quarter's attitude *vis-à-vis* the outside world becomes both defensive and aggressive. Defensive, because the primary function of the quarter is to defend the community formed by its residents from attacks by outsiders. Aggressive, because the quarter is, primarily, a symbolic referent that 'exists only through its opposition to another quarter';[43] aggressive, also, because the best way to ensure the physical security of the quarter's residents is to make sure that outsiders won't come in. In any case, the protective, integrative, and defensive functions of the quarter are always accompanied, at least potentially, by an aggressive, intolerant stance in relation to the outside world.[44]

Seen from this perspective, what happened in Lebanon after 1975 is not unique. The war simply has eroded the stabilizing, functional aspects of neighbourhood solidarities (self-regulation, integration, the thwarting of horizontal solidarity . . .) and exacerbated their pathological, destabilizing, disintegrative potential. As quarters had to defend themselves against outsiders, they also started to assume an avowedly antagonistic position with regard to outside forces. In such a context, as Seurat has suggested in his remarkable study of the Bab Tebbane quarter in Tripoli, the quarter becomes the territorial base of an 'urban *'asabiyya*', the only place where individuals can trust and identify with one another.[45] Drawing on the work of Claude Cahen on cities in the Islamic world in the medieval period, Seurat is quick to remind his reader that a fundamental element of an urban *'asabiyya* 'is the enmity it bears toward the neighbouring *'asabiyya*'.[46] In such a context, the politics of the city can easily become a confrontation of urban *'asabiyya*. As the individual's identification with his quarter intensifies, so may his tendency to reject the outsider.

Seurat's study also suggests that, once such a process is under way, a mythology of the quarter can develop. In it, the quarter is seen not only as the location where a beleaguered community fights for its survival, but also as a territorial base from which the community may set out to create a utopia, a world where one may live a 'pure' and 'authentic' life, in conformity with the community's traditions and values. The neighbourhood community may even be invested with a redemptive role and mission (such as the defence of Sunni Islam in the case of Bab Tebbane). Hence the dialectic, highlighted by Seurat, between identity and politics. Politics implies negotiation, compromise, and living side by side with 'the other'. Heightened feelings of identity, however, may lead one to a refusal to compromise, if negotiation comes to be perceived as containing the seeds of treachery that may undermine the traditions, values, and 'honour' of one's community.[47] In such a context, violence and polarization become inevitable: precisely the phenomena that have plagued Lebanon for more than a decade.

Sectarian loyalties

To assert that sectarian affiliations have been reinforced by the war is, in many respects, documenting the obvious. It is, nonetheless, an affirmation worth belabouring, given some of the curious and pervasive features and consequences of Lebanese confessionalism. Lebanon's political history is replete with instances where sectarian loyalties evolved a dynamic of their own and became the most compelling forces underlying some of the major socio-cultural and political transformations in society. Even during periods of relative stability and normality, confessional allegiances have almost always operated, touching virtually all dimensions of everyday life. All the momentous events in a person's life cycle continue to be shaped by sectarian affiliation. It is a reality one cannot renounce. Early socialization, access to education, employment, welfare, hospital care, as well as many other vital services and personal benefits, are mediated through or controlled by sectarian foundations or agencies. Even a person's civil rights and duties as a citizen are, largely, an expression of one's sectarian identity. The *sine qua non* of the state is, after all, an embodiment of a pact—transfigured at times into a sacred covenant— between the various sects to preserve this delicate balance.

Although the two decades of rapid socio-economic change which preceded the outbreak of the war had ushered in some of the inevitable manifestations of secularization (behaviourally, if not institutionally), the residues of 12 years of civil unrest and random violence have eroded many of them. At least the burgeoning class identities depicted, and at times heralded, by many observers prior to the outbreak of the civil war[48] have been grossly undermined. Indeed, sectarian sentiments and their associated loyalties appear to have reasserted themselves more powerfully than ever before. Military and economic reasons have doubtless played a crucial role in this process, as affiliations with militias rapidly became the most effective means for ensuring one's physical security, as well as providing access to vital goods and services.[49]

More pressing perhaps, given public unease and fear, is the role of sectarian organizations in dispensing relief and shelter and attending to much of the war-stricken needs of the homeless and traumatized. In this context, it is scarcely surprising that sectarian mobilization and the accompanying exacerbation of religious tensions and passions should become more pronounced.

Indeed, confessional loyalties have become so intense that they now account for much of the bigotry and paranoia permeating the entire social fabric. More surprising, they bear an inverse relationship to the degree of religiosity. Preliminary results of a survey on the socio-psychological effects of the war reveal that while the religiosity (measured by the extent of changes in beliefs and the practice of religious duties) of a selected sample of the Lebanese people has been declining, their confessional and religious biases and prejudices are becoming more pronounced.[50] This implies, among other things, that religion is not resorted to as a spiritual force to restore one's sense of well-being, but as a means of communal and ideological mobilization.

The Lebanese are today brandishing their confessionalism, if we may invoke a dual metaphor, as both emblem and armour. As emblem, because one's confessional identity has become the most viable medium for asserting one's presence and securing vital needs and benefits. Without it, one is, literally, rootless, nameless, and voiceless. One is not heard or recognized unless one's confessional allegiance is disclosed first. It is only when one is placed within a confessional context that one's ideas and assertions are rendered meaningful or worthwhile. As armour, because it has become one's shield against real or imagined threats. The more vulnerable the emblem, the thicker the armour. Conversely, the thicker the armour, the more vulnerable and paranoiac other communities become. It is precisely this dialectic between threatened communities and the urge to seek shelter in cloistered worlds which has plagued Lebanon for so long.

Intense as sectarian affiliations appear to be at the moment, it is still unclear whether they are those loyalties which, in the long term, stand to benefit most from Lebanon's protracted turmoil. Massive population shifts have been accompanied by the reintegration of displaced groups into more homogeneous, self-contained, and exclusive communities. These are based not only on communal solidarities, but also on territorial, and, to a lesser extent, on familial and other forms of allegiance. What has been badly damaged in Lebanon is the idea that communities which differ in their beliefs, values, history, and traditions, can nevertheless share a territory and a common project, thanks to a political framework which preserves their specificity while enabling them to live together.[51] Many actors on the Lebanese scene now seem to refuse to see their community mingle freely with other communities in a 'public' space, arguing that such a situation goes against the need to preserve the identity, 'purity', or 'authenticity' of the community to which they belong.

In this context, one may understand why it is territorial solidarities which, in the long term, may be most strengthened by the war. When community feelings have grown so strong that communities feel uneasy, to say the least, at the prospect of interacting freely with one another, only two alternatives exist. The first is for one community to attempt to impose its will on the others. In Lebanon, this is the strategy that has been adopted by many groups; for several complex reasons, it has always ended in failure. The second is for each community to attempt to endow itself with its own territory; although each community may perceive such a strategy to be suboptimal, it also may realize that it is better adapted to the Lebanese reality, in which no group seems capable of imposing its will on others more than transiently.[52]

Concluding inferences

This paper has focused on urban informal networks to argue that the very forces of clientelism, parochialism, particularism, and communalism which prior to the civil war seemed capable of holding Lebanon together, have also been responsible for sustaining the current war. More poignantly, they have provided most of the dynamic that accounts for the intensity, ferocity and protracted character of violence. At least three broad inferences can be drawn.

The first concerns the way the Lebanese have coped with the threatening horrors of a Hobbesian jungle. Lebanon, despite its many peculiarities, seems to share with other countries a set of individual and collective responses to widespread fear and anarchy.[53] When the cruelties of the public world become more menacing, threatened and traumatized groups seek refuge in their tested and secure primordial ties and affiliations. Hence the family, locality and confessional communities allay some of their vulnerabilities, and provide the needed psychic, social and economic supports and cushions. They do so, however, only by eroding civility, increasing distance between groups, and sharpening further the segmented character of society. In short, what enables at one level disables at another. The same forces that sustain the social identity of certain groups also prompt them on occasion to violate and betray normative standards. The Lebanese is being demoralized, in other words, by the very forces that are supposed to make him or her a more human and social being. In other words, the elements that account for the resourcefulness, prosperity, cultural awakening and solidarity of certain communities are also the elements that fragment the society and weaken its civic and national loyalties. The formation and deformation of Lebanon are, so to speak, rooted in the same forces.

Secondly, the formation of cloistered communities is accompanied and sustained by 'ideologies of enmity'.[54] All such ideologies are modes for the legitimization of violence in the name of autonomy, identity, authenticity, or self-defence. Rival groups engage in mutual debasement. Their media have developed elaborate and effective strategies for such mutual denegration. Each group depicts the 'other' as the repository of all evil. The consequences of the 'demonization' of other groups[55] have been significant and damaging. All the unacknowledged and undesirable attributes of one's own group are projected onto the 'other'. By evoking such imagery, the 'other' is transformed into a public menace and a threat to security. In this context, aggression against the 'other' assumes a purgative value. It becomes an act of liberation, the only way to preserve or restore integrity and dignity. Terror and violence masquerade as virtue.

Finally, social and intellectual historians remind us that a fascinating transformation in the historical evolution of most societies involves their passage from a relatively 'closed' to a more 'open' system: membership and access to privileges and benefits are no longer denied by virtue of limitations of religion, kinship, or race. Such openness accounts for much of the spectacular growth in the philosophical, artistic, and political emancipation of contemporary societies.[56] What Lebanon has been experiencing is the reversal of this transformation, often believed to be natural and inevitable. The country is, once again, creating closed communities. The boundaries and horizons within which people circulate and interact are continuing to shrink.

Notes

1. The concept of 'networks' is used in this paper to designate the informal 'structures' formed by individuals or loosely organized groups of individuals linked to one another by interpersonal bonds. The definition is borrowed from Harrison White and Charles Tilly (see C. Tilly, *From Mobilization to Revolution* (Reading, 1978)). Networks involve frequent face-to-face contacts, physical proximity, and, as a rule, rather intense forms of solidarity and commitment. This study will focus on three types of networks: those based on sectarian ties; those built around residential (quarter/neighbourhood) affiliation and loyalty; and patron-client clusters.

2. See for example L. T. Fawaz, *Merchants and Migrants in Nineteenth Century Beirut* (Cambridge, 1983), and A. Hourani, 'Ottoman reforms and the politics of notables', in W. Polk and R. Chambers eds, *The Beginnings of Modernization in the Middle East* (Chicago, Ill., 1968).

3. See M. Hudson, *The Precarious Republic* (New York, 1968), and S. Khalaf and P. Kongstad, 'Urbanization and urbanism in Beirut: some preliminary results', in L. C. Brown ed., *From Madina to Metropolis* (Princeton, NJ, 1973).

4. For evidence, see S. Khalaf, 'Adaptive modernization, the case for Lebanon', in C. A. Cooper and S. S. Alexander eds, *Economic Development and Population Growth in the Middle East* (New York, 1972).

5. E. Shils, 'The prospect for Lebanese civility', in L. Binder ed., *Politics in Lebanon* (New York, 1966).

6. M. Johnson, *Class and Client in Beirut* (London, 1986), p. 79.

7. A. Hottinger, '"Zu'ama" in historical perspective', in L. Binder ed., *Politics in Lebanon*, p. 96.

8. Johnson, *Class and Client in Beirut*, p. 50.

9. R. Owen, 'The political economy of Grand Liban, 1920–1970', in R. Owen ed., *Essays on the Crisis in Lebanon* (London, 1976), p. 29; Johnson, *Class and Client in Beirut*, p. 131.

10. It is well known that under the presidencies of Fu'ad Shihab and Charles Helou many *qabadayat* were artificially promoted by the Deuxième Bureau and manipulated by it in order

to undercut the traditional patrons. Subsequently, when Sulayman Franjieh came into power in 1970, the *qabadayat* became largely independent of state control (and started to be clientelized by the Palestinian organizations, and the Libyan, Iraqi, Syrian, Saudi, and Egyptian governments). One cannot over-emphasize the instability created by such an absence of continuity at the political centre, the constant strife between urban patrons, and the loose and shifting coalitions between political actors.

11. On *caciques*, see W. A. Cornelius, *Politics and the Migrant Poor in Mexico City* (Stanford, Calif., 1975).

12. C. Liauzu, 'Sociétés urbaines et mouvements sociaux: état des recherches en langue anglaise sur le "Middle East" ', *Maghreb-Machreq* 111 (1986) 41–2.

13. Johnson, *Class and Client in Beirut*, p. 106.

14. Liauzu, 'Sociétés urbaines', p. 42.

15. C. Maksoud, 'Lebanon and Arab nationalism', in L. Binder ed., *Politics in Lebanon*, p. 241.

16. T. Khalaf, 'The Phalange and the Maronite community', in R. Owen ed., *Essays on the Crisis in Lebanon*, p. 45.

17. See S. Khalaf, *Lebanon's Predicament* (New York, 1987), pp. 170–84.

18. J. P. Entelis, *Pluralism and Party Transformation in Lebanon* (Leiden, 1974), p. 66.

19. See the introduction by Kamal Salibi.

20. See for example T. Khalaf, 'The Phalange and the Maronite community', p. 44, and M. Farouk-Sluglett and P. Sluglett, 'Aspects of the changing nature of Lebanese confessional politics', *Peuples Méditerranéens* 20 (1982) 62.

21. Johnson, *Class and Client in Beirut*, pp. 133–5.

22. W. Khalidi, *Conflict and Violence in Lebanon* (Cambridge, 1979), p. 73.

23. Ibid., p. 73.

24. See A. Norton, *Amal and the Shi'a* (Austin, 1987), and S. Nasr, 'Roots of the Shi'a movement', *Merip Reports* (June 1985).

25. Johnson, *Class and Client in Beirut*.

26. Khalaf, *Lebanon's Predicament*, p. 174.

27. Fouad Ajami, *The Vanished Imam* (Ithaca, NY and London, 1986).

28. K. W. Deutsch, 'Social mobilization and political development', *American Political Science Review* 55 (1961).

29. L. Z. Yamak, 'Party politics in the Lebanese political system', in Binder ed., *Politics in Lebanon*, p. 162.

30. L. Binder, 'Political change in Lebanon', in Binder ed., *Politics in Lebanon*.

31. A. Hottinger, ' "Zu'ama" in historical perspective', p. 99.

32. G. Salamé, *Lebanon's Injured Identities* (Oxford, 1986), p. 15.

33. For further details, see Johnson, *Class and Client in Beirut*.

34. The emergence of Amal to a position of prominence can really be traced back to 1978. It is only then that a series of events—particularly the disappearance of Sadr, the Iranian revolution, and the Israeli invasion—combined to turn the movement into the primary actor in the Shi'i community. For further details, see Norton, *Amal and the Shi'a*.

35. G. Salamé, *Lebanon's Injured Identities*, p. 16.

36. Ibid., p. 12.

37. A. Abu Khalil, 'Druze, Sunni and Shiite political leadership in present-day Lebanon', *Arab Studies Quarterly* 7.4 (1985).

38. J. Mack, 'Some thoughts on the nuclear age and the psychological roots of anti-Sovietism', *Psychoanalytic Inquiry* 6.2 (1986).

39. J. Mack, 'Foreword' to *Cyprus: War and Adaptation*, ed. V. Volkan (Charlottesville, Va, 1979).

40. Norton, *Amal and the Shi'a*, p. 11.

41. Abu Khalil, 'Druze, Sunni and Shi'i political leadership', pp. 38 and 54.

42. J. Abu-Lughod, 'The Islamic city—historic myth, Islamic essence, and contemporary relevance', *International Journal of Middle East Studies* 19 (May 1987).

43. M. Seurat, 'Le quartier de Bâb Tebbâné à Tripoli (Liban)', in CERMOC (Centre d'Etudes et de Recherches sur le Moyen-Orient Arabe Contemporain), *Mouvements Communautaires et Espaces Urbains au Machreq* (Beirut, 1985).

44. Abu-Lughod, 'The Islamic city'.

45. M. Seurat, 'Le quartier de Bâb Tebbâné'.

46. Ibid, p. 57.

47. Ibid, and J. F. Clément, 'Ce que le Liban m'a appris', *Esprit* 115 (June 1986).

48. See C. Dubar and S. Nasr, *Les Classes sociales au Liban* (Paris, 1976), and E. Picard, 'Science politique, orientalisme et sociologie au chevet du Liban', *Revue Française de Science Politique* (August 1977).

49. On this and other symptoms of public demoralization, see S. Khalaf, *Lebanon's Predicament*, pp. 238–98.

50. These results are part of a research carried out by Salim Nasr and Samir Khalaf under the auspices of the American University of Beirut.

51. See A. Hourani, *The Emergence of the Modern Middle East* (Berkeley, 1981), p. 175.

52. We have benefited here from the reading of O. Mongin, 'Penser la politique contre la domination au Proche-Orient', *Esprit* 115 (June 1986).

53. See for example J. E. Corradi, 'Toward societies without fear', mimeograph paper prepared for the conference on 'The Culture of Fear in Military Regimes of the Southern Cone', held in Buenos Aires, 30 May–1 June 1985; J. Mack, 'Some thoughts'; and C. Pinderhughes, 'Differential bonding from infancy to international conflict', *Psychoanalytic Inquiry* 6.2 (1986).

54. J. Mack, 'Some thoughts'.

55. J. Mack, 'Foreword'.

56. R. A. Nisbet, *The Social Bond* (New York, 1970).

11

The Termination of Protracted Social Conflict in Lebanon
An Analytical Perspective

GHASSAN T. RAAD

Introduction

We are daily reminded by newspaper and television news that we live in an era of intense conflict, with the nuclear threat, border clashes, terrorist attacks, civil wars and violent revolutions. I shall address here one specific kind of conflict that is culturally or identity bound; is communal in nature; is rooted in severely divided multi-ethnic and heterogeneous societies; fluctuates in the intensity and frequency of its violent outbursts; and spills over into all domains, internal and international. Conflict of this kind, suppressed over long periods, bursts into violence when triggered.

This category of conflict is referred to as 'protracted social conflict' (PSC), and is very common in the Third World. Empirical data collected by the American-Lebanese professor Edward Azar of the University of Maryland, the director of the Center for International Development and Conflict Management (CIDCM) suggests that 90 per cent of conflicts since the second world war have taken place within the Third World and have been protracted social-ethnic rather than strategic conflicts (i.e. conflicts between states).

Protracted social conflicts are ideological in nature, with strong preferences for secession, national liberation, the rights of self-determination, autonomy or equal rights. They are characterized by: '(1) temporal protractedness, (2) fluctuation in intensity and frequency, (3) conflict spillover from one realm to another, (4) a tendency towards partial equilibrium, (5) absence of explicit termination, and (6) blurred demarcation between internal and external sources of conflict.'[1]

Protracted social conflicts are rooted in highly volatile and contested issues such as identity, distribution of justice, and ethnicity or nationalism. They arise from very unequal socio-economic structures, characteristic of the developing world where the channels of mediation and arbitration are either absent, inefficient or blocked. According to PSC theory, conflict is situated within the totality of the social system composed of structures determined by its specificity and historical position.

Protracted intercommunal conflict (PIC) is a sub-type of the general category of protracted social conflicts. This type of conflict, which exists for example in Lebanon, Northern Ireland, Sri Lanka, or the Punjab province in India, becomes increasingly more complex and difficult to resolve over time.

How can societies, like Lebanon, which are locked in a vicious cycle of violence, turn from war to peace? In other words, how are protracted social conflicts resolved? To answer this question, a definition of the essence of PSC and its systemic properties is necessary.

Protracted social conflict: roots and properties

Protracted social conflicts have two major sources: a deformed and polarized environment; and the denial or unfulfilment of basic needs, including security (physical, economic and cultural), identity and recognition.

Deformed and polarized environment

The deformed environment of PSCs has three major features:

1. Deeply divided heterogeneous, multi-ethnic societies with severe social cleavages of a religious, linguistic, tribal, regional, cultural, ethnic, racial, ideological, social or economic nature.
2. Those social cleavages tend to be cumulative/superimposed instead of cross-cutting. In any society, religion, culture identity and languages superimpose. The more layers of cleavages there are, the deeper the divisions between the communities. In Lebanon we have a case of cumulative, superimposed cleavages.
3. Empirically observed systemic properties.

The first property is the failure of post-independence nation-states to fulfil the basic needs of all its ethnic communities. Such failure is attributed to the following factors:

(a) Inherited disjointed social systems—socio-economic and political—of ex-colonial powers.

(b) Legacy of colonial policy of 'divide and rule': skewed economic development; and unjust treatment of some ethnic communities and preferential treatment given to some others.

(c) Structural socio-economic inequalities leading to victimization and the feeling of relative deprivation by some ethnic groups. As the perception of being marginalized grows, alienation increases as does the fear of eventual assimilation or coercive integration by the numerically dominant community, bringing about the destruction of a distinct 'identity group'.

(d) Population shifts, growth and pressures in the Third World. These are connected to resource scarcities and maldistribution of socio-economic reward, causing malnutrition, illiteracy, inadequate medical care, housing shortages and unemployment.

The second property is the inadequate, imported Western models of development stressing one dimension of uneven economic growth, resulting in further chronic poverty and a widening gap in the level of development between the communities, leading to intercommunal violence and 'scapegoating' (i.e. the tendency to blame other communities for the underdevelopment of one's own).

The third property is the awareness of victimization by marginalized communities and their resolve to redress historical grievances benefiting from favourable conditions to challenge the status quo.

Denial or unfulfilment of basic needs

John Burton wrote:

> Classical thinking led us to believe that conflict was about interests only. For that reason it was that individuals could be socialized and coerced. What both theory and application revealed was that protracted conflicts, which are the major concern in world politics, are primarily over non-negotiable values. They are concerned with human and identity needs such as those listed by Sites. This being the case, it is impossible to socialize the individuals over any length of time into behaviors that run counter to the pursuit of security, identity, and other aspects of development.[2]

It was found at the Center for International Development and Conflict Management (CIDCM) at the University of Maryland, College Park, that major conflicts involve non-negotiable needs such as those for security, identity and recognition.

These human needs for security, identity and recognition cannot be denied or repressed. Conflicts involving *needs* are different from those involving *interests*. Lebanon has been the victim of conflicts over needs which are not responsive to the traditional bargaining and negotiation techniques of conflict-resolution processes as evidenced

by 13 years of violence in Lebanon. We read in one pamphlet
produced by CIDCM:

> The reason why intractability and escalation occur is because, while
> parties experience their own inalienable needs, they attribute
> motives to the other side that are merely interests expressed, for
> example, as expansion for aggression. In a situation like this, parties
> try to coerce or deter one another by threat, without conceding that
> they are dealing with needs that are not negotiable.

Triggers of PSCs

I shall simply list the trigger conditions conducive to intercommunal
violence, without elaboration:

1. Demographic communal imbalance.
2. External interference:
     (a) direct;
     (b) indirect.
3. Disintegration of legitimate state authority and power.
4. Emergence of charismatic leadership and mobilization of movements to destabilize the system.

Now I would like to address the second part of my presentation.

The termination of PSCs

There are several methods to terminate PSCs, ranging from extreme,
negative, violent methods to positive, democratic, peaceful ones. The
following is a brief description of each.

Negative methods

Ethnic hegemony. This is a repressive method of dominance where
one major ethnic group attempts to force the integration or
assimilation of a minor group. For example, the treatment of ethnic
minorities by dominant Russians in the Soviet Union, particularly
the Baltic peoples in the annexed states of Estonia, Latvia and
Lithuania. A related method of dominance is to confer second-class
citizen status to some ethnic communities: for example, apartheid in
South Africa.

Forced displacement. This method is applied to some ethnic communities through the use of terror, massacres, violent threats and

intimidation. The Armenian genocide in Turkey and the Jewish holocaust in Nazi Europe are examples.

Partition or secession. There are several examples in recent history: Cyprus has been *de facto* partitioned; Bangladesh seceded from Pakistan which seceded from India.

Protracted communal violence. This is one way of drawing attention to the ongoing and unresolved conflict. The examples are numerous and include Lebanon and Northern Ireland.

Positive methods

There are some positive methods for conflict resolution that depend on successful management and the containment of conflict. Many of these approaches stress the traditional legalistic settlement of conflict through the use of sanctions, rewards or United Nations mediation. Consociational democracy, as advocated by Lijphart, Daadler, Hanf and others, has merits and should be seriously considered in some deeply divided societies where the conditions for its success are present: a multiple balance of segments where the segments are of approximately equal size; a relatively small total population; external threats perceived as a common danger by the different segments; the presence of some national loyalties; the absence of extreme socio-economic inequalities among the segments; the relative isolation of the segments from each other; and traditions of political accommodation that predispose the segments to power sharing.[3]

What alternative is there for conflict resolution when one or more of these conditions are absent?

I would like to draw our attention to an alternative approach which is gaining momentum in the United States, and I shall develop the following key notions: the transformation of conflict situations; development diplomacy; 'facilitation' or Track II diplomacy.

The transformation of conflict situations

I would like to make some observations here. Empirically oriented students of conflict have tended to focus conflict theory on interaction between the elite as opposed to between the disadvantaged or victimized, and on the management or containment of conflict rather than on transformation of conflict situations. Conflict researchers concentrated on conflicts between major powers during the 'strategic balance of terror' era. Today, international conflict has shifted toward the Third World. Therefore, the focus of our conflict research must shift to an extremely intense type of conflict, protracted social conflict. The notion of PSC provides a richer paradigm in analysing conflict, as it attends to the realities of the Third World where conflict is intimately linked to issues of inequitable distribution both between and within societies.

Neither of the dimensions of protracted social conflict—interstate strategic or intrastate (social/structural)—can be understood without linking them to the concept of development as a potential means of transforming societies experiencing protracted social conflict. Those societies are characterized by 'poverty, inequality, police state regimes, acute problems of population growth and overt violence—all inter-acting in a vicious circle'.[4] The goal of any meaningful development must be the reduction of inequality and the structural victimization produced by the social system:

> Structural victimization is the condition of rank inequality and disequilibrium in the system which has emerged as a by-product of the historical development of a specific social system. It is reality that permeates every level of social existence. An individual is vic-timized whenever a beneficial action or choice is structurally denied him. Significantly, the victim need not be consciously aware of the source or the occurrence of his victimization in order for it to take place . . . An example from American history is the de facto denial of civil and human rights to black Americans as a consequence of the institution which originally imported them to America—slavery.[5]

This concept of structural victimization will be useful to link development and social conflict in general. Only through the elimination of the roots of victimization by transforming conflict situations can we reduce outbreaks of violence and create favourable conditions for a stable and long-lasting peace. Development diplomacy is one way of achieving such an objective.

Development diplomacy

Because protracted social conflicts differ from other types of conflict in their focus on group identity and personal identity in relation to the power and privileges associated with each group, the effective management of conflicts requires political and economic development to redress communal grievances and satisfy identity needs. Therefore, the major objectives of development diplomacy consist in achieving the following ends:

1. Reduction of structural inequalities.
2. Shift in developmental strategy.
3. Alternation of external economic ties to reduce economic depend-encies on the outside actors.

4. Progressive reforms in socio-political structures, to include:
    (a) redistribution of power among social forces;
    (b) institution building and consensus among competing communal groups.

The cause of underdevelopment in the Third World is the notion of dependency. This situation of unhealthy dependency and skewed economic development should be corrected through multi-ethnic, rather than bilateral arrangements. Development diplomacy should become an integral part of global political and economic reform movements.[6] In essence, development diplomacy must aim at inducing economic participation, the effective involvement of victimized groups, as opposed to marginalization and discrimination. Such a strategy is more conducive to conflict resolution than are the traditional legalistic methods, because it *severs* the causal links between underdevelopment and structural inequalities; and because it rights the communal imbalance on the development scales and heals institutional paralysis.

Facilitation or Track II diplomacy

Joseph Montville, the research director of the Center for the Study of Foreign Affairs at the US Department of State, is credited with the use of the term Track II diplomacy defined as the 'unofficial non-structural interaction. It is always open minded, often altruistic, based on best case analysis.'[7] Therefore, Track II diplomacy is unofficial, informal interaction between members of adversary groups or nations aiming at developing strategies, influencing public opinion, organizing human and material resources in ways that might help resolve their conflict.[8]

According to Burton:

> Second track diplomatic conflict resolution seeks to deal with the underlying conditions that give rise to conflict. It is not an idealistic diplomacy that simply wishes well for all conflict resolution that substitutes for court, mediators, and peace-keeping forces the tried techniques of facilitation of conflict resolution. It is a means of bringing parties to disputes together in an analytical framework controlled by a panel of facilitators to ensure there is no power bargaining, no proposals by a mediator, no proposals by parties, until there is a thorough analysis of the total situation by the parties, from which they can deduce options that fully meet their requirements. In essence, track two is an approach that analyses the needs, values, and interests of the parties.[9]

This approach to problem solving has three distinct aspects, according to Montville:[10]

1. Problem-solving workshops. These bring together leaders of conflicting groups or nations or their representatives to: develop workable personal relationships in microcosm; understand the dimension of conflicts from the adversary's perspective; develop strategies for dealing with the conflict as a shared problem requiring reciprocal and co-operative efforts.

2. Influencing public opinion. This is a psychological task aimed at reducing the sense of victimhood of the parties and rehumanizing the image of the adversary. If this step is successful there will emerge a climate of opinion within each antagonistic community that will make it safe for political leaders to take positive steps.

3. Co-operative economic development. This will provide incentives, institutional support and continuity to political and psychological advances.

Recommendations for conflict resolution in Lebanon today

Based on this theoretical model of protracted social conflict resolution, these observations might be made.

Lebanese Christians' fears of Islamic arabism, which they perceive as a threat to their long-cherished cultural and religious values and their distinct way of life, should be seriously examined. Their fears should be properly assessed to determine whether or not they have valid historical foundations. Lebanese Muslims' suspicion of Christian intentions and lack of genuine commitment to Arabs' causes should be thoroughly examined to determine whether or not they are justified.

The overwhelming majority of Lebanese have the desire to coexist, I believe, providing the following principles of intercommunal co-existence are understood and accepted by the major communities of Lebanon.

1. The outcome of power struggles in a multi-ethnic society can never be a zero-sum game, as no single community can hope to achieve decisive victory in multi-communal societies. The 13 years of continuous strife in Lebanon should prove this point conclusively.
2. It is in the mutual interests of all Lebanese communities to work for the preservation of a just and equitable plural model in Lebanon. It will be a disaster to either Islamize or Christianize Lebanon. The blend of the two religious cultures provides a unique civilization itself.
3. The Western model of 'one man, one vote' is unworkable in

a multi-ethnic society. If applied, there would not be democracy but ethnic hegemony of the numerically dominant community controlling the state's apparatus and subjugating the remaining ethnic communities.

4. Under no circumstances should any community in Lebanon, in the short or long term, be suppressed, marginalized or coercively silenced, as alienation will breed more violence.

5. All Lebanese communities should be given enough incentives in the form of security guarantees in the future of Lebanon to induce them to take an active part in the peace-building process.

Notes

1. Edward E. Azar, 'Protracted social conflict: ten propositions', in John Burton and Azar eds, *International Conflict Resolution: Theory and Practice* (Sussex, 1986), pp. 28–39.

2. John W. Burton, 'The history of international conflict resolution', in Edward E. Azar and Burton eds, *International Conflict Resolution*, p. 51.

3. Arendt Lijphart, 'Consociation: the model and the application in divided societies', in Desmond Rea ed., *Political Cooperation in Divided Societies: a Series of Papers relevant to the Conflict in Northern Ireland* (Dublin, 1982), p. 83.

4. Edward E. Azar, 'Development diplomacy', in Joyce Starr and Addeone S. Calliegh eds, *A shared Destiny: Near East Regional Development and Cooperation* (New York, 1983), p. 96.

5. Ibid. p. 96.

6. Ibid.

7. John W. Macdonald, 'Observations of a diplomat', in E. E. Azar and J. W. Burton eds, *International Conflict Resolution*, p. 143.

8. See John V. Montville, 'The arrow and the olive branch', in John Macdonald and Diane B. Bendahmone eds, *Conflict Resolution: Track Two Diplomacy*, Department of State Publication, Foreign Service Institute, Center for the Study of Foreign Affairs, 1987.

9. John W. Burton, 'Track two: an alternative to power politics', in J. Macdonald and D. B. Bendahmone eds, *Conflict Resolution*, p. 72.

10. See 'The arrow and the olive branch'.

12

Comment l'Etat a-t-il été compris au Liban?

DOMINIQUE CHEVALLIER

Observation: in recent works written by young Lebanese, the affirmation of the eternity of Lebanon, the focus on class struggle in Lebanon, or indeed any other ideological presupposition concerning Lebanon, very often make an abstraction of the idea and the reality of the state.

Inter-Lebanese polemics become much more violent the more the state is put into parentheses. How does the current situation, so dramatic, shed light on the problems that arose between 1830 and 1975?

What form would Lebanon assume among the Arab states which succeeded the Ottoman state? An Arab kingdom or an independent and protected Lebanon with Christian predominance? Significance of a testimony: the uneasy nostalgia of a Lebanese today looking back on the years 1918–20.

Was the proclamation of Grand Liban by General Gouraud, on 1 September 1920, clear? Reminder of the text: a state with its administrative attributes, its territory and its borders. The French Republic and its model of a secular nation, parliamentary and liberal; the colonial French empire and its models.

Social and community culture in the political and economic life of the Lebanese Republic.

Power and its forms: familial, solidary ('tribal'), confessional and regional. Some examples of political ascents and public behaviour in twentieth-century Lebanon.

The dates 1936, 1943, 1958 and 1967 in the history of Lebanon. Comparison between the Lebanese state 'with an Arab face' and other Arab states which emerged from the Ottoman state.

Territory, borders and the role of the Lebanese state in the crises of the Middle East.

Sincerity of attitudes and surrealism of judgements; what is Lebanon in the consciousness of the Lebanese?

Mon propos a d'abord pour but de poser des questions destinées à alimenter notre réflexion commune. Il est bien évident que, lorsque nous débattons de conflits et de consensus au Liban de 1830 à 1975, nous avons constamment présent à l'esprit le drame actuel. Il commande notre problématique. C'est pour cette raison que je veux me demander avec vous: 'Comment l'Etat a-t-il été compris au Liban?'

J'ai été également amené à formuler cette interrogation après avoir lu, ces derniers mois, des thèses qui ont été écrites par des Libanais (mais qui n'ont pas été préparées sous ma direction). Les plus significatifs de ces travaux ont été rédigés par des enseignants d'une trentaine d'années dont l'inexpérience scientifique constitue déjà, hélas! un témoignage. J'ai été choqué en constatant à quel point, chez eux, il y a une dissolution du sens de l'Etat, une absence de référence à l'Etat. Dans une recherche sur la France et la politique libanaise de 1919 à 1943, l'auteur fait quasi abstraction de la notion d'Etat—ce qui est quand même surprenant! Une autre thèse focalise tout sur la lutte de classes, avec les méchants exploiteurs et les bons exploités, sans que jamais soit évoqué le cadre spatial et juridique dans lequel vit cette société d'exploiteurs et d'exploités.

Or, remarquons-le, lorsque la réalité de l'Etat est gommée, lorsque la date historique de la création de l'Etat—le 1er septembre 1920—est par conséquent ignorée, il est facile d'affirmer l'éternité du Liban. Il suffit de rejeter les questions permettant d'étudier la naissance et la formation d'une conscience libanaise, ou la fondation de l'Etat libanais à un moment bien précis, pour proclamer que le Liban est éternel de l'Antiquité à nos jours. Parallèlement, si l'Etat est né au Liban, alors que le pays est cependant cité pour discourir sur des conflits sociaux et politiques qui s'y déroulent, ceux-ci sont replacés et compris dans un ensemble qualifié soit d'arabe, soit d'islamique, mais dont la consistance n'est pas pour autant définie par une analyse des conditions culturelles, économiques et institutionnelles. Dans l'un et l'autre cas, l'incantation idéologique cache fort mal la vacuité totale du savoir et du raisonnement. Ce qui est plus grave dans de telles démarches, c'est que l'homme est occulté, parce que les sociétés et leurs moyens échappent à la connaissance. Les polémiques qui se développent depuis plusieurs années entre partis ou entre communautés, entre factions libanaises, tirent ainsi leur violence de la mise entre parenthèses de l'Etat.

Soyons donc, quant à nous, plus lucides, plus francs, plus directs: les Libanais ont-ils su assumer un Etat de droit? Comment ont-ils vécu et compris les institutions d'un Etat de droit? Quelles traditions étatiques trouvent-ils dans leur histoire?

En quoi la situation présente, si poignante et si dangereuse, éclaire-t-elle les problèmes qui se sont posés entre 1830 et 1975? A quelles expériences se réfère-t-elle?

Vous connaissez le beau livre d'Ahmad Beydoun, *Identité confessionnelle et temps social chez les historiens libanais contemporains* (Beyrouth, 1984). Les attitudes intellectuelles des historiens des différentes communautés religieuses et des différents horizons politiques y sont présentées avec une grande intelligence; leurs arguments y sont médités avec une rare sensibilité. Poursuivons le questionnement.

Qu'a représenté le Liban parmi les Etats arabes qui ont succédé à l'Etat ottoman après la première guerre mondiale? Je dis bien l''Etat' (*dawla*) ottoman, et pas seulement l'Empire ottoman, car la réalité constitutive de l'Etat et de son gouvernement était très fortement ancrée dans la conscience comme dans l'existence des Ottomans. Or, la société de la Montagne libanaise d'abord, mais aussi celle de Beyrouth et des vieilles 'échelles', et celles des différents districts qui, à côté de ceux de la *mutasarrifiyya* du Mont Liban, ont été incorporé au Grand-Liban, toutes ces sociétés étaient-elles aptes à prendre la relève de l'Etat ottoman? Et comment?

Ces questions peuvent se poser de façon analogue pour d'autres pays du Proche-Orient. Pour l'Egypte, par exemple, où il existait une vieille tradition étatique et une initiative moderniste qui ont souvent servi de modèle aux élites dirigeantes libanaises, qu'il s'agisse d'hommes d'affaires, d'hommes politiques ou d'intellectuels. Pour l'Irak aussi, où l'Etat ottoman a été relayé par des cadres administratifs et militaires qui en étaient issus; même s'ils sont devenus nationalistes arabes et s'ils ont partagé les responsabilités avec de puissants notables locaux, ils avaient été formés dans le moule étatique et administratif ottoman. Pour la Syrie encore, où l'Etat a été assumé par des notables des villes et des grands propriétaires fonciers qui, à l'occasion des réformes entreprises dans l'Empire ottoman au dix-neuvième siècle, avaient renouvelé et affirmé leur pouvoir économique, leur pouvoir administratif et, en milieu musulman sunnite, leur pouvoir communautaire.[1] La comparaison est possible entre tous ces cas (auxquels il faudrait évidemment ajouter beaucoup de nuances); mais chacun d'eux offre, cependant, une réponse particulière.

Qu'en est-il de l'Etat au Liban? Menée depuis 1920, l'expérience aura bientôt soixante-dix ans. Elle a été ponctuée en 1945, à la fin de la seconde guerre mondiale, par la constitution de la Ligue des Etats arabes dont le Liban a été l'un des membres fondateurs. Durant les décennies qui ont suivi cet événement ayant force de symbole, les différents Etats arabes ont accentué leurs caractères propres, chacun pour son compte, chacun en tant qu'Etat distinct des autres, à travers de proclamations unitaires arabes, nationalistes arabes, parfois arabes et musulmanes. C'est au nom de l'idéal unitaire du nationalisme arabe que l'Etat en Egypte, en Syrie et en Irak, s'est à la fois rénové et consolidé dans l'élaboration de sa propre indépendance politique et économique, de sa propre souveraineté territoriale, et de sa propre légitimité qui a été légalisée par l'équipe ayant pris le pouvoir. La période 1958 à 1961, au cours de laquelle l'Egypte et la Syrie ont été associées au sein de la République arabe unie, n'a fait que confirmer, par sa brièveté, cette évolution.

Pour un esprit occidental insuffisamment averti, il peut sembler paradoxal que des proclamations unitaires arabes, dont la fonction théorique serait d'effacer les frontières d'Etat, aboutissent en fait à les consolider, donc à promouvoir une personnalité collective qu'incarne—ou que veut incarner—l'Etat sur un territoire défini, et internationalement reconnu. Cette situation n'est pourtant contradictoire que par rapport à une certaine vision rationaliste; elle résulte de la logique interne de structures sociales et mentales très anciennement élaborées en milieu arabe, et complétées par la construction et la justification légale du pouvoir au nom de la révélation transcendantale de l'Un, donnée par l'Un, sans que pour autant disparaissent les groupes cloisonnés initiaux, berceaux nécessaires de l'aspiration à l'unité.

Au lendemain de la première guerre mondiale, il y a eu un choix à faire pour fixer l'avenir du Liban. Deviendrait-il une province autonome, comprenant une population en majorité chrétienne, dans le cadre d'un royaume arabe? Ou bien devait-il acquérir l'indépendance, grâce à la protection éventuelle d'une puissance mandataire, la France?

Cette interrogation continue d'habiter des Libanais d'aujourd'hui; elle s'exprime dans une nostalgie de la période 1918 à 1920, celle des espérances mais aussi du choix. Ainsi forme-t-elle la trame de l'émouvant récit de Gérard Khoury, *Mémoire de l'aube* (Paris, 1987). Cet auteur, parti d'une recherche historique, a abouti à la rédaction d'un roman—peut-être pour mieux rendre ses propres états d'âme. La mise en scène de ses personnages, des chrétiens et des Français notamment, l'a amené à transformer le décor réel en mythe. Voici une famille maronite, de modeste origine montagnarde, qui obéit à de mêmes rythmes culturels de sociabilité que les milieux musulmans voisins, mais qui traîne la peur et l'humiliation ancestrale des minoritaires; ses membres citadinisés espèrent que la France leur permettra d'échapper à un Etat dominé par l'Islam. Leur ami français, un officier des services de renseignement, pense, quant à lui, qu'une autonomie libanaise dans le cadre d'une vaste fédération syrienne, qui pourrait être monarchique, serait la meilleure solution. Ce premier couple franco-libanais est croisé par un second qui lui donne la réplique; un journaliste du *Temps*, agent officieux, superficiel et combinard, se montre un actif partisan d'un Liban indépendant du reste de la Syrie; il est l'ami d'une grande famille grecque-orthodoxe de Beyrouth, qui cultive sa pérennité par l'occidentalisation, mais qui, en son sein, entretient une vision désespérée de l'avenir des chrétiens en Orient, même dans un cadre étatique constitué pour eux.

Ce roman est attachant par son ambiguïté sans cesse renouvelée. Les rivalités entre la France et l'Angleterre aiguisent les revendications, se disant nationales, de quelques bourgeoisies. Les élites chrétiennes sont à la recherche d'une forme d'Etat que ne sent pas la masse de la population, parce que celle-ci vit la question du pouvoir à travers ses consciences confessionnelles. Replacée à l'intérieur d'une telle situation, la fiction de Gérard Khoury offre une double face toute levantine. Elle peut être interprétée comme un regret de l'occasion manquée qu'aurait été un royaume arabe pour tous. Mais elle manifeste aussi une irrépressible nostalgie de cette 'aube' que fut la présence française aux côtés des maronites.

Finalement, ce livre répercute le cri d'un maronite qui s'identifie par sa fidélité à la France. Le personnage sympathique est l'officier français; les braves gens, longuement décrits, sont des maronites. Les autres se contentent d'être au mieux des esthètes, au pire des affairistes, mais toujours des ombres. Dans le dernier chapitre, tout se décompose. Ce livre, écrit en 1984 à 1986, aurait-il eu la même tonalité s'il avait été conçu avant les épreuves qu'ont subies les Libanais depuis les années 1970? L'auteur veut témoigner pour une vérité du Liban, tout en décrivant, au bout du compte, la création du Grand-Liban comme une affaire mondaine, rondement menée à Beyrouth. L'imaginaire répand son parfum. La réalité exhale d'autres effluves.

La proclamation du Grand-Liban par le général Gouraud, le 1er septembre 1920, a-t-elle été claire? Le discours qu'il a prononcé ce jour-là, sur le perron de la Résidence des Pins, est-il bien compris aujourd'hui? Il est fréquent d'entendre dire que Gouraud a proclamé le Grand-Liban, mais de ne pas entendre parler de l'Etat. Evidemment, le haut-commissaire français a utilisé un pathos dans le goût du temps. Ecoutons son envolée oratoire:

> Par devant tous ces témoins de vos espoirs, de vos luttes et de votre victoire, c'est en partageant votre fierté que je proclame solennellement le Grand-Liban, qu'au nom de la République française, je le salue, dans sa grandeur et dans sa force, du Nahr el-Kébir aux portes de la Palestine et aux crêtes de l'Anti-Liban . . .

Pour les musulmans, il a pris soin d'ajouter plus loin: 'Le Grand-Liban est fait au profit de tous.'[2]

D'emblée, il a défini le Grand-Liban à partir d'un territoire pour que soit reconnue la base concrète d'un Etat. Sa déclaration serait incompréhensible sans les textes juridiques qui l'ont accompagnée. Pourquoi sont-ils si souvent ignorés alors qu'ils ont été à nouveau publiés récemment? . . .[3] La proclamation du 1er septembre a été précédée, le 31 août 1920, d'un arrêté qui a précisé, sans équivoque possible, que c'était bien un Etat qui était créé:

> Le général Gouraud, haut-commissaire de la République française en Syrie et Cilicie, Commandant en chef de l'armée du Levant,

Vu le décret présidentiel du 8 octobre 1919,

Attendu que la France, en venant en Syrie, n'a poursuivi d'autre but que celui de permettre aux populations de la Syrie et du Liban de réaliser leurs aspirations les plus légitimes de liberté et d'autonomie,

Considérant qu'il importe, pour ce faire, de restituer au Liban ses frontières naturelles telles qu'elles ont été définies par ses représentants et réclamées par les voeux unanimes des populations,

Que le Grand-Liban ainsi fixé dans ses limites naturelles pourra poursuivre, *en tant qu'Etat indépendant,* au mieux de ses intérêts politiques et économiques, avec l'aide de la France le programme qu'il s'est tracé,

Pour ces motifs:

Arrêté:

Art. I.—*Il est formé, sous le nom d'Etat du Grand-Liban, un territoire comprenant* . . .

Suit l'énumération et la description des districts qui composent le Liban tel qu'il reste aujourd'hui internationalement reconnu. J'ai souligné les passages où le mot 'Etat' a été mentionné dans cet arrêté, car ils consacrent explicitement la fondation d'un Etat. Dès le lendemain, le 1er septembre 1920, un autre arrêté du haut-commissaire a détaillé la réglementation provisoire de l'administration du Grand-Liban:

Considérant qu'en attendant la mise en vigueur de son statut organique qui sera établi en conformité des articles 94 et 96 du traité de Sèvres (10 août 1920) et du mandat prévu par ces articles, il importe de donner *à l'Etat du Grand-Liban* une organisation administrative conforme aux aspirations des populations, pour leur permettre de réaliser, avec l'aide de la France, le programme d'indépendance et d'autonomie qu'elles se sont tracées . . .

Ce texte a défini l'ensemble des organes exécutifs, administratifs et consultatifs dont le Liban était doté à l'intérieur de frontières établies en même temps. Ces institutions étaient certes provisoires, et soumises à l'autorité du haut-commissaire et des fonctionnaires nommés par le gouvernement français, mais le Liban a bien alors reçu les attributs d'un Etat de droit; un territoire, un pouvoir exécutif et administratif, une capitale, et le système judiciaire maintenu en place.

Il est, en outre, utile de préciser que l'Etat du Grand-Liban n'a pas été créé à la place d'un Etat existant, mais à un moment où un vide avait été formé au Levant du fait de la dislocation de l'Empire ottoman, puis de l'effondrement de l'éphémère Royaume de Syrie, survenu à la suite de la bataille de Maysalun, le 24 juillet 1920. Cette situation politique et juridique était évidemment la conséquence d'opérations militaires où les troupes françaises avaient été efficacement engagées; mais elle résultait aussi de tous les pourparlers poursuivis, après la 'Grande Guerre', pour recomposer de nombreux pays et pour en reconnaître l'existence par des arrangements internationaux. Dans ce large mouvement, la brève chronologie qui vient d'être évoquée circonscrit bien l'événement: 24 juillet 1920, bataille de Maysalun; 10 août 1920, signature du traité de Sèvres; 1er septembre 1920, proclamation de l'Etat du Grand-Liban.

La mentalité façonnée par les débats de ses concitoyens, Gouraud avait utilisé l'expression de 'frontières naturelles', tandis que l'administration française y propulsait sa propre logique juridique. Mais des chrétiens libanais avaient déjà emprunté la notion de 'frontières naturelles' pour justifier l'extension territoriale qu'ils réclamaient avec l'indépendance. En effet, le territoire du nouvel Etat a été revendiqué, et donc composé, par des Libanais. Au cours des siècles précédents, leurs ancêtres avaient mis en valeur la 'Montagne' par des cultures arbustives dont ils commercialisaient les produits (soie, huile, tabac . . .) pour se procurer des monnaies et acheter de quoi se nourrir, notamment des grains. Aussi leur fallait-il avoir accès aux ports de la Méditerranée et aux plaines céréalières que dominait directement le pouvoir ottoman; celui-ci maintenait, par ce moyen, son contrôle sur des zones que leur relief rendait pourtant peu accessibles. Pour tenter d'échapper à cette durable contrainte, les notables de la Montagne druze et maronite avaient longtemps rêvé de mettre la main sur ces débouchés et sur ces ressources.

Leur ambition se transforma en mythe inaugural dans la mesure où elle contribua à forger une conscience libanaise. Voilà qu'elle trouvait l'occasion de se réaliser! L'Etat libanais a pu être créé grâce à l'appui de la France et de son armée, mais il n'a pris consistance que parce qu'une aspiration 'libaniste' existait. Des paysans, des artisans et des clercs lui avaient donnée ses assises populaires; une nouvelle élite du négoce, de la vie publique et de l'esprit avaient adapté son espoir à la modernité.

La République française a, bien entendu, offert son modèle d'Etat-nation laïc, parlementaire et libéral, même si, dans le cadre de son empire colonial, elle acceptait d'autres solutions, monarchiques par exemple, comme en Tunisie et au Maroc. Le gouvernement français a agi, et légitimé son action, en projetant sur les populations du Levant les idéaux de la société et les mécanismes du système qui étaient les siens. Les instructions de Briand à Henry de Jouvenel, rendues publiques en décembre 1925, sont révélatrices à cet égard:

Les droits des habitants de la Syrie et du Liban seront définis conformément aux principes sur lesquels sont fondées les libertés de l'Occident, qu'il nous appartient de faire entrer dans les lois et dans les moeurs de l'Orient syrien: liberté de conscience, liberté individuelle, égalité devant les tribunaux et droit de propriété, conformément à la Déclaration des Droits de l'Homme ... Le mandat a le pouvoir que suppose sa responsabilité, pour conseiller, contrôler les gouvernements de la Syrie et du Liban, redresser leurs décisions, y suppléer en cas de défaillance, dans les matières touchant aux intérêts essentiels des Etats et aux obligations internationales.[4]

Des ambiguïtés et un double langage ont été ainsi entretenus auprès des Libanais, au-delà même de la durée du mandat et donc de l'arbitrage impératif que le gouvernement français s'était alors réservé. Si le régime et les idéaux de la Troisième République ont inspiré les juristes qui ont élaboré la constitution libanaise en 1926, ils n'en ont pas moins précisé, dans l'article 95, que: 'A titre transitoire et conformément à l'article premier de la Charte du mandat, et dans une intention de justice et de concorde, les Communautés seront équitablement représentées dans les emplois publics et la composition du Ministère, sans que cela puisse cependant nuire au bien de l'Etat.'[5] Cette disposition a soumis la puissance mandataire aux réalités locales, et non l'inverse. L'Etat du Grand-Liban en devenant la République libanaise, a conservé dans sa pratique constitutionnelle et législative, un vécu social et communautaire qui n'avait jamais cessé de guider les comportements de ses habitants.

En effet, contrairement à une interprétation parfois répandue, le mandat n'a pas institué le 'confessionnalisme'. Il a seulement hérité d'une répartition des responsabilités selon l'importance des communautés religieuses. Ce système, résultat d'une adaptation réalisée au dix-neuvième siècle, avait eu pour but d'égaliser le statut des communautés dans l'Empire ottoman. Mais, dans sa conception, il était d'abord le produit d'une organisation de création très ancienne puisqu'elle se confond avec les origines de l'exercice du pouvoir dans les Etats soumis à la loi islamique, et donc avec celles des droits reconnus aux fidèles des religions révélées non musulmanes, le christianisme et le judaïsme. Les diverses populations de ces pays avaient sauvegardé leur identité ou leurs privilèges grâce à leur solidarité confessionnelle; elles y restaient spontanément attachées, à travers leurs réclamations comme à travers les changements. Les réformateurs ottomans du siècle dernier, soucieux d'assurer leur autorité, avaient concilié des principes et des pratiques, du passé et du présent, pour parvenir à moderniser l'administration et la justice tout en maintenant la personnalité des communautés.

Cette mesure, avec la conscience de soi qui lui servait de support dans chaque regroupement (y compris parmi les imaginaires nationaux en gestation), trouva son application dans la représentation administrative et législative. Pour cette raison majeure, qui a été évidemment liée à un ordre public approuvé par la puissance mandataire, les législateurs libanais ont inscrit dans leur constitution une clause prolongeant de bien vieilles habitudes communautaires et sociales. Indissociables du mental collectif et de conduites quotidiennes, elles se sont coulées dans la modernité jusqu'à nos jours.

L'organisation confessionnelle a elle-même coiffé la structure des familles et des clans patriarcaux dont l'agencement fut esquissé bien avant l'apparition de l'Islam, du christianisme et du judaïsme; peut-être remonte-t-elle au néolithique, ou même encore plus loin. Cette structure a dicté des types identiques de solidarités parentales et 'tribales' chez les chrétiens de différents rites, comme chez les musulmans de toutes filiations. Au cours des millénaires, puis des siècles, elle s'est adaptée aux différents systèmes qui se sont succédés; elle a évolué avec eux et orienté leur évolution.[6]

Les solidarités et les hiérarchies qu'elle a commandées se sont perpétuées jusque dans les mouvements politiques contemporains. Elles sont improprement appelées 'féodalités'; mais il faut prendre ce terme pour ce qu'il vaut dans le langage de bois des idéologies, pour ce qu'il tente de désigner: des rassemblements dont la coloration politique actuelle cache des réflexes très anciennement acquis. L'autorité se fonde toujours sur la *'asabiyya*, sur la tendance au regroupement solidaire de la famille, puis de la communauté confessionnelle; elle s'étend sur l'aire occupée par leurs membres. Il n'est que d'observer tant d'exemples d'ascensions politiques et d'attitudes publiques dans le Liban du vingtième siècle.

Qu'il y ait aussi des différences, c'est certain. Mais elles se complètent, comme les strates d'une même histoire. Les réactions des notables sunnites ou grecs-orthodoxes de vieilles souches n'épousent pas nécessairement les mêmes contours que les ambitions d'hommes politiques maronites dont le rôle est plus récent. Les uns véhiculent les souvenirs d'anciennes fidélités impériales; les autres perpétuent, ou rappellent, les moeurs d'une société montagnarde cloisonnée.

Passant à Beyrouth à la fin de mai 1987, j'ai revu un de ces sunnites éminents qui est né au début de notre siècle et qui en garde la distinction. Au cours de l'entretien, il a suivi mon regard sur les impacts de balle dont les combats du mois de février précédent, à Beyrouth-Ouest, avaient constellé les murs de sa maison. Il a soupiré: 'Du temps de l'Empire ottoman, on ne se battait pas comme ça!' Boutade? Sa nostalgie témoigne de sa volonté de rétablir un Etat multicommunautaire qui doit exister pour tous, quelles que soient leurs origines confessionnelles.

Mais pour faire carrière politique au Liban, il a fallu choisir ses alliances et ses clientèles, autrement dit ses opportunités solidaires. Camille Chamoun, décédé récemment, venait d'une famille modeste, n'ayant qu'un rayonnement très faible; il a donc pris pour assise sa communauté confessionnelle afin de donner à ses ambitions des dimensions suffisamment larges. Muni de cette référence, il s'est allié, au lendemain de la seconde guerre mondiale, au druze Kamal Jumblat et au grec-orthodoxe Ghassan Tuéni. Devenu un des leaders maronites, il a été élu président de la République en 1952. Il est possible qu'il ait contribué à affaiblir ensuite sa propre position en laissant Kamal Jumblat et Ghassan Tuéni subir un échec aux élections législatives de 1957.[7]

D'autres ont attaché le destin de leur famille à un renouvellement social à l'intérieur de catégories communautaires. Les maronites et les chiites ont, par exemple, connu de telles expériences grâce à la force montante des cadres moyens qui désiraient participer au pouvoir politique, économique, universitaire . . . Leurs revendications ont été exposées dans le programme de partis qui se sont réclamés d'idéologies modernes, inspirées ou provoquées par des modèles occidentaux. Toutefois, l'action de ces mouvements n'est devenue efficace que lorsqu'elle a été prise en main par quelques familles (une même constation peut être faite en Syrie avec laquelle un parallélisme structural n'est pas difficile à établir). Dans le cas des phalangistes, les Gemayel ont imposé leur rôle en utilisant un cadre politique nouveau, mais avec tout ce que cela comporte, à l'intérieur de la société libanaise, de ralliements et de fidélité personnelle à une famille, mais aussi de divisions au sein de clans familiaux et confessionnels.

Un titre de cheikh conforte une direction politique aux perspectives novatrices. Un leadership confessionnel se situe par rapport au pouvoir. Les traditions vivantes des élites citadines et des montagnards se sont rencontrées dans l'essor et le renouvellement d'une vie politique très active. L'Etat libanais y a-t-il acquis une réelle consistance depuis sa fondation en 1920? Sa cohérence existe-t-elle dans les actes et surtout dans la conscience des Libanais? Ceux-ci ont-ils le sentiment d'être les vrais citoyens d'un Etat, ou seulement les participants de plusieurs rassemblements solidaires qui aboutissent à faire le Liban?

Il n'est pas indifférent de rappeler des étapes essentielles de l'histoire libanaise contemporaine telles qu'elles ont été symbolisées par quelques dates: 1936, 1943, 1948, 1958 et 1967. En 1936, les négociations franco-libanaises, contrepoint des négociations franco-syriennes, ont confirmé la pérennité de l'Etat libanais. Au nom de l'Islam, Riyad el-Solh, s'y est rallié avec éclat. Le Pacte national de 1943, même s'il a été trop restreint à un dialogue entre maronites et sunnites, a confirmé cette volonté des chrétiens et des musulmans de vivre ensemble. Cependant, la création de l'Etat d'Israël en 1948, en provoquant l'exode de Palestiniens et l'arrivée de nombreux réfugiés au Liban, a mis en cause, à moyen terme, la nouvelle cohésion libanaise. Les Palestiniens ont eu le légitime souci de protéger leur personnalité; ils ont clamé l'existence de leur propre entité, parallèlement à celles dont la conscience se manifestait dans les autres pays arabes, y compris à travers le nationalisme arabe. A partir du Liban, ils ont revendiqué leur territoire qui n'était pas celui du Liban. La guerre de juin 1967 fut pour eux une immense blessure en même temps qu'une grande leçon; après cette défaite arabe, leur présence, justifiée par la tradition d'accueil et de voisinage, s'est doublée d'actions politiques et militaires qui ont aussi eu pour conséquence d'impliquer et d'ébranler les institutions intérieures du Liban et son système libéral.

Les réformes entreprises en 1958, à la suite de l'élection du général Fouad Chehab à la présidence de la République, ont été pourtant décisives pour assurer une meilleure participation des musulmans à la vie de l'Etat libanais, et pour donner à tous les citoyens libanais, à quelque confession qu'ils appartinssent, le sentiment qu'ils avaient bien leur place dans cet Etat. Les efforts qui ont été alors réalisés ont paradoxalement mis en relief une difficulté: la recherche d'un équilibre entre chrétiens et musulmans a contribué à maintenir le pouvoir de notables, notamment en milieu musulman, alors que leurs homologues étaient renversés par de nouvelles équipes dirigeantes dans les pays arabes voisins, comme l'Egypte, la Syrie et l'Irak. Le problème a été posé avec d'autant plus de gravité que la rapide croissance démographique et ses effets—migrations intérieures, urbanisation, émigration—ont autorisé d'autres couches de Libanais, chez les chiites par exemple, à vouloir jouer un rôle actif dans l'essor de la République libanaise.

La société issue de la 'Montagne' libanaise—disons, pour simplifier, d'abord celle des druzes et des maronites, mais incompréhensible sans la présence des sunnites et des autres communautés—a légué quelques comportements déterminants à la vie politique, constitutionnelle et administrative; elle n'est pourtant pas parvenue à s'accomplir au niveau d'une nouvelle élaboration gouvernementale et civique. Les ruptures démographiques, économiques et technologiques, dont les conséquences ont été fondamentales, ont souligné ce phénomène. La convivialité libanaise se grippe en 1975. Est-ce l'organisation sociale, économique et confessionnelle du pouvoir qui est en cause, ou plus profondément l'Etat? Les autres Etats arabes, construits après la disparition de l'Empire ottoman, se sont renouvelés et affermis en se distinguant bien les uns des autres, mais presque toujours au nom d'un idéal transcendantal qui a été commun à plusieurs d'entre eux en même temps. Dans le Liban 'à visage arabe', pour reprendre la formule de 1943, y a-t-il eu moindre résistance de l'Etat parce que son pluri-confessionnalisme libéral et ses structures familiales ont entraîné une sclérose sociale de la direction politique? Cette grave et épineuse question a été posée des phalangistes aux communistes, des réformistes chehabistes aux islamistes.

Toutefois, qu'on le veuille ou non, il existe une réalité de l'Etat libanais, même dans les parcellisations actuelles des pouvoirs de fait, puisqu'il est internationalement reconnu en droit, et qu'il s'inscrit avec son territoire, ses frontières, son armée et son administration dans la configuration de l'Orient méditerranéen et arabe. Il y marque son originalité par la distribution de son peuplement: près de la moitié de la population libanaise est chrétienne et elle occupe dans le monde arabe, à majorité musulmane, une position qui dépasse cette proportion. La singularité de cette situation doit toujours être présente à l'esprit dans la recherche d'une solution pacifique et juste aux conflits qui déchirent le Liban.

En France, j'ai vu des étudiants libanais chrétiens pleurer de désespoir en disant qu'il n'y a plus d'Etat dans leur pays. Les étudiants musulmans sont aussi bouleversés, minés par l'inquiétude, mais ils ne sont pas hantés par l'angoisse des 'minoritaires'. En fait, l'Etat est là, mais c'est la nature du gouvernement, l'application des lois, l'exercice du pouvoir central, qui sont contestés. La composition pluri-communautaire de la population du Liban, les caractères de sa croissance, ses positions dans les crises secouant le Moyen-Orient depuis 1948 . . . tout a contribué à faire de ce pays un microcosme de l'ensemble des mutations vécues par les peuples de l'Orient arabe, sans qu'il soit allé lui-même jusqu'au bout de ces changements, sinon dans la guerre. D'où son sort si tragique, qui surprend aussi par la vérité des attitudes et le surréalisme des jugements.

Que reste l'Etat dans la conscience des Libanais? L'opinion libanaise manifeste plus que jamais le désir de quelque chose d'autre que les totalitarismes parcellaires et que les interventions 'périphériques' qui se sont substitués à la légalité. Secouant la peur et la lassitude, de nombreuses manifestations en ont témoigné depuis plusieurs années: la journée du drapeau, les réunions professionnelles intercommunautaires, les protestations communes contre les prises d'otages, les émeutes contre la dépréciation de la monnaie et la hausse vertigineuse des prix, les chaînes et les défilés pour la paix . . . Bref, il y a eu un appel à ce qui règle une société par delà les clans familiaux et communautaires, par delà les partis et les factions, par delà les clivages sociaux. Il y a eu, de fait, un appel à l'Etat.

Le consensus n'est plus à espérer, comme jadis, dans la théorie d'une unanimité religieuse, puisque le Liban se définit par sa pluralité. La liberté et l'égalité ne peuvent y être assurées que dans la tolérance et le respect mutuel, en évitant donc que certains soient des protecteurs et d'autres des protégés. Après tant de combats fratricides, c'est de l'Etat que les humiliés attendent la justice et l'ordre. Les Libanais ont-ils fini par éprouver la nécessité de cet Etat sans savoir comment rétablir son autorité? Ont-ils su le situer dans les alliances régionales et internationales?

Si jamais le Liban, Etat internationalement reconnu en droit, venait à être amputé, à être partagé ou même à disparaître, les territoires et les frontières de tous les Etats de la région, quels qu'ils soient, seraient mis en cause. Peut-être que certains incendiaires espèrent réaliser leurs ambitions par cette politique du pire, mais imaginons à quelles nouvelles catastrophes elle aboutirait dans la zone stratégique du Moyen-Orient, et à l'échelle mondiale. Faut-il, en particulier, rappeler que la France et l'Europe sont directement concernées par la paix à l'est et au sud de la Méditerranée, et par conséquent par le rôle et la stabilité que doit retrouver l'Etat libanais.

Petit Etat multi-communautaire, le Liban assume aujourd'hui dans le sang, le deuil quotidien, dans la détresse du peuple, des conflits intérieurs, régionaux et internationaux, qui ne cessent de réagir les uns sur les autres. S'il parvient à les résoudre, s'il rétablit la concorde entre les siens dans le respect des diversités, son exemple permettra de mieux trouver une issue pacifique à d'autres conflits. Sa pluralité sera communicative; elle rayonnera dans les complémentarités régionales comme dans les relations entre l'Orient arabe et l'Europe.[8]

Que les misères qu'endurent les Libanais et que les doutes qui habitent leur coeur donnent encore plus de force à mes paroles d'espoir, celles d'un ami. Malgré les rejets et les exclusivismes identitaires, qui aurait l'audace d'oublier que l'Etat libanais, au cours de bientôt soixante-dix ans d'existence, a non seulement recueilli les diverses formes communautaires d'une culture sociale au passé si lointain, mais a signifié un profond désir de vivre ensemble? Son destin dépend d'une volonté commune.

Notes

1. Cf. Hanna Batatu, *The Old Social Classes and the Revolutionary Movements of Iraq* (Princeton, 1978). Zouhair Ghazzal, *Les Fondements de l'économie politique de Damas durant le XIXème siècle: structures traditionnelles et capitalisme*, thèse de Doctorat, Université de

Paris-Sorbonne (Paris IV), 1986. Dominique Chevallier, *La Société du Mont Liban à l'époque de la révolution industrielle en Europe* (Paris, 1971; 2ème éd. 1982).

2. Edmond Rabbath, *La Formation historique du Liban politique et constitutionnel* (Beyrouth, 1973), pp. 352 et 353. Il est intéressant de comparer les termes de cette proclamation avec ceux que Kamal Jumblat a utilisés quarante ans plus tard. Cf. Chevallier, *La Société du Mont Liban*, p. 22.

3. Antoine Hokayem et Marie-Claude Bittar, *L'Empire ottoman, les Arabes et les grandes puissances, 1914–1920* (Beyrouth, 1981), pp. 354–67.

4. Rabbath, *La Formation historique du Liban*, p. 364. Aristide Briand était alors président du Conseil des ministres, et Henry de Jouvenel venait d'être nommé haut-commissaire de la République française en Syrie et au Liban. Voir aussi: Pierre Fournie, 'L'administration française au Levant (1918–1930)', *Positions des thèses*, Ecole de Chartres (Paris, 1987), pp. 87–94.

5. La rédaction en reste la suivante: 'Article 95 (tel que modifié par la loi constitutionnelle du 9 novembre 1943, article 5). A titre transitoire et dans une intention de justice et de concorde, les communautés seront équitablement représentées dans les emplois publics et dans la composition du ministère, sans que cela puisse cependant nuire au bien de l'Etat.' Cf. Edmond Rabbath, *La Constitution libanaise. Origines, textes et commentaires* (Beyrouth, 1982), p. 517.

6. Voir Chevallier, *La Société du Mont Liban*, ch. VI.

7. Dominique Chevallier, 'Politique et religion dans le Proche-Orient. Une iconographie des maronites du Liban', *Revue d'histoire moderne et contemporaine*, t. X, oct–déc 1963. Camille Chamoun, *Crise au Moyen-Orient* (Paris, 1963). Kamal Jumblat, *Pour le Liban* (Paris, 1978). Ghassan Tuéni, *Une Guerre pour les autres* (Paris, 1985).

8. Voir ce que j'ai déjà écrit à ce sujet: Dominique Chevallier (sous la dir. de), *Renouvellements du monde arabe 1952–1982. Pensées politiques et confrontations internationales* (Paris, 1987), pp. 196–7.

13

The Problem of Authoritative Power in Lebanese Politics
Why Consociationalism Failed

MICHAEL C. HUDSON

Introduction

Few would quarrel with the proposition that Lebanon is a difficult country to govern. Outside rulers—the Turks and the French—found this to be the case, and indigenous leaders from Ma'nid princes to modern-day presidents have had to cope almost continually with crises that threatened the very cohesion of the political order. The reasons, I think, have little to do with political socialization or 'Levantine' personalities; if the Lebanese display a conspicuous cynicism toward their national politicians and institutions, it is learned, not inculcated. I would identify three other important factors.

First, it is clear that Lebanon is a divided society with a fragmented political culture. This means that there are numerous subcommunities whose members are locked in by what Geertz called 'primordial' affiliations: the kind one does not choose to enter and cannot easily escape.[1] These groups have a strong sense of self-identity nurtured by ethnic, sectarian, and kinship bonds. Putting it a little too simply, we could describe Lebanese political culture as marked by strong vertical cleavages. Even the sense of national loyalty expressed by leaders of these communal fragments is not as strong evidence for an integrated *national* community as one might suppose, taking it at face value, because the definition of 'Lebanon' is, to say the least, filtered through a Shi'i, Maronite, or other ideological optic.

The second factor is socio-economic inequity, a product of the inability of the liberal state to rectify growing subjective perceptions of discriminatory performance. It is true, as Harik has shown,[2] that in comparative terms, inequality in Lebanon is less than in many other Third World countries; yet we know not only from the IRFED Report of the 1960s[3] but also from recent events that the neglect of south Lebanon and the Biqa', as well as the slum belt around Beirut, unquestionably facilitated the disintegration of the fragile national consensus.

Thirdly, government in Lebanon is complicated by a history of external interventions. Just as the Turkish period was marked by 'rule by consuls', modern Lebanese politics have been coloured by French, American, Egyptian, Syrian, Israeli, Palestinian, and Iranian 'connections'; and Lebanese elites have been delegitimized in the eyes of important segments by their political, economic, and cultural 'special relations' with outsiders. Certainly, the unsettled regional environment has contributed to Lebanon's vulnerability: in a sense it is one of the last contested battlegrounds in the 'war of Ottoman succession'. The failure, so far, to establish a stable state system in the eastern mediterranean (due in large part to the unsolved Palestine problem) has made Lebanon—a 'power vacuum' for the reasons just described—a virtually irresistible field of competition for neighbouring states whose legitimacy and stability is not yet established.

Lebanon is not just a difficult country to govern; it is also difficult to study. I am not referring to the practical aspect: until the civil war, Lebanon was if anything 'over-studied' because it was so accessible, while now for many of us it is as unapproachable as Chernobyl. What I mean is that the scholars working on Lebanon were for the most part surprised by the collapse and since then have been divided among themselves as to its causes and possible solution. Writing in 1976, Albert Hourani recalled a conference on Lebanon in Chicago in 1963[4] in which the mood was decidedly positive, even euphoric, about Lebanon's success as a stable democracy, and then remarked that 'Anyone who has turned to that book during the last months of civil war in Lebanon, in the hope that it would help him to understand what was happening, must have felt that something had been left out of it.'[5]

For the last 12 years we have argued about whether the causes were primarily external or internal: if internal were they mainly sectarian or socio-economic; if external were the Palestinians, Syrians, or Israelis most to blame? Was confessionalism as a political system a positive bulwark against chaos or actually a cause of it? Was the Lebanese elite skilled at conflict management or, on the contrary, so short-sighted and corrupt that it brought destruction upon itself? Is the best way out the restoration of (strong) central government or devolution into a cantonal system? Any attempt to answer such questions requires some careful thinking, or rethinking, about the nature of power and authority in contemporary Lebanon. In particular, it suggests that we look again at the logic of the 'power sharing' arrangements that so impressed students of Lebanese politics in the 1960s. Some scholars argued that Lebanon's 'traditional liberal pluralism' represented a successful application of an especially interesting form of power sharing known as 'consociational democracy'.

Lebanon's experiment with consociationalism

The term 'consociational democracy', coined by Arendt Lijphart in the late 1960s, denotes 'government by elite cartel designed to turn a democracy with a fragmented political culture into a stable democracy'.[6] Lijphart was unsatisfied by Gabriel Almond's typology of political systems which drew a dichotomous distinction between a culturally homogeneous-majoritarian democratic model, characterized by cross-cutting group affiliations, and a culturally fragmented type conducive to immobilism and even dictatorship. 'Consociational democracy' was presented as a third type, based on the experience of the smaller West European states which seemed to function with reasonable democracy, stability, and efficacy. Lijphart's consociational democracy is defined by four elements:

1. Government by a 'grand coalition'.
2. The mutual veto or 'concurrent majority' rule.
3. Proportionality as the principle of representation.
4. A high degree of autonomy for each segment to run its own internal affairs.[7]

A consociational democracy will work if the following conditions are present:

1. Distinct lines of cleavage.
2. A multiple balance of power.
3. Popular attitudes favourable to a grand coalition.
4. An external threat.
5. Moderate nationalism.
6. Relatively low total load on the system.[8]

The main examples of consociationalism are Austria, the Netherlands, Belgium and Switzerland, but in the Third World Malaysia and Lebanon were also cited by Lijphart and other 'consociationalists'. One of the most intriguing ideas embedded in the consociational approach was the notion of political engineering: man-made formulas and procedures could mitigate the 'blind forces' of society and culture.

Clearly, consociationalism seems like a good prescription for the Lebanese body politic, with its well-known infirmities. But before we prescribe it, we need to ask several questions. First, is consociationalism also a good *description* of the Lebanese system (at least at an earlier time), as Lijphart and other consociationalists suggested? If so, how well did the medicine work, and were there possibly negative side effects that might have helped hasten the political life-threatening disease that now grips the country? If not, then would a strong dose of consociationalism now save the patient? Let us tackle each question in turn.

I am inclined to argue that the Lebanese system was, on the whole, consociational during most of the post-1943 independence era, with the exception of the Shihabist period in the 1960s. [9] The core element of consociationalism—government by grand coalition, or elite cartel—seems clearly present. The 'mutual veto' rule also appears to be operative in a practical if not strictly legal way, given the distribution of high offices among the major sects, and the difficulties which an attempt by Christians to override Muslims (or vice versa) would (and did) create. However, one's view about the presence of this feature will depend on precisely which units or segments had (or should have had) mutual veto powers: for example, perhaps the Sunni establishment could 'veto' a course of action, but could the Shi'is or Druzes? The answers are not clear-cut. As for the proportionality principle, the National Pact and the ingenious construction of the electoral system gave structural impetus for including (or at least not excluding) any sizeable minority. The problem here of course was that the empirical basis for the actual proportions became increasingly less believable. Whatever the deviations of Lebanese reality from the model (and I shall come back to them in a moment), I think that the ghosts of Michel Chiha and other philosophers of the liberal system, were they to study the contemporary consociational democracy theory, would agree with it—in spirit at least.

Now, assuming that the liberal system was essentially consociational, how do we evaluate its importance in explaining Lebanon's 'stable democracy' (or the lack, or lapse, of it)? Clearly, there are two very different dependent variables here. From 'the glass is half full' perspective, the variable is three decades of more or less stable democracy; from 'the glass is half empty' perspective, the thing to be explained is political immobilism and collapse. Looking at Lebanon as a political success story, the conventional wisdom identifies key consociational elements as necessary, though not sufficient, conditions: above all, the elite cartel, mutual veto, and proportionality. The philosophy of Lebanon's founding fathers—that the country's vertical (sectarian) cleavages must be accommodated, at least for some time—is quintessentially consociational. If we can confidently assume that the country would have split apart had there not been this accommodation, then we may be impressed with the potency of the consociational remedy. But how confident are we about that assumption? After all, consociational practices were in full flower just preceding modern Lebanon's two worst breakdowns, in 1958 and 1975. It is possible, of course, that we are just indulging in a *post hoc ergo propter hoc* fallacy, but I am more inclined to suspect that this sequence is a clue to one of the unintended, possibly lethal, side effects of consociational practices. Would the country have split apart after independence had Lebanon adopted a system of majority rule? Would the country have split apart without designating the top three 'presidencies' according to sect? Were the major issues during the liberal republican era resolved by compromises within the 'grand coalition'? Was there a pattern of communal hostility that was managed and mitigated by communal elites reaching accommodations among themselves? I do not believe that the literature on this period establishes these points concretely.

The fact that consociational elements were present during a period of democratic stability does not warrant our assuming that they caused it. One can just as easily entertain contrary interpretations. For example, Brian Barry, a sceptic about the efficacy of consociationalism in general, questions whether the consociational procedures rather than other factors accounted for the democratic stability of the relatively small universe (between two and four cases) of consociational democracies: 'The Duke of Clarence was drowned in a butt of Malmsey, but we should be unwise to deduce therefrom that water would not have been just as effective . . .'[10] Perhaps the absence of political instability was not due to consociational practices but simply to the relative absence of communal antagonism. Indeed, until the mid-1970s, with an occasional exception, Lebanese political turmoil was not basically sectarian. This argument leads one to ask whether the myth of communal antagonism was propagated by a feudal–upper bourgeois elite cartel as a rationale to justify its hegemony. And Barry's comment on the post-second world war Austrian case is instructive: he suggests that general prosperity rather than a consociational model might have accounted for its democratic stability.[11] Could not the same be said for Lebanon? Here, lest I be accused later of trying to have it both ways, let me say that while rising aggregate levels of economic well-being might ease political tensions in general, highly uneven economic growth (as also occurred in Lebanon) could induce perceptions of relative deprivation in certain sectors that could have destabilizing consequences.

To summarize: if Lebanon was, descriptively, essentially consociational during the liberal-republic periods, it has not been clearly established that its consociational devices significantly accounted for such democratic stability as it enjoyed. But, as I argued in *The Precarious Republic*, one can make a case that these devices induced a degree of immobilism that prevented government from dealing with socio-economic and ideological challenges.[12] From this point of view, trying to explain why the glass is half empty, consociationalism is a cause of breakdown and chaos. The elite cartel, bound by its own parochialisms, not only failed to deal with these challenges (in terms of policy) at the mass level but also allowed itself to become deeply divided by them.

At this point, proponents of consociationalism as a prescriptive political palliative for divided societies might well say that this only shows that Lebanon was not really a consociational system after all; and they might go on to argue that if only Lebanon would adopt *true* consociationalism, it might recover and indeed go on to achieve genuine democratic stability. Dekmejian finds the consociational approach relevant to the segmented political cultures in Lebanon and throughout the Middle East: 'once the Middle Eastern states and their modernizing elites outgrow their "beginning of ideology" phase of heightened nationalism, they may well find consociationalism a worthy model to emulate—a model that may better fit their respective segmented "mosaics".'[13] He agrees that Lebanon fits the consociational model in important ways, but he also discerns ways in which Lebanon deviates from it and suggests that these deviations are so significant that 'it is not at all clear as to whether Lebanese consociationalism will survive to witness this new phase of social and political modernity.'[14] Drawing both on Lijphart and Eric Nordlinger's work, [15] Dekmejian discerns the main characteristics of consociationalism to be the following:

1. The elite cartel.
2. Controlled competition.
3. Cohesion in subcultures.
4. A multiple balance of power.
5. Circumscribed state power.
6. System legitimacy and elite effectiveness.
7. Passive electorate and private bargaining.
8. High encapsulation (of segments) and low mobilization.
9. Minimal environmental turbulence.[16]

The most serious deviations from the model, Dekmejian argues, involve the elite cartel: Maronite refusal to cede some of its dominance to the Muslim sects disrupted the elite harmony stipulated in the model; and the limited scope of elite recruitment allowed horizontal class antagonisms to weaken the stipulated elite management of masses within each segment. He also suggests that the period of Lebanon's experience with consociationalism was relatively short, compared to the European cases; that the state lacked sufficient coercive control (an important point); and that Lebanon's regional environment was highly turbulent, thus contradicting his ninth condition.

Paul Salem goes even further, arguing that in the past Lebanon's political system was not really consociational at all but 'presidential', and that the concentration of power in the presidency was destabilizing.[17] He recommends a 'genuine' consociational solution for Lebanon whose key features would be territorial autonomy for the major segments, a collegial (and weakened) presidency, a wider scope for local government, and the strengthening of elites through strong (probably sectarian) parties with real power in their respective areas.

An evaluation of Lebanese consociationalism

Perhaps most students of Lebanese politics would agree that the founders of the liberal republic wrote a *prescription* for a kind of 'consociational engineering'. A realistic *description* reveals some important deviations from the model—but not enough, in my view, to justify claiming that Lebanon did not actually undergo a consociational 'experiment'. Be that as it may, one should ask why the deviations occurred. Were they just miscalculations in the prescription, correctable by some institutional tinkering? Or were they the result of deep socio-cultural forces?

The importance of this question is obvious: if the consociational medicine was, in reality, only a political placebo, then it has yet to be tested on this patient; or, if the past dosage was insufficient, then there might be a case for prescribing a stronger one. This, I take it, is the view of moderate pro-consociationalists like Dekmejian or enthusiastic ones like Salem. However, one could also argue that the deviations show that the necessary and sufficient conditions for consociational democracy did not exist, whatever the constitutional doctors might prescribe; or, worse, that the consociational prescription actually exacerbated instability and fostered the eventual breakdown. In this case, to advocate even purer consociational devices would be as sensible as increasing the dosage of penicillin to a patient whom we now realize is allergic to the substance.

The most fundamental deviations from the model are to be found in the elite cartel or 'grand coalition'. One objection is that not all of the significant segments were properly represented in the coalition; Shi'is, for example, were possibly only 'junior partners'. A second difficulty is that sectarian communities were not always internally cohesive: there were often deep intra-sect divisions on both the elite and mass levels. Another anomaly, perhaps, is that the stipulated accommodation between elite segments broke down often enough to make some observers conclude that the 'coalition' was more apparent than real. Elite longevity and continuity (which certainly existed) was not the same as elite co-operation; and one can look at a variety of issues, especially in foreign policy, over the years which brought the dominant Maronites into severe conflict with the non-Christian elites. A further deviation involves vertical linkages within segments between elites and followers. 'Counter-elites' sprang up, usually with a leftist, Arab nationalist or extreme religious ideology, both within and across sectarian segments. Elites could not control their 'flocks'. Another related deviancy was disrespect for the state, which often lacked authority as well as coercive capabilities.

The dynamic behind all of these deviancies was social change and domestic turmoil. Increasingly, the uneasy (elite) agreement on the key question of the *distribution* of power among sects within the elite cartel came to be challenged both on the elite and mass levels, and consociational democracy theory does not provide a means for establishing or modifying it. Furthermore, Lebanese society was becoming mobilized behind a variety of political identities and ideologies other than sect. Members of the elites were not immune to these currents, and so conflict broke out at the elite level, within as well as between sectarian communities. The resulting deadlock and immobilism prevented the Lebanese government from undertaking reforms that might have mitigated the rising tensions. If the 'immobilism' argument is valid, however, the argument also made by proponents of the 'consociationalism has never been tried' school, to the effect that Lebanon suffered from an authoritarian 'presidential' system, seems anomalous: even the strongest president—Shihab —could not prevail over Lebanon's traditional pluralism.

An important 'external' deviancy was regional turmoil: according to consociational theory there should either be a common external threat that would tend to unite fractious communities or else 'low environmental turbulence'. But Lebanon's regional environment was neither calm nor binding in its domestic ramifications. How could a fragile, fractious coalition of notables, representative (in a flawed way) of sects but in terms of their social class position and interests not very representative of changing Lebanese society, steer Lebanon firmly through the shoals of regional politics?

These 'deviations' do not show that consociationalism has never been tried in Lebanon, and they do not argue for 'giving it a chance'. Certainly the major sects, including the Shi'is, were built into the grand coalition formula. If intra-sectarian cleavages were important, then either the usage of sects as 'pillars' of Lebanon's consociational system was inappropriate—though nobody would deny that such usage was fundamental to the Lebanese formula—or else Lebanon's sectarian elites were inadequate for the leadership task thrust upon them by the system. However much intra-elite quarrelling there may have been, few would argue that the identity or stability of the ruling elite coalition was in question. If the elites had increasing difficulty controlling their 'flocks', which is true, this fact cannot be used to deny that the logic of the Lebanese system required sectarian elites to exert discipline over their 'masses'.

What these deviations actually show is that a conscious effort to apply consociationalism failed because changing socio-economic and political conditions and regional tensions would not support it: the elite cartel became increasingly divided, and the exercise of sectarian veto power induced paralysis and increased frustration; the legitimacy of the specific sectarian proportions sank disastrously; non-sectarian actors found themselves severely handicapped in playing 'the game' of Lebanese politics; presidential authoritarian tendencies were checked not only by the cleavages in Lebanese society but also by the weakness of the Lebanese state; and external factors, instead of inducing internal cohesion, actually exacerbated internal divisions. If Lebanese consociationalism had been 'working properly', the Israeli-Palestinian conflict should have induced Lebanese national solidarity instead of its opposite. The logic of the Lebanese system required that the principles of elite cartel, mutual veto, proportionality and all the rest be accepted by the politically relevant strata in Lebanon as legitimate. And they probably were, for the most part, until the late 1950s when two counter-trends set in: first, elements of the traditional elite became increasingly disenchanted with the arrangements; and second, the 'politically relevant strata' in Lebanon began to expand to include previously unmobilized and uninfluential elements, of which the 'disinherited' Shi'is organized by Musa al-Sadr and the organizations forming the Lebanese National Movement were the principal examples. For the Lebanese body politic the medicine of consociationalism was beginning to lose its sedative effect.

We would be spared these convoluted discussions if consociational theory were better specified and if Lebanese realities were less complex. Parsimony, precision, and elegance are the hallmarks of powerful theory. Lijphart is careful to define consociational democracy in terms of only four characteristics: grand coalition, mutual veto, proportionality, and segmental autonomy. But he, and others, then add on a number of 'conditions' (listed above) which are necessary or helpful for consociational-democratic stability; these no doubt add verisimilitude, but the more there are the less powerful and applicable the theory becomes. If, in a descriptive sense, Lebanon had been a complete consociational democracy, and if it had been unambiguously stable over time, then we could simply say that (1) the Lebanese case supports the validity of the model in general and (2) perhaps the case supports the applicability of 'consociational engineering' to similar cases. This is essentially what Lijphart himself concludes about Lebanon up to 1975.[18] But, of course, Lebanon in the liberal republic phase was not perfectly consociational, nor was it—by a long shot —unambiguously stable. So one is left to interpret and argue.

Dekmejian's interpretation is that Lebanon was rather consociational but by the mid-1970s obviously on the edge of disaster; but he is unwilling to ascribe the disaster to the theory. In order to save the theory, he first specifies so many identifying characteristics and conditions (listed above) that he makes it almost uninteresting—but he is only following Lijphart and Nordlinger. It would hardly be surprising that a case embodying all nine of them would indeed be stable (and democratic, in a sense), but it would be hard to find very many in the real world. Then he discovers enough important deviations in the Lebanese case to justify arguing that consociationalism, if applied properly, still might be helpful for bringing stability to Middle Eastern politics, even perhaps to chaotic Lebanon.

I go along with much of Dekmejian's argument, but I am not convinced that consociational democracy, in the sense of prescriptive constitutional engineering, will do much for Lebanon or for other divided societies in the Middle East, though I agree that the problem of primordial identity groups and their representation is a key element in the region's legitimacy problem. Indeed, on the general level, Lijphart is rather cautious about attributing too much power to consociational devices: he concludes his book with a schematic diagram which suggests that the consociational model may prove moderately successful in moderately plural societies (more so than the classical majoritarian model), but that the probability of success declines rapidly in extremely plural societies (though it is still better than in the majoritarian model, which has zero probability of success in such circumstances).[19] Most writers on Lebanon, I believe, would agree that its society is 'extremely plural'. With its several sectarian 'pillars' and the hostilities that have grown between them there are sufficient grounds for questioning the adequacy of a consociational strategy; and this is without even considering the horizontal socio-economic cleavages and several other complicating factors. To me, the Lebanese case shows that consociational devices at best do not have a great deal of potency in building legitimacy and stability. At worst, they may actually have exacerbated divisions and hastened the collapse. One need only look at Fouad Ajami's study of Musa al-Sadr,[20] which depicts the confessional system from a deprived Shi'i perspective as a barrier to justice and 'a share of the pie', a formula cynically manipulated by the 'elite cartel' to cream off the spoils—all of which turns the proclaimed virtues of this system upside down. Is this really a model to emulate, to try again?

The authority problem: power sharing and alternative models

The problem of power sharing, and political participation more broadly, is perhaps the most serious obstacle in the way of achieving political legitimacy in most Third World and Middle Eastern countries. There is no shortage of explanations for the problem: poverty, maldistribution of wealth, the colonial legacy, rapid modernization, divided political culture, and even the 'newness' of political institutions. Weakly legitimized political orders, however, are not necessarily unstable; while political change may be irregular and occasionally violent, most Third World countries display one form or another of authoritarian rule—bureaucratic, populistic, praetorian, or traditional. For a student of Lebanon it is interesting to note that most of these countries do not disintegrate into violence and chaos; even if the power is not shared to the general satisfaction, it at least remains concentrated so that order—even if not legitimate—is more or less preserved. But in a few countries (and not only in the Third World) even these authoritarian 'solutions' do not work, either to establish legitimacy or stability.

Lebanon is, perhaps, a textbook case (but mercifully rare) of a near-total collapse of a country's political order. In Lebanon there was, if you will, a double failure: first, a failure to achieve even rough authoritarian stability in line with the general Third World model; and second, a failure to maintain a *legitimate* power-sharing order. In the absence of a sufficient *concentration* of power—in the state and regime—the legitimacy of the *distribution* of power does become a necessary condition of political stability. If the 'traditional liberal system' (1943–58 and 1970–5) constituted a 'power sharing' model, the Shihabist era (1958–70) constituted a 'strong state' alternative. Both models failed. Lacking both an effective concentration and a legitimate distribution of power, the Lebanese political system over the past decade has evolved in terms of a third model, neither statist nor consociational, which we might dub the 'non-state model', and whose motto might well be *e uno plura*.

Lebanon's unhappy experience with consociationalism raises the larger question of the efficacy of 'power sharing' formulas for deeply divided societies. Power sharing refers to formulas, mechanisms, devices, processes. Who governs and how absolutely? What are the units of representation? Are certain districts and communities guaranteed representation? One goes back to the Aristotelian typology; one looks at doctrines of separation of powers, federalism, confederalism, and cantonal schemes. One studies electoral systems. In authoritarian political systems—such as most of those in the Middle East—power is not shared very much at all, and when it is, it is shared among a small circle. In deeply divided societies, the problems of power sharing are especially acute. As we have seen, the 'consociational solution', whereby fixed shares of power are allotted to separate communities, whose elites then conduct political activity jointly, seemed to address the problem of developing authoritative power in the fragmented political cultures of the Levant rather nicely. Unfortunately, however, several of the successor states to the Ottoman empire in the Levant display a tendency towards authoritarianism (both bureaucratic and patriarchal) as well as being deeply divided. Regimes which are often identified with an ethnic, sectarian or tribal minority or dynasty, seize control of the state apparatus and use it to thwart power sharing. In such environments the need for power sharing is as obvious as the obstacles to achieving it. The question arises: in such circumstances can power-sharing formulas work in the absence of a strong state? The Lebanese case suggests that the answer is an emphatic *no*. But can they work in the presence of a strong state? The examples of Lebanon's Arab neighbours also suggest a negative answer.

Power-sharing formulas would appear to have a chance only where the state is not only strong but also is, and can remain, autonomous; for when it becomes more or less indefinitely the instrument of only a particular segment, class, stratum or interest it cannot acquire the legitimacy necessary to regulate intersocietal tensions and conflicts. Classical Marxists denied the autonomy of the state; neo-Marxists[21] and non-Marxist political economists[22] allow for the possibility, at least occasionally; and liberal pluralists (for whom the state is essentially a kind of neutral market-place of ideas and interests) assume that, collectively, satisfactory outcomes over time (win some, lose some) will reveal (or create) an underlying harmony. Unless and until society in the Middle Eastern countries takes on more 'civic' characteristics and a certain autonomy of its own *vis-à-vis* both its own particularistic segments and also the state, it is hard to be optimistic about the prospects for power-sharing formulas.

While a number of factors contributed to Lebanon's disaster, one that needs more consideration and which may help explain the magnitude of that disaster is the weakness of the Lebanese state. This would seem to be an unremarkable, even trivial, proposition were it not for the resurgence of interest among social scientists in what some see as the 'neglected' concept of the state.[23] Students of the Middle East have also shown new interest in the state.[24] Some have attached great importance to the growth of the state from the 1950s to the

1970s. Now some are talking about the retreat of the state and an associated new crisis of legitimacy. Scholars of Lebanon are divided as to the strength and significance of the Lebanese state: Harik, for example, imputes historical durability and meaning to the Lebanese state[25] while more sceptical observers have expressed doubts about its strength either on symbolic or bureaucratic-structural grounds. Without making the mistake of reifying or romanticizing the term, we nevertheless should take another look at the Lebanese state within the Lebanese socio-cultural and regional contexts.

What happens when neither the power-sharing (consociational) nor hegemonic etatist (authoritarian) models work? In Lebanon, as we know all too well, the irresistible forces of social change, political protest and ideological ferment collided with the immovable object of a confessional-consociational constitution, and since the state lacked sufficient authority and coercive power, a Hobbesian nightmare of chaos broke out. A different kind of logic, a certain dog-eat-dog rationality, an environment of worst-case expectations and self-confirming prophecy came to drive Lebanese political behaviour. The law of the jungle and the rules of classical international politics were used to describe and explain political behaviour. Thus, a new model emerges: what Waltz calls the 'self-help' system, in which autonomous actors pursue their security and other interests in an environment of anarchy, uncertainty, and danger.[26] This model is distinguished from the other two by the absence of a state, in the Weberian sense, with its monopoly of force and the rule of law. Of course, the application of an 'international politics' model to Lebanon is not really 'new'—I made the analogy myself years ago, as did others, and we applied it to Lebanon of the 'good old days'. With the hindsight of the last 12 years of violence, however, we can now appreciate what genuine anarchy really is; from today's perspective Lebanon of the liberal (consociational) period possessed more 'stateness' than some of us thought at the time.

The Lebanese political system since 1975 has taken on fairly regular and stable characteristics. To be sure, it is a comparatively 'decadent' system inasmuch as it displays high levels of violence and low levels of policy performance, which have led to a near-catastrophic decline in the quality of life. Nevertheless, one can argue that it is a distinctive system and not necessarily a transition phase or purely formless behaviour. In a nutshell, effective power has now devolved from the state and regime to several authoritarian communities structured around militias. While not completely demarcated in terms of territory, the major groupings clearly possess their own 'turf'. Two external powers—Israel and Syria—also possess turf and play both direct and proxy roles. It makes sense to analyse the main players in the Lebanese 'game' as if they were states, with security interests, foreign policies, and alliances. Yet we know that the Lebanese situation is not purely analogous to an international model, even if it is much more so now than it was during the liberal period. This being the case, the work being done at the international level now on 'co-operation under anarchy'[27] and 'international regimes' [28] might prove fruitful in application to 'non-state Lebanon', particularly with respect to the following question: if this third model is likely to endure, then what can be done to reduce conflict and induce some measure of co-operative behaviour among the several 'sovereign' actors?

It would be interesting for students of deeply divided societies to take a fresh look at the political transformation of Lebanon by examining these three models of government that have emerged since independence: the traditional-liberal model, 1943–58 and 1970–5; the Shihabist strong-state model, 1958–70; and the non-state model, which has been taking form since 1975 and, I suspect, will be with us for a long time to come. And it might prove fruitful to do so in terms of three bodies of evolving political theory: the 'consociational democracy' approach, the 'bring the state back in' approach, and the 'co-operation under anarchy' approach of some neo-realist and functionalist theorists of international relations.

Lebanon's future and the need for a new model

The rate for the Lebanese pound to the US dollar in spring 1988 is about 368; stocks of basic commodities are dwindling; and the news reports from Lebanon offer no immediate or even distant hope of improvement. Little wonder that we look with a certain nostalgia at the Lebanon of the liberal-traditional and statist periods. The present degradation of Lebanese politics seems to reveal a perverse dialectic: Shihabism was generated as the antithesis to a poorly legitimized and clumsily executed elite consociationalism, but the reaction to a similarly clumsy experiment in *étatisme* was not, unfortunately, the synthesis of power sharing and power concentration that ideally is what Lebanon needs but rather a crude perversion—a caricature—of the old consociational model.

My intention in this paper has not been to discredit power-sharing approaches in general or the consociational model in particular, but only to indicate their limitations. As Theodor Hanf remarked in the 1987 Oxford conference on Lebanon, 'Consociationalism is a fair-weather model'—perhaps more successful in contemporary Austria or Switzerland than in Lebanon. The liberal system in Lebanon proved ultimately to be worse than 'precarious', but we should also remember that it had several constructive features. For a time, it probably did soften, or at least postpone, sectarian hostilities. Moreover, there were indications that, like a butterfly trying to emerge from its cocoon, the system might develop beyond its consociational framework toward a more genuinely democratic model. The electoral system, for example, did seem to become more representative and effective with time, and sectarian stereotypes seemed to be receding. There was considerable latitude for political expression and organization on a non-sectarian basis, even though the traditional elite generally succeeded in keeping 'radical outsiders' at bay. The 1958 crisis forced a substantial reorientation of the system in the direction of building a state apparatus and executive that would come to terms with the immobilism that gripped domestic affairs and the erratic swings in foreign policy orientation occasioned by sectarian and ideological polarities. The Shihabist experiment came close to success, but while it may have made progress in developing the apparatus of the state, it seems not to have fared so well in inculcating a general sense of its moral worth—it could not elicit the legitimacy from enough key elite and mass constituencies to re-establish a more liberal and participatory order. Instead, the resurgence of the parochial, traditional elitism in the Frangieh period and the subsequent civil war brought about the 'non-state model', a caricature of consociational democracy in that there was not the accommodative intra-elite behaviour or the elite–mass discipline that defines consociationalism, nor was there the practice of representation, participation, and accountability that is required for democracy, either between or within communal segments.

If a consociational model requires a 'withered state' [29] in order to perform its basic function of lubricating communal relations, and yet if a strong state is essential to provide the security that consociational devices are supposed to deliver for communal segments (not to mention the development and equity for society as a whole), then the positive synthesis is impossible to achieve and Lebanon's dilemma is inescapable. But is the incompatibility actually this absolute? Perhaps after further analysis of the Shihabist experiment and its failure, some ingenious political doctor will discover or invent a fourth model that will provide both the distribution and concentration of power that a deeply divided society like Lebanon's requires for legitimate, stable government.

Notes

1. C. Geertz, 'The integrative revolution: primordial sentiments and civil politics in the new states', in Geertz ed., *The Interpretation of Cultures* (New York, 1973), pp. 255–310.

2. I. Harik, 'Lebanon: anatomy of conflict', *American Universities Field Staff Reports*, no. 49.

3. Republique libanaise, Ministère du Plan, Mission IRFED, *Besoins et Possibilités de Développement du Liban*, 2 vols (1960–1).

4. Published as *Politics in Lebanon*, ed. L. Binder (New York, 1966).

5. A. Hourani, 'Ideologies of the mountain and the city', in R. Owen ed., *Essays on the Crisis in Lebanon* (London, 1976), p. 33.

6. A. Lijphart, 'Typologies of democratic systems', *Comparative Political Studies*, 1.1 (1969) 3–44.

7. A. Lijphart, *Democracy in Plural Societies* (New Haven, Conn., 1977), p. 25.

8. A. Lijphart, 'Typologies of democratic systems', pp. 25–30.

9. For an extended discussion of this point, see M. C. Hudson, 'The Lebanese crisis and the limits of consociational democracy', *Journal of Palestine Studies* 5.3/4 (1976) 109–22.

10. B. Barry, 'Political accommodation and consociational democracy', *British Journal of Political Science* 5.4 (1975) 492.

11. Ibid. pp. 495–6.

12. M. C. Hudson, *The Precarious Republic: Political Modernization in Lebanon* (New York, 1968, repr. Boulder, Col., 1985), pp. 87–105, 325–31.

13. R. H. Dekmejian, 'Consociational democracy in crisis: the case of Lebanon', *Comparative Politics* 10.2 (1978) 251–66.

14. Ibid. p. 264.

15. E. A. Nordlinger, *Conflict Resolution in Divided Societies* (Cambridge, Mass., 1972).

16. Dekmejian, 'Consociational democracy in crisis', pp. 253–8.

17. P. Salem, 'The political framework for a stable Lebanon' [revised version of a paper published in *Panorama of Events* (Beirut)] (1984).

18. Lijphart, *Democracy in Plural Societies*, pp. 147–50, 180.

19. Ibid. pp. 237–8.

20. F. Ajami, *The Vanished Imam: Musa al Sadr and the Shia of Lebanon* (New York, 1986).

21. See H. Alavi, 'The state in postcolonial societies: Pakistan and Bangladesh', *New Left Review* 74 (July–August 1982) 59–82.

22. For example see J. Waterbury, *The Egypt of Nasser and Sadat* (Princeton, NJ, 1983).

23. See T. Skocpol, 'Bringing the state back in: strategies of analysis in current research', in P. Evans, D. Rueschmeyer and T. Skocpol eds, *Bringing the State Back In* (Cambridge and New York, 1985), pp. 4–37.

24. See L. Anderson, 'The state in the Middle East and North Africa', *Comparative Politics* (1987) 1–18; G. Ben-Dor, *State and Conflict in the Middle East: Emergence of the Postcolonial State* (New York, 1983); E. Ozbudun, 'Modernization of political structures: the Ottoman empire and its successor states', typescript, Ankara University (1986); and Waterbury, *The Egypt of Nasser and Sadat*.

25. I. Harik, 'The origins of the Arab state system', paper prepared for conference on 'Nation, State and Integration in the Arab World' (Greece, 1984).

26. K. N. Waltz, *Theory of International Politics* (Reading, Mass., 1979), p. 91 and ch. 6.

27. See for example, *World Politics* 38.1 (1985), a special issue on 'Cooperation Under Anarchy', esp. K. A. Oye, 'Explaining cooperation under anarchy: hypotheses and strategies', pp. 1–24; and R. Axelrod and R. O. Keohane, 'Achieving cooperation under anarchy: strategies and institutions', pp. 226–54.

28. See S. D. Krasner ed., *International Regimes* (New York, 1983).

29. M. Kerr, 'Political decision-making in a confessional democracy', in L. Binder ed., *Politics in Lebanon*, pp. 187–91.

14

Partage du pouvoir
Dilemme et perspectives d'évolution: le cas du Liban

ANTOINE N. MESSARRA

The Lebanese case sheds a fundamental theoretical light on the *proporz*, or the proportionality rule, and its application modalities in power-sharing systems.

A rigid application of the proporz can comprise four principal risks: (1) it classifies citizens; (2) it violates the principle of equal opportunity; (3) it overloads the administration with useless offices designed to ensure equilibrium of the communities rather than efficiency; (4) it paralyses the decision-making process because simple majority is not enough to reach a decision.

The three presidential posts in Lebanon, that of the republic, that of the government and that of the parliament, are not equivalent as to their nature, their powers, their functions, and not at all as to their symbolism. To try ingenuously to make them equal, even with compensatory techniques, would be to square the circle. The three posts are not equivalent and cannot be so in a political system which is well managed according to the elementary principles of functional differentiation.

A multiple balance system, such as the Lebanese one, is required to choose from three options: a ceiling system (*suquf*) with certain offices permanently secured to particular communities; a mille-feuille system (*mushabbak* or *muhasasa*) with a superposition of additional offices; an open proporz system with organized or semi-organized alternation and regulation mechanisms.

The rule of the proporz can evolve in five directions: its application at the global level; its application at the decision-making level, excluding offices of high technicity; the adoption of temporized proporz, by alternation or rotation; the suppression of the rule in particular communities; the determination of a quota open to all without consideration of community.

An egalitarian strategy of parity implies a national and evolutionist vision of the system, so that no one community may hold the biggest share.

We can, according to the Lebanese institutional debate, distinguish three compensatory mechanisms: an open compensation by rotation, or alternance, organized or semi-organized; compensation by attribution (an option which is refused by the Maronite political leadership as regards the first presidency); compensation by superposition, i.e. by the creation of additional offices.

The over-confessionalization of the three presidencies puts at risk the rebuilding of the state as a neutral space or bridge over which all citizens and all communities may pass.

Le principe de majorité, dont il faut rétablir la signification par un retour aux écrits des philosophes et théoriciens de la démocratie, n'est pas une notion arithmétique, mais se situe sur une chaîne de participation, allant de la liberté d'expression, au droit de vote, à la constitution de groupements politiques, à la participation aux ressources collectives et jusqu'à la présence effective dans les rouages de l'état et les apparcils décisionnels.

Si le système concurrentiel assure la participation, c'est grâce à la chance d'alternance qu'a la minorité politique exclue du pouvoir de devenir majoritaire par un retournement de l'opinion et grâce au processus électoral. Pour éviter l'exclusion permanente et assurer la participation politique dans les systèmes consociatifs, de concordance, de proporzdémocratie ou, dans une perspective plus large, consensuels,[1] les moyens institutionnels consistent notamment en l'adoption de systèmes électoraux proportionnels, la formation coutumière de cabinets de coalition ou en l'affectation, suivant des règles formelles ou des pratiques coutumières, d'un quota de représentation au sein des organisations gouvernementales ou de certaines d'entre elles, ce qu'on appelle *proporz* ou proporzdémocratie.[2]

La proporz, qui est un système de *partage garanti* du pouvoir (*power-sharing*) est appliquée en vertu d'un texte constitutionnel ou par coutume dans plus de trente pays, dont la Suisse, la Belgique, l'Autriche, les Pays-Bas, le Canada, la Malaisie, la Colombie, Chypre (en vertu de la Constitution de 1960), la Tchécoslovaquie, l'Inde, la Viêt-Nam, la Nouvelle-Zélande, les Iles Fidji, le Sri Lanka, le Zimbabwe (jusqu'à septembre 1987), l'Ile Maurice, partiellement en Afrique du Sud, et même aux Etats-Unis d'Amérique dans la haute cour.[3] Le modèle de la proporz assure l'égalité et parfois la sur-représentaion de la minorité, afin de procurer protection et sécurité accrues aux petits segments. Dans certains cas, la représentation n'est pas porportionnelle au nombre ou à la masse du groupe, mais est fixée d'avance relativement à un équilibre politique. Aussi certains groupes se verront-ils accorder un nombre de représentants plus large que celui d'un groupe numériquement supérieur, comme en Belgique. On explique cette pratique par le fait que les sociétés multicommunautaires recherchent leur équilibre dans une égalité politique entre les groupes malgré la différence numérique.

Comment partager cependant, face à des revendications communautaires et suivant les règles et les contraintes de la proporz? Pour répondre à cette question, d'après le cas libanais, il faut éviter, du moins dans un but méthodologique, de lier le problème théorique et empirique que nous soulevons ici avec les guerres (au pluriel) au Liban depuis 1975. Dire que le système de la proporzdémocratie a échoué au Liban et, à partir de cete affirmation, conclure à l'échec inéluctable de la proporzdémocratie, c'est présupposer que les systèmes exclusive-ment concurrentiels bénéficient d'une valeur normative, à la fois générale et absolue. Or tout système politique contient les germes de sa propre corruption à défaut de mécanismes permanents de contrôle et de régulation.

Une problématique de l'égalité

Tout système politique risque de réserver ses faveurs à une élite à défaut de contrepoids qui en assurent le contrôle et la régulation. 'Allons enfants de la fratrie', titrait le journal *le Monde* à propos de l'élite dirigeante française.[4] Une application rigide de la proporz peut comporter quatre principaux risques: elle classifie les citoyens, porte atteinte à l'égalité des chances devant les emplois publics, surcharge l'administration de postes inutiles destinés à assurer moins l'efficience que l'équilibre communautaire, et paralyse la décision puisque la majorité simple ne suffit pas à faire aboutir une décision. Le Liban n'a pas cependant le monopole des inconvénients de la règle de participation. Dans la ville de Moutier, située dans le nouveau canton du Jura, séparé de Berne, ville dont la population est mi-catholique, mi-protestante, on voulait nommer une infirmière. Finalement, on en a désigné deux pour l'équilibre communautaire.[5]

Le grand risque d'un système de proporz rigide est dc développer une perception inégalitaire. Cette perception, quand elle est politisée et entretenue par une idéologie de la supériorité ou de la pureté de l'allégeance, est génératrice de conflit. Aucun Noir n'a accédé jusqu'à présent à la présidence des Etats-Unis et aucune femme n'a encore été élue présidente de la République en France, mais l'absence de toute disposition juridique ou coutumière formelle fait que tous les citoyens se perçoivent égaux en droit dans la compétition politique. Aucune femme au Liban n'a accédé jusqu'à présent à un poste ministériel bien qu'il n'y ait aucune disposition juridique et aucune règle coutumière qui empêche cet accès. Au cas où une règle juridique est instituée pour empêcher les femmes de détenir un portefeuille ministériel, des mouvements féministes de revendications se formeront pour réclamer alors le 'droit' à l'égalité. L'égalité réclamée est souvent une égalité en dignité, expression de l'appartenance à une même citoyenneté. Heribert Adam parle de '*self-esteem*' (estime de soi) qu'il faut cultiver chez les divers groupes dans les sociétés segmentées ou multicom-munautaires.[6]

Une proporz rigide où des postes déterminés sont en *permanence* et comme *de droit* accordés à des communautés données ne peut être qu'un règlement provisoire, parce que, avec le temps, il favorise la politisation des clivages et suscite chez les citoyens des autres communautés des perceptions inégalitaires. A un colloque franco-libanais organisé sous les auspices du Sénat français, le 12 février 1987, Marwan Hamadé, journaliste et ancien ministre, pose clairement le problème au moyen d'un exemple concret, le sien: 'Je suis druze, druze de père, catholique de mère, marié à une sunnite, et j'ai un beau-frère et des neveux orthodoxes. Savez-vous que dans cette famille chacun de nous, tout libanais qu'il soit, ne bénéficie pas aux yeux de la loi des mêmes droits civiques . . . Face aux exégètes du pluralisme, je dirai que notre projet, pour sauver le Liban, n'est pas de consacrer la différence, mais d'établir l'égalité.'[7]

Deux exemples significatifs, ceux des Iles Fidji et de la Yougo-slavie, montrent l'acuïté de la revendication d'égalité dans les systèmes fondés sur la proporz. Un Fidjien d'origine indienne déclare: 'Je suis un immigré de troisième génération. Je n'ai aucun lien particulier avec l'Inde, je me considère comme Fidjien, et on me propose de demeurer à vie un étranger. La pilule est difficile à avaler.'[8] En Yougoslavie, la collégialité et l'alternance visent à régler le problème de l'égalité entre nationalités. Le système de rotation suscite cependant des perturbations dans la classe politique. Aussi entend-on des propositions tendant au retour à l'élection d'un président de la république pour une période de quatre ans.[9]

Les plafonds, les mille-feuilles ou un système consensuel évolutif et ouvert

L'élaboration d'une théorie de la proporz dépend de trois variables: le nombre des segments dans la société, le degré de mobilité des clivages et les enjeux (postes et ressources) objets de compétition.

Quant au nombre des segments, plus ce nombre est élevé, plus difficile est le partage et d'une manière telle qu'aucun segment ne se trouve ou s'estime lésé. Quand un système de concordance est composé de deux grandes communautés d'une importance numérique presque égale, comme en Belgique, un partage paritaire et un système rotatif peuvent être institués de sorte qu'aucune des deux grandes communautés ne se perçoive d'un rang inférieur. Dans un système composé de deux ou trois communautés d'importance numérique inégale, comme à Chypre et aux Iles Fidji, le partage est plus complexe. Dans un système à balance multiple comme au Liban, composé de 17 communautés officiellement reconnues et toutes minoritaires ou, en pratique, de trois grandes minorités (maronite, sunnite et chiite) et quatre petites minorités (grecque-orthodoxe, grecque-catholique, druze et arménienne), le partage se heurte au maximum d'écueils: risques d'inégalité, de morcellement du pouvoir, de blocage de la décision et de rigidité institutionnelle qui irait sans doute à l'encontre de l'évolution sociale et des allégeances entrecroisées (*overlapping memberships*) des citoyens.

Quant au degré de mobilité des clivages, la revendication à plus d'égalité se développe à mesure que les citoyens se sentent plus intégrés dans la société. La revendication des chiites à une part plus grande ou plus juste dans le système est la résultante d'une politique de développement socio-économique et culturel depuis surtout le mandat du président Chehab.[10]

Quant à la troisième variable relative aux enjeux, c'est-à-dire les ressources et les postes à partager, le plus souvent les parts ne sont pas divisibles et équivalentes. Les sièges parlementaires sont considérés comme équivalents les uns aux autres, et par conséquent divisibles sur base de la proporz à travers les différents segments. En Suisse, l'élection d'un gouvernement par le parlement crée une situation analogue en ce sens que les sièges du Bundesrät (conseil fédéral) sont considérés comme équivalents les uns aux autres, et par conséquent divisibles sur la base de la proporz. Mais l'application de la proporz au niveau du gouvernement entraîne de plus grandes difficultés, du fait que les postes gouvernementaux individuels sont considérés comme ayant des valeurs différentes. La plus grande difficulté surgit lorsqu'un seul poste est à remplir, par exemple celui de président. Dans ce cas, on a recours à l'un des deux processus suivants: soit la proporz par alternance ou rotative, que Jürg Steiner appelle 'la proportionnalité dans sa dimension temporelle'[11] ou la proporz par compensation dans le cas où l'inconvénient imposé à un segment peut être compensé par le choix préférentiel qui lui serait donné dans une autre décision. Les inconvénients de la proporz rejaillissent certes au niveau de la décision politique. Dans les décisions relatives aux individus, il est relativement aisé de procéder à un équilibrage. Par contre les problèmes politiques ne sont pas structurés de façon que l'on puisse les réduire à un nombre d'unités considérées comme équivalentes les unes aux autres. Aussi faudra-t-il recourir aux divers processus de négociation avec la participation de tous les groupes.

Les trois présidences au sommet au Liban, celles de la République, du Gouvernement et de la Chambre, ne sont pas égales, quant à leur nature, leur pouvoir, leurs fonctions et surtout leur symbolisme. Chercher à les égaliser de force avec des ingéniosités techniques et compensatoires, c'est la quadrature du cercle. Les trois présidences ne sont pas égales et ne peuvent l'être pour une bonne gestion de la politique suivant les règles élémentaires de la différenciation des fonctions. Aussi, un système à balance multiple, c'est-à-dire composé de sept communautés principales comme au Liban, est affronté à un choix parmi les trois options suivantes d'efficience bien inégale.

Première option: le système des plafonds

Depuis 1943, la règle de la proporz s'est trouvée figée. Cette fixité aurait pu être expliquée par les besoins de la concorde, de l'équilibre ou des garanties démocratiques. Mais une idéologie persistante et structurée justifiait cette pratique par la supériorité numérique, l'antériorité historique ou la pureté de l'allégeance. Des juristes développaient des arguments formels sur les attributions légales de telle ou telle présidence et en assimilant ces attributions à la garantie de l'identité. Il en est découlé des fantasmes psychologiques attachés aux trois présidences ou à certaines d'entre elles et une perception politique collective qu'il s'agit de droits, de privilèges et de garanties sectaires réservés à des communautés de premier rang. Preuve en est que le système électoral libanais accorde 20 sièges au parlement aux sunnites et 19 aux chiites. Il s'agit de rien moins que de marquer une supériorité. Certes, nul ne dira que la Grande-Bretagne enfreint les principes de l'égalité parce que tout Britannique ne peut pas devenir roi d'Angleterre. Mais si nul ne conteste la royauté en Grande-Bretagne, c'est parce que la royauté représente le pont sur lequel passent tous les citoyens et tous les groupes sans exception. Mais nul ne peut accepter l'idéologie d'un sang royal supérieur qui justifie la détention d'une haute fonction. Le summum du système des plafonds serait de consigner dans un texte constitutionnel, en tant que droit reconnu, intangible et inconditionnel, que le chef de l'état est maronite, le chef du gouvernement sunnite et le chef du législatif chiite. Ce serait alors perçu comme un monopole et un droit en faveur d'une communauté, alors qu'il s'agit d'un consensus nécessairement subordonné à la capacité du détenteur à sauvegarder ce consensus et à être un agent d'unité et de concorde.

De multiples raisons, d'ordre consensuel, conjoncturel ou structurel, liées en partie à l'environnement, expliquent des aménagements particuliers au niveau du pouvoir au sommet au Liban, mais un système rigide cristallise une idéologie identitaire de la première présidence préjudiciable à la présidence même et à sa capacité de négociation et d'arbitrage. Une idéologie de la présidence maronite de la république s'est déployée au mépris du bon sens, suscitant les fantasmes, les peurs, ou les frustrations, alors que le président de la république au Liban est loin d'être un monarque absolu.

En vertu de cette idéologie, il ne faudrait plus accepter l'accession à la présidence de la république d'un candidat de compromis—fruit d'un consensus islamo-chrétien—peu représentatif de sa propre communauté et donc forcé, de par son assise même, à être un arbitre neutre ou impartial. C'est l'idéologie du président 'fort' au sens de son appartenance et de sa représentativité communautaire. Or le corollaire d'un consensus sur la communauté du chef de l'état implique une autre conception de la 'force' du président de la république. Le président n'est 'fort' que par le large soutien dont il bénéficie auprès de toutes les communautés. Un président qui ne serait 'fort' qu'auprès de sa communauté est vite bloqué dans son action par le veto du chef du gouvernement. Il cristallise une perception sectaire de la présidence et alimente un sentiment de frustration auprès des autres communautés. L'identification entre présidence maronite et état libanais contient les germes de la remise en question du Pacte national de 1943. Une telle idéologie communautaire, poussée jusqu'à ses extrêmes limites, aboutit à une volonté d'accaparer l'état et, quand une telle démarche ne réussit pas, à usurper l'état. Aucune communauté n'assume exclusivement la responsabilité d'une telle idéologie. Pour rectifier la conception de la force présidentielle, le président Amin Gemayel affirme: 'Un président peut être chrétien, mais pas pour les chrétiens. Il doit faire prévaloir l'intérêt national.'[12] L'idéologie qui identifie le président de la république à sa communauté ou aux communautés chrétiennes s'exprime aussi par l'exigence d'une '*entente absolue et permanente* avec la présidence de la République et l'instauration de processus de négociation *continus et permanents*' entre lui et les forces politiques considérées comme représentatives des communautés chrétiennes.[13] Cette idéologie est en rupture avec toute une tradition politique selon laquelle la force de la première magistrature découle du soutien profond dont elle jouit de la part de toutes les communautés, par la personne même du président, son histoire politique, ses affiliations et sa capacité de négociation et d'arbitrage. Toute autre idéologie de la force présidentielle porte en germe la condamnation de l'affectation de la première présidence à la communauté qui laisse se développer une telle idéologie.

Deuxième option: le système des mille-feuilles

Le système de la proporz se trouve dans différents projets envisagés depuis 1976 au Liban poussé jusqu'à ses extrêmes limites. C'est comme le gâteau mille-feuilles mais sans le goût ni la saveur. On superpose des fonctions et des attributions pour une communauté par-ci et une communauté par-là. On rogne des attributions par-ci et des attributions par-là, dans un but compensatoire, pour que les communautés soient satisfaites. On ajoute d'autres feuilles aux mille-feuilles. C'est la *muhasasa* qui effrite l'autorité alors que l'exigence est de la reconstituer et de la renforcer. Cela confessionnalise davantage le système au nom de la déconfessionnalisation, le rigidifie encore plus et crée de nouveaux privilèges. Or, un système à balance multiple a besoin de chefs qui symbolisent l'unité du pays et un pouvoir central politiquement efficient qui freine les appétits d'hégémonie. Pour satisfaire les chiites on va créer des vice-présidences. On se plaignait du bicéphalisme, ce sera alors le multicéphalisme. C'est la proporz mille-feuilles, c'est-à-dire le multicéphalisme et le surplus de fragmentation. Ce multicéphalisme ira en s'accroissant, car la création de postes artificiels et des attributions artificielles peut-il satisfaire toutes les communautés dans un système à balance multiple comme celui du Liban? Pour l'étude de ce processus mille-feuilles, on étudiera le cas du onzième round des négociations libano-syriennes, commencées le 18 janvier 1987 et interrompues le 26 mars, puis reprises le 10 mai et de nouveau interrompues après cette séance, et cela en ce qui concerne l'aspect institutionnel interne du problème libanais.

Les artifices de l'équilibrage ou l'Etat-chrysanthème

Pour équilibrer le système de manière à satisfaire les communautés chiite et druze, les artifices juridiques suivants sont avancés au cours des négociations libano-syriennes:

A. En ce qui concerne le Conseil des ministres et l'équilibrage maronite-sunnite

1. La limitation du vote en Conseil des ministres, à l'exclusion du président maronite de la république (8 mars).[14]
2. La réunion du Conseil des ministres sous la présidence du chef sunnite du gouvernement, avec l'exigence d'une majorité qualifiée pour les décisions (15 février).
3. La distinction entre deux types de Conseils des ministres, celui présidé par le président maronite de la république et qui décide de certaines affaires importantes dont la nature est à déterminer, et celui présidé par le chef sunnite du gouvernement. Des objections ont été formulées à l'encontre de cette proposition: il y a là une source de conflit sur la qualification juridique des projets et sur l'instance habilitée à régler le conflit (15 mars).
4. La réunion du gouvernement sous la forme d'un Conseil de cabinet et sous la présidence du ministre orthodoxe le plus âgé, une fois par semaine. Les projets de décrets sont transmis au président de la république et au chef du gouvernement pour approbation (7 avril).
5. L'élection du chef sunnite du gouvernement par la Chambre, ce qui accroît l'influence du chef chiite de l'Assemblée et réduit l'influence présumée du président maronite de la république dans cette désignation (10 mars).

6. La création de six portefeuilles de ministres d'état pour six grandes communautés (maronite, sunnite, chiite, druze, grecque-catholique et grecque-orthodoxe), la communauté arménienne étant souvent exclue. Ces six ministres d'état forment un conseil qui statue sur les affaires importantes. En cas de conflit, ces affaires sont transmises au Conseil des ministres (3 février).
7. L'équilibrage par les bâtiments grâce à la réunion du Conseil des ministres au Sérail, siège de la présidence sunnite du gouvernement et non pas au Palais de Baabda, siège de la présidence maronite de la république, de sorte que le Conseil des ministres ait un bâtiment indépendant avec des fonctionnaires qui en relèvent directement (2 avril).

B. En ce qui concerne la communauté chiite

8. La création d'une vice-présidence chiite de la république, proposition timidement avancée (18 janvier).
9. L'affectation d'une vice-présidence du gouvernement à la communauté chiite (18 janvier).
10. La prorogation de la durée du mandat du président chiite de la Chambre pour quatre ans afin d'équilibrer par la durée le décalage tel que perçu au niveau des postes et des attributions. Cette proposition s'est heurtée à l'objection que chaque mandat présidentiel a connu en pratique le même chef du législatif.
11. La signature par le président chiite de la Chambre des décrets relatifs à la nomination du chef du gouvernement et à la formation du cabinet. Cette proposition a été critiquée parce qu'elle enfreint le principe de la séparation des pouvoirs exécutif et législatif (8 février).
12. La désignation du président chiite de la Chambre en tant que membre du Conseil supérieur de la Défense (9 février).
13. L'affectation permanente du portefeuille ministériel des Finances à un chiite dont le contreseing est exigé pour la promulgation des lois et décrets co-signés par le président de la république et le chef du gouvernement. Cette proposition aurait été refusée par le ministre chiite, Nabih Berri, qui réclame une participation plus effective au sein du Conseil même des ministres (20 janvier et 9 février).

C. En ce qui concerne la communauté druze

14. La création d'un Sénat dont la présidence est confiée à un druze (17 février).

Le défaut de ces équilibrages et de leurs artifices juridiques est que les risques de blocage se trouvent multipliés par un usage fréquent du veto désormais bien institutionnalisé en faveur de l'un ou l'autre des présidents, vice-présidents ou ministres d'état. En outre, tous ces équilibrages s'inspirent en fait d'une idéologie majoritaire, sous couvert de concordance, puisqu'ils ne prennent en considération pour le partage du pouvoir au sommet que les trois grandes minorités maronite, sunnite et chiite. On ignore par ailleurs les modalités d'aménagement constitutionnel de ces équilibrages hybrides qui bouleversent les catégories et les différenciations connues dans les théories constitutionnelles.

Face aux projets de création de petits royaumes communautaires, les quatre petites minorités (grecque-orthodoxe, grecque-catholique, druze et arménienne), sans être revendicatives et sans nourrir une ambition présidentielle (un ancien ministre qualifie la première présidence de 'cadeau empoisonné' au cas où elle est proposée à sa communauté), expriment le refus à la fois de leur exclusion et de ce fromagisme à outrance ou de cette société par actions. La communauté druze, par la voix de Walid Jumblat, se désintéresse de l'ensemble des négociations institutionnelles: 'Je ne vois pas pourquoi la petite communauté druze n'y aurait pas ses droits. J'ai donc réclamé la création d'un sénat. Ils ne veulent pas, tant pis. Mois je ne me sens pas concerné par cette affaire.'[15] Dans un système à balance multiple livré à une *muhasasa* outrancière, les sept petites minorités sont relativement privilégiées, mais les dix autres s'estiment exclues, sinon fortement lésées. L'étude publiée par le Conseil consultatif de la communauté syro-catholique est la plus explicite sur la notion d'égalité.[16]

On pourrait certes étendre le système mille-feuilles aux dix-sept communautés libanaises, grandes et petites, au moyen de calculs subtils et d'artifices juridiques ingénieux, mais quelle en est la conséquence sur la prise de décision et sur l'efficience du pouvoir? La multiplication des risques de blocage par les vetos et les conflits de compétence et de qualification affaiblit non seulement la fonction du président (maronite) de la république, mais l'ensemble de l'appareil étatique. Il se crée de la sorte un Etat-chrysanthème dont chacun arracherait une poignée de pétales sans se soucier de la fleur elle-même.

Troisième option: une proporz avec quelques mécanismes régulateurs pour éviter les risques d'accaparement ou d'hégémonie et inspirée des exigences du consensus et non par des droits

Un système ouvert de participation n'est pas nouveau au Liban, puisqu'il a été appliqué avant le Pacte national de 1943. Il est aussi appliqué d'une manière coutumière dans les élections municipales, les élections aux conseils des syndicats et des organisations professionnelles, la formation d'associations volontaires, et les conseils d'administration des grandes sociétés. Les Ordres des avocats de Beyrouth et de Tripoli constituent les exemples typiques d'un modèle évolutif de concordance.

Le problème de l'ouverture du système libanais de participation se pose en fait d'une manière aiguë aux communautés musulmanes et druze. Les maronites représentent la plus grande minorité parmi les communautés chrétiennes et le leadership politique maronite, toutes les fois où il est consensuel, n'est ni contesté ni envié par les autres communautés chrétiennes. Mais il n'en est pas de même chez les deux communautés musulmanes et la communauté druze. Les chiites et les sunnites sont deux grandes minorités presque égalitaires, mais la communauté sunnite détient un poste décisionnel alors que les chiites se sentent exclus.[17] Dans la psychologie politique orientale, valoir politiquement, c'est être un chef ou un président au sommet.

Un système fermé et cloisonné de proporz, au lieu d'inciter les segments à la coopération, finit par dresser les communautés les unes contre les autres, car chaque communauté, sûre du poste qu'elle détient, cesse de pratiquer avec les autres communautés une politique qui lui fait gagner du soutien. On en arrive à cette situation paradoxale où le chef de l'état est accusé d'islamisme s'il pratique une politique d'entente, où les conflits intracommunautaires provoquent autant de victimes que les conflits intercommunautaires, et où le chef du gouvernement se trouve en pratique désigné par Dar al-Fatwa. Un système dont la finalité est la participation cesse, en cas de plafonnement impératif, de favoriser la coopération. Le document constitutionnel du 14 février 1976 stipule que 'les trois présidents représentent tous les Libanais'. Mais le dilemme est dans la détermination des processus institutionnels qui permettent de réaliser cette condition et d'éviter que les communautés ne se barricadent dans des postes qui leur sont affectés de façon permanente et impérative.

Cadre d'évolution de la proporz

Quelles sont les perspectives d'évolution de la règle de la proporz? L'article 95 de la Constitution libanaise est d'une souplesse telle qu'il impose par lui-même une évolution dans le cadre de la participation et non en dehors d'elle. Il stipule: 'A titre transitoire et dans une intention de justice et de concorde, les communautés seront équitablement représentées dans les emplois publics et dans la composition du ministère sans que cela puisse cependant nuire au bien de l'Etat.' On peut notamment comparer cet article à l'article 30 de la Constitution indonésienne du 30 septembre 1956 qui parle du 'droit de participer' et à l'article 16 de la Constitution indienne du 26 novembre 1949 qui stipule que 'rien n'empêche l'Etat de prendre des dispositions pour l'affectation de postes administratifs en faveur de toute classe défavorisée de citoyens dont l'Etat estime que leur représentation est insuffisante dans les services de l'administration publique.'

La règle de la proporz ou de participation peut évoluer dans cinq directions:

1. *Application de la règle à l'échelle globale.* Appliquer la règle à l'échelle de toute l'administration, de l'ensemble de l'armée et non à chaque train de nomination ou d'avancement limite les inconvénients à l'encontre des particuliers, tout en assurant l'équilibre souhaité au niveau national. Aux résultats d'un concours administratif, le nombre des admis des communautés chrétiennes peut être plus élevé. A un autre ou d'autres concours, l'équilibre sera rétabli.

2. *Application au niveau décisionnel, à l'exclusion des postes de haute technicité.* La limitation de la règle de participation aux postes décisionnels réduit les inconvénients de la règle. Les postes de haute technicité comme ceux de gouverneur de la Banque du Liban, de magistrat, de professeur d'université . . . ne peuvent être affectés suivant des considérations d'équilibre. De fait, la règle de la proporz est destinée à assurer un équilibre politique aux postes de décision gouvernementale. La détermination de ces postes peut être du ressort du Conseil des ministres.

3. *L'adoption d'un système par alternance ou rotatif.* La proporz dans sa dimension temporelle évite l'accaparement d'un poste par un seul segment et l'identification idéologique entre le poste et la communauté qui le détient. La rotation peut être de trois sortes, écrite ou coutumière, limitée à quelques segments de la société ou ouverte aux principaux segments, préordonnée ou compétitive avec éventuellement des mécanismes régulateurs. L'un de ces mécanismes réside dans l'interdiction de la détention d'un poste par un membre d'une même communauté durant plus de deux mandats successifs.

4. *Suppression partielle de la règle à l'égard des communautés chiite, sunnite et druze.* Si ces communautés veulent réellement la suppression de la règle, cela est possible . . . à leur égard. Les communautés chrétiennes conserveront un quota garanti de 50 pour cent des sièges. Quant aux autres communautés, elles pourraient être régies par un système exclusivement concurrentiel avec ses avantages et ses inconvénients.

5. *Détermination d'un quota ouvert à tous, sans considération communautaire.* Le parlement pourrait comporter dix sièges ou plus, affectés à des représentants sans considération communautaire. Ce procédé corrige les inconvénients du système actuel.[18] La proportion pourrait augmenter avec le temps.

Président arbitre pour tous ou président honoraire?

L'impératif de participation et, en même temps, les risques du plafonnement et des mille-feuilles quant à l'efficience étatique étant reconnus, il s'agit de déterminer les alternatives d'une évolution du système libanais à balance multiple de partage du pouvoir. Quelles sont ces alternatives en ce qui concerne les trois présidences et la première en particulier, la représentation parlementaire et les hauts postes décisionnels?

Un retour à la formule ouverte des trois présidences d'avant 1943 dans laquelle il serait alors possible à un druze d'être chef du gouvernement pourrait être considérée comme, *techniquement*, la formule la plus appropriée permettant d'éviter le plafonnement et les mille-feuilles et, surtout, de maintenir aux trois présidents leurs pleines attributions. Une telle formule où aucune des trois présidences n'est de droit *garantie* à une communauté est à la fois compétitive et coopérative. Elle contraint les leaders de la communauté sunnite à mieux pratiquer une politique d'entente avec les autres com-munautés—au lieu des sommets communautaires isolés—pour qu'ils puissent assurer l'accès à la présidence du gouvernement d'un leader sunnite. Les leaders de la communauté druze, pour accéder à la présidence de la Chambre ou du gouvernement, devront aussi se faire accepter par les autres communautés. L'ouverture, totale ou partielle, des trois premières présidences implique cependant des mécanismes régulateurs afin de contourner le risque d'un retour à la monopoli-sation. L'un des mécanismes régulateurs réside dans l'interdiction que l'une des présidences soit détenue par un membre d'une même communauté durant plus de deux mandats successifs.

La décision d'ouverture, totale ou partielle, avec des mécanismes régulateurs que le président Salim Hoss appelle 'régulateurs consoci-ationnels' (*dhawabit tawafuqiyya*)[19] implique une vision d'ensemble, et non sectaire, du problème de la participation. Un politicien qualifie ainsi la démarche particulariste: 'On se distribue des parts entre maronites, sunnites et chiites en laissant aux autres des restes de droits ou aucun droit significatif.'[20] Une volonté de supériorité, en s'arrogeant le droit de distributeur de parts, se manifeste au cours d'une importante réunion où un leader proclame la position suivante: 'Nous avons accepté la parité islamo- chrétienne et ce n'est pas à nous de trouver une part aux chiites. L'ensemble des chrétiens et l'ensemble des musulmans décideront respectivement du partage convenable.'[21] Aussi la modalité d'ouverture du système au niveau des trois présidences pose-t-elle un nouveau dilemme: est-il égalitaire d'ouvrir le système à l'intérieur de certaines communautés seulement? Ces communautés accepteront-elles d'ailleurs une compétition interne non exigée des autres?

A défaut d'ouverture, c'est-à-dire si la rigidité du Pacte de 1943 est maintenue, on peut envisager deux perspectives: celle d'un président maronite mais avec une remise en question radicale de l'idéologie de la présidence, et celle d'un président maronite mais plutôt honoraire.

La perspective d'un président maronite (ou chrétien), mais au-dessus des communautés et avec une capacité de négociation, d'arbitrage et surtout d'unification, est dans la logique d'un système multicommunautaire où le chef de l'état devrait être comme un roi, comme en Belgique, ni Flamand, ni Wallon, un chef pour toutes les communautés, symbole de l'unité et de la pérennité de la patrie.[22] Pour défendre leur présence et leur participation, les maronites et plus généralement les chrétiens, devraient tabler sur leurs ministres au gouvernement, leurs députés, leurs partis et non s'identifier à la première présidence, acculer la première présidence à s'aligner, à devenir partisane. Il est aussi dans la logique d'un système de concordance que le chef de l'état, même maronite, soit perçu comme en dehors des enjeux du partage du pouvoir comme pour le chef de gouvernement sunnite. Quand l'idéologie dominante considère le chef maronite de l'état comme un enjeu dans le partage du pouvoir et non comme un chef et arbitre pour tous, d'autres communautés s'estiment en droit de réclamer des parts égales alors que le partage du pouvoir doit être axé à d'autres niveaux.

Le président de la république a toujours été la victime d'une perception qui gêne son efficience, sa qualité de chef pour tout le Liban et tous les Libanais. Quand un chef d'état oeuvre avec ténacité pour tout le Liban, il en est qui l'appellent Mohamad . . . Une telle plaisanterie finit par coûter cher à l'autorité de la première présidence et son prestige. C'est alors que d'autres se disent: 'Du moment qu'il est *votre* président, partageons équitablement!'

L'attachement à toutes les attributions du chef de l'état et l'existence d'une tête au sommet de l'état, comme il a été souligné au cours du dixième round des négociations libano-syriennes en mars 1987, implique l'exercice par le président d'une fonction d'arbitrage au-dessus des communautés et un minimum de coopération inter-communautaire, de sorte que les élites de la communauté à laquelle la première présidence est affectée ne se comportent pas comme s'il s'agissait d'un droit ou d'un statut privilégié justifié par des considérations de supériorité, d'antériorité historique ou de pureté de l'allégeance. Tenter d'usurper ou de contester la fonction unificatrice de la présidence maronite et des institutions communautaires officielles de cette communauté, développer une idéologie inégalitaire (en contradiction d'ailleurs avec la réalité constitutionnelle) et se livrer parfois à des conflits armés intracommunautaires compromettent le caractère consensuel de la première présidence.

L'autre perspective d'équilibrage, en fait trop coûteuse, consiste à isoler de facto le président de la république (l'homme de Baabda) et à transférer le pouvoir au Conseil des ministres pour faire du président de la république une sorte de président honoraire. Le système de la présidence honoraire aurait été tenté durant le boycottage par des ministres du Palais de Baabda. Sans doute les raisons de ce boycottage ne sont pas d'origine exclusivement interne. Mais les trois moyens utilisés peuvent se transformer en usage constitutionnel si le processus de réforme des institutions demeure bloqué. Le premier moyen réside dans les 'rencontres ministérielles à l'hippodrome' commencées après l'initiative-programme du 1er août 1986 du chef de l'état et interrompues après le 23 septembre 1986. Le second moyen est celui de la 'réunion ministérielle au Parlement' du 24 avril 1987 sur convocation du président de la chambre. Le troisième moyen, continu, réside dans les 'décrets ambulants' ou le Conseil des ministres par correspondance.

Parité et triple parité

Au niveau de la représentation parlementaire, un système paritaire ou quasi paritaire, ou évoluant vers la parité, avec un pourcentage de sièges sans affectation communautaire et appelé à augmenter éventuellement avec le temps, peut susciter une perception consensuelle (et non 'numérique') du système. Une proporz égalitaire, ouverte et évolutive, ne peut cependant s'accommoder que de la grande circonscription électorale, seule compatible avec l'esprit du collège électoral unique où des candidats de diverses communautés sont élus par des électeurs de diverses communautés.

Dans ce débat sur l'inégalité, c'est la parité (*munasafa*) entre musulmans et chrétiens au parlement au lieu de la proportion en vigueur de cinq musulmans sur six chrétiens, qui est préconisée. On propose aussi la triple parité (*muthalatha*), c'est-à-dire l'égalité de représentation au parlement entre les trois grandes minorités maronite, sunnite et chiite, au lieu de la représentation en vigueur, respectivement de 30, 20 et 19 députés. La parité semble inévitable, mais la *muthalatha* est contestée. On voudrait que le partage inter-rites se fasse à l'intérieur de chacune des deux grandes communautés musulmane et chrétienne, et par un consensus à l'intérieur de chacune de ces communautés. Or une parité ou quasi parité peut aussi être instituée entre les quatre petites communautés grecque-orthodoxe, grecque-catholique, arménienne et druze. Cela implique une vision nationale et évolutive d'ensemble sans qu'un segment ne s'attribue une droit supérieur de 'partageur'.

'Acceptons la parité en attendant d'avoir la majorité', penseraient peut-être certains. Une déclaration comme celle-ci justifie l'opposition contre une parité absolue ou sans mécanismes régulateurs. 'Ce qui a été approuvé à Lausanne, affirmait un leader, constitue une réforme transitoire . . . Nous nous sommes entendus par un compromis déterminé. Acceptons-le en tant que transitoire et réclamons ensuite davantage.'[23] Or un système est sécurisant et légitime quand la conscience collective croit à sa stabilité et à ses constantes. La revendication d'égalité, avancée à l'encontre de certaines communautés chrétiennes, peut et doit aussi être avancée à l'encontre de toute idéologie islamique qui, comme au Soudan ou ailleurs, entendrait imposer la *shari'a* ou un statut de *dhimmi* à des non-musulmans libanais. Une stratégie de l'égalité est globale.

Conclusion

Quand une proporz de plafonnement cesse de bénéficier d'un large consensus, il faut, soit établir un système exclusivement concurrentiel, en fait non démocratique et qui bouleverse tout le système, soit trouver des mécanismes compensatoires pour assurer l'égalité. On peut, d'après le débat institutionnel libanais, distinguer entre trois mécanismes compensatoires (*tawazunat*): la compensation ouverte par rotation ou alternance, la compensation par les attributions (compensation refusée par le leadership politique maronite en ce qui concerne la première présidence), et la compensation par superposition ou mille-feuilles par la création de postes supplémentaires.

Le rêve de vivre sans changement, en s'accrochant à des cadres juridiques le plus souvent formels mais perçus comme des droits sûrs et éternels, est révolu. Le Liban est certes un pays otage de puissances régionales et internationales, mais on ne peut, afin d'étouffer toute volonté de changement, nier le dilemme institutionnel interne.

La régulation des conflits internes dans les sociétés multicommunautaires s'opère soit par un *changement des hommes* avec assimilation forcée, transferts de population ou même génocide; soit par un *changement de la géographie* au moyen de l'annexion ou du partage quand il est possible; soit par un *changement des institutions* grâce à un partage du pouvoir.

Toute recherche qui vise à élucider des aspects souvent confus et par suite controversés et conflictuels à propos des modalités de partage du pouvoir ouvre la voie à des solutions originales et démocratiques pour les sociétés où le partage du pouvoir, combinant à la fois les processus coopératifs et compétitifs, est synonyme d'unité, d'efficience et de stabilité.

Notes

1. L'étude que nous publions ici constitue une version condensée de la communication à la Conférence. Pour une bibliographie relative aux systèmes consensuels:

(i) Arend Lijphart, *Democracy in Plural Societies: a Comparative Exploration* (New Haven et Londres, 1977); *Democracies: Patterns of Majoritarian and Consensus Government in Twenty-One Countries* (New Haven et Londres, 1984); *Power-sharing in South Africa* (Berkeley, 1985), bibliographie pp. 137–71.

(ii) Les actes des deux premières rencontres internationales, sous la direction de Theodor Hanf et avec la participation d'auteurs de l'école consociative. La première, sur le thème: 'Violence et régulation des conflits dans les sociétés plurales', dans le cadre du congrès annuel de l'European Consortium for Political Research, à Fribourg-en-Brisgau, du 20 au 25 mars 1983; la seconde sur le thème: 'Education et régulation consociationelle des conflits dans les sociétés plurales', organisée par Arnold–Bergstraesser–Institut (Fribourg-en-Brisgau), à Metzéral (France) du 25 au 30 mars 1983.

(iii) M. P. C. M. Van Schendelen, 'Systemic bibliography on consociationalism', dans Van Schendelen, (sous la dir. de), *Consociationalism, Pillarization and Conflict-Management in the Low Countries, Acta Politica* XIX (January, 1984) 161–75.

(iv) Antoine N. Messarra, *Le modèle politique libanais et sa survie. Essai sur la classification et l'aménagement d'un système consociatif* (Beyrouth, 1983), bibliographie pp. 501–12.

(v) Theodor Hanf, Antoine N. Messarra et Heinrich R. Reinstrom, *La Société de concordance. Approche comparative* (Beyrouth, 1986).

2. Gerhard Lehmbruch, *Proporzdemokratie. Politisches System und politische Kultur in der Schweiz und in Österreich* (Tübingen, 1967).

3. Antoine N. Messarra, 'Un modèle consociatif au Proche-Orient arabe. Approche comparative du système politique libanais', dans *Droit, institutions et systèmes politiques. Mélanges en hommage à Maurice Duverger* (Paris, 1987).

4. *Le Monde*, 28–9 avril 1985.

5. Rapporté par Ramez Salamé au cours d'une rencontre internationale du Réarmement moral en 1986.

6. Heribert Adam, 'Combatting racism', dans *Education in Culturally Segmented States, Zeitschrift für erziehungs—und sozialwissenschaftliche forschung* 1 (Frankfurt, 1984), t. 2, pp. 239–99.

7. Marwan Hamadé, 'Une solution par l'égalité, plutôt qu'un règlement par la différence', *l'Orient-Le Jour*, 14 au 19 mars 1987, 16 mars 1987.

8. Francis Deron, 'Mélanésiens et Indiens: la déchirure', *le Monde*, 21–2 juin 1987.

9. Paul Yankovitch, 'M. Lazar Moïsov devient président de la présidence', *le Monde*, 17–18 mai 1987.

10. Boutros Labaki, '*Mawazin al-qiwa bayna al-tawa'if wa-takawwun al-sira'at al-ta'ifiyya fi Lubnan*', *al-Waqi'* 5–6 (octobre 1983) 215–44.

11. Jürg Steiner, 'The principles of majority and proportionality', *British Journal of Political Science*, t. 1 (1970) 63–70.

12. Entretien avec Françoise Chipaux, *le Monde*, 14 février 1986. Le Président Fouad Chehab aurait affirmé aux membres d'une institution communautaire maronite venus lui présenter des doléances: 'Je suis président maronite, mais pas pour les maronites.'(Rapporté par le Professeur Antoine Khair au cours d'un débat.)

13. Déclaration parue dans *al-Nahar*, 12 mars 1987.

14. La date entre parenthèses renvoie à des informations de presse, notamment *al-Nahar* et *al-Safir* du jour indiqué.

15. Interview, *Magazine*, 28 mars 1987.

16. Communiqué de la communauté syro-catholique, *al-Nahar*, 27 mai 1984.

17. Elizabeth Picard, 'De la communauté classe à la résistance nationale. Pour une analyse du rôle des chiites dans le système politique libanais', *Revue française de science politique* (décembre 1985) 999–1027.

18. Antoine Messarra, *La structure sociale du Parlement libanais*, Publications de l'Université libanaise, Institut des sciences sociales, no. 18 (Beyrouth, 1977), pp. 118–21.

19. Salim Hoss, '*Al-ta'addudiyya wa-al-'adadiyya bayna al-ta'ayush wa-al-'aysh al-mushtaraq*', al-Safir, 7, 8, 9 novembre 1986.

20. *Al-Nahar*, 3 février 1987.

21. Ibid., 18 janvier 1987.

22. José-Alain Fralon, 'Profession: roi des Belges', *le Monde*, 29 janvier 1987, 6–7.

23. *Al-Nahar*, 17 septembre 1984.

15

Myths and Realities
of the Lebanese Conflict

GEORGES CORM

Any situation involving violence calls for the forging of mythologies
that aim to justify the death of innocent people. The mobilization of
aggressiveness for war is first of all an ideological mobilization. The
word is what kills first, for no one would take a life spontaneously
without prior conditioning. In massacres, collective liquidations or
forced movement of civilian populations, an even stronger psychological mobilization is required than in a classic war where regular
armies confront each other. The justification of violence becomes
necessary not only to make the criminal acts possible but also to enable
the perpetrators to find support and protection in public opinion,
allowing them to continue their career as murderers with impunity.

The Lebanese case is a striking example of a situation where crimes
against humanity have been committed for more than 12 years by local
factions whose leaders are turned into heroes of mythological causes.
They find support in the so-called enlightened public opinion,
although their declared causes bear no relation to the reality of
violence in the field or to its objectives. The ideological blindness in
the face of the real issues behind the violence in Lebanon has become
so complete after 12 years that the authors of these crimes against
humanity, claiming to be inspired by religion, honour, nationalism and
social and political justice, have no difficulty finding material and
moral support outside Lebanon.

Does not, after all, the greatest encouragement to those responsible
for violence in Lebanon arise from the sense of powerlessness of the
public in democratic countries? This feeling is rationalized by the
misconception that Lebanon is a country genetically condemned to
drown in violence: the product of French imperialism, a transient jewel
in the Middle East, but condemned to die after terrible suffering. In
fact, this feeling is created by a permanent and insidious distillation of

the fighting factions' ideological doctrines. The function of these mythological doctrines, regardless of their pseudo-realistic appearance, is to make the unbearable acceptable: the massacre of civilians, using different techniques of violence, by a handful of cynics and madmen who become professionals of crimes against humanity.

The violence in Lebanon, in spite of illusions created by the mass media and international ideological passions, is not the violence of religious communities in war against each other. It is a war led by wild militias, resulting from regional destabilization, against the Lebanese civilian population, martyrizing it because it refuses to submit to their order which aims to divide the Lebanese territory into religious ghettos to the profit of the leading regional actors of the Middle Eastern conflicts. It is the silent and non-violent resistance of the Lebanese population that leads to so many civilian victims of snipers, artillery shells, car bombs, and gangs of kidnappers—whose hostages may never be released. The Lebanese refuse to admit that the country has died, despite the daily sacrifice of its children since 1975 who defy the militias which pretend to defend them while breaking inter-communal links that are the basis of the very historical existence of Lebanon and the Lebanese people.

This non-violent struggle of the Lebanese people is not recognized by world opinion. First, because all non-violent Lebanese people are defined in the mass media by clichés and according to simplifications based on analyses of the Lebanese conflict which justify violence and crime. Second, because the mass media pay attention, almost exclusively, to the violence itself. In this mass media political show, the victim cannot be of any interest: only the violent person is allowed to be heard and is worthy of attention. Furthermore, each innocent civilian, although a victim of militia violence for 12 years, is considered a dangerous terrorist, or at least a potentially violent person by virtue of belonging to one community or another. Militia leaders, however, are heroes of Christian, Muslim, Druze, Shi'i or Maronite causes who may be heard, received, and allowed freedom of movement in democratic countries in the service of their causes.

The wish of the large majority of Lebanese people is to be able to continue their non-violent resistance to the militia order. But this is constantly overshadowed by the simplifications and clichés propagated by the major regional powers as they try to control the Middle East, using the Lebanese militia forces as instruments. These simplifications and clichés, the basis of mythologies justifying the crimes committed against the Lebanese civilian population, aim to reinforce the idea of a Lebanon that is genetically condemned and which cannot be saved from its own demons. This idea places the responsibility on all the Lebanese, collectively and without distinction, overshadowing the responsibility of those directly accountable for the massacres, the forced movement of populations, and the kidnapping. Such a view of the conflict overestimates the local causes, reinforcing the Lebanese people's sense of responsibility for their misfortunes, and under-estimates the regional and international causes, so allowing the responsibility of the major actors in the Middle Eastern conflict— those who provoked, brought about and contributed directly or indirectly to the rise of the militia order on Lebanese territory to the detriment of the central state institutions and the unified transcom-munal society—to be eclipsed. For this reason, before describing the civilian population's non-violent struggle for the survival of a unified and transcommunal society, we should demonstrate this double game which underestimates the broader regional and international issues concerning Lebanon and overestimates local issues. This is the game which imposes a vision of a country condemned to chaos, concealing the non-violent resistance of the population against the militia order.

Let us say immediately that there is not and there could not be a strictly local issue in Lebanon capable of creating so many crimes against the civilian population. It should be remembered that Lebanon's area is only 10,500 sq. km and that its territory has no natural resources. Its 3 million inhabitants barely represent one third of the urban area of any major capital such as Cairo or Paris. As we shall see, this tiny country is held to ransom only because, due to the establishment of the militia order, the Lebanese religious communities became over the years the hostages of the major regional and inter-national actors fighting for regional hegemony. In fact, these actors use the Lebanese scene, by means of the militias, to score points, to further their plans for hegemony in the Middle East, and to play their appalling and bloody games.

Misinterpretation and overestimation of the local issues

We cannot look in detail here at all the misinterpretations and distortions of the Lebanese reality as they appear in the mass media and in articles and works inspired by the militias and their external protectors.[1] We shall look at two of the major arguments which aim to show that Lebanon could never be an ordinary country, in other words a country at peace.

Divisions in the population

It is common to speak in terms of ethnic groups confronting each other in Lebanon and having contradicting socio-cultural and religious values which cannot find ground for conciliation. Based on such a simplistic assumption, violence in Lebanon appears inevitable, a natural phenomenon which can only come to an end when the ethnic groups are separated and protected by powerful foreign forces for which they have affinity: for example, Christians by the Christian Western powers; Shi'is by Shi'i Iran. This approach is flawed, for three reasons.

First, there are no basic divisions in Lebanon: there are religious communities, which should not be mistaken for ethnic groups. There are churches of oriental Christianity which took root during the first centuries of Christianity; there are the two branches of Islam, Sunnism and Shi'ism, as well as a heterodox sect of Islamic origin, the Druze.

Second, language, culture and customs (clothing, music, food) are common to these communities. All attempts to find genetic or racial differences between the Lebanese people from different communities, such as measurement of skulls, blood groups, have failed. In fact, the common ethno-cultural heritage among Lebanese people is the Aramaic language, which has characterized the Palestinian, Syrian and Lebanese regions of the Middle East since ancient times. In Lebanon, this Aramaic heritage, in any case similar to the Arab heritage, was quickly arabized with the Arab conquest in the seventh century; Syriac and Greek remained for the different Lebanese churches languages of worship and liturgy.

Third, two ethnic groups exist in Lebanon which represent about 8–10 per cent of the population: Armenians (7–8 per cent) and Kurds (2–3 per cent). Newcomers to the Lebanese land, they arrived at the beginning of the twentieth century as a result of Turkish persecution. These two large groups have their own language and the Kurds have family and tribal traditions which are totally separate from the Arab structures in Lebanese society.

Socio-political divisions certainly exist in Lebanon as in any other society, but they are not as they are portrayed in the mass media. The main division is at the level of historical differences that exist between the rural society in Mount Lebanon and the urban society in the coastal cities (Tripoli, Beirut, Sidon, Tyre). Without going into detail, let us say that Maronites, Druzes and Shi'is constituted the original population of the Mountain—a poor, semi-arid region with limited water resources. The Sunnis and the Greek Orthodox since the sixth and seventh centuries have formed the population of the cities. Poor farmers living under a feudal transcommunal hierarchy based on tribal-like structures and patricians on the one hand; Ottoman empire civil servants, religious and trade notables on the other.

Mandatory France created the State of Greater Lebanon in 1920 with the difficult marriage of the Mountain and the City. Though difficult—as everywhere else—the marriage was not impossible. Lebanon, as other Third World countries and before that industrial Europe, initially had to face a decline in agriculture and consequently a massive migration of its rural population to cities, especially Beirut. But two historical events made this meeting between the Mountain and the City even more difficult. First, the closing of the country's southern border with Palestine which became the Israeli state in 1948. This accelerated the decline of the economy of Lebanon's southern areas which had been structured on the basis of intensive trade with Palestine. Second, the end of the economic union between Lebanon and Syria, a legacy from the French mandate, in 1950. In fact, while Syria tended to adopt an active policy of industrialization, Lebanon, which aimed to develop its role as a regional commercial entrepôt, wanted to maintain low customs tariffs. This affected the movement of exchanges between Syria and Lebanon and had a negative effect on the country's northern and eastern areas bordering Syria. In both cases the rural population which suffered most of these new trade barriers was that of the Mountain with its majority Shi'i community. This raises a question about the state's role in a development policy aimed at offsetting these negative elements and at equitably redistributing the fruits of the rapid expansion of the economy that Lebanon would experience from 1950 to 1970.

The nature and role of the Lebanese state

The Lebanese state has not failed more than any other state in the region, or in the Third World, in its task of economic development. Despite its liberal ideology, the state at the beginning of the 1950s began a traditional policy of developing the infrastructure in the country. This policy was developed through the work of President Fu'ad Shihab (1958–64). Shihab modernized the country in all fields, inspired by the Abbé Lebret, founder of the Research and Training Institute for development, who was entrusted with the task of elaborating a general development plan for the country. A social security system was set up, in addition to programmes for land reclamation and for the development of the city of Tripoli. The Litani dam, intended to provide irrigation to the Biqa' region and the south, was completed. It should be pointed out that the investment in this dam was equivalent, given the size of Lebanon, to the Aswan dam in Egypt and the Euphrates dam in Syria. This is not to mention the development of other parts of the infrastructure, such as roads, telecommunications, and the expansion of the port of Beirut.

One cannot therefore claim that the Lebanese state neglected its responsibilities concerning development. Its work between 1950 and

1970 can in fact be favourably compared with that of neighbouring countries. It cannot be maintained that the Lebanese conflict was the result of the state's deficiencies and its class policy. The Lebanese state did not adopt a strong policy of social egalitarianism, and this is particularly evident in the fiscal field dominated by indirect taxes; but those among the neighbouring countries who did adopt egalitarian policies developed a state bourgeoisie whose parasitism and corruption have been as detrimental as the social inequalities in Lebanon.

It is interesting to note that it was only during President Shihab's term in office that one could evoke, through the operation of army and security machineries, the supremacy of the Maronite community. Yet, the charge of Maronite hegemony was not raised until later, when the Maronite successors of General Shihab lost control over the entire state machinery, and, together with the other Maronite, Druze and Sunni notables, broke the relative hegemony of the army and security forces. The period of Lebanese contemporary history called 'Shihabist' is, anyway, a period when no voice was raised to contest the head of state's policy in the name of a larger participation of Muslim communities in their country's management. The general's internal and foreign policies were met in fact with a popular consensus, apart from the circle of the Christian and Muslim traditional political notables whose control over the country's political life had already started to decline.

In fact, the problem in Lebanon was never fundamentally the leaders' religion, but rather on the one hand of the policies implemented, and on the other hand of the monopolization of power by a leading elite of 40 to 50 Christian and Muslim families which had existed since the end of the French mandate. We should note that if the head of state belonged to the Maronite community according to the tradition stemming from the 1943 National Pact, this same tradition called for the president of the chamber of deputies to be chosen from Shi'i notables, and the prime minister from Sunni notables. The Lebanese political system is in fact a parliamentary system even if the president of the republic enjoys strong prerogatives as head of the executive. Furthermore, the Christian deputies in the chamber of deputies were never unquestioning supporters of the president of the republic. The Lebanese political system does not allow the hegemony of one community; if this had really existed, the events which led to the complete destabilization of the country in 1975 would never have occurred.

On the contrary, it was this climate of freedom and the weakness of the army and security forces after the departure of General Shihab in 1964 which allowed the country's destabilization under the sway of broader regional influences. This is not to say, however, that Lebanon

was a country without problems, but only that there was little time to
adjust to and assimilate the tensions, imbalances and shortcomings
which are also common to other societies before the regional
conditions that destabilized the country appeared in 1967, the date of
the Arab defeat (in June) by the Israeli army.

In conclusion, Lebanese society was not genetically flawed; it
certainly was not to settle quarrels between Lebanese notables of one
community or another about church towers and minarets that so many
foreign armies have occupied Lebanon since 1975. These armies
include the Syrian, Saudi, Yemeni and Libyan contingents of the Arab
Deterrent Force of 1976, as well as the Multinational Force (US,
French, Italian, English) formed in 1982 in the wake of the Israeli
invasion, and the different contingents of the United Nations Interim
Force in Lebanon (UNIFIL) deployed in south Lebanon in 1978.

The emergence of the Lebanese militia is more the result of regional
tensions than of a civil war which was smouldering in the very
foundations of Lebanese society. It is true that the militia strikes its
roots in a sociologically fertile ground, but its basic line of division is
not the opposition between Christian and Muslim communities. This
ground is that of the Mountain—a rural world where a large number
of the militia members are recruited. The only militia forces active
today are the ones that claim to be acting in the name of the three
historical communities of the Mountain: the Maronite, Druze and Shi'i.
They are the ones who seized the Lebanese cities to reshape them to
their advantage—the revenge of the Mountain on the City—and who
demarcated Mountain territories through the Israeli invasion of 1982.

Underestimation of regional issues

The underestimation of regional issues prevents the recognition of a
major function of the Lebanese conflict: Lebanon provides a battle-
field, and can be used by local and international forces fighting for
the domination of the Middle East as an area of experimentation.
One should not forget that in this region of the world, with its highly
strategic geographic situation and oil reserves, the question of the
Ottoman empire's succession remains as persistent as ever. As early as
the nineteenth century the region was subject to the greed of
international forces under various pretexts, one of which was the
protection of minorities. In the nineteenth century, the contradicting
French and English interventions in the affairs of the Levant had
already led to the destabilization of Lebanon between 1840 and 1860.[2]

The interference by the great powers of the time (Austria and Prussia
in addition to France and England), as they tried to dominate the

Middle East and the Balkan region, was generally classified under the label of the 'Orient Question'. Nineteenth–century writings also played down colonial rivalry for political hegemony by overemphasizing the local ethno-religious divisions, which were maintained by these powers through various means and used to justify their interference.

It is not necessary to go into the details of these classical colonial policies which lasted until 1956, the year of the French–English–Israeli expedition against Nasser's Egypt. Let us simply recall the Sykes–Picot Agreement which divided the Arab provinces of the Ottoman empire into zones of French and English domination; and also the Soviet effort to carve out for itself under cover of both world wars supporting states on the Turkish and Iranian territories; and finally the famous 1917 Balfour Declaration whereby the English granted the Zionist movement the 'right' for Jewish communities throughout the world to occupy the Palestinian territories that had belonged to the Ottoman empire.

If the emergence of a unitarian, secular Arab nationalist movement, incarnated by Nasserism and Ba'thism, appeared for a moment during the 1960s to have the authority to inherit naturally the succession of the Ottoman empire, this movement quickly broke down under the weight of a number of factors.

The first of these factors was undoubtedly the military supremacy acquired by the Israeli state in the region, allowing it to occupy and colonize numerous Arab territories, many more than the plan for Palestine's division confirmed by the United Nations in 1947 had stipulated. Israel is a geographic and demographic dwarf in the Middle East but a military giant due to Western and specifically US protection, which has created a disequilibrium in the region. By obtaining through the Camp David Accords of 1978–9 the military neutralization of Egypt in the Arab–Israeli conflict concerning the restitution of the Sinai occupied in 1967, Israel became a superpower in the region, the real successor to the Ottoman empire in the military field; this set back the cause of Arab unity among the different peoples of the region who had fought throughout the first half of the century for liberation from European colonial powers.

The second factor was the increase of inter-Arab rivalries from the beginning of the 1960s. In fact, if the hegemony of Nasser's Egypt over the region came to an end as a result of its military defeat by Israel in 1967, it had never really succeeded in imposing itself securely on the entire region. Two sources of opposition should be mentioned here: Saudi Arabia, and the countries dominated by the Ba'thist ideology. Saudi Arabia worked to undermine Arab unitary and essentially secular aspirations by resorting to Islamic values, endorsing a reactionary fundamentalism hostile to any idea of modern secular nationalism. For this purpose, it financed the expansion of Muslim brotherhoods throughout the Arab world. The setting up of the Conference of Muslim States in 1969 under the auspices of Saudi Arabia, Pakistan and Morocco was a counterbalance against the influence of the League of Arab States which was dominated by Nasser's Egypt and the anti-imperialist Ba'thist ideology. The Ba'thist ideology found support in Syria and Iraq and worked for a long time to surprise Egypt on its 'left' by reinforcing its anti-imperialist campaign. Yet, this opposition was itself a victim of the breakdown of relations between Syria and Iraq which would lead to great hostility between the two countries in the 1970s, and in the 1980s was manifested by Syrian support of Iran in its war with Iraq.

The third factor was the result of the first two: the emergence of various Palestinian armed movements after the 1967 defeat who were later manipulated by the contradicting influences of various Arab governments. When the Palestinians were driven out of Jordan in 1970, they found refuge in Lebanon and tried to mark their claims with guerrilla actions against the State of Israel from the country's borders. Furthermore, at least two of these movements will later be openly Marxist-Leninist and have close ties with the Soviet Union.

The fourth factor was the attitude of the United States, whose policy has been to deny the Soviet Union any role in the Middle East in spite of its geographical proximity. This policy failed hopelessly during the 1950s and 1960s when the USSR established itself firmly, due to mistakes committed by Western powers in Egypt, Syria and Iraq. But as a result of the Arab military defeat in 1967, the United States was able to reduce considerably Soviet influence in the region. It did this by making every effort to convince Israel to find an honourable settlement of the Palestinian problem on the condition that Arab countries abandoned Soviet influence. Egypt did so between 1972 and 1974, when it entered the American sphere of influence in the military field. The total absence of a Soviet reaction to the invasion of Lebanon in 1982 reflects the results of the American policy, compared with the decisive Soviet intervention during the preceding Israeli invasions in the region in 1956, 1967 and 1973.

Finally, the fifth factor was the ambitions of Iran. These ambitions had already been manifested at the time of the shah who wanted to be the fifth world power and military protector of the Arab-Persian Gulf. The shah's ambitions were, in fact, realized by Khomeini's regime which became a key regional power, not only as a result of its military victories in the conflict with Iraq, but also due to its active presence in Lebanon since 1982, the date of the Israeli invasion. As a result of the kidnapping of Western hostages in Beirut, the Lebanese Hizbullah (the political-military organization directly financed by Iran), have succeeded in substantially reorienting the policies of Western countries.

The Lebanese conflict started in the spring of 1975 when the regional situation grew more explosive. It became clear that Egypt was alone in being favoured by the United States in an attempt to settle bilaterally its dispute with Israel. The Palestinian movement was nervous as it had made no progress in gaining rights in spite of being recognized by the international community in 1974. Differences increased among the different groups and a serious rift emerged between those who supported a negotiated solution with Israel under the only possible umbrella of the United States and those who opposed such a settlement. As Lebanon was the only Arab country adjoining Israel from which Palestinian armed groups could launch attacks, the most contradicting pressures began to be exercised upon this small territory; this is not to mention the severe military retaliations by the Israeli air force against the Lebanese and Palestinian civilian populations, which had started in 1969 and which culminated with the invasion of Lebanon in 1982.

The Lebanese militias then became active in the Middle East under the auspices of the regional and international forces: militias of the Right, recruited by the Phalangist Party or by Camille Chamoun, former president of the republic, famous for his close ties with Western powers; and militias of the Left, recruited by the Nasserist Lebanese parties, the four parties close to the Soviet Union (the Syrian Popular Party, the Progressive Socialist Party of Kamal Jumblat, the Communist Party and the Organization of the Communist Lebanese). The militias of the Right attacked the Palestinian armed groups in Lebanon, especially those of Marxist allegiance; the militias of the Left had to defend them. The Lebanese war broke out: a 'Spanish war' for the whole Middle East.

From then on, the events and the pace of the war became woven with the struggles for supremacy in the region. Thus, for example, Syria's entry into Lebanon in 1976, in a game from which it had never entirely been excluded, aimed to mark its presence on the only territory where Palestinian activism was able to operate, in order to control this expansion on the one hand, and to increase its own regional importance on the other. But the Syrian action was swiftly countered by the Israelis, Egyptians and Iraqis, all of whom and for different reasons were hostile to the extension of the Syrian influence in the region.

It is impossible in this restricted framework to make all the correlations between the evolution of the regional situation and the internal developments of the Lebanese conflict. Let us just recall 1977 when for a short moment, as a result of Jimmy Carter's election to the US presidency, a dialogue was initiated between the principal forces working in the region. Carter had a meeting with Hafez Assad, the Syrian president, in Vienna. Subsequently, President Anwar Sadat of Egypt held discussions with Assad and there was some talk of convening an international conference for the settlement of the Arab–Israeli conflict and of including the Soviet Union. Lebanon has known peace: 1977 was a year without violence. But as soon as the Egyptian president went to Jerusalem alone and prepared a separate peace with the State of Israel, Lebanon again became destabilized. From the spring of 1978 fighting started again in Lebanon and has not stopped; as the regional tensions have increased, so has the manipulation by the Lebanese and Palestinian militias.

If we consider that since 1973 there has been no major Israeli–Arab war endangering world stability and increasing the risk of confrontation between the two superpowers as there was in 1956, 1967 and 1973, this is certainly because the Lebanese territory served as a limited zone of confrontation between regional and international forces aiming at ensuring, restoring or developing their hegemony over this highly strategic region of the world. This is why Israel, by invading Lebanon in 1982 and besieging Beirut, had broken the rules of a cruel but delimited game. By trying to make the Lebanese state—placed by the Israeli army under the control of the Phalangist militia—sign a peace treaty, under the auspices of the US and similar to that of Camp David, Israel could only expect to produce a violent reply from all forces (Soviet bloc, Iran, Syria) hostile to the strengthening of the Israeli-American hegemony over the Middle East. The Multinational Force, though mainly the Lebanese, paid the price. The militia order became fiercer than ever: each actor on the Lebanese stage trying through the militias to secure a piece of this war-torn country.

The intensification of the militia order was made with the consent of the Israeli forces since arms passed through Israeli–occupied zones to reach the militias opposed to the Phalangist Party: to the militias having, henceforth, an exclusively community allegiance (Amal and Hizbullah, Shi'i, the Progressive Socialist Party (PPS), Druze), as well as to the anti-Syrian Palestinian groups. The Shi'i militias, therefore, opposed these secular parties of the Left; however, encouraged by the Syrians, they also opposed as fiercely the reconstituted Palestinian groups.

Since the Israeli invasion and the failure to include Lebanon in the US–Israeli sphere of influence through the abortive treaty of 17 May 1983, it became clear that the militias were assuming exclusive community allegiances, and this was exacerbated by the considerable influences Iran could suddenly wield. The Lebanese communities, taken as hostages by their militias but then identifying with them to the profit of the forces working in the region, acquired a very strong political symbolism. Thus, the political-military status of the Maronite community became, through the strength or weakness of the militias claiming to represent it, a symbol of the influence of the United States and Western powers; the status of the Shi'i community through Amal and Hizbullah became a symbol of the Syrian and Iranian influence; the status of the Druze community became a symbol of Syrian and Soviet influence. Nevertheless, the restoration of Palestinian armed groups indicate that the Palestine Liberation Organization (PLO) should always be taken into account.

This is why no Lebanese or Palestinian militia can remain active; they must continually reaffirm their presence on Lebanese soil, as their movements reflect the dynamics of all regional conflicts: East–West, inter-Arab, Israeli-Arab, Iraqi-Iranian, Iranian–French and conflicts with the United States. From 1982–4 these militias fought mainly, not according to the Islamic–Christian division, which was never the driving force behind the conflict, but inside community territories which they carved up for themselves and which they claimed to protect in order to ensure and expand their domination. Thus, factions of Christian militias have fiercely confronted each other since 1978 to try to dominate the Christian community, especially the most important community, the Maronites. Fighting has raged between militias of Islamic allegiance throughout the last few years, especially in western Beirut; not to mention the fighting between Amal and the Palestinians. It was the intolerable violence of the confrontation between Amal and the Palestinians which led to the recall of the Syrian army in that part of the Lebanese capital which had become 'Muslim'.

All this violence has added to the suffering of the civilian population which, nevertheless, continues to resist the militia order relentlessly and with non-violent means. The Lebanese people know, anyway, that the war between the militias is not their struggle. This is why we hear the Lebanese speak so often of the 'conspiracy' against their country, to which Western observers always reply with obvious annoyance that the Lebanese can only accuse others of their suffering to free themselves of any responsibility. The leaders of these militias certainly bear a heavy responsibility which observers have not clearly denounced. But the violent regime that has been established in Lebanon since 1975 is definitely the result of regional destabilization, as the political geography of tomorrow's Middle East and the zones of influence of the regional and international powers are being drawn and tested on this small territory of 10,000 sq. km. In particular, the attempt to divide the country into microstates according to religious allegiances is an experience which some would like to extend in future to other pluralist states in the region such as Syria, Iraq, Kuwait and even Egypt.[3] The increasing tension between Sunnis and Shi'is all over the region owing to the Iran–Iraq war has facilitated this division by community from which Iran and Israel have profited most.[4]

What will tomorrow's Middle East be like? What share of influence will both the superpowers have? What borders and what strength of military power will Israel have? What will Iran's share be, bearing in mind that it is not an Arab country? Will there be a place for a Palestinian state? Will Syria and Iraq be able to retain the whole of their territories whose borders were drawn by the Sykes–Picot Agreement in 1917? Finally, who will watch over the security of the world's largest cheap energy reservoir, the countries of the Arab peninsula whose states and demography are particularly fragile? These are the real issues at stake in Lebanon, where each actor scores points on the Lebanese scene through the Lebanese and Palestinian militia order progressively established since 1975. These geopolitical issues are the ones which are overshadowed by those put forward as internal Lebanese issues: the balance of the communities and the distribution of power in a small, miserable territory without resources and with 3 million inhabitants.

If internal issues are exaggerated to such an extent in the presentation of the Lebanese conflict, it is in order to demonstrate how difficult it is for the Lebanese to live together, and therefore the necessity of dividing the territory. It is to prevent the carving up of their country that the Lebanese people have for 12 years conducted a silent and non-violent struggle, which has been ignored by the world media.

The Lebanese resistance to the militia order

From the beginning of the conflict in 1975, the Lebanese people have been subject to four principal techniques of violence. It is because they refuse to submit to the implicit order of these forms of violence that the civilian population has paid such a high price in terms of the destruction of property, injury and loss of life.

The first technique involves teams of specialized snipers who operate the different militias. The snipers' task is to divide the country's rural areas into community ghettos, imprisoning the civilian population. Lying on the roofs of houses in cities and villages, or behind hills in mountainous areas, snipers are instructed to open fire on anyone crossing between the zones demarcated by their guns.[5] Yet since 1975 the Lebanese people have every day refused to accept this injunction by the militia to restrict their movement in the cities and villages of their country. For this they pay a very heavy price.

The second technique of violence has been used since 1975. Known as 'flying road-blocks', mobile teams of militiamen take a position on a street or route and stop, without warning, any passer-by to 'check' his or her religious identity. Those who have the misfortune not to belong to the community favoured by the militiamen attempting to take control of a particular zone, are kidnapped and often tortured, or 'disappear'. It is estimated that at least 15,000 people have been victims of these road-blocks and may never return home; to this may be added the victims killed by the snipers, numbering around 10,000, and all those maimed and wounded. The civilians who insist upon travelling between zones must not only escape the snipers' guns but must also succeed in avoiding the militias' road-blocks.

But who are these Lebanese who insist on defying the militia order? They are armies of patriots who continue to ensure the basic services throughout the country, and refuse to accept the division of the territory: taxi drivers, doctors, ambulance drivers, civil servants, teachers, electricians, bakers, distributors of newspapers, and simply all those who refuse to live in artificial ghettos and consider that they should defy, even at the cost of their lives, this savage and senseless militia order.

The third technique of violence is the shelling of civilian areas using heavy artillery. In a daily routine since 1975, from the afternoon until the next morning, militiamen of each zone open fire on zones held by other militia, not on their batteries but on residential buildings, hospitals and schools. Here again, a war is directed against the civilian population which is used to demonstrate that the absolute evil comes from the other community ghetto.[6] Such attacks have resulted in the death of over 60,000 people. Like the snipers and the flying road-blocks, this form of attack continues to claim victims every day.

The fourth technique of violence, appearing in 1978, is the car bomb. They are intended as 'messages' sent by the militias or their regional international protectors to each other through the militia order. This 'message', according to the zone in which it explodes, indicates that one militia or the other, or its foreign protector, is following a policy which exceeds the normally accepted limits of violence in Lebanon. The message is aimed at the civilian population and directly at other militias, as in most cases the car bomb is placed in heavy traffic and timed to explode during the rush hour. Car bombs have claimed at least 3,000 or 4,000 victims between 1980 and 1987.

This brief account of the techniques of violence in Lebanon shows to what extent this war is a militia war conducted against civilians of all communities, and is not a war between communities as it is so

conveniently portrayed by the mass media in the West. When militias
failed to separate the Lebanese people according to the different
communities and shut them up in ghettos, the Israeli army helped
them to do so successfully during its three-year occupation of Lebanon
(1982–5). This is how in the Shuf, a zone where Druzes and Maronites
live together, and in the south of Lebanon, a zone where Christians
from different communities live alongside Shi'i and Sunni Muslims,
the Christian population was moved twice by force, in 1980 and 1985.

Unfortunately, all these crimes against humanity have not been
denounced as such, except selectively to discredit one militia and
exculpate another. The militia order as a whole has not been denounced
as the perpetrators of these crimes. Even worse, the political mass media
pictures of Lebanon have reversed the roles: militia leaders responsible
for collective crimes against the civilian population are made heroes of
Christian or Muslim causes, important personalities with whom
democratic states deal, sometimes officially receiving them, even at the
highest political level. And yet, the ordinary Lebanese people who
struggle in a non-violent way for the survival of a unified country find
they are portrayed in international public opinion as genetically violent.
The militia population in Lebanon did not exceed 10–12,000 men in
1982, the date of the Israeli invasion; that is, about 0.3 per cent of the
population. With the increase in militia activity as a result of the Israeli
invasion, this number rose to approximately 20,000 men; that is, 0.7 per
cent of the population. The militias therefore represent only a small
percentage of the Lebanese population.

Of course many Lebanese not recruited in militia ranks can
sometimes talk vehemently about their fellow citizens in other
communities. As the victims of 12 years of intercommunal violence
and militia propaganda this talk is the product of the militia order. But
it is the behaviour which should be noted and the behaviour
contradicts the words. This is revealed by the mutual assistance of the
great majority of Lebanese of all religions as they struggle against the
militia order, to operate a country unified by its public services, its
schools and universities, its banks and its national airline company.
The reality is disliked by all those who consciously or unconsciously,
through what they say or write about Lebanon or through the links
they establish with the militia order, have become parties in this order,
accomplices to the crimes against humanity.[7]

What hope for Lebanon?

There is certainly no hope in the short term for a real improvement in
the situation. The discussions which have nervously begun to propose

an international conference on the Middle East seem, up till now, to have been opportunistic political manoeuvres, and we can base no serious hope on them. In addition, an unprecedented financial crisis is shaking the Lebanese economy which had withstood the shocks of the conflict until 1982. But the Israeli occupation, the forced movement of populations it precipitated, as well as the problems created by the militia have led to the devaluation of the Lebanese pound. The population's standard of living is falling daily and the country is threatened with starvation.[8]

But in the longer term, several factors allow for a less disastrous scenario.

1.   Even though the morale of the population has been worn down by the crisis, its capacity for resistance survives. The Lebanese struggle for their country's unity despite all obstacles. The attempts of the militia order to divide Lebanon have failed. The central administration, the principal public services, including those managed privately, continue to function to some extent throughout the country. This is the result of the sacrifice that the Lebanese have been willing to make, if necessary with their lives.[9] The Lebanese army is still there: the dreadful blows it has received have not led to its complete disintegration. It will be a decisive factor in the future.

2.   There is a great number of Lebanese emigrants who maintain close ties with the country and help those of their families who remain. Many of them have made large fortunes in Africa and in the Arab oil-exporting countries during the last ten years. This will also be a decisive factor in Lebanon's future.

3.   During 12 years of war, none of the powers aspiring to regional hegemony have succeeded through the militia order in completely controlling any of the communities, or in making any into a pliable instrument in the service of its policy. The reason for this is very simple: community allegiance has not extinguished the diversity of natures and opinions of the Lebanese people existing in one community. Community loyalty does not dictate the ideological and political behaviour of the Lebanese. Only a deeply racist mentality, such as the militia order tries so hard to instil in Lebanon, can give the illusion that a perfect homogeneity of nature and behaviour exists within each religious community. The consequence of this racist view would be that the Lebanese communities can only maintain and nourish differences between each other, inevitably leading to the division of the country unless one community can succeed in dominating the others.

Notes

1. See Georges Corm, *Géopolitique du conflit libanais* (Paris, 1986).
2. See ibid., ch. 7.
3. Let us recall that the French mandate for a few years had divided Syria into microstates by community. As for Israel, an entire school of thought dreams of dividing the Middle East along religious lines; this would be the best justification of the Israeli state, which was itself erected according to religious adherence (see ibid., ch. 7 and Georges Corm, *Le Proche-Orient eclaté: de Suez à l'invasion du Liban, 1956–1982* (Paris, 1983), ch. 7).
4. On the occasion of the Irangate scandal, Israel had to justify very clearly the motives of its key role in the arms supplies to Iran by putting forward the reason that it was necessary for it to weaken at any cost the surrounding Arab societies.
5. The sniper is remunerated according to the number of victims, the allowance for a dead person being double that for a wounded one.
6. One night of routine shelling inside Beirut costs 2 or 3 million dollars: this shows the amounts of money involved which exceed by far what the militias can obtain by demanding ransoms from the civilian population.
7. This applies especially to those journalists, excited by the militias' adventure and arguments, who claim to be experts on Lebanon by virtue only of their contacts in the militia. The civilian population seldom attracts the media's attention, which must always attend the scene of violence.
8. The militia order also unfortunately becomes an almost compulsory intermediary in the reception and distribution of international aid.
9. I should mention here the attempts to take collective action against the militia order, especially the marches crossing districts divided by the militias to try to reunite them. Militiamen fired into the crowd in 1976. In 1984 they established an artillery barrage to stop a march of as many as 3–400,000 people from both sides of Beirut who had planned to meet at the 'green line' dividing the city into two zones. Let us note the movement to delete the specification of community affiliation on identity cards: advocates of the movement were beaten up by militiamen who argued that it was shocking that people should be 'ashamed' of their religious identity. Strikes occur more and more often, but militiamen try to bring them under their control. We should also note that Lebanese women are very active in these movements.

16

Espace urbain, espaces politiques: ville, état et communautés à Beyrouth vers 1975
Eléments pour une problématique

NABIL BEYHUM

The intention of this paper is to stand back from the general discussion: instead of investigating the variations on the theme of conflict and consensus, it aims to tackle the transformations to which Lebanese society has been subjected and thus understand each consensus and each conflict as being partial, momentary and open to reinterpretation. Rather than placing the emphasis on institutions, an attempt is made to begin to look at the social problems of Lebanon; the paper thus seeks to examine the manifestations and institutions of the state in the sociological dimensions of their interventionism. Finally, the paper also tries to distance itself from a theme which is implicit, or in counterpoint, in the title of these discussions, that of the identification of the present situation as a breakdown in consensus; the view offered here is that the present situation is a crisis of Middle Eastern space and national space, articulated on a specifically urban crisis, or around urban stakes.

The question asked is therefore that of the organization of the spaces which make up Lebanon and of the transformation of these spaces in contemporary history. An attempt is made to fix the times which marked the Lebanese experience and accompanied the rapid growth of Beirut. In this framework, the role of the institutions of state is questioned, as is the specific contribution of Shihabism to the City–Mountain–State trilogy.

Préambule: ville, état et identités

> The most important event in Lebanese history after 1920 was the transformation of an agrarian republic into an extended city-state, a metropolis with its hinterland, and political events can only be understood in this context.
>
> What happened was not simply that the population flowed into Beirut from the villages of the mountain . . .
>
> A. Hourani

La violence au Liban est en fait le thème non-dit de nos investigations dans l'histoire: nous essayons souvent de retrouver dans le passé, que parfois nous figeons,[1] les causes d'une situation actuelle qui semble se refuser à une explication immédiate. Notre propre problématique n'échappe pas à cette quête implicite quand elle essaie de délimiter un espace: la ville, et un temps: celui des années 1970 et 1980. Partant, il est difficile de ne pas assumer explicitement la coupure qu'entraîne un tel choix: dire la ville, en deçà ou au-delà du pays, dire le pays à partir de la ville, dire les dernières années qui ont précédé l'explosion des violences, sans retourner jusqu'aux mythes d'émergence de l'espace national.

Or dire Beyrouth n'est plus facile: M. Gilsenan rappelait récemment que de toutes les villes d'Orient c'est celle qui impose le silence.[2] Comment dire cet espace, cette société, en 1970 à 1975? Quelle mémoire faut-il forcer pour retrouver ce qui semble ne plus exister, n'avoir jamais existé? Qu'est-ce qui peut résister au raz de marée réel, mais aussi théorique, qui a emporté la ville? Des destructions physiques et des délires des discours, lesquels font-ils aujourd'hui de la simple tentative de souvenir, de reconstitution intellectuelle, une entreprise téméraire et . . . baroque?[3] Ne sommes nous pas parfois en train de nous surprendre à adopter des démarches d'archéologues?

Mais il y a sans doute quelque chose de plus grave. Aujourd'hui tout discours sur Beyrouth est sciemment interdit: par les acteurs locaux dominants, par les acteurs externes dominants, par la défaite qui domine ceux qui vivent la violence quotidienne. Tout discours sur Beyrouth se heurte aussi à des conceptions réductrices de la société. Trop souvent les a priori qui dominent les analyses bloquent les débats car ils ne peuvent prendre la mesure de la crise de la société. Ce débat même, sur le consensus et le conflit, n'est-il pas déjà dès le départ piégé? N'identifie-t-on pas souvent le premier terme à l'état, l'autre aux identités, en oubliant que du consensus au conflit peuvent se décliner toutes les gammes des relations?

Le premier discours, dominant surtout avant 1975, est celui ayant les institutions étatiques comme horizon. Horizon tout autant positif que négatif, car elles seraient dans certaines versions un absolu intouchable, dans d'autres au contraire le lieu de l'immaturité fondamentale de la formation sociale. Il est ainsi implicitement assumé que l'état, et ses institutions, constitueraient la voie royale vers la connaissance de la société, à la fois lieu du consensus social mais aussi du conflit. Discours contradictoire, insuffisant surtout, où les enjeux des conflits se réduiraient à empêcher ou à favoriser un réaménagement de la distribution des postes administratifs censé traduire des rapports de nombre, appelés improprement 'démographiques' dans un certain langage produit par la guerre elle-même.

L'état, et les rapports politico-juridiques, deviennent ainsi les seuls déterminants, car les seules solutions, à des problèmes bien plus vastes. Les institutions sont idéalisées, leur force est survalorisée, y compris quand elle apparaît comme négative, en revanche les conditions d'émergence des pouvoirs sont pudiquement voilées, alors que disparaît toute notion de planification de la gestion de la société, si l'on excepte bien sûr l'intermède chehabiste. Si la défaite de ce courant de pensée a été le fait de son incapacité à raisonner en termes sociaux, c'est qu'il a été incapable de concevoir la guerre au moment où elle s'installait, il n'a pu l'appréhender ni à plus forte raison s'y opposer. Ainsi dans cette problématique, le débat a été épuisé par une seule question, non pas que faire de ou avec l'état, quelle politique engager, mais seulement 'qui' va constituer le politique (ou quelle combinaison de qui). Bien que sa formulation soit un élément contraire, opposé à la guerre, ce courant de pensée reste à notre avis loin de concevoir la paix, du moins tant qu'il n'accepte d'approfondir, prolonger et enrichir, sa vision de la société civile.

Le second thème est plus pernicieux. Il s'est imposé après 1975. C'est celui de la permanence et de la fixité des identités religieuses comme autre horizon. Le consensus et le conflit deviennent alibi et essence, et renvoient à des identités stables et irréductibles, que certains courants intellectuels avaient précédemment sous-évaluées, et qu'ils redécouvrent aujourd'hui plus 'vraies' que l'état, en fait seules vraies, par compensation de la cécité précédente. Ici aussi, une instance, le culturel ou l'idéologique, occulte le social: la religion, conçue presque comme origine raciale, parfois affublée des oripaux de la culture, de la civilisation ou de l'idéologie de mobilisation, est le référent principal du discours.

Le consensus (toujours soupçonnable) et le conflit (toujours vrai) apparaissent comme les seuls termes des relations: la différence entre les acteurs devrait se résoudre à se nier pour servir le consensus ou à entrer en conflit pour s'affirmer. La multiformité du corps social, la multiplicité des identités selon le contexte, l'acceptation de la différence, la compétition entre les groupes, la recomposition de ces mêmes groupes ne seraient plus perceptibles. La tautologie narcissique se nourrissant de la permanence des identités tient lieu d'analyse. Ces dernières parlent d'elles-mêmes, elles sont stables dans le temps, inchangeables malgré la transformation du monde ambiant, éternelles et figées dans leur opposition constitutive, par ces oppositions catégoriques, absolues, réductrices l'histoire n'est plus qu'une compulsion répétitive appauvrissante. Ce discours ne peut qu'entretenir la guerre, qu'il pose implicitement comme a-priori fondateur de la société, même dans les versions les plus douces. Cette version identitaire a comme corollaire l'analyse de l'espace libanais en termes de 'Grand-' et de 'Petit-' Liban, le second étant supposé plus contrôlable, parce que plus homogène sur le plan des identités religieuses. Encore une fois la question est celle du 'qui', et non pas celle de la politique à entreprendre.

Comme construction intellectuelle, ce thème se retrouve dans la réalité, dans l'appréhension que font les individus de leur vécu quotidien, dans les idéologies les plus répandues. Mais n'implique-t-il pas aussi des solutions magiques, imaginaires, c'est à dire ne répondant qu'à des tentatives de justification et de légitimation, et donc mise en oeuvre d'une méconnaissance des mécanismes de formation et de transformation des identités, le poids du contexte dans leur évolution?

De fait, réduire la société à n'être qu'une manifestation répétitive d'identités pérennes ou enfouies, n'est pas seulement théoriquement contestable, mais nous prive surtout de précieux instruments d'analyse. Ni la sphère du juridique, ni l'essentialisme des acteurs, ne suffisent à rendre compte de rapports sociaux, et d'institutions, qui n'ont pas nécessairement l'état pour centre, de formes culturelles qui ne se réduisent pas à des identités religieuses—presque totémiques—immobiles.

Ces rapports et ces formes initient des dynamiques qui témoignent à la fois d'une grande tradition moyen-orientale de citadinité,[4] tout autant que de grandes traditions et tendances démocratiques des mouvements sociaux dans la Montagne. Mais ni la montagne, ni la ville n'étant des entités stables et étrangères, leur compétition n'étant pas un jeu à somme nulle, leur opposition n'est plus à l'ordre du jour, elles sont désormais surclassées par cet entre-deux des banlieues, ni ville, ni montagne.

C'est donc de ce phénomène d'émergence des banlieues entre ville et montagne, événement certes mais dans la longue durée, lieu où s'élaborent de nouveaux rapports sociaux, que nous voudrions partir: la ville double sa population tous les vingt ans (parfois quinze) jusqu'en 1975, alors que le pays ne double la sienne que tous les trente ans. Il importe de prendre la mesure des transformations induites dans la société libanaise par ces mouvements de population des campagnes vers la ville, parfois lents et continus sous l'emprise de la contrainte économique, d'autres fois rapides et saccadés sous l'emprise des acteurs politiques régionaux, et qui aboutissent à des mouvements sociaux de grande ampleur. Leur somme fait que près de la moitié de la population du pays se retrouve à Beyrouth vers 1970.

Or le mouvement vers la ville suppose déjà un cheminement qui n'est pas seulement physique ou géographique: aller à la ville est aussi aller vers une autre forme de société, vers un modèle spécifique de rapports sociaux que nous pourrions résumer par le concept trop négligé de citadinité, ou plutôt de citadinités car elles ne pourraient s'appréhender qu'au pluriel, tant la tradition est susceptible d'être transformée par les apports nouveaux.

Pour constituer les éléments de cette problématique, nous chercherons à savoir s'il y a une continuité ou rupture entre l'organisation de l'espace urbain avant et après 1975. Plutôt que de réécrire l'histoire des identités, ou des institutions censées les transcender, nous essayerons d'analyser la structure de l'espace urbain de Beyrouth en 1970, l'organisation des modes de vie et la projection des communautés dans l'espace urbain, enfin les sens différents des rapports inter-communautaires, pour avancer quelques propositions sur la violence dans sa forme quotidienne.

Deux mises en garde méthodologiques s'imposent au préalable. On peut ne pas tenir pour acquis et légitime le fait que nous évitions de traiter en profondeur des crises constitutives de l'espace moyen-oriental ou de l'espace national. Ce n'est certes pas pour les méconnaître, mais dans l'espoir de les reconnaître autrement: la constitution de l'espace urbain en objet spécifique d'étude pourra, peut-être, éclairer ces autres paliers d'une lumière supplémentaire.

De même il pourrait sembler que nous assumions trop vite l'idée que les acteurs sont comparables. Or ils se posent, et ils sont posés par les discours dominants, comme dissemblables, à la limite uniques. C'est là un choix, de vie et de théorie. Un autre est-il possible? Peut-on, par delà l'hétérogénéité proclamée irréductible, fouiller les zones de convergence et de parallélisme?

La ville en 1970

A Beyrouth chaque idée habite une maison.
A Beyrouth chaque mot est une ostentation.
A Beyrouth l'on décharge pensées et caravanes.

N. Tuéni

Beyrouth a été fait de temps forts.[5] Celui de la *soie* qui lui donnera la suprématie sur Saïda au dix-neuvième siècle, celui de construction de la route vers *Damas*, renforcé par l'agrandissement des quais du port, puis la voie ferrée, celui de la *famine* qui affirmera la dépendance à l'égard de l'extérieur. Puis viendra le temps des *indépendances*, celui des capitales et des frontières, qui fonctionnera—à l'encontre de toutes les appréhensions des commerçants beyrouthins inquiets—en faveur de l'expansion de la ville au Moyen-Orient. Car ce fut le temps de la mort des villes palestiniennes et particulièrement de Haïfa, la puissante concurrente de Beyrouth qui s'évanouira, tout comme Alexandrie la magnifique ou Alep la superbe succombant devant les capitales. Ce fut enfin le temps du *pétrole* qui ne finit pas de s'écrire et qui participa tant à l'expansion de la ville, que peut-être à sa mise à mort.

Ces temps multiples se sont écrits dans la population multiforme de la ville[6] aux mille origines et aux mille mythes d'origine.[7] Ils se sont écrits dans la pierre en détruisant l'ancien pour bâtir plus loin, plus haut. Ils se sont aussi écrits dans le foisonnement de formes de vie[8] tout autant que dans l'économie de cette ville à l'étroit dans son aire d'influence levantine, que dire de ses frontières nationales,[9] mais marquée cependant par sa fonction de capitale.

Ainsi Beyrouth ne saurait sans dommage être réduit à une de ses origines, à un de ses temps, à une de ses activités, à une de ses populations,[10] à un de ses déterminants. Résumé de l'espace moyen-oriental et de l'espace national, résumé des temps de la région, la ville n'était que multiformité. S'agissait-il d'un vulgaire assemblage d'éléments épars, ou un ordre, des ordres, présidaient-ils à organiser cet espace?

Structures de l'espace urbain

La lecture de l'espace de la ville ne peut partir que des formes perceptibles dans l'organisation physique, pour s'y appuyer et retrouver ensuite l'organisation sociale. Ainsi, par un premier survol, il est possible de dégager deux principes qui organisent l'espace urbain, et non un seul, dans les années 1970: celui présidant à l'expansion du tissu urbain en cercles concentriques et celui de la concentration communautaire en moitiés opposées[11] à l'image de ce que fut pour un temps court le cas de la montagne.

Le premier principe, si oublié aujourd'hui, organisait la ville en cercles (ou en arcs de cercle) concentriques, marquant le Temps de la ville et l'histoire de son expansion.

Dans un premier cercle se trouvait le centre-ville, entouré par la ville-municipe qui s'étendait vers l'Ouest, puis les banlieues autour de la nouvelle et de l'ancienne route vers Saïda, de la route vers la Montagne et de la route vers Tripoli, enfin s'ébauchait un quatrième cercle fait d'îlots encore mal reliés.

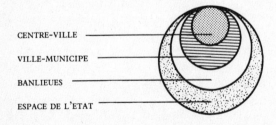

CENTRE-VILLE
VILLE-MUNICIPE
BANLIEUES
ESPACE DE L'ETAT

Schéma 1   *La structure de l'espace urbain en 1975*

Le centre-ville, qui recouvre les limites historiques de la vieille ville, a été très peu décrit. A part les indispensables travaux de géographie humaine d'André Bourgey,[12] seuls des travaux trop partiels ont été dédiés à la description du fonctionnement des souks de Beyrouth, mais aussi des ensembles fonctionnels constituant le centre-ville: le symbolisme religieux, l'organisation des échanges, l'espace bancaire, la gare routière, l'articulation sur le port, les centres de loisir.[13]

Porte symbolique de la ville, où aboutissaient tous les transports routiers et où se retrouvaient représentés tous les quartiers, toutes les régions du pays, tous les pays du Moyen-Orient. Les aires de stationnement au nombre d'une cinquantaine, garages spécialisés vers un quartier, une région, une capitale ou un pays, couvraient en effet le pays et le Moyen-Orient par les mailles d'un réseau serré. Le centre-ville était tout autant la porte de la ville par son adossement au port donc noeud d'une circulation maritime méditerranéenne, qu'il l'était par sa gare routière, à la fois noeud de la circulation intra-urbaine puisque passage obligé d'un quartier de la ville à l'autre, et de la circulation dans l'espace national et moyen-oriental.

Lieu de l'activité économique de la ville, un actif sur trois y travaillait alors que seulement un habitant sur 42 y résidait, il se présentait aussi, en contrepoint des quartiers d'habitat plus structurés communautairement, comme un espace ouvert à tous les citadins, tout autant qu'aux étrangers de passage avec ses khans et hôtels, cafés et restaurants, retraçant en ces quelques centaines de mètres carrés la géographie sinon l'histoire du Liban, du Moyen-Orient et déjà du monde: le café de Palestine, les voitures d'El-Alamein, le Parisiana, le Hammam Fleur de Syrie, la fontaine Hamidiyé, etc. . . . .

La ville-municipe s'organisait dans un second cercle, fruit de l'irruption de la vieille ville en dehors de ses murs. La plupart de ses quartiers dataient du début du vingtième siècle, mais les immeubles étaient en constante rénovation, en exceptant bien sûr les écoles et les édifices publics. La circulation était organisée de telle façon que de Mousseitbé ou d'Achrafié on dévalait toujours vers le centre-ville, la place de l'Etoile, la place Debbas et bien sûr la place des Canons recevant les rues venant des différents quartiers. Pour passer d'un quartier à l'autre, il fallait changer de véhicule dans le centre, et nous le verrons plus loin l'organisation de la circulation urbaine n'est pas sans incidence sur l'organisation sociale.

Résidence d'une petite-bourgeoisie citadine, vivant du et avec le centre-ville, ces quartiers ne seront reliés entre eux que dans les années 1960–1970 par des rues transversales, allant d'Est en Ouest et ignorant peut-être le centre qui entre-temps s'était étendu.[14] C'est dans les années 1950, en même temps que fut mis en place l'aéroport, que se passa l'événement marquant la recomposition de cet espace: *la ruée vers l'Ouest*, vers la modernité de Ras-Beyrouth. Le centre-ville s'étendit à Hamra, s'appuya sur l'American University of Beirut, se constitua des bourgeoisies arabes et des activités commerciales dont le centre de gravité se déplaçait du Levant vers le Golfe, et se traduisit par l'émergence d'une organisation communautaire et professionnelle encore plus chatoyante et luxuriante que celle de la vieille ville.[15]

Les banlieues, troisième cercle de l'expansion urbaine, étaient aussi témoins de l'expansion de la ville vers le Nord-Est et le Sud.[16] La ceinture de misère, décrite et décriée dans les années 1970, était très présente. Malgré les tentatives de l'occulter par des murs de la honte qui l'entouraient, elle se signalait pour ainsi dire par défaut. Elle était faite de points ou de taches de taudis, habitat précaire s'il en fût et soumis au harcèlement des incendies d'origine inconnue.

Mais, dans ce cercle les plus grandes surfaces étaient couvertes par les quartiers résidentiels des années 1960, tout en hauteur et offrant les possibilités maximum—à Beyrouth—d'une exploitation du bâti par sa location à une *moyenne* et *petite bourgeoisie* venant tout juste d'être urbanisés. Ces quartiers comme ceux de Aïn el-Rommaneh, Forn el-Chebbak, Chiah Ghobeïré, Haï el-Jédid, ne vivaient pas d'activités nécessairement articulées sur le centre-ville, mais étalées sur l'ensemble de l'agglomération ou parfois concentrées en banlieue.

Le dernier cercle n'était qu'ébauche autour des puissantes formes étatiques: la caserne-école militaire de Fayadiyé, le palais présidentiel de Baabda, la télévision de Hazmié et le complexe du ministère de la défense de Yarzé. Faut-il placer là les puissants bâtiments des Jésuites à Jamhour? La continuité fonctionnelle est frappante. Autour de ce noyau dur 'institutionnel', une série d'îlots résidentiels voyaient le jour, faits de villas indépendantes dans le style anglo-saxon.[17] En se multipliant de l'extrême Sud à l'extrême Nord autour de la ville, ils organisaient un nouveau cercle qui était en passe de devenir très vite celui du pouvoir et de la richesse.

Cette concentration spatiale, pouvoir et richesse, avait la particularité d'être issue de la période de l'autonomisation du politique grâce au boom pétrolier et aux retours d'émigration. Dans ce cadre-là, les activités économiques principales n'avaient plus rien à voir avec le centre-ville ou sa version modernisée de Ras-Beyrouth, et la production citadine de valeurs. Ils proposaient de fait une autre modernité repérable dans le bâti, la nouvelle urbanisation s'employait à la colonisation des franges entre la ville et les pentes de la montagne, parfois à l'implantation d'industries.

La grande division, la césure, qui marquait physiquement le paysage urbain, était en 1970 à 1975 la ligne de fracture qui séparait le second cercle du troisième, d'un côté le centre-ville et la ville-municipe, de l'autre les banlieues avec les ceintures de misère, de richesse et de pouvoir. La ligne de partage des étendues sablonneuses succédant à Ramlet el-Baïda pour suivre les collines ensablées jusqu'à la forêt de pins en enjambant les espaces de la cité sportive et de l'hippodrome, pour enfin accompagner le cours du fleuve, où l'impression de séparation était encore plus sensible par le fait même de la hauteur de la colline d'Achrafié d'un côté, et de l'aplatissement de l'espace extra-municipe. Cette ligne, suivant à peu près la frontière administrative, ne connaissait qu'une seule solution de continuité par les camps palestiniens qui semblaient illustrer l'exception plutôt que la règle. La ligne de fracture Ouest-Est rendait physiquement perceptible l'importance du premier principe d'organisation de l'espace urbain, celui de la superposition des couches de population selon les époques de leur arrivées en ville. Un des effets de la guerre sera son remplacement par une autre ligne, Nord-Sud, alors relativement invisible bien que toujours présente.

Modèles de relations communautaires: ville et état

> that law is personal and determined by who one is, not territorial and determined by where one is.
>
> C. Geertz

La ville-métropole et la ville-capitale

Qu'est donc la Ville? C'est certes au premier abord un espace physique fait de bâti, mais c'est surtout un espace social à construire. Le danger est peut-être d'en faire un absolu: la Ville vécue est pour certains de ses habitants, à certains moments de l'histoire, un référent magique, non pas une partie de la société, un ensemble de groupes, une forme ou une structure sociale, mais une identité rigide et absolue, à la limite une volonté collective s'exprimant d'une façon monolithique. La fameuse 'critique' de Weber concernant la ville orientale est justement minée par une conception sous-jacente, celle de l'adéquation totale entre hétérogénéité physique—la ville est distincte de son environnement—et personnalité sociale: elle devrait posséder ses institutions municipales propres et cohérentes, elle est l'expression d'une seule communauté bourgeoise, sinon 'quelque chose'[18] lui manquerait. Mais c'est peut-être plus là un enjeu qu'une règle, comme le relève Michel Seurat dans le débat de Weuleresse et Lapidus.[19]

Or la ville ne peut être qu'un objet virtuel à construire[20] par l'activité de réflexion, car si elle n'est pas seulement située du côté physique, elle ne peut non plus se concevoir seulement à travers un nominalisme réducteur: elle n'est pas donnée une fois pour toutes, elle n'est pas un de ses groupes, ni leur somme, ni les seules fonctions qu'ils assument. Elle ne peut être appréhendée que comme rapports entre des groupes se faisant et se défaisant dans l'économique, le politique, ou le symbolique. Sa composition n'est pas donnée une fois pour toutes, mais constitue en elle-même un des enjeux des rapports et conflits des groupes.

L'espace physique nous servira donc à reconnaître l'organisation de l'espace social, sans jamais faire l'hypothèse d'une adéquation totale, mais en émettant celle de corrélations structurelles: la grande opposition qui structurait l'espace social de Beyrouth relayait la grande césure qui divisait l'espace physique en 1970. Ainsi, la-ville-en-dehors-de-la-ville devenait de plus en plus visible à travers l'urbanisation du quatrième cercle. La tension entre le premier cercle (le centre-ville) et le dernier (la ceinture de la richesse et du pouvoir) reflétait la compétition entre deux centres, celui de la Ville et celui de l'Etat.

Cette tension entre deux centralités était en fait une divergence entre deux principes d'organisation sociale, entre deux ordres sociaux tentant chacun de devenir dominant. La ville-métropole régionale et la ville-capitale faisaient à elles deux l'agglomération beyrouthine sans que les principes les régissant ne soient les mêmes. Certes, le plus souvent, l'opposition n'était pas la seule règle, la complicité étant aussi parfois de mise, mais l'un des deux principes ne pouvait qu'être remis en question par l'autre. Il ne s'agit pas ici seulement de conflit ou de consensus entre deux groupes se reconnaissant dans l'un ou dans l'autre, bien qu'à l'occasion ceci fut une des traductions possibles, mais d'une compétition continue pour la prééminence, parfois relais de celle de l'espace-montagne et de l'espace-ville, où consensus et conflits n'étaient que partiels et momentanés, remis en question et remettant en question la définition même des identités.[21]

Notre hypothèse essentielle est que l'organisation traditionnelle par communautés, peut-être héritée de l'époque ottomane, ou même de périodes historiques antérieures,[22] fonctionnait en 1970 selon deux principes différents, deux symboliques distinctes: le principe d'organisation du pouvoir et le principe d'organisation de la ville, le niveau du politique et le niveau de l'économique, le niveau institutionnel formel et celui des institutions moins visibles mais que révèle l'analyse de l'espace social de la ville, celui des statuts politiques et celui des spécialisations professionnelles, la manipulation des structures communautaires comme point d'appui dans la lutte pour le pouvoir et l'utilisation de la communauté comme réseau compétitif de relations commerciales entre les villes. Ainsi, les relations communautaires, et donc 'la' communauté, prenaient un sens dans l'ordre étatique et en avaient un autre dans l'ordre urbain.[23]

Cette distinction des principes internes qui structuraient la société, a pris des formes spécifiques à travers la différenciation moderne entre la dynamique territoriale de l'Etat-Nation et la dynamique d'une ville métropole moyen-orientale (succédant à toute une série de maillons d'un réseau urbain en disparition). La problématique des frontières à tracer entre un espace interne et un espace externe, différait de la problématique de la circulation des biens, des messages et des personnes à travers les frontières par l'organisation de réseaux inter-urbains. Car si la ville-capitale organise la citoyenneté à travers des rapports de pouvoir, la ville-métropole spécifie la citadinité à travers des rapports de négoce.[24]

Si l'état peut se présenter comme le degré zéro des communautés, la pudeur des communautés comme l'a si joliment appelée Ahmad Beydoun,[25] la ville, et surtout le centre-ville sont par définition un autre lieu de la présence simultanée—et . . . pudique—de ces communautés. En quoi ces deux principes d'articulation des communautés diffèrent-ils?

Les modes de vie dans la ville

Il existe toute une tradition urbaine qui se démarque du pouvoir des états dans le Moyen-Orient. La sociologie, la science politique et l'historiographie modernes auraient intérêt à ne pas négliger cette distanciation en identifiant villes et états. Cette tradition de citadinité s'élabore à partir de lieux spécifiques qui fondent une démarcation subtile: ni opposition-conflit, ni accord-fusion, mais autres lieux, autres rapports.

Il est évident que le principe de citadinité ne recouvre pas toute l'agglomération beyrouthine. Il est le plus fort au centre, et il va en s'atténuant vers les périphéries où se renforce au contraire le principe d'état. Le principe de la ville structurait cependant par ses effets l'agglomération en modes de vie, qui à leur tour découpaient quatre espaces sociaux différents, représentant des rapports sociaux distincts. Deux d'entre eux se situaient dans la ville-municipe, ceux de la citadinité traditionnelle et de la citadinité moderne, deux autres dans les banlieues, celui de la nouvelle urbanité centrée autour de l'état, et celui de l'urbanité tout aussi nouvelle mais marginalisée à la fois par l'état et par la ville. C'est le premier mode de vie qui reste pour nous la matrice de l'organisation sociale de la ville, le noyau d'où émerge la citadinité, ce qui ne le met pas nécessairement en conflit avec les autres. La ville, avec son droit de cité devait se démarquer de la citoyenneté: 45 pour cent des habitants de l'agglomération ne relevaient du droit de citoyenneté que par leur exclusion, ils étaient étrangers.[26]

La citadinité traditionnelle se déployait dans l'espace du centre-ville et de la ville-municipe, elle était déterminée par l'importance des activités de négoce, petit et grand, et par celle de la structure différenciée de l'espace dans laquelle se meuvent les citadins. Ce mouvement quotidien du citadin allant des quartiers résidentiels, et en général à dominance communautaire, vers un centre d'activités économiques multiforme communautairement, organisant l'échange économique, est fondateur de la citadinité traditionnelle. La symbolique qui en résulte est une force d'attraction très puissante: c'est un sens très efficace qui se situe en marge de la citoyenneté ou de la modernité.

La division communautaire fait référence ici à la grande division des activités économiques de la ville historique: pour les musulmans (les sunnites) le commerce de l'alimentation, pour les chrétiens (les orthodoxes) le commerce de produits finis, habits et autres. Cette division n'est pas fortuite, elle est au coeur de l'organisation urbaine, car elle implique un principe de proximité, de distinction des identités malgré cette proximité et de réciprocité entre les communautés, aucune d'elles ne pouvant se passer des autres dans la vie quotidienne. Même si les quartiers d'habitation restaient séparés, les formes de ravitaillement impliquaient le rapport à l'autre.

Au fur et à mesure de l'expansion urbaine, cette distribution devient plus complexe. Ainsi viennent s'ajouter d'autres spécialités professionnelles et d'autres communautés, les commerces de bijoux et d'horlogerie et le petit artisanat témoignant de la concentration des arméniens, des noyaux très anciens mais limités de maronites, chiites et druzes, et surtout d'une importante bourgeoisie grecque-catholique et d'une vieille communauté juive. Ce commerce de détail se double souvent d'un commerce triangulaire impliquant des amplitudes et des échelles plus larges, vers d'autres pays et d'autres villes de la région, à travers des réseaux dépendant largement des structures confession-nelles, des alliances de mariage, ou de migrations de la parentèle.

Pour cela il fallait réinterpréter les liens familiaux et communau-taires dans des termes permettant d'entretenir des réseaux d'échange et de correspondance. Ce qui implique en retour un traitement paradoxal de l'identité: en assignant des références à ce qui est soi, en le définissant à travers les rapports à l'autre, on le dégage en quelque sorte du déterminisme des liens de sang, on le produit comme Autre. Différence et réciprocité, émiettement et contiguïté, négoce et négociation, voisinage et compromis, la citadinité traditionnelle se caractérisera par ces termes, au point que pour la critiquer on identifiera le compromis à la compromission.

C'est un compromis qui permet de comprendre la luxuriance de la multiformité de la vie sociale des villes moyen-orientales tradition-nelles, que le colonialisme n'a fait qu'accentuer. Beyrouth survivra à l'indépendance, devant laquelle ont succombé les villes de la région, en gardant cette richesse faite de différences posées les unes à côté des autres, de tolérance générale et de télescopage des temps, qui constituent l'espace social où les réseaux commerciaux ont pu proliférer, et les identités se relativiser.

Le mode de vie quotidien semble se caractériser, comme l'a noté Clifford Geertz au sujet des souks de Sefrou,[27] par la rétention d'information, mais aussi par un contrôle étroit de la circulation de la monnaie et une réduction des dépenses apparentes frisant parfois l'avarice. Si la multitude de petits échanges commerciaux, d'opérations fractionnées, dominent cet espace, les figures les plus caractéristiques de ce milieu sont celles du *petit commerçant* local, véritable *médiateur* (*wasit*) au plan social prolongeant sa fonction aux plans foncier et du négoce régional (*simsar, simsar bida'a*). Cependant en égard à l'importance prise par la propriété foncière et aux problèmes de sa transmission par héritage, ainsi qu'aux problèmes commerciaux, l'avocat, intercesseur,[28] va devenir de plus en plus une figure centrale de ce mode de vie.

C'est l'espace social d'une population qui sans se constituer en grande bourgeoisie, n'est cependant pas exposée aux vicissitudes de la vie, une certaine quiétude marquant son rythme de vie. Car l'expansion continue de l'urbain facilite l'émergence d'une *petite bourgeoisie, souvent appuyée sur une valorisation symbolique de son espace de vie*, mais aussi sur la propriété foncière en constante réévaluation. C'est celui d'une population qui vit (1) en deçà de l'état, dans son espace réduit, mais fortement différencié en public et privé, en centre et quartiers de résidence, et (2) au-delà de cet état, à travers les villes de la région et du monde. C'est une population qui a du monde, et de son propre espace urbain une connaissance exacte et utile: celle des circuits de commerce. C'est aussi une population qui a de l'espace économiquement inutile une méconnaissance forte.

Un autre mode de vie va s'installer dans l'Ouest de la citadinité moderne: le rôle de l'Université américaine, véritable centre d'attraction moyen-oriental, se traduira par l'intronisation des diplômes comme voie d'accès à la profession. La mode, surtout en habillement, est le second élément qui fera la prospérité et la structure de ce mode de vie, où Hamra gagnera une réputation moyen-orientale, sans commune mesure avec son poids économique réel. Enfin, il se structurera autour de relations commerciales, mais aussi de services bancaires, éducatifs ou médicaux, atteignant grâce à l'aviation et aux télécommunications des régions bien plus vastes que le Levant et son hinterland immédiat. C'est la *modernité* qui caractérise ce mode de vie, modernité revendiquée le plus souvent et non pas réellement pensée, modernité d'avant-garde politique parfois, phare régional, mais aussi souvent fuite en avant.

La figure dominante de cet espace est de fait celle du *banquier*, qui propose un autre type d'urbanité que celui du petit commerçant du centre-ville, mais à laquelle il faudrait ajouter celle opposante de *l'artiste*, le plus souvent marqué politiquement à gauche, mais créateur lui aussi de valeurs, selon une autre conception de l'échange. C'est un espace marqué lui aussi d'une dualité fonctionnelle, celle de la recherche de la richesse et de la demande esthétique, la mode se retrouvant à l'intersection des deux. Ce mode de vie est-il en continuité avec le précédent? A l'analyse la différence est évidente, la rupture moins certaine.

En plus des sunnites et des orthodoxes venus de l'espace plus traditionnel, de chiites et de maronites en nombre plus réduit mais présents de très longue date en ville, les communautés qui le caractérisent, sont en majeure partie des communautés de réfugiés, massivement intégrées à la vie urbaine, se retrouvant en priorité à Beyrouth, exceptionnellement dans des villes secondaires, et souvent elles-mêmes d'origines citadines anciennes, comme les catholiques alépins, ceux d'Alexandrie ou de Palestine. Il faut y ajouter les arméniens, les protestants, des sunnites et des orthodoxes de l'intérieur levantin, beaucoup d'étrangers au Moyen-Orient, les *ajnabis-ajanib*s.

Notre hypothèse est que l'aspect international et moderne des rapports dans cet espace, est au moins partiellement une réinterprétation de la citadinité traditionnelle: le fonctionnement des communautés-nationalités comme communautés citadines, c'est à dire comme réseaux et spécialisations professionnelles sur le modèle du centre-ville. La question qui se pose est le fonctionnement de cet espace social comme espace politique: manipulation de l'état contre la ville traditionnelle, utilisation de la ville pour limiter l'emprise sociale de l'état? L'analyse est loin d'être close.[29]

Le troisième mode de vie est celui des marginaux, *nouveaux urbains*, la plupart du temps réfugiés installés en majorité à Beyrouth ou en zones urbaines, c'était aussi parfois des 'paysans dépaysannés'[30] arrivant en ville des zones périphériques et se retrouvant concentrés dans des ghettos. Certains groupes en sortiront vers la ville moderne après un laps de temps en général assez long, comme par exemple les paysans dépaysannés maronites de la gare de triage de Karm el-Zeïtoun. Mais la plupart se verront concentrés dans des camps ou un habitat bidonvillaire.

Sans rapports avec le centre-ville, en dehors du cercle des professions traditionnelles ou modernes par manque de qualifications, de capitaux ou de réseaux, ces populations étaient réduites à constituer une main-d'oeuvre non-qualifiée à bas prix et donc surexploitée en particulier par certaines industries naissantes; elles constituaient le type-même du sous-prolétariat. La misère des Kurdes, des Palestiniens, des apatrides, avant eux des Arméniens, et bientôt des chiites de Naba'a, de la Quarantaine, de Borj-Hammoud et de Maslakh sera ignorée. Tout autant cependant que celle des ex-paysans maronites de Karm el-Zeïtoun ou de Dora, ou celle du petit peuple urbain. Mais dans le cas du sous-prolétariat des banlieues, la situation sera aggravée pour certains par l'exclusion dont les frappait le principe de citoyenneté. Ces populations étaient pénalisées par leur incapacité à accéder à la nationalité malgré leur présence dans la cité, leur style de vie ne pouvait être caractérisé que par la *précarité* qu'ils savent imposée à la fois par la volonté de l'état et la démission de la ville.

Analphabétisme,[31] manque d'hygiène, problèmes de santé, chômage, sous-équipement du point de vue des services urbains,[32] dans ces quartiers se glissant entre ville et banlieue vivait une population qui faisait l'expérience anticipatrice du ghetto, certes imposé. La concentration par groupes ethniques ou communautaires ne laissait apparaître aucune figure polarisante, sauf peut-être celle du *médecin militant*, qui au début des années 1970 commencera, grâce à l'effervescence politique ambiante, à se manifester comme investi d'un certain capital symbolique. Ce n'est que bien plus tard, après 1982, que l'homme de religion le surclassera.

Il y avait cependant une autre forme de nouvelle urbanité, décrite en partie par Khuri[33] et mettant en jeu un phénomène de reconfessionnalisation, ou plutôt de relativisation du poids des structures sociales ayant fonctionné dans la montagne, comme la famille étendue, vers une sur-valorisation et une redécouverte de l'origine régionale ou confessionnelle comme unité de solidarité.

Cette forme de *nouvelle urbanité*, en contrepoint de la citadinité traditionnelle et de la marginalité, *prenait appui sur l'état*, mythe et institutions, pour assurer la réussite de sa transition vers la ville. Cumulant plusieurs ressources, allant des retombées de l'émigration vers les Amériques ou l'Afrique, bientôt le Golfe du pétrole, à l'accès facile à des postes de fonctionnaires qui lui permettaient de se constituer en classes moyennes nouvelles. Cette population se caractérisait aussi par des concentrations très fortes dans l'habitat, et surtout par une propension à la *surconsommation* ostentatoire, dans une sorte de compétition intra-communautaire, mais sans doute aussi par réaction à, et pour se démarquer de, la déchéance d'autres nouveaux venus à la ville.

S'il est une figure dominante dans cet espace c'est bien celle du *maître d'école*, régnant sur la voie de passage royale vers le monde adulte et vers l'emploi dans la ville, traduisant donc à la fois la maturation biologique et le passage géographique à la ville par une transition sociale.

Il est nécessaire à ce point de faire le point sur le thème si répandu de 'l'hégémonie maronite'. S'il est vrai en effet qu'une certaine concentration maronite est perceptible dans les postes de l'état, en particulier les postes-clés, il est cependant nécessaire de faire la part des choses en ce qui concerne le poids effectif de la communauté dans la société. On ne peut parler là d'hégémonie, ni dans les quartiers de la ville, ni dans le centre-ville, ni dans les activités économiques. Socio-économiquement la communauté maronite n'a jamais atteint en ville plus que le statut d'une petite et moyenne bourgeoisie dominant, numériquement et seulement numériquement, dans les activités salariées principales, mais seulement dans ces activités-là: l'administration, la banque et les écoles.

Or ce poids, certes important, dans ces activités est loin d'être essentiel dans la dynamique générale de l'économie. Ce n'est de toute façon pas l'état, qui est le vecteur de cette intégration urbaine, mais bien le système d'enseignement des écoles catholiques qui a permis à cette classe moyenne néo-urbaine de se constituer. La mesure du rôle réel de l'état dans la société indique les limites de l'efficacité de son action en faveur de l'intégration de la communauté maronite: à peine fournira-t-il de meilleurs équipements urbains dans les quartiers maronites de la banlieue. L'hégémonie, réelle sur l'appareil d'état, apparaît donc plus limitée dans la société.

Quelle fonction a eu ce mythe de l'hégémonie maronite? Probablement celui d'assurer une solidarité de la communauté, car ce mythe était omniprésent dans cette communauté-même avant qu'il ne devienne un reproche véhiculé par les autres communautés. Solidarité mythique certes, au sens d'un mythe fort qui est une volonté de traduire un principe dans la réalité, et probablement moins fictive qu'on ne ne veut le croire parfois. N'empêche que cette hégémonie est avant tout symbolique. Se croire privilégié dans la société grâce à l'état, se sentir tenu de lutter pour conserver cette voie royale vers l'intégration dans la ville est cependant un mythe dangereux. Pour commencer, il conforte l'étrangeté de la communauté 'hégémonique' dans sa société. Il produit le rejet des autres communautés citadines et montagnardes.

Mais surtout, quand les nouvelles générations dans d'autres communautés néo-urbaines s'adresseront à l'état pour assurer leur intégration, elles risqueront de n'y trouver qu'une possibilité de promotion illusoire, mais non pas réelle, l'état étant incapable de l'assurer à lui seul. Et elles se sentiront peut-être d'autant plus flouées. Ne seront-elles pas alors tentées de se rattraper en passant d'une hégémonie symbolique à des totalitarismes absolus? A la suite, en miroir d'une certaine jeunesse maronite, ne seront-elles pas tentées de se passer de l'état pour conquérir le territoire, c'est à dire de passer d'une image de domination à une déception rageuse destructrice de pans entiers de la société?

Les degrés de citoyenneté ou le principe d'état

Le rôle de l'état comme acteur social a souvent été appréhendé à travers des brumes idéologiques, le modèle idéal se confondant avec le réel, ce qui était implicitement affirmé consistait en sa parfaite adéquation avec la société. Aussi, rarement les conditions sociales de la production de l'état ont-elles été questionnées. Pour notre part, nous ne nous limiterons pas à la logique et la cohérence interne des institutions idéalisées, mais chercherons à prendre la mesure de leur poids dans la société, nous ne rejetterons pas les idéologies qui se forment à partir ou autour de l'état mais chercherons à déterminer leur efficacité sociale.

Au prisme de la ville et en regard des effets de l'état et plus généralement du Politique sur l'intégration urbaine, des tendances contradictoires peuvent être ainsi décelées:

1. D'un côté il y a certainement un effet de facilitation de l'intégration urbaine grâce au maintien, contre la logique dominante d'une économie sauvagement libérale, d'une loi sur les loyers extrêmement favorable aux locataires favorisant la présence physique en ville des classes moyennes.
2. Mais d'un autre côté, se déploient des effets d'accentuation de la différenciation symbolique entre les nouvelles populations urbanisées et les autres, par le maintien de structures archaïques dans la représentation parlementaire ou l'organisation administrative: la plupart des 'nouveaux urbains', parfois installés en ville depuis plus d'une génération, continuaient à voter dans leur région d'origine; les municipalités de banlieue dépendaient elles du *muhafazat* de la montagne, les passerelles pour une coordination avec la municipalité de la ville étaient rares, ce qui favorisait la bipolarisation de l'espace urbain, et rendait plus difficile l'identification à la ville des nouveaux-venus.

Mais surtout, il est nécessaire de se demander si le mythe social de l'état n'a pas fonctionné autrement que son modèle idéal, 'unitaire', ne l'impliquait. L'état vécu, réel, c'est à dire paradoxalement celui de sa symbolique sociale, se traduisait par l'existence d'au moins *quatre degrés de citoyenneté* dans la société et non pas comme principe d'unification de cette même société. Il a proposé à la société un modèle de hiérarchie à mi-chemin entre l'implicite et l'explicite.

Il y eut ainsi des *citoyens de plein droit*, de vrais Libanais, des Libanais de coeur, et qui le devenaient effectivement puisque supposés tels. Un second degré fut celui des *citoyens d'adoption*, des Libanais naturalisés, clients donc, ou supposés clients de la première catégorie. Un troisième degré était celui des Libanais de jure, mais ne jouissant pas dans la symbolique de la citoyenneté du degré premier, un doute étant entretenu quand à leur qualité, qui n'est pas sans relation avec leur appartenance à un sous-espace interne symboliquement *périphérique*. Un dernier degré était celui des *non-citoyens*, degré extrême, celui de la non-jouissance des droits relevant de la citoyenneté.

Cette classification des communautés comportait cependant des incertitudes. En particulier, la position des communautés de vieux citadins est difficile à délimiter: tout en n'étant pas partie prenante du premier degré, elles ne s'acceptaient cependant pas comme clientes (second degré) et remettaient souvent en question le fonctionnement du système. Mais ce principe de hiérarchie fonctionnait surtout en négatif, comme exclusion des populations de la ceinture de misère, doublant l'exclusion sociale dont ils étaient victimes, ne les structurant comme communautés que négativement. En fait le territoire d'exercice de ces principes se situait dans la ville des banlieues, structurées ainsi en unités bien plus conflictuelles que celles de la ville-municipe qui elle se situait en marge de l'état.

Pourquoi le modèle idéal de l'état n'a-t-il pas fonctionné en créant une nation de citoyens? Il ne nous appartient pas d'apporter une réponse à ce problème, simplement de rappeler que ce modèle, bien que dominant dans le monde depuis 1945, n'est pas le seul possible du Politique—historiquement s'entend—et qu'il ne semble pas mieux fonctionner en Afrique ou en Asie du Sud-Est, et bien sûr dans tout le reste du Moyen-Orient. S'agit-il du décalage dû à l'imposition d'un modèle du politique ne correspondant pas à la structure sociale?

La crise urbaine vers 1970

> Pour aller au paradis, ou en enfer, il faut se rendre dans un grand milieu: la ville. Elle offre cette liberté de choix.
>
> D. Chevallier

Une situation de crise très particulière existe dans la ville de 1970: les vieux mécanismes d'intégration urbaine mis en place par les deux grandes communautés citadines, les orthodoxes et les sunnites, pour intégrer les nouveaux urbains de même confession ne suffisent plus. La vieille division professionnelle n'arrive plus à absorber ni les nouvelles générations, ni les membres de communautés nouvelles. Le statut de ces dernières est instable: elles n'appartiennent ni à l'ordre urbain, ni à l'ordre étatique.

Les communautés les plus fraîchement urbanisées sont pénalisées par leur unique spécialisation agricole, inutile par définition en ville. De plus:

1. Elles arrivent massivement, des villages entiers se vident, essentiellement sous la pression de l'armée israélienne, c'est à dire de l'intervention de l'espace moyen-oriental dans l'espace national, et s'installent en ville provoquant un accroissement des besoins et de la consommation de bâti, d'équipements et de biens.
2. Et ce en un temps particulièrement court et exigeant des solutions immédiates à des situations dramatiques.
3. A travers une situation politique particulièrement tendue, qui se caractérise par une opposition entre Ville et Etat, où chacun des deux termes tentera et de résoudre une partie de leurs problèmes et de les manipuler contre l'autre. A ce stade la ville peut imprudemment se délier de la responsabilité de ceux qui se pressent à ses portes, pour la rejeter sur l'état. Ce dernier ne fait qu'accentuer, parfois sciemment, la *marginalité,* sinon l'exclusion, des nouveaux venus.

Ainsi, la crise de l'emploi, celle de l'habitat, celle de l'accès à la consommation, celle de l'enseignement public traduisent en 1970 une crise urbaine particulièrement décisive, même si, ou paradoxalement parce qu'elle se situe dans une période d'expansion économique et non pas de récession. La ville est en effet en bouillonnement. La plèbe urbaine rassemble tous les marginaux, mais aussi les tenants de la citadinité traditionnelle contre un état qui représente de plus en plus un pôle de défi communautaire. La ville est incapable d'offrir à ses communautés un sens à leur présence, une fonction les constituant, qu'en opposition à l'état.

L'agitation, à la fois celle des quartiers traditionnels et celle des syndicats modernes, ne va cependant jamais jusqu'à l'irrémédiable, jusqu'à la réécriture de nouveaux principes d'organisation sociale dans l'espace. La centralité urbaine est sauvegardée tout en étant investie comme lieu symbolique de l'opposition à l'autre centralité, l'étatique. La Rue de Beyrouth devient le symbole d'un certain état d'esprit anarchisant.

D'un autre côté, l'exemple de l'intégration maronite est à la fois méconnu, délégitimé et lui-même en crise: l'urbanisation de la communauté ne s'arrête pas et l'école n'est plus réellement un vecteur d'urbanisation réussie. Un flot continu, bien que moins rapide, continue à couler de la montagne vers la ville. Les secteurs de l'emploi qui recrutaient dans ses rangs, grâce à un niveau d'instruction élevé, sont de plus en plus saturés, alors même que la compétition s'accroît avec l'accès aux diplômes d'autres jeunes, originaires de régions maronites périphériques ou tout simplement d'autres confessions, en particulier à travers l'Université libanaise.

Le déclassement menace à terme les nouvelles générations de la petite et moyenne bourgeoisie maronite. La définition de la communauté risque de perdre tout sens. Il est compréhensible que s'affirme en son sein toute une mythologie radicalement conservatrice, repliée sur l'affirmation privilégiée de l'identité, et centrée autour d'une meilleur efficacité de l'appareil d'état, du Politique en général plutôt que de l'éducationnel, comme dernier recours pour échapper *au déclassement.*

Situation d'autant plus difficile, que l'émigration en Afrique commence à fermer ses portes aux Libanais et même à les renvoyer, le plus souvent avec leurs avoirs il est vrai, mais c'est là un autre problème. L'accès réduit à la ville n'est pas seulement un problème de richesse, c'est aussi celui de l'accès à une certaine symbolique. Du haut des collines de la richesse entourant Beyrouth, et dont une grande partie du bâti était due aux émigrés retournés, on pouvait se sentir encore plus exclu de la ville, et parfois concevoir cette exclusion comme une plus grande injustice, que celle dont fait les frais la ceinture de misère. *Le politique, plus particulièrement le pouvoir d'état, devient un axe essentiel de la réalisation de soi, c'est à dire de définition d'un sens propre.*

Or cette crise s'inscrit dans des crises plus vastes. La crise légitimité des Etats-Nations du Moyen-Orient va de pair avec un renforcement paradoxal du politique, comme instance et comme appareils. Ce paradoxe traduit bien les effets de la situation moyen-orientale, doublement déterminée par la crise post-guerre de 1967 et par les retombées de la hausse des prix du pétrole après 1973. La première lance le défi du modèle d'une société monocommunautaire et conquérante à des sociétés toujours multicommunautaires et empêtrées dans leurs problèmes de sous-développement. L'idée d'une corrélation entre la 'purification' des identités religieuses et la voie royale vers la réussite fait lentement son chemin. Quand au pétrole, il permet par le jeu de la redistribution à tous les états et institutions politiques de la région de s'autonomiser par rapport à leurs société, sinon de les menacer, en tout cas de *marginaliser les multitudes de petits réseaux de commerce* qui fondaient la citadinité traditionnelle. En tout cela le cas libanais est moins particulier qu'une première appréhension le ferait penser.

Crise dans et de l'espace urbain, sur-déterminée par les crises de l'espace moyen-oriental et de l'espace national: c'est une crise de la centralité dans la ville doublée d'une crise de l'accès à la centralité de certaines catégories d'habitants de Beyrouth, ou même crise du maintien dans l'espace urbain d'autres catégories, incapables pour s'y reproduire d'en assimiler les règles, ou de les modifier en leur faveur. Ces catégories marginales, méprisées et manipulées pour fournir l'essentiel de la troupe, vont cependant peu à peu se retrouver en position de contrôle du terrain.

Du système urbain au système milicien ou les années de violence

> Il n'y a pas de salut pour tous ces perdants, que là où ils ont recours à la violence, à l'agression, à la guerre.
>
> F. Braudel

L'une des questions qui se posent avec le plus d'insistance n'est-elle pas celle des causes de la violence que connait le Liban? Du Liban-scène de la violence des autres, au Liban-enjeu de conflits entre groupes, au Liban-objectif et victime des forces du mal, au Liban-résistant à toutes ces forces, autant d'explications qui se veulent contradictoires, exclusives, uniques. Mais est-il vrai que les années de violence ne sont que l'une, quelconque, de ces explications? Ne faut-il pas rechercher dans des phénomènes aussi complexes une multiplicité des déterminants, plutôt que de tenter d'en investir une seule d'une signification ultime, d'ailleurs plus idéologique qu'explicative? N'y a-t-il pas dans la simplification outrancière un a priori refusant la connaissance dans ce qu'elle a de plus dérangeant, de remise en cause, d'autant plus que l'objet de connaissance est lui-même dérangeant? Le mécanisme même de la connaissance intellectuelle ne se transforme-t-il pas en une tentative de juguler la remise en cause qu'introduit un objet si lassant à force de répétition, si insaisissable à force de changement, plutôt qu'en une revendication d'un discours nuancé permettant sa découverte à travers ses multiples facettes?

Peut-on encore remettre en question la complémentarité des facteurs externes qui fragilisent la scène libanaise, l'archaïsme de certaines institutions et mentalités en contradiction avec l'évolution moderne bien que s'en réclamant? Ne doit-on pas s'interroger aussi sur les situations qui ont fait identifier l'autre comme force du mal, et qui ont par la symbolique de la victimisation ou de la résistance occulté l'étude des conditions qui ont permis la permanence d'une violence quotidienne? Plutôt que de se réfugier dans des explications simples en termes de grandes religions-identités s'opposant éternellement, la chrétienne et la musulmane, ou de grandes classes-identités reprenant le même processus, la grande-bourgeoisie et les classes populaires.

N'est-il pas possible d'identifier partout, c'est à dire dans chacune

des identités religieuses, une petite-bourgeoisie néo-urbaine menacée
de déclassement et un sous-prolétariat péri-urbain marginalisé, qui
surmontent dans la guerre leur crise, créent et imposent leur vision
de la société, l'urbaine en particulier, conçue comme un ensemble
de territoires leur permettant tant de recontrôler leurs communautés
propres, de s'imposer aux communautés citadines de la même
religion, et d'instaurer un rapport spécifique entre l'autre groupe—
l'autre territoire—et son propre groupe—son propre territoire—
exclusion et intégration plus volontaristes donc que simples sur-
vivances d'un passé? Tout l'intérêt de la question serait de savoir
comment se mobilise la population derrière ces groupes les plus
décidés, et quand commence-t-elle à se détacher d'eux puis à s'opposer
à leurs pouvoirs, c'est à dire quand ces groupes représentent-ils
la société ou une partie d'entre elle, et quand rentrent-ils en conflit
avec elle, et non pas s'ils la représentent ou pas. Il est illusoire, parce
que réducteur, de s'enfermer dans les pièges de la continuité
identitaire.

Ainsi, la guerre pouvait-elle être autre que rupture? En deçà de
l'ordre étatique, au-delà du système urbain, va s'instaurer et s'imposer
non pas seulement le désordre, mais un nouvel ordre, celui des
territoires de la violence quotidienne. Cet ordre va tracer une autre
forme d'organisation de l'espace: la trop fameuse ligne de démarcation
va devenir prégnante, elle va poser la limite de deux cercles qui
s'opposent en place et lieu des cercles concentriques.

Presque perpendiculaire à la césure des couches d'urbanisation que
nous avons rencontrée plus haut, la ligne de démarcation va s'imposer
pour redessiner le paysage, au point d'en épuiser la signification. Le
paysage urbain est différent: de plus en plus la ligne de césure de
l'avant-guerre, celle qui sépare la ville-municipe des banlieues, va
avoir tendance à être gommée, effacée, comblée. La nouvelle division
va passer par une ligne précédemment de haute densité d'urbanisation,
la rue de Damas, creusant dans le tissu urbain une ligne de vide, allant
jusqu'au centre, énorme trou noir, béance par laquelle la nouvel ordre
voit le jour.[34] Cette rupture spatiale est aussi rupture du mode
d'organisation sociale dominant.

De part et d'autre de cette ancienne-nouvelle ligne naissent les
territoires censés résumer des identités religieuses: ils impliquent en
fait une recomposition de chaque communauté en faveur de ceux qui
veulent la défendre et l'affirmer comme cadre unique de référence. Les
anciens marginaux sont ceux qui ont apparemment le moins à perdre
et le plus à gagner de la constitution des communautés en autarcie
spatiale. Ces territoires impliquent donc une autre conception des
rapports inter-communautaires, à la fois perversion du principe d'Etat
et de celui de la Ville:

1. Ces territoires, qui s'opposent, fondent dans un même ensemble spatial une partie de la montagne et une partie de la ville, avec comme solution de continuité la banlieue, annulant par là-même sa précarité. La structure physique, la morphologie de la ville, en est grandement affectée.

2. La division qui se veut conservatrice, défense d'une identité, repli sur elle, est en fait un bouleversement radical, une interprétation particulière de l'identité, une conquête d'autres espaces pour l'assujettissement d'autres identités.[35]

3. L'organisation communautaire de l'espace est bouleversée: ce qui caractérise la nouvelle organisation est la disparition des zones de mixité communautaire doublée de l'homogénéisation supposée des quartiers et effective des zones-territoires. Unification des territoires et division de la ville, les deux mouvements apparaissent comme un seul mais sont dissociables à l'analyse. La division de la ville est le sens de l'émergence des identités, ce qui est présenté comme résurgence (d'identités) est dès l'abord réinterprétation (de la ville), nous verrons plus loin que cette réinterprétation est fonctionnelle, qu'elle sert un projet expansionniste de certains groupes.

4. L'homme unidimensionnel de la modernité fait une apparition particulière à Beyrouth: l'identité se réduit de plus en plus au territoire. Sans disparaître tout à fait, les autres systèmes de référence perdent de leur efficacité. Les modes de vie urbains, et les systèmes symboliques qui les structurent, sont à des degrés divers remis en question: un nouveau mode de vie apparait comme dominant, celui de l'ordre milicien, avec ses trois figures. Celle du milicien circulant librement dans son territoire, mais interdit de circulation dans l'autre, celle du réfugié obligé à un déplacement forcé, celle du civil essayant de comprendre les nouvelles règles du déplacement dans l'espace urbain. La logique qui domine l'espace de la ville est celle de l'exclusion de l'Autre, et de l'incorporation du Même dans le territoire.[36] Elle se double d'une logique de miroir, le territoire-autre est souvent l'image négative de soi, mais aussi ce contre quoi, ce comme quoi, ce par quoi on se légitime et on se construit. Chaque territoire se reconstruit cependant comme autosuffisant économiquement, du moins est contraint de se vouloir ainsi, rendant par là même inutile le rapport à l'autre, qu'à travers le miroir de l'imaginaire.

Cette approche nous permet de classer les milices en deux catégories:

1. Celles qui se limitent à des projets de défense locale et qui finiront par disparaître dans le temps ou à s'épuiser dans de micro-espaces, ce sont celles d'une petite-bourgeoisie et de classes populaires citadines, ou au contraire conservant des structures trop montagnardes ou rurales, elles perdent assez vite le contrôle de leur terrain.

2. Celles qui ajoutent à cette fonction de défense une fonction de conquête de l'espace urbain qui leur permet de durer dans le temps. Que les plus fortes milices se soient constituées dans les communautés nouvellement urbanisées, qu'elles aient reconstitué leurs communautés pour en pousser une partie vers la guerre ne peut se comprendre ni seulement en réponse à une stratégie de l'état—certaine s'est mobilisée pour le défendre, les autres pour le transformer—ni à la nature belliqueuse de ces communautés.

Nul atavisme ne peut, et ne doit, être invoqué: méthodologiquement ce serait retomber dans la thèse des identités essentialistes. Si certaines communautés laissent se développer une dynamique guerrière dans leur sein et se battent plus que d'autres, autrement que d'autres, si les états-majors de ces milices arrivent à mobiliser une partie de la population qui n'est pas seulement complice ou victime, c'est avant tout à cause du contexte dans lequel elles sont placées: petite-bourgeoisie déclassée ou sous-prolétariat néo-urbain vivant un faisceau d'exclusions. Chaque territoire, l'Est comme l'Ouest, est témoin de l'expansion que réalisent en son sein ces catégories sociales à travers la milice. Sortant des quartiers de banlieue, elles envahissent chacune une partie de la ville-municipe, au nom de sa défense. Pour elles, se posait un problème d'intégration urbaine que la violence quotidienne—division rituelle de la ville mais aussi destruction des lieux de la mixité proclamée fausse—a semblé pouvoir résoudre par une méprise tragique: *défendre la ville pour s'en approprier une partie, la diviser pour la figer et ne pas en être délogé.*

La destruction des zones de mixité—et en premier lieu le centre-ville—est la condition d'apparition des territoires, et non seulement sa conséquence, car à travers ces espaces deux ordres sociaux se disputent l'organisation de la société: la citadinité et la territorialité. Ce n'est qu'en détruisant les lieux du premier, que le second peut s'imposer, et imposer sa requalification de la société. La violence globale n'est plus seulement instrumentale, moyen de tenir le pays, mais légitimatrice d'une transformation de la société urbaine. Elle est devenue nécessaire à la justification de la police des territoires 'libérés'.[37] Elle seule permet de marginaliser l'Etat et d'occuper la Ville. Le propre de l'intelligence des états-majors des milices est d'avoir compris qu'elles pouvaient puiser dans cet immense réservoir humain des banlieues pour mobiliser des troupes, pour atteindre des objectifs qui au début se définissaient dans l'espace moyen-oriental ou national, mais qui au palier du social se traduisent très vite par la conquête de la ville, la revanche prise sur elle.

Or si cette conquête fascine, elle coûtera très cher aussi, car la ville a sa Règle, elle n'est pas que le bâti à conquérir, mais une société.

Soumettre sa population et la marginaliser, ne veut pas dire avoir soi-même accès à une centralité supérieure. Si la ville n'offre pas de résistance quand elle est prise, du moins là où l'on si attend le plus c'est à dire sur le terrain des armes, en revanche elle se dérobe, elle s'évanouit sous les pas du milicien. Multiforme, elle est antithétique par nature à la domination. Une autre lecture plus simple est cependant toujours possible: la conquête de la ville, apparemment si aisée, n'a-t-elle pas été en fait si violente qu'elle s'est traduite par la destruction immédiate, physique, économique, sociale et symbolique de l'objet convoité?

On ne saurait cependant oublier qu'à l'intérieur même de cette dynamique dominante, qui recompose d'une façon si dure les relations inter-communautaires dans la ville, il existe une seconde recomposition *intra-communautaire* cette fois. Ce mouvement de la milice pour le contrôle violent de l'espace urbain a comme condition une restructuration intra-communautaire et un renouvellement des élites communautaires, qui se fait au dépens tant des vieux leaderships urbains que montagnards qui sont systématiquement marginalisés ou détruits. Il assure l'émergence à partir de l'entre-deux de la ville et de la montagne d'une petite bourgeoisie néo-urbaine combattante et progressant vers les classes moyennes au prix de féroces opérations de police.

Mais il assure aussi la promotion d'une nouvelle bourgeoisie parasitaire et à consommation ostentatoire, se nourrissant de la guerre, et se passant complètement des réseaux commerciaux traditionnels. Nous ne le dirons jamais assez, c'est dans leurs propres communautés, dans leurs propres élites citadines et rurales qui tiennent à certaines formes de rapports inter-communautaires, que les milices censées les défendre font le plus de ravages, car le principe qu'elles ont mis en oeuvre pour la division de la ville se retrouve dans les luttes de pouvoir à l'intérieur du territoire.[38]

Rendre Etranger l'Autre interne, l'expulser à l'extérieur du territoire, est en effet le principe fondateur de *toutes* les milices communautaires. Quand la définition de ce qui est interne et de ce qui est externe est si mouvante, peut-on encore soutenir, au nom d'un quelconque artifice intellectuel de compensation et de méconnaissance, de rejet de la responsabilité et de démission, que nous n'avons pas affaire, entre autres choses, à une guerre civile? Cette guerre a touché prioritairement des civils, elle s'est réalisée principalement à travers des acteurs ne constituant pas d'organisations militaires officielles, elle a eu, entre autres, des enjeux de pouvoirs internes, spécifiquement urbains. Que cette guerre civile se soit passée à l'ombre d'une ou de plusieurs guerres nationales,[39] et d'une ou de plusieurs guerres régionales[40] est certain. Que le déclencheur en soit externe n'est pas questionnable. Mais il n'en reste pas moins que quand elle devient quotidienne elle pose question sur les rapports internes à la société.

En guise de conclusion: ville, état et milice

> Peu importe, du point de vue qui est ici le nôtre que ce soit un bienfait pour l'humanité ou une malédiction pour le monde . . . notre but consistait à illustrer . . . cette vérité que les morts règnent toujours sur les vivants.
>
> J. Schumpeter

Que la réunion qui se tient ici à Oxford[41] soit impossible à tenir à Beyrouth, par le fait même des milices respectives qui contrôlent les territoires d'où nous venons, devrait être une illustration suffisante d'une guerre qui se pose au départ comme mécanisme de défense des groupes sociaux, et se perpétue comme agression contre une certaine forme de culture et de rapports sociaux, de convivialité. S'il appartient aux politiques d'avoir honte de leur histoire, et de la déguiser, il est du ressort des sciences sociales de l'assumer et de l'écrire, autant que faire se peut, en dehors des mythes dominant l'instant.

Faut-il voir dans ces fractures une crise de la citadinité moyen-orientale qui n'arrive pas à s'insérer dans un projet de modernité étatique, et donc l'anticipation de l'avenir d'autres villes? Est-ce au contraire la ponctuation d'un mouvement antérieur, Beyrouth ne serait-il ainsi que la dernière ville de l'Empire ottoman? Ou est-ce simplement le temps qui manquait, l'urgence, qui a imposé cette douloureuse brutalité de la recomposition de l'espace et de la société?

La ville n'est-elle synonyme que de richesse? N'est-elle pas aussi réciprocité, démocratie si l'on veut? Reconnaissance et acceptation de la différence, mais aussi relativisation de ces différences en les sachant un des niveaux de définition des identités, support des interactions et non pas de la séparation spatiale et des exclusions? A trop ignorer cette règle, les acteurs sociaux n'y ont pas gagné, même s'ils se sont sentis à un moment transfigurés par l'identité 'retrouvée'. Il y a quelque part une escroquerie intellectuelle à parler de ce retour aux sources: le discours qui revendique l'identité est celui qui la reconstruit, le fait même de le tenir la fait advenir. Ce discours sur Soi s'est construit à partir de l'exclusion de l'Autre, de son meurtre symbolique et réel. Or expulser l'Autre pour tracer les limites du Soi, faire de l'Autre un Etranger à rejeter, n'est-il pas avant tout tuer une partie, sans doute la plus riche, de soi-même?[42]

En conclusion, trois séries de questions se posent.

1.   La ville peut-elle *se* retrouver et dépasser la crise du système milicien actuel, mais aussi se transformer, sortir de son égoïsme et assumer les responsabilités dues à l'accueil des migrants, se laissera-t-elle aveugler par les fausses joies de la revanche ou retrouvera-t-elle sa tolérance tout en retrouvant les moyens d'équilibrer les différents pouvoirs? Certes les capacités de cette ville à retrouver son rôle économique de métropole régionale en sont la condition de départ, mais n'y a-t-il pas aussi, dans la citadinité perdue, une importante dimension symbolique à mettre en relief, à rebâtir, ou à recréer? Le rôle des communautés citadines, leur responsabilité dans la construction de l'avenir est immense, tout autant qu'était secondaire leur rôle dans la violence.

2.   N'est-ce pas donc vers un état plus en adéquation avec la société, un état social, un état tenant compte dans l'application des principes du droit de citoyenneté de ceux du droit de cité, un état plus respectueux de la société civile et limitant les empiètements du politique, que se situe sinon une solution, du moins la condition de la permanence dans le temps de la paix civile? N'est-il pas absurde de prétendre intégrer des groupes en les repoussant violemment, en les soumettant, ou en leur faisant miroiter des rêves de suprématie? Ou l'état peut-il, comme la ville, les assumer dans un même espace pour les relativiser? Les reconnaître pour en faire une richesse, et non un danger? Les concevoir dans des rapports de réciprocité?

3.   L'ordre milicien, enfin, pourra-t-il un jour être amené à se poser la question du coût de sa reproduction? Dès que le miroir des territoires est devenu parfait, dès qu'il a renvoyé des images identiques, il s'est fêlé. La crise de l'ordre milicien est aujourd'hui patente, et aussi meurtrière que l'a été son émergence. Ces mois-ci, la violence contre l'Autre ne s'est-elle pas prolongée dans tous les territoires comme violence contre le Soi?

Notes

1. Quand ce n'est pas dans la génétique, voir la critique que fait G.Corm ici même de cette approche 'génétique'.

2. M. Gilsenan, *Imagined cities of the East* (Oxford, 1986).

3. Nous faisons bien sûr référence au si beau montage de M. Buheiry à l'AUB sur 'Beirut Baroque'.

4. Quelques travaux novateurs de jeunes chercheurs, malheureusement aujourd'hui disparus, ont balisé l'étude de cette voie; il s'agit bien entendu des travaux d'A. Abdelnour et de M. Seurat. Voir A. Abdelnour, *Introduction à l'histoire de la Syrie urbaine* (Beyrouth, 1982); M. Seurat, 'Le quartier de Bâb Tabbâné à Tripoli (Liban), étude d'une 'Asabiya urbaine', dans CERMOC, *Mouvements communautaires et espace urbain* (Beyrouth, 1985), pp. 45–86.

5. Voir en particulier les exposés qui nous ont précédé de Boutros Labaki sur l'économie et ses temps, et cel d'Antoine Messarra sur les institutions.

6. L. Fawaz, *Merchants and Migrants in Nineteenth Century Beirut* (Cambridge, Mass., 1983).

7. Des origines andalouses et marocaines, voire maltaises des sunnites, aux tribus arabes dont seraient originaires les orthodoxes, en passant par l'origine libanaise affirmée et syrienne occultée des maronites, à celles multiples des druzes, spécifiques des arméniens et sacralisées des chiites . . . sans compter le mythe du retour palestinien.

8. Voir entre autres: M. Buheiry, *Beirut's Role in the Political Economy of the French Mandate: 1919–39*, Centre for Lebanese Studies, Oxford, 1987.

9. J. Ducruet, *Capitaux européens au Proche-Orient* (Paris, 1964).

10. Ainsi Beyrouth n'est et ne sera, et surtout n'a jamais été une ville 'musulmane' ou 'chrétienne', l'un à l'exclusion de l'autre, comme certaines polémiques inutiles ont essayés de l'y réduire. Comme toute ville, c'est un lieu de rencontre avec l'Autre, et c'est les modalités de cette rencontre qu'il s'agira d'étudier. L'imposition de la logique des nombres, celle des états, sur celle de la multiformité ne peut mener qu'à méconnaître sa spécificité. La question des nombres est comme on le sait très contestée, il n'en reste pas moins que quelques remarques de bon sens qui devraient être rappelées: aucune communauté n'est majoritaire dans l'agglomération, certaines sont plus visibles, parfois elles comptent politiquement plus dans la ville; elles sont alors plus comptées, par un glissement classique dans les mythes dominant le Liban. Ne peut-on en conclure que la seule hypothèse de travail valable est qu'aucune communauté ne dépasse à elle seule 25% de la population du Grand Beyrouth? Que l'addition de deux des communautés, n'importe lesquelles, ne suffit pas à atteindre 50%.

11. Par manque de place, nous ne nous arrêterons ici que sur le premier; l'étude détaillée de l'autre sera faite dans le cadre d'un autre travail. Il faut cependant avoir présent à l'esprit que les deux principes étaient concomitants.

12. A. Bourgey, 'La guerre et ses conséquences géographiques au Liban', *Annales de géographie* 521 (1986) 1–37; 'L'évolution du centre de Beyrouth de 1960 à 1977', dans Dominique Chevallier (sous la dir. de), *L'Espace social de la ville arabe* (Paris, 1979).

13. Une étude du mouvement social pour le compte de la Direction Générale de l'Urbanisme et dirigée par A. Kahi, ainsi que des passages d'un fascicule sur la reconstruction, un travail de mémoire de maîtrise de C. Ghorra lui ont été consacrés; S. Nasr en a partiellement parlé dans un de ses articles. A. Kahi (sous la dir. de), *Le Centre-ville de Beyrouth en 1974, mouvement social* (Beyrouth, 1980); S. Nasr, 'Les formes de regroupement traditionnel (familles, confessions, communautés régionales) dans la société de Beyrouth', dans Chevallier (sous la dir. de), *L'espace social de la ville arabe*.

14. Le travail de Jad Tabet sur Beyrouth est explicite sur ce point. Il allie une grande rigueur à une extraordinaire finesse dans l'interprétation des formes spatiales et du symbolisme. J. Tabet, 'Beyrouth et la guerre urbaine: la ville et le vide', dans *Peuples méditerranées* 37 (1986) *Villes tourmentées*.

15. Se peut-il que la thèse sur le remplacement du centre-ville par Hamra, et de l'inévitable dépérissement du premier préalable à sa disparition brutale, soit valable? Un nombre d'activités restaient au centre-ville, mais surtout le type d'organisation dans Hamra la moderne n'était pas vraiment différent de celui du centre-ville; bien qu'apparaissant comme international, cet espace utilisait les catégories de classement du centre-ville ancien. Voir à ce sujet l'étude de Khalaf sur Ras-Beyrouth et Hamra, ou les remarques de Ducruet, d'un intérêt exceptionnel pour l'anthropologue à travers une lecture au deuxième degré, sur les sociétés anonymes qui ne l'étaient pas vraiment. S. Khalaf et P. Kongstadt, *Hamra of Beirut, a Case of Rapid Urbanization* (Leiden, 1973); Ducruet, *Capitaux européens*.

16. Le travail de base que Khuri a consacré à deux de ces quartiers (Chyah Ghobeïré et Chyah Aïn el-Rommaneh) est certainement une référence trop peu connue dans les milieux

de la recherche francophone; il s'agira de le consulter pour l'intelligence de la vie sociale de ces espaces. F. I. Khuri, *From Village to Suburbs. Order and Change in Greater Beirut* (Chicago, 1975).

17. Bourgey, 'L'Evolution du centre de Beyrouth'.

18. M. Weber, *La Ville* (édité en français, Paris, 1982).

19. Seurat, 'Le quartier de Bâb Tabbâné'.

20. H. Le Fèvre, *Le Droit à la ville* (Paris, 1968).

21. La question du 'confessionnalisme' par exemple a été maltraitée (et mal traitée) par l'indistinction où l'on a voulu plonger ces deux principes. Vouloir dériver le modèle de la confession de celui de l'une d'entre elles est inconséquent: qu'y a-t-il de commun entre la taille, la structure, le mode de projection sur l'espace de la confession maronite et celle des protestants, ou entre les structures politiques internes, la place du symbolisme, l'implantation rurale ou urbaine de la communauté sunnite et de la druze? Comment apprécier la place des communautés externes à la définition juridique de la confession comme par exemple les palestiniens, les kurdes ou les apatrides? Etant donné que le juridique ne découpe qu'une partie de la réalité, comment apprécier les effets des rapports de nombre, des différences de projection dans l'espace, des structures organisationnelles ou des activités économiques qui récusent ce statut d'équivalence et de similitude juridique implicitement assumé? Certaines confessions-communautés sont parfois le lieu de vraies et fortes solidarités, d'autres ne sont qu'un espace social où sont regroupés par défaut, dirait-on, des ensembles dispersés. Certaines assument et revendiquent cette identité confessionnelle, d'autres se sentent exclues à travers elle et cherchent à l'ignorer et à en fuir; d'autres enfin se posent en dehors ou à côté. Ces attitudes sont elles-mêmes fonction des contextes, donc des moments et non pas de la durée. Voir à ce sujet une approche originale des confessions dans le système politique: J. Farès, *Les Conflits confessionnels dans l'histoire du Liban moderne* (Beyrouth, 1980), en arabe.

22. A. Raymond, *Grandes villes arabes à l'époque ottomane* (Paris, 1985); I. Lapidus, *Muslim Cities in the Later Middle Ages* (Cambridge, Mass., 1967).

23. Que l'on ne voit ici nul a priori critique ou apologétique. Remettre à l'honneur l'étude des structures de l'Empire ottoman en coupant court à la tradition libano-centriste des historiens ne peut que faire progresser une meilleure compréhension du cas libanais, périphérique certes mais suffisamment autonome dans cet immense empire que l'on se rappelle aujourd'hui si peu centralisé. Le Liban qui a du se faire historiquement à travers le mythe fort de l'arrachement et de l'opposition à l'empire vermoulu, est typique de problèmes à naître dans d'autres parties de cet empire vaste. Malgré cet effort dirigé de fait contre les manifestations de la turquification de l'empire dans ces dernières décades, le Liban est peut-être resté plus proche et structurellement toujours attaché à certains des modèles du passé ottoman que par exemple l'actuelle Turquie. Il est heureux que ce colloque ait été l'occasion de deux communications proposant de nouvelles lectures de l'histoire de cet empire et de ses provinces.

24. Voir aussi l'insistance de Ducruet sur l'impossibilité de concevoir des investissements économiques selon la seule logique de l'état territorial et la préférence qui lui est corrélée de concevoir les activités économiques dans un espace moyen-oriental. Ducruet, *Capitaux européens*.

25. A. Beydoun, *Identité confessionnelle et temps social chez les historiens libanais contemporains* (Beyrouth, 1984).

26. Bourgey, 'L'Evolution du centre de Beyrouth'.

27. C. Geertz et al., *Meaning and Order in Moroccan Society. Three Essays in Cultural Analysis* (Cambridge, 1979).

28. Le *qabaday*, autre intercesseur de la ville, repéré par Johnson par exemple, n'est pas la figure centrale de cet espace même s'il en est le plus haut en couleur; le *qabaday* n'a qu'un rôle minime dans le centre-ville et fonctionne comme protecteur des quartiers résidentiels. M. Johnson, 'The political bosses and their gangs. Zu'ama and Qabadaiyyat in the Sunni

Muslim quarters of Beirut', dans E. Gellner and J. Waterbury, *Patrons and Clients* (London, 1977), pp. 207–24. Plus récemment: M. Johnson, *Class and Client in Beirut, The Sunni Muslim Community and the Lebanese State, 1840–1985* (London, 1986).

29. Elle renvoit bien sûr aux thèses de la bourgeoisie périphérique. Voir à ce sujet: M. Amel, *Du mode de production colonial* (Beyrouth, 1976), en arabe; C. Dubar et S. Nasr, *Les Classes sociales au Liban* (Paris, 1976).

30. P. Bourdieu et S. Abdelmalek, *Le Déracinement* (Paris, 1964).

31. Le taux d'analphabètes à Beyrouth était plus élevé que l'on ne le croit généralement: 16% pour les hommes de plus de dix ans et 31% pour les femmes de plus de dix ans en 1970.

32. F. Awada, *Les Services urbains à Beyrouth-Ouest durant la guerre. Questions sur la pénurie. Mémoire d'urbanisme* (Paris VII, 1985).

33. Khuri, *From Village to Suburbs*.

34. K. Salibi, *Crossroads to Civil War* (New York, 1976).

35. Voir W. Charara, 'Les guerres d'assujettissement'. Si Charara ne 'voit' pas la ville, il n'empêche que sa description des rapports politiques entre communautés combattantes est extrêmement précise.

36. La thèse de B. Osmat est significative à ce sujet: B. Osmat, 'Coexistence impossible, lectures dans les idéologies de la guerre' (thèse soutenue à Paris-Sorbonne, 1983).

37. Voir l'ambiguité fantastique des textes de P. Kemp, fascination pour la ville et identification de celle-ci à un territoire résument le tout. Kemp trouve la ville là où elle n'est plus, dans le territoire, et participe bien involontairement à sa disparition, alors que W. Charara pris d'un malaise comparable avec sa ville 'indécidable', ne cesse d'y rechercher les marques de la territorialité. Chez ces deux auteurs la passion de la ville n'a d'égal que son dérobement face aux concepts utilisés. P. Kemp, 'La cité-état, Beyrouth entre deux formes de combat', *Esprit*, numéro spécial, *Le Proche-Orient dans la guerre* 5–6 (1982) 53–67; W. Charara, *La Ville indécidable, Beyrouth entre la parenté et la résidence* (Beyrouth, 1985), en arabe.

38. Voir G. Corm, *Géopolitique du conflit libanais* (Paris, 1986).

39. De défense nationale, ou autour d'enjeux nationaux comme le système de pouvoir et de décision tel que l'a analysé Messarra ici même.

40. Il n'a sans doute existé que très peu de conflits purs de la civilité et dans l'histoire, la résistance française dans les années 1940 a été une guerre civile et la guerre d'indépendance américaine a été aussi par certains aspects une guerre civile. Les guerres civiles elles-même peuvent déboucher sur des conflits internationaux: la venture napoléonienne est l'exemple parfait de la guerre civile qui se transforme en guerre de défense nationale puis en guerre de conquête nationale. Séparer artificiellement les plans pour disqualifier les responsabilités internes ne facilite pas la reconstruction de l'avenir; la politique de l'autruche ne produit ni consensus, ni réconciliation. De même, méconnaître en retour l'importance des mécanismes internationaux en assimilant les rapports inter-libanais à une autarcie relève de l'inconséquence méthodologique et du jugement moral le plus irresponsable.

41. Réunion pour l'organisation de laquelle nous nous devons de remercier le Centre for Lebanese Studies.

42. Le document le plus expressif quant à ces potentialités est sans doute le très beau roman de G. Khoury, *Mémoire de l'aube* (Paris, 1987).

17

The Role of the South in Lebanese Politics

ALI EL-KHALIL

South Lebanon is at the root of the Lebanese political problem. It embodies the basic elements of the Lebanese crisis caused mainly by the Israeli occupation, but also a confessional political system lacking equality and social justice. It is the key to the Lebanese settlement, aspiring to liberate the national homeland from without and the human individual from within. It symbolizes the Lebanese problem, and must play a distinct role in its solution. South Lebanon occupies a basic position in the Middle Eastern question.

Southern Lebanon is the front line of defence not only for Lebanon but for all Arabs. It faces almost alone the shelling and raids of Israeli military operations. It is the base of the noble and heroic resistance holding the torch of confrontation before the aggressors. This struggling land is without the minimum support required to maintain its momentum for resistance. South Lebanon is the home of Jabal 'Amil, which has produced leading men devoted to knowledge, worship, austerity and dignity; men of standing willing to shed their blood and sacrifice their lives to defend their honour, culture, liberty and the independence of their country.

During the days of the emirates and after the Ottoman rule in 1516, this area, with the exception of occasional incursions, was left alone even after the Ottomans established the *wilaya* (province) of Sidon in the mid-seventeenth century; and it was not until the late eighteenth century that the area started to resist governor Ahmad Pasha al-Jazzar's harshness and suppression. His rule led to ruin, poverty, flight, and even the burning of massive libraries full of valuable books, documents and manuscripts. And after a quarter of a century of struggle, misery and persecution, al-Jazzar's tyrannic system came to an end.

The people of that area played a significant role in the awakening of the Arab movement with the close of the nineteenth century. No Arab

nationalist congress or meeting was held without representatives from
Jabal 'Amil and the rest of the southern regions of Lebanon, which
offered martyrs and heroes to the cause of emancipation and freedom.
Replacing Ottoman rule, the French mandate was equally rejected,
resisted and confronted by the popular struggles for independence.

The south has been a deprived region in Lebanon both before and
after the creation of Greater Lebanon and with independence. Even
during the early years of independence, the villages of the south were
deprived of the minimum basic rights. Only a few of them had schools,
roads, medical centres or hospitals, electricity, or water (even though
the Litani river runs through the region). It was not until Fu'ad
Shihab's regime (1958–64), which was the first rule coloured with
étatisme, that some reforms were introduced. That regime tried to
strengthen the institution of the state *vis-à-vis* the oligarchs, feudal
chieftains and warlords, and tried to help the neglected parts of the
country.

The poor economic and social conditions prevailing in the south as
a result of many years of neglect had turned it into a depressed area
materially and psychologically; and oppression usually leads to
explosion. Such conditions led to an exodus from the south to the
ghettos of Beirut and its surroundings. The southerners were the main
human source of the poverty belt around the capital, Beirut, and
wealth and poverty existed side by side. It is true that the middle class
in Lebanon is larger than its equivalent in similar traditional social
orders. Yet in the early 1960s statistics highlighted the social
inequalities in the Lebanese economy, which depends mainly on the
service sector, by revealing that the top 4 per cent of the people
possessed 32 per cent of the national income; whereas the bottom 50
per cent owned only 18 per cent, leaving 46 per cent of the people with
50 per cent of the national income.

The early 1970s witnessed strikes motivated by the desire for social
reforms; the demands centred on medical insurance, housing, a
minimum wage, the education system and the cause of the tobacco
planters, who called for the right to form a union and wanted higher
prices for their crops grown mainly in the south. At that time the
average annual income of the small tobacco grower was about one
tenth of that of the service-sector worker. Early in 1973 two demonstrations were organized, one in Beirut and the other in Nabatiyya
in the south, to support the tobacco-growers' demands. During these
demonstrations two people were killed and several others injured as a
result of clashes with the security forces. The political economy of
tobacco has always been a southern problem, reflecting the social
inequalities among regions and the economic imbalance between the
service sector and the agricultural sector.

Since disorder in Lebanon started in 1975, when the civil war broke out, economic and social conditions have continually deteriorated and we are entering a period of social unrest and of widespread poverty after 13 years of war which has left complex economic problems. It has caused tremendous damage to our infrastructure; a severe cut in production in various sectors; a division in the markets (resulting in a sharp decline of economic activity); a drainage of capital and human resources; a continuous growth in expenditures and decline in revenues (leading to the acceleration of public debt); and rising inflation accompanied by fiscal disorder—the US dollar's parity with the Lebanese pound, which was in the range of 2.20–3.00 before 1975, has recently reached 300; and the per capita income, which was about $1,500, that is higher than some European countries, is now in the range of $100–120, placing Lebanon among the poor countries of the world. It is true that essential reforms should be introduced in the fiscal and economic policies, and that we should rely, in addition to the national domestic savings and investments, on foreign aid and loans to slow down the drastic economic collapse. However, in order to return to normalcy the economic conditions, like all the other problems facing us, require political stability which can only be reached by solving the Lebanese crisis.

South Lebanon has been a battleground in the face of the continuous Zionist aggression. It has paid a heavy price in that confrontation, and has been exposed to many Israeli military attacks, conquests and occupations. The Israeli invasion of southern Lebanon in mid-March 1978, entitled the 'Litani Operation', resulted in the formation of the so-called 'Security Belt' zone; the zone is a slip of land along the border about 5–10 km wide, covering an area of 5–600 sq. km and controlled by Israeli agents. The Israeli invasion of Lebanon on 5 June 1982—leading to the first occupation of an Arab capital, Beirut—has become a watershed in contemporary Middle Eastern history. It was not, as was claimed, a war waged in the interests of 'Peace for Galilee', but rather against the Lebanese land, people and identity, causing widespread destruction, defying the principles and codes of international law and morality, and challenging the international community.

The occupation led to a relentless war in which the southerners and their resistance groups fought the Israeli occupying army with zeal, fury and courage, as many operations demonstrate. On 16 October 1983, the day of 'Ashura, unarmed crowds in Nabatiyya clashed with the Israeli armed forces and drove them away. On 4 November, in the city of Tyre, a suicide driver struck the Israeli headquarters, killing dozens of Israeli soldiers; a similar operation a few weeks earlier had destroyed the previous headquarters in Tyre and killed and injured more than 200 Israeli soldiers. Several more suicide missions followed and southern Lebanon witnessed more than 900 attacks against the Israeli soldiers in 1984, forcing their withdrawal. The Israelis maintain their occupation of the Security Belt, where resistance operations continue to secure the complete liberation of the national land.

The future of peace in the Middle East depends on the direct or indirect Israeli occupation of south Lebanon and the rest of the occupied Arab lands. Israel is an enemy with aggressive long-range designs in the area and its attitude towards Lebanon cannot be separated from its hostility to the Arabs. Israel has, among others, the following objectives in Lebanon and its south.

1. To occupy the Lebanese land south of the Litani river, for its abundant water resources and fertile plains, and for its strategic position, making it a stand-in for Israel's borders and facilitating its attacks on the Lebanese resistance movement and the PLO.
2. To destabilize the country by deepening the sectarian conflicts, and interfering in our internal politics by instigating trouble and creating problems (the crime of the assassination of Premier Rashid Karami is an example of this strategy). The fragmentation of Lebanon along sectarian lines would set a precedent which could be followed throughout the whole region. This objective was made clear by Ben Gurion as early as 1954, when he described Lebanon as the weakest link and the first target of such a plot. To ensure its own survival, the Israeli strategy in the Middle East is based on the division of the area into small ethnic or confessional entities; the Israeli military forces will then not need to occupy wider territories to maintain their aggressive policies—when they cannot even control the occupied territories of the West Bank and Gaza Strip.
3. To conclude a unilateral peace settlement with Lebanon, since Israel's policy has been to try to negotiate separate treaties with each of the Arab states in turn, in order to splinter the Arabs.
4. To destroy the Lebanese experience, based on the coexistence of its 17 sects, which is the dignified answer to the Israeli experience rooted in the Zionist ideology which proclaims that the Jew cannot exercise his or her Jewishness except in a Jewish state.
5. To erase and liquidate Lebanon as an independent entity, because it is the most important state in the region in the field of services, culture, education and technical expertise, and this threatens the Israeli role and poses a challenge to its future.

It is believed that one of the major motives of the Israeli occupation in 1982 was to strike a death blow against the Lebanese economy, which has declined ever since, and to dislocate the people of the south and drive them northward.

Hence, in order to settle the question of south Lebanon and consequently the Lebanese crisis, we have to achieve the dual national goals of liberating our national soil from without, from the Israeli occupation, and our citizen from within, by introducing basic political, economic and social reforms. To this end, we resort to all the available means at our disposal, the most important of which are the resistance movement, international law, and political reforms.

The resistance movement

The achievement of Israel's aggressive objective in Lebanon has been prevented by the courageous defence of our people on the border and of the national resistance. The resistance movement has gained world-wide acclaim, and received tremendous momentum from wide popular support, since it emerged in the late summer of 1982. It has forced the occupying army to withdraw from most of the land it occupied in 1982, although Israel remains in the Security Belt zone, which serves as a base for the implementation of its expansionist designs, sowing division and discord and disrupting national reconciliation.

The resistance movement will continue to struggle until the complete liberation of our national soil from the traces of direct and indirect occupation. Modern history has recorded a rare example of this type of determined resistance in the Lebanese struggle for national liberation, and in the immediate results and achievements which it has yielded.

At this juncture, we should reiterate the necessity of differentiating between resistance and terrorism. Israel has committed atrocities in the occupied territories of the West Bank and Gaza Strip by storming villages, destroying houses, shooting innocent citizens and carrying out similar criminal and brutal actions which have turned the people into extremists. These people are not terrorists as Israel calls them: they are fighting against an occupying force. We are not terrorists; we are freedom fighters. And there is a vast difference between terrorism, whether at the individual or collective level, and the right to struggle for liberation; the former is condemned, and the latter is praised and should be supported.

As occupation continues, moderation has been discredited and extremism validated; violence breeds violence, and action calls for reaction. Extremism stems from a political condition that forces, in an offensive manner, problems upon the people of the region. So violence is the product of regional and international conflicts exploding in Lebanon, rather than a question of conflicts between Muslims and Christians, who have lived together for hundreds of years and have never fought a religious war; and even wars which have been given such colouring were the result of the involvement of foreign powers. Thus, the Lebanese are not accountable for such conflicts, except inasmuch as they allowed themselves to be the tools of the struggle.

Whereas the sectarian strife and conflict are shameful and harmful, the war against the Israeli occupation is a source of national pride and the only war worth fighting. The Israelis benefit from our internal conflicts, and they realize this; Yitzhak Rabin stated, after the deployment of Syrian units in West Beirut in February 1987, that resistance in the south was expected to mount again after the situation in the city achieved security.

International law

We support the United Nations Security Council Resolutions on south Lebanon, and insist upon their implementation; in particular, Resolution 425 which calls for the immediate withdrawal of the Israeli forces from all the Lebanese lands; for strict respect of the territorial integrity and political independence of Lebanon within its internationally recognized boundaries; and for the establishment of a United Nations Interim Force in Lebanon (UNIFIL) for the purpose of confirming this withdrawal, and assisting the government of Lebanon in ensuring the return of its effective authority throughout its territories. While Israel has refused to comply with the will of the international community embodied in these resolutions, the Security Council has reiterated on several occasions its strong support for their complete implementation, as revealed by its official records.

Lebanon's ambassador to the UN has aptly expressed the Lebanese view in his statement on 19 January 1979:

> we accuse Israel of, beyond any doubt, obstructing international peace-keeping, in continued defiance of UN resolutions and the universal consensus. We also accuse Israel of trying to establish vicarious occupation of southern Lebanon, usurping authority through mutineers and mercenaries, not only to prevent the restoration of Lebanese sovereignty, but with the express purpose of disrupting our society and, through the destabilization of Lebanon, imperilling the chances of peace in the whole Middle East.

In his report on UNIFIL in April 1986 the Secretary General of the United Nations stated that the 'security zone'

> is not a legitimate means of meeting Israel's security concerns; nor is it an effective one. It is not legitimate, because it contravenes

Council Resolution 425, and it is not effective, because it has been fiercely attacked and has been used as a base for attacking Israel across the international frontiers.

In a speech delivered at the Security Council on 17 January 1986, the British representative stated:

> The council does not accept that Israel may flout the UN charter by invading and occupying another state or any part of its territory . . . We remain firmly committed to the sovereignty, unity, independence and territorial integrity of Lebanon within its internationally recognised borders . . . The presence of Israel and Israeli-backed forces in place of UNIFIL provides a constant provocation to the Lebanese population who wish to see their country free of foreign occupation.

However, it is not enough simply to adopt these resolutions and to renew the mandate of UNIFIL; it is necessary that all the permanent members of the Security Council, especially the United States which has supported the Israeli policy, give full support and backing to the international force in order for it to fulfill its task, so that the resolutions may be put into effect, and the United Nations may live up to its commitment to the maintenance of international peace and justice.

Political reforms

We cannot possibly introduce basic political reforms, leading to economic and social reforms, without the elimination of the confessional system; the Lebanese communities must devote much less thought and energy to serving their own interests and much more to serving the national interest. The sectarian divisions in Lebanon have been strengthened in recent years by the sectarian political system, which is a delicate mechanism that has often used violence in its operations. Unless all citizens have equal rights and duties, the divergences and differences are likely to arise.

As far as all religions aspire to serve man whom they call to God, they are united in purpose. But the divergences, discord and strife have emerged due to the system of political confessionalism, which has given the impression that Lebanon is a country of deep religious antagonisms. The political exploitation of sectarianism in a fractured social order, the internal disturbances and fighting, and the emergence of new sources of troubles, have led to the weakening of the state.

Sectarianism or 'confessionalism', a feeling of political, social, cultural and religious loyalty to a certain religious sect, has undermined the national consciousness of the Lebanese people, broken their social solidarity, and divided their state and society. It is legally recognized, and it manifests itself in the institutions of the state as well as in the various aspects of society.

Political sectarianism has been associated with the history of Lebanon. Lebanon has never had a religiously homogeneous population, but has been an asylum for religious minorities even before the Ottoman rule in 1516. The sectarian structure had existed during the days of the emirates, but started taking shape with the establishment of the *qa'imaqamiyyatan* in 1842, dividing Mount Lebanon into two districts: the northern district headed by a Maronite *qa'imaqam* (governor), and the southern district headed by a Druze *qa'imaqam*. The sectarian antagonisms, which were encouraged by the Ottomans as well as by the Western powers acting as the protectors of one side or the other, led to the clashes of 1860. They resulted in the Protocol of Mount Lebanon of 1861—later amended in 1864 and signed by the Ottoman empire and the European powers—establishing the *mutasarrifiyya*, governed by a Christian *mutasarrif* appointed by the Europeans and responsible to the Ottomans. He was assisted by an Administrative Council (*majlis edara*) of 12 representatives, reflecting the sectarian division of the six major sects of the population.

During the French mandate and with the creation of the State of Greater Lebanon in 1920 (adding to Mount Lebanon the provinces in the north, east, south and the coastal cities inhabited mainly by Muslims) sectarianism became more and more entrenched in public life. The 1926 Constitution, especially article 95, perpetuated the customary system of confessional representation, so that seats in the executive and legislative branches of government as well as appointments in the civil service were distributed along sectarian lines. Sectarianism has also been incorporated into the electoral law, and the personal status law involving questions of inheritance, marriage and divorce.

The National Pact in 1943 provided for sectarian balance and sectarian fraternity. It bridged the gap between the two wings of Lebanon, and provided a compromise formula for the distribution of political power among the various sects, in a multi-confessional society, within the framework of a liberal parliamentary democracy. The pact balanced divergences among the Lebanese. Whereas the Muslims had looked predominantly towards the Arabs for linkage and identity, the Christians had looked towards the West. The compromise reached was to give up both inclinations, and to belong to an independent, sovereign Lebanon with an Arab face; that is, no merger with the Arab national environment, and no dependence on Western protection. The National Pact had originally aimed at progressively replacing the sectarian spirit by the national; but unfortunately, regimes and events following independence did not allow such a transformation.

Sectarianism is absolutely incompatible with the notion of the modern state. It is a serious threat to the binding force in society since it interferes with national loyalty and weakens it, by creating a double loyalty to the state and to the sect. The citizen then addresses the state through his or her sect, while seeking public appointment or discussing the distribution of shares, benefits and rights. Hence the sectarian system cannot provide sound, democratic public institutions fit for a modern state.

How can we abolish sectarianism? The vast majority of people and most leaders, at least outwardly, deplore the contemporary confessional nature of the Lebanese state; but they differ in their outlook on the timing as well as the means of dismantling it. Sectarianism should be eradicated in such a way that the harm this entails will not be greater than the harm that would have ensued had it continued. Its elimination from the electoral law, the top positions and ministerial posts and the civil service recruitment—according to a realistic timetable—could lead to the replacement of political sects by political parties, and the confederation of sects by the national state.

It is true that the majority of Lebanese work for a settlement involving security, reunification, reforms, liberation and sovereignty. But the framework for reforms has not yet taken shape, due to the numerous and varying proposals discussed at different levels and introduced by various groups, ranging from federalism and confederalism to secularism and a unitary state. However, Lebanon's national identity was confirmed in the Geneva talks for national reconciliation held in November 1983, when Lebanon was described as 'Arab in its identity, being a founding member of the League of Arab States'.

I believe that nothing short of the establishment of a democratic parliamentary republic, with a freely organized economic system in a unitary, independent state, can secure the future of modern Lebanon. The New Deal which should be agreed upon to rebuild Lebanon ought to abolish sectarianism; build the state of institutions rather than the state of individuals and clans; establish political centralization and administrative decentralization; have an Arab character; strengthen our distinct and special relations with Syria for mutual national benefits and interests; and agree that the solution of the Lebanese crisis starts with the liberation of the south where a common enemy occupies our land.

In conclusion, the organic link between a solution in Lebanon and a settlement in the whole of the Middle East must be acknowledged, for the external participants in the Lebanese conflict are key protagonists in the regional and international conflicts struggling to form a settlement in the area. Yet it is in the interests of the Lebanese, the Palestinians and the Arabs to separate the timing—but not the context—of a solution to the Lebanese crisis from that of the conflict in the Middle East, as the solution of the Lebanese crisis would be the first stage towards a regional settlement: a healthy, unified, sovereign Lebanon will serve the Lebanese, Palestinian and Arab causes better than a fragmented, weak and sick Lebanon. As long as the conflict in Lebanon goes on, it is unlikely that a regional accord will be reached in the area, and its continuation endangers not only the Lebanese themselves but also the security and stability of the whole region.

The Lebanese problem stands in the way of the liberation of southern Lebanon, Jerusalem, and the rest of the occupied Arab territories, and does nothing to help Arab co-operation and co-ordination in the face of the common enemy, Israel, which is the real threat. The threat of this common enemy regulates the relationship between the Lebanese, the Palestinians and the Arabs, and leads them to work for a common cause; and such a co-ordination is the most efficient means to achieve results. At the same time, efforts should be exerted at the international level to bring about the liberation of all the occupied territories.

Select Bibliography

Abraham, A. J., *Lebanon at Mid-Century: Maronite–Druze Relations in Lebanon 1840–1860* (Washington, 1981).

Abu Fadil, H., *al-Barlaman* (Beirut, 1985).

Abu Khalil, A., 'Druze, Sunni and Shiite political leadership in present-day Lebanon', *Arab Studies Quarterly* 7.4 (1985).

Abu-Lughod, J., 'The Islamic city: historical myth, Islamic essence, and contemporary relevance', *International Journal of Middle East Studies* 19 (May 1987).

Abu Shaqra, Hussayn Ghadban and Abu Shaqra, Yusuf Khattar, *al-Harakat fi Lubnan ila 'ahd al-mutassarrifiyya,* ed. Arif Abu Shaqra (Beirut, 1952).

Adas, Michael, 'Market demand vs. imperial control: colonial contradictions and the origins of agrarian conflict in south and southeast Asia', in E. Burke ed., *Global Crises and Social Movements: Artisans, Peasants, Populists and the World Economy* (Boulder, Co., 1988).

Ageron, Charles-Robert, *Les Algériens musulmans et la France*, 2 vols (Paris, 1968).

A Handbook of Syria (Including Palestine) (London, *c.*1920).

Ajami, Fouad, *The Vanished Imam: Musa al Sadr and the Shia of Lebanon* (Ithaca, NY, and London, 1986).

Akarli, E. D., 'Problems in Ottoman politics under Abdulhamid II, 1876–1909', Ph.D. thesis, Princeton University, 1976.

——, *Cebel-i Lübnân'da Mutasarrıflık Düzeni, 1861–1915*, Bosphorus University doçentship thesis, Istanbul, 1981.

——, 'Taxation in Ottoman Lebanon, 1861–1915', *Abhath* (American University of Beirut, forthcoming).

——, 'Ottoman documents concerning the governorate of Mount Lebanon, 1861–1918', in *Studies on Turkish–Arab Relations: Annual 1986* (Istanbul, 1987).

Alavi, H., 'The state in postcolonial societies: Pakistan and Bangladesh', *New Left Review* 74 (July–August 1982).

Anderson, L., 'The state in the Middle East and North Africa', *Comparative Politics* (1987) 1–18.

Andrew, Christopher M. and Kanya-Forstner, A. S., *France Overseas: the Great War and the Climax of French Imperial Expansion* (London, 1981).

al-'Aqiqi, Antun Dahir, *Thawra wa-fitna fi Lubnan*, ed. Yusuf Ibrahim Yazbak (Damascus, 1938).

Atiyah, N. W., 'The attitude of the Lebanese Sunnis towards the State of Lebanon', Ph.D. thesis (unpublished), University of London, 1937.

'Awad, Walid, *Ashab al-fakhama: ru'asa lubnan* (Beirut, 1877).

Awada, F., *Les Services urbains à Beyrouth-Ouest durant la guerre. Questions sur la pénurie. Mémoire d'urbanisme* (Paris VII, 1985).

Axelrod, R. and Keohane, R. O., 'Achieving cooperation under anarchy: strategies and institutions', *World Politics* 38.1 (1985) (special issue on 'Cooperation under Anarchy') 226–54.

Aya, Roderick, *The Missed Revolution: the Fate of Rural Rebels in Sicily and Southern Spain, 1840–1950*, Papers on European and Mediterranean Societies no. 3 (Amsterdam, 1975).

Azar, Edward E., 'Development diplomacy', in Joyce Starr and Addeone S. Calliegh eds, *A Shared Destiny: Near East Regional Development and Cooperation* (New York, 1983).

——, 'The theory of protracted social conflict and the challenge of transforming conflict situations', in Dina Zinnes ed., *Conflict Process and Break Down of International Systems* (Denver, Co., 1983).

——, 'Protracted social conflict: ten propositions', in John Burton and Azar eds, *International Conflict Resolution: Theory and Practice* (Sussex, 1986).

—— and Burton, John W., 'Lessons for great powers relations', in Azar and Burton eds, *International Conflict Resolution: Theory and Practice* (Sussex, 1986).

—— and Moon, Chung In, 'Managing protracted social conflict in the Third World: facilitation and development diplomacy', *Millennium: Journal of International Studies* 15.3 (1986) 339–406.

Baer, Gabriel, 'Submissiveness and revolt of the fellah', *Studies in the Social History of Modern Egypt* (Chicago, Ill., 1973).

——, 'Fellah rebellion in Egypt and the Fertile Crescent', *Fellah and Townsman in the Middle East* (London and Totowa, NJ, 1982).

—— and Gerber, Haim, *The Social Origins of the Modern Middle East* (Boulder, Co., 1987).

Barry, B., 'Political accommodation and consociational democracy', *British Journal of Political Science* 5.4 (1975).

Batatu, Hanna, *The Old Social Classes and the Revolutionary Movements of Iraq* (Princeton, NJ, 1978).

Bells, R. B., *Christians in the Arab East* (Athens, 1973).

Ben-Dor, G., *State and Conflict in the Middle East: Emergence of the Postcolonial State* (New York, 1983).

Besoins et possibilités de développement du Liban, 2 vols, Republique libanaise, Ministère de plan, Mission IRFED, 1960–1.

Beydoun, A., *Indentité confessionelle et temps social chez les historiens libanais contemporains* (Beyrouth, 1984).

Beyhum, M. I., *al-'Ahd al-mukhadram fi Suriya wa-Lubnan* (Beirut, n.d.)

Binder, L., 'Political change in Lebanon', in Binder ed., *Politics in Lebanon* (New York, 1966).

—— ed., *Politics in Lebanon* (New York, 1966).

al-Bish'alani, Istifan, *Lubnan wa Yusuf Karam* (Beirut, 1924).

Blok, Anton, 'Mafia and peasant rebellion as contrasting factors in Sicilian latifundism', *European Journal of Sociology* 10 (1969) 95–116.

——, *The Mafia of a Sicilian Village* (New York, 1974).

Blondel, Edouard, *Deux ans en Syrie et en Palestine (1838–1939)* (Paris, 1840).

Bourdieu, Pierre, *The Algerians* (Boston, Mass., 1962).

——, *Esquisse d'une theorie de la pratique* (Paris et Genève, 1972).

—— and Abdelmalek, S., *Le Déracinement* (Paris, 1964).

Bourgey, A., 'L'Evolution du centre de Beyrouth de 1960 à 1977', in D. Chevallier ed., *L'Espace social de la ville arabe* (Paris, 1979).

——, 'La Guerre et ses conséquences géographiques au Liban', *Annales de géographie* 521 (1986) 1–37.

Brown, Carl L., *International Politics and the Middle East* (Princeton, NJ, 1984).

Browne, Walter L. ed., *The Political History of Lebanon, 1920–1950. Documents on Politics and Political Parties under French Mandate, 1920–1936*, vol. I (Salisbury, NC, 1976).

Bruneau, André, *Traditions et politique de la France au Levant* (Paris, 1932).

Buheiry, Marwan R., 'Bulus Nujaim and the Grand Liban ideal, 1908–1919', in Buheiry ed., *Intellectual Life in the Arab East* (Beirut, 1981).

—— ed., *Intellectual Life in the Arab East* (Beirut, 1981).

——, 'Beirut's role in the political economy of the French Mandate, 1919–1939', Papers on Lebanon no. 4, Centre for Lebanese Studies, Oxford, 1987.

Burke III, Edmund, *Prelude to Protectorate in Morocco: Precolonial Protest and Resistance, 1860–1912* (Chicago, Ill., 1976).

Burton, John W., 'The history of international conflict resolution', in Edward E. Azar and Burton eds, *International Conflict Resolution: Theory and Practice* (Sussex, 1986).

——, 'Track two: an alternative to power politics', in John Macdonald and Diane B. Bendahmone eds, *Conflict Resolution: Track Two Diplomacy*, Department of State Publication, Foreign Service Institute, Center for the Study of Foreign Affairs, 1987.

Carne, John, *Syria, the Holy Land, Asia Minor, etc., Illustrated* (London, 1836–8).

Chamoun, Camille, *Crise au Moyen-Orient* (Paris, 1963).

Charles-Roux, F., *France et chrétiens d'Orient* (Paris, 1939)

Cherif, Mohamad, 'Expansion européenne et difficultés tunisiennes de 1815 à 1830', *Annales E.S.C.* 25.3 (1970) 714–45.

——, 'Les mouvements paysans dans la Tunisie du XIXe siècle', *Revue de l'Occident musulman et de la Méditerranée* 30 (1980).

Chevallier, Dominique, 'Aux origines des troubles agraires libanais en 1858', *Annales* XIV (1959) 35–64.

——, 'Politique et religion dans le Proche-Orient. Une iconographie des maronites du Liban', *Revue d'histoire moderne et contemporaine* X (Oct.–Dec. 1963).

——, 'Western development and Eastern crisis in the mid-nineteenth century: Syrian confronted with the European economy', in W. R. Polk and Richard Chambers eds, *The Beginnings of Modernization in the Middle East* (Chicago, Ill., 1968).

——, *La Société du Mont Liban à l'époque de la révolution industrielle en Europe* (Paris, 1971; 2nd edn 1982).

—— ed., *Renouvellements du monde arabe (1952–1982). Pensées politiques et confrontations internationales* (Paris, 1987).

Churchill, Charles Henry, *The Druzes and the Maronites under the Turkish Rule from 1840 to 1860* (London, 1862).

——, *Mount Lebanon: a Ten Years' Residence from 1842 to 1860* (New York, 1973).

Clark, Samuel, *Social Origins of the Irish Land War* (Princeton, NJ, 1979).

Clément, J. F., 'Ce que le Liban m'a appris', *Esprit* 115 (June 1986).

Corm, Georges, *Le Proche-Orient eclaté—Suez à l'invasion du Liban, 1956–1982* (Paris, 1983).

——, *Géopolique du conflit libanais* (Paris, 1986).

Cornelius, W. A., *Politics and the Migrant Poor in Mexico City* (Stanford, Calif., 1975).

Corradi, J. E., 'Toward societies without fear', mimeograph paper prepared for the conference on 'The Culture of Fear in Military Regimes of the Southern Cone' (held in Buenos Aires, 30 May–1 June 1985).

Cuinet, Vital, *Syrie, Liban et Palestine: Géographie administrative statistique, descriptive et raisonnée* (Paris, 1896).

Cunningham, A. B., *The Early Correspondence of Richard Wood 1831–1841* (London: 1966).

Dahdah, N., *Evolution historique du Liban*, 3rd edn (Beirut, 1967).

Daher, M., *L'Histoire socio-politique de la République libanaise sous mandat français: 1926–1943*, 2 vols (Paris, 1980).

Darwazah, M. I., *Hawl al-haraka al-'arabiyya al-wahida* (Sidon, 1950).

Davison, R. H., *Reform in the Ottoman Empire 1856–1876* (New York, 1963, 1973).

Dawn, C. D., *From Ottomanism to Arabism* (Chicago, Ill., 1973).

Dekmejian, R. H., 'Consociational democracy in crisis: the case of Lebanon', *Comparative Politics* 10.2 (1978) 251–66.

Delpart, Raymond, *Liban. L'évolution du niveau de vie en milieu rural 1960–1970* (Ministry of Planning, Beirut, 1970).

Deutsch, K. W., 'Social mobilization and political development', *American Political Science Review* 55 (1961).

Du Hays, C. R., *Les Armées françaises au levant 1919–1939,* vol. I (Château de Vincennes, 1978).

Dubar, C. and Nasr, S., *Les Classes sociales au Liban* (Paris, 1976).

Ducruet, J., *Capitaux européens au Proche-Orient* (Paris, 1964).

Entelis, J. P., *Pluralism and Party Transformation in Lebanon* (Leiden, 1974).

Farah, Caesar E., 'The Lebanese insurgence of 1840 and the powers', in *The Journal of Asian History* 1 (1967) 105–32.

——, 'The Quadruple Alliance and proposed Ottoman reforms in Syria, 1839–1841', in *International Journal of Turkish Studies* 2 (1981) 101–30.

Farouk-Sluglett, M. and Sluglett, P., 'Aspects of the changing nature of Lebanese confessional politics', *Peuples méditerranéens* 20 (1982).

Fawaz, Leila Tarazi, *Merchants and Migrants in Nineteenth Century Beirut* (Cambridge, Mass., 1983).

Fournie, Pierre, 'L'Administration française au Levant (1918–1930)', *Position des thèses* (Paris, 1987).

Gaunson, A. B., *The Anglo-French Clash in Lebanon and Syria, 1940–45* (London, 1987).

Geertz, C. ed., *Old Societies and New States* (New York, 1967).

——, 'The integrative revolution: primordial sentiments and civil politics in the new states', in Geertz ed., *The Interpretation of Cultures* (New York, 1973).

Geertz, C., *Meaning and Order in Moroccan Society. Three Essays in Cultural Analysis* (Cambridge, 1979).

Ghannagé, Elias, 'La redistribution des revenus au Liban', in ILO, *L'Economie libanaise et le progrès social* (Beirut, 1955).

Ghazzal, Zouhair, 'Les Fondements de l'économie politique de Damas durant le xixème siècle: structures traditionelles et capitalisme', Doctoral thesis, Sorbonne (Paris IV), 1986.

Gilsenan, M., *Imagined Cities of the East* (Oxford, 1986).

Gould, Andrew, 'Pashas and brigands: Ottoman provincial reform and its impact upon the nomadic tribes of southern Anatolia, 1840–1885', Ph.D. thesis (unpublished), University of California, LA, 1973.

Guys, Henri, *Beyrouth et le Liban: relation d'un séjour de plusieurs années dans ce pays,* vol. II (Paris, 1850).

Hajjar, Joseph, *L'Europe et les destinées du Proche-Orient 1815–1848* (Paris, 1970).

——, *Le Vatican: la France et le catholicisme oriental (1878–1914)* (Paris, 1979).

al-Hakim, Yusuf, *Bairut wa-Lubnan fi 'ahd al-'Uthman,* 2nd print. (Beirut, 1980).

Hallaq, H., *Dirasat fi tarikh Lubnan al-mu'asir* (Beirut, 1985).

——, *Mu'tamar al-sahil wa-al-aqdiya al-arba'* (Beirut, 1985).

Hanf, Theodor, Messarra, Antoine N. and Reinstrom, Heinrich R., *La société de concordance. Approche comparative* (Beirut, 1986).

Hanna, Abdallah, *Qadiyat al-zira'iyyah wa-harakat al-fallahiya fi Suriya wa-Lubnan, 1820–1920.*

Haqqi, Isma'il, *Lubnan: Mabahith 'ilmiyya wa-ijtima'iyya,* ed. Fu'ad Ifram al-Bustani (Beirut, 1970).

Harik, Ilya F., 'Lebanon: anatomy of conflict', *American Universities Field Staff Reports* 49.

——, *Politics and Change in a Traditional Society: Lebanon, 1711–1845* (Princeton, NJ, 1968)

——, *Al-tahawwul al-siyasi fi tarikh Lubnan al-hadith* (Beirut, 1982).

Havemann, Axel, *Rurale Bewegungen im Libanongebirge des 19. Jahrhunderts* (Berlin, 1983).

Hokayem, Antoine and Bittar, Marie-Claude, *L'Empire ottoman, les Arabes et les grandes puissances, 1914–1920* (Beirut, 1981).

Hottinger, A., 'Zu'ama' in historical perspective', in L. Binder ed., *Politics in Lebanon* (New York, 1966).

Hourani, Albert H., *Syria and Lebanon: a Political Essay* (London, 1946)

——, 'Lebanon: the development of a political society', in L. Binder ed., *Politics in Lebanon* (New York, 1966).

——, 'Ottoman reforms and the politics of notables', in W. Polk and R. Chambers eds, *The Beginnings of Modernization in the Middle East* (Chicago, Ill., 1968).

——, 'Ideologies of the mountain and the city', in Roger Owen ed., *Essays on the Crisis in Lebanon* (London, 1976).

——, 'Lebanon from feudalism to nation-state', *The Emergence of the Modern Middle East* (London, 1981).

——, 'Lebanon: the development of a political society', *The Emergence of the Modern Middle East* (London, 1981).

——, *The Emergence of the Modern Middle East* (London, 1981).

——, 'Political Society in Lebanon: a Historical Introduction', Papers on Lebanon no. 1, Centre for Lebanese Studies, Oxford, 1986.

Howard, H. N., *The King–Crane Commission* (Beirut, 1963).

Hudson, M. C., *The Precarious Republic: Political Modernization in Lebanon* (New York, 1968, 1985).

——, 'The Lebanese crisis and the limits of consociational democracy', *Journal of Palestine Studies* 5.3/4 (1976) 109–22.

——, *Arab Politics: the Search for Legitimacy* (New Haven, Conn., 1977).

Hurewitz, J. C., *Diplomacy in the Near and Middle East: a Documentary Record*, 2 vols (Princeton, NJ, 1956).

Ismail, Adel ed., *Documents diplomatiques et consulairs relatifs à l'histoire du Liban*, vol. 18 (Beirut, 1979).

Issawi, Charles, *An Economic History of the Middle East and North Africa* (New York, 1982).

Jalabert, Henri, *Un montagnard contre le pouvoir: Liban 1866* (Beyrouth, 1975).

al-Jisr, B., *Mithaq 1943* (Beirut, 1978).

Johnson, M., *Class and Client in Beirut* (London, 1986).

Johnson, M., 'The political bosses and their gangs. Zu'ama and Qabadaiyyat in the Sunni Muslim quarters of Beirut', in E. Gellner and J. Waterbury eds, *Patrons and Clients* (London, 1977).

Joseph, Rick, 'The material origins of the Lebanese conflict of 1860', B.Litt. thesis (unpublished), Oxford.

Jouplain, M. (pseud. of Bulus Nujaim), *La Question du Liban, Etude d'histoire diplomatique et de droit international (1908)*, 2nd edn (Jounieh, 1961).

Journal of Peasant Studies 13.2 (1986), special issue: 'Everyday Forms of Peasant Resistance in South-East Asia'.

Jumblat, Kamal, *Pour le Liban* (Paris, 1978).

Kadri, A., *Mudhakkirat 'an al-thawra al-'arabiyya al-kubra* (Damascus, 1956).

Kahi, A. ed., *Le Centre-ville de Beyrouth en 1974, mouvement social* (Beyrouth, 1980).

Kalla, Mohammad Said, 'The role of foreign trade in the economic development of Syria, 1831–1914', Ph.D. thesis (unpublished), American University, 1969.

Karam, Georges A. ed., *Qadiyat Lubnan 1918–1920* (Beirut, 1985).

Karpat, Kemal, 'The Ottoman emigration to America, 1860–1914', *IJMES* 17.2 (1985) 175–209.

Kawtharani, W., *Al-ittijahat al-ijtima'iyya al-siyasiyya fi Jabal Lubnan wa-al-mashriq al-'arabi, 1860–1920* (Beirut, 1976).

Kerr, Malcolm H. trans., *Lebanon in the Last Years of Feudalism, 1840–1868: a Contemporary Account by Antun Dahir al-'Aqiqi, and Other Documents* (Beirut, 1959).

——, 'Political decision-making in a confessional democracy', in L. Binder ed., *Politics in Lebanon* (New York, 1966).

Khair, Antoine, Le moutaçarrifat du Mont-Liban (Beirut, 1973).

Khalaf, Samir, 'Adaptive modernization: the case for Lebanon', in C. A. Cooper and S. S. Alexander eds, *Economic Development and Population Growth in the Middle East* (New York, 1972).

——, *Persistence and Change in 19th Century Lebanon: a Sociological Essay* (Beirut, 1979).

——, *Lebanon's Predicament* (New York, 1987).

—— and Kongstadt P., *Hamra of Beirut: a Case of Rapid Urbanization* (Leiden, 1973).

—— and Kongstad, P., 'Urbanization and urbanism in Beirut: some preliminary results', in L. C. Brown ed., *From Madina to Metropolis* (Princeton, NJ, 1973).

Khalaf, Tewfik, 'The Phalange and the Maronite community: from Lebanonism to Maronitism', in Roger Owen ed., *Essays on the Crisis in Lebanon* (London, 1976).

Khalidi, Rashid Ismail, *British Policy Towards Syria and Palestine 1906–1914* (London, 1980).

Khalidi, Tarif ed., *Land Tenure and Social Transformation in the Middle East* (Beirut, 1984).

Khalidi, W., *Conflict and Violence in Lebanon* (Cambridge, 1979).

Khater, Akram, 'Silk, shaykhs, peasants and merchants: the impact of silk production on the society of Mount Lebanon in the 19th century', MA thesis (unpublished), University of California, Santa Cruz, 1986.

Khater, L., *'Ahd al-mutasarrifiyya fi Lubnan, 1861–1918* (Beirut, 1973).

al-Khazin, Sim'an, *Yusuf Bey Karam fi al-Manfa* (Tripoli, Lebanon, 1950).

Khoury, G., *Mémoire de l'aube* (Paris, 1987).

Khoury, Philip S., *Syria and the French Mandate: the Politics of Arab Nationalism, 1920–1945* (Princeton, NJ, 1987).

al-Khuri, Bishara K., *Haqa'iq Lubnaniyya*, 3 vols (Beirut, 1961).

Khuri, F. I., *From Village to Suburbs. Order and Change in Greater Beirut* (Chicago, Ill., 1975).

Krasner, S. D. ed., *International Regimes* (Ithaca, NY, 1983).

Labaki, Boutros, *La Soie dans l'économie du Mont Liban*, 2 vols (Paris, 1979).

——, 'Mawazin al-qiwa bayna al-tawa'if wa-takawwun al-sira'at al-ta'ifiyya fi Lubnan', *Al-Waqi'* 5–6 (October 1983) 215–44.

——, *Introduction à l'histoire économique du Liban* (Beyrouth, 1984).

——, 'L'Emigration libanaise en fin de période Ottomane', *Hannon* 19 (1987) 7–32.

Lamartine, Alphonse de, *Voyage en Orient*, vol. VII of *Oeuvres complètes de M. de Lamartine* (Paris, 1840).

Lammens, Henri, *La Syrie, précis historique*, 2 vols (Beirut, 1939).
Lapidus, I., *Muslim Cities in the Later Middle Ages* (Cambridge, Mass., 1967).
Lawson, Fred H., 'Rural revolt and provincial society in Egypt, 1820–1824', *IJMES* 13.2 (1981) 131–53.
Leary, Lewis Gaston, *Syria the Land of Lebanon* (New York, 1913).
Le Fèvre, H., *Le Droit à la ville* (Paris, 1968).
Lewis, Norman N., *Nomads and Settlers in Syria and Jordan, 1800–1980* (Cambridge, 1987).
Liauzu, C., 'Sociétés urbaines et mouvements sociaux: état des recherches en langue anglaise sur le 'Middle East'', *Maghreb-Machreq* 3 (1986).
Lijphart, Arendt, 'Typologies of democratic systems', *Comparative Political Studies* 1.1 (April 1968) 3–44.
——, *Democracy in Plural Societies* (New Haven, Conn., 1977).
——, 'Consociation: the model and the application in divided societies', in Desmond Rea ed., *Political Cooperation in Divided Societies: a Series of Papers relevant to the Conflict in Northern Ireland* (Dublin, 1982).
Loheac, Lyne, *Daoud Ammoun et la création de l'Etat libanais* (Paris, 1978).
Longrigg, S. H., *Iraq 1900–1950* (Beirut, 1968).
Louis, Wm Roger, *The British Empire in the Middle East, 1945–1951* (Oxford, 1984).
Macdonald, John W., 'Observations of a diplomat', in E. E. Azar and J. W. Burton eds, *International Conflict Resolution: Theory and Practice* (Sussex, 1986).
—— and Bendahmone, Diane B. eds, *Conflict Resolution: Track Two Diplomacy*, Department of State Publication, Foreign Service Institute, Center for the Study of Foreign Affairs, 1987.
Macdonald, Michael, *Children of Wrath: Political Violence in Northern Ireland* (Cambridge, 1986).
Mack, J., Foreword to *Cyprus: War and Adaption*, ed. V. Volkan (Charlottesville, Vir., 1979).
——, 'Some thoughts on the nuclear age and the psychological roots of anti-Sovietism', *Psychoanalytic Inquiry* 6.2 (1986).
Mahafza, A., *Mawqif faransa wa-almaniya wa-italiya min al-wihda al-'arabiyya 1919–1945* (Beirut, 1985).
Maksoud, C., 'Lebanon and Arab nationalism', in L. Binder ed., *Politics in Lebanon* (New York, 1966).
al-Mallah, Abdallah, *Mutasarrifiyya Jabal Lubnan fi 'ahd Muzaffar Pasha, 1902–1907* (Beirut, 1985).
Marlowe, John, *Perfidious Albion: the Origins of Anglo-French Rivalry in the Levant* (London, 1971).

McDowell, David, 'The Druse Revolt, 1925–1927, and its background in the late Ottoman period', B.Litt. thesis (unpublished), Oxford.

Meo, L., 'The separation of Lebanon from Greater Syria', Ph.D. thesis (unpublished), Indiana University, 1961.

Messarra, Antoine N., *La structure sociale du Parlement libanais*, Publications de l'Université libanaise, Institut des sciences sociales, no. 18 (Beirut, 1977).

——, *Le modèle politique libanais et sa survie. Essai sur la classification et l'aménagement d'un système consociatif* (Beirut, 1983).

——, 'Un modèle consociatif au Proche-Orient arabe. Approche comparative du système politique libanais', in *Droit, institutions et systèmes politiques. Mélanges en hommage à Maurice Duverger* (Paris, 1987).

Migdal, Joel, *Peasants, Politics and Revolution* (Princeton, NJ, 1974).

Mizhir, Y., *Tarikh Lubnan al-'amm*, vol. II (n.d.)

Mongin, O., 'Penser la politique contre la domination au Proche-Orient', *Esprit* 115 (June 1986).

Montville, John V., 'The arrow and the olive branch', in John Macdonald and Diane B. Bendahmone eds, *Conflict Resolution: Track Two Diplomacy*, Department of State Publication, Foreign Service Institute, Center for the Study of Foreign Affairs, 1987.

Moore, Barrington Jr, *Social Origins of Dictatorship and Democracy* (Boston, Mass., 1966).

Mufarrij, F., *al-Mu'tamar al-'arabi al-qawmi fi Bludan* (Damascus, 1937).

Muzhir, Yusuf, *Tarikh Lubnan al-'amm* (Beirut, 1955).

Naff, Alixa, 'A social history of Zahle, the principal market town in nineteenth-century Lebanon', 1972 Ph.D. thesis, University of California, LA (Ann Arbor, Mich., 1973).

Nasr, S., 'Roots of the Shi'a movement', *Merip Reports* (June 1985).

Nisbet, R. A., *The Social Bond* (New York, 1970).

Noradounghian, G., *Recueil d'actes internationaux de l'empire Ottoman*, 4 vols (Paris, 1902).

Nordlinger, E. A., *Conflict Resolution in Divided Societies* (Cambridge, Mass., 1972).

Norton, A., *Amal and the Shi'a* (Austin, 1987).

Nour, Antoine Abdel, *Introduction à l'histoire urbaine de la Syrie Ottomane (XVIe–XVIIIe siècle)*, Publications de l'Université Libanaise, Section des Etudes Historiques, XXV (Beirut, 1982).

O'Sullivan, Katherine, *First World Nationalisms: Class and Ethnic Nationalisms in Northern Ireland and Quebec* (Chicago, Ill., 1986).

Owen, Roger ed., *Essays on the Crisis in Lebanon* (London, 1976).

——, 'The political economy of Grand Liban, 1920–1970', in Owen ed., *Essays on the Crisis in Lebanon* (London, 1976).

——, *The Middle East in the World Economy, 1800–1914* (London and New York, 1981).

Oye, K. A., 'Explaining cooperation under anarchy: hypotheses and strategies', *World Politics* 38.1 (1985) (special issue on 'Cooperation under Anarchy') 1–24.

Ozbudun, E., 'Modernization of political structures: the Ottoman empire and its successor states', typescript, Ankara University, 1986.

Paige, Jeffery, *Agrarian Revolution* (New York, 1975).

Pannikar, K. M., *Asia and Western Dominance* (London, 1953).

Picard, Elizabeth, 'Science politique, orientalisme et sociologie au chevet du Liban', *Revue française de science politique* (August 1977).

——, 'De la communauté classe à la résistance nationale. Pour une analyse du rôle des chiites dans le système politique libanais', *Revue française de science politique* 6 (December 1985) 999–1027.

Pinderhughes, C., *Psychoanalytic Inquiry* 6.2 (1986).

Polk, William R., *The Opening of South Lebanon: 1788–1840* (Cambridge, 1963).

Popkin, Samuel, *The Rational Peasant* (Berkeley, Calif., 1979).

Porath, Yeheshua, 'The peasant revolt of 1858–1861 in Kisrawan', *Asian and African Studies* 2 (1966) 77–157.

Porter, J. L., *Five Years in Damascus*, vol. 2 (London, 1855).

Puaux, G., *Deux années au Levant. Souvenirs de Syrie et du Liban 1939–1940* (Paris, 1952).

Puryear, Vernon J., *Napoleon and the Dardanelles* (Berkeley, Calif., 1951).

Qal'aji, Q., *Jil al-fida* (Beirut, n.d.)

Qarqut, D., *Tatawur al-haraka al-wataniyya fi Suriyya: 1920–1939* (Beirut, 1975).

Raymond, A., *Grandes villes arabes à l'époque ottomane* (Paris, 1985).

Rabbath, Edmond, *La Formation historique du Liban politique et constitutionnel* (Beirut, 1973).

——, *La Constitution libanaise. Origines, textes et commentaires* (Beirut, 1982).

Rinn, Louis, *Histoire de l'insurrection de 1871* (Algiers, 1891).

Robin, N., *L'Insurrection de la Grande Kabylie en 1871* (Paris [1901]).

Rustum, Asad, *Lubnan fi 'ahd al-mutasarrifiyya* (Beirut, 1973).

Saba, Paul, 'The development and decline of the Lebanese silk industry', B.Litt. thesis (unpublished), Oxford, 1977.

——, 'The creation of the Lebanese economy: economic growth in the nineteenth and early twentieth centuries', in Roger Owen ed., *Essays on the Crisis in Lebanon* (London, 1976), pp. 1–22.

Safa, Elie, *L'Emigration libanaise* (Beirut, 1976).

Salamé, G., 'Lebanon's Injured Identities', Centre for Lebanese Studies, Oxford, 1986.

Salem, P., 'The political framework for a stable Lebanon', *Panorama of Events* 35 (Beirut, 1984).

Salibi, Kamal, *The Modern History of Lebanon* (London, 1965).

——, 'The 1860 upheaval in Damascus as seen by al-Sayyid Muhammad Abu'l Hasibi, notable and later *Naqib al-Ashraf* of the city', in W. R. Polk and R. L. Chambers eds, *Beginnings of Modernization in the Middle East* (Chicago, Ill., 1968).

——, *Crossroads to Civil War: Lebanon 1958–1976* (Delmar, NY, 1976).

——, *A House of Many Mansions* (London, 1988).

Salih, Shakeeb, 'The British–Druse connection and the Druse rising of 1896 in the Hawran', *Middle Eastern Studies* 13 (1977) 251–7.

al-Sauda, Yusuf, *Fi sabil al-istiqlal* (Beirut, 1967).

Scheltema, J. F. trans., *The Lebanon in Turmoil; Syria and the Powers in 1860: Book of the Marvels of the Time concerning the Massacres in the Arab Country, by Iskander Ibn Yaq'ub Abkarius* (New Haven, Conn., 1920).

Schiller, Linda Schatkowski, *Families in Politics, Damascene Factions and Estates of the 18th and 19th Centuries* (Stuttgart, 1985).

Schlicht, Alfred, 'The role of foreign powers in the history of Lebanon and Syria from 1799 to 1861', in *The Journal of Asian History* 14 (1980) 97–126.

Schmeil, Yves, *Sociologie du système politique libanais* (Grenoble, 1976).

Schneider, Jane and Schneider, Peter, *Culture and Political Economy in Western Sicily* (New York, 1976).

Scott, James C., *The Moral Economy of the Peasant* (New Haven, Conn., 1976).

——, *Weapons of the Weak: Everyday Forms of Peasant Resistance* (New Haven, Conn., 1985).

Seurat, M., 'Le Quartier de Bâb Tebbâné à Tripoli (Liban)', in *Mouvements communautaires et espaces urbains au Machreq* (Beirut, 1985).

Sharara, Waddah, *Fi usul Lubnan al-ta'ifi* (Beirut, 1975).

Shils, E., 'The prospect for Lebanese civility', in L. Binder ed., *Politics in Lebanon* (New York, 1966).

Shorrock, William I., *French Imperialism in the Middle East: the Failure of Policy in Syria and Lebanon, 1900–1914* (Madison, Wis., 1976).

Sivers, Peter Von, 'Rural uprisings as political movements in early colonial Algeria (1851–1914)', in Edmund Burke III and Ira M. Lapidus eds, *Islam, Politics and Social Movements* (Berkeley, Calif., 1988).

Skocpol, Theda, *States and Social Revolutions* (Cambridge, 1979).

——, 'Bringing the state back in: strategies of analysis in current research', in P. Evans, D. Rueschmeyer and Skocpol eds, *Bringing the State Back In* (Cambridge and New York, 1985).

Slama, Bice, *L'Insurrection en 1864 en Tunisie* (Tunis, 1967).

Smilianskaya, I. M., 'The disintegration of feudal relations in Syria and Lebanon in the middle of the nineteenth century', trans. *Economic History of the Middle East, 1800–1914: a Book of Readings*, ed. Charles Issawi (Chicago, Ill., 1966).

——, *Al-Harakat al-fallahiyya fi Lubnan*, trans. Adnan Jamus, ed. Salim Yusuf (Beirut, 1972).

Solh, A., *Hizb al-istiqlal al-jamhuri* (Beirut, 1970).

Solh, K., *Mushkilat al-infisal wa-al-ittisal*, pamphlet published in Beirut, 1937.

Spagnolo, John P., 'French influence in Syria prior to World War I: the functional weakness of imperialism', in *The Middle East Journal* 23 (1969).

——, *France and Lebanon 1861–1914*, St Antony's Middle East Monographs no. 7 (London, 1977).

——, *France and Ottoman Lebanon, 1861–1914* (London, 1977).

Steiner, Jürg, 'The principles of majority and proportionality', *British Journal of Political Science* 1 (1970) 63–70.

Steppat, Fritz, 'Some Arabic manuscript sources on the Syrian crisis of 1860', in J. Berque and D. Chevallier eds, *Les Arabes par leurs archives (XVIe–XXe siècle)* (Paris, 1976).

La Syrie et le Liban en 1922 (French report during the French mandate) (Paris, 1922).

Tabet, J., 'Beyrouth et la guerre urbaine: la ville et le vide', in *Peuple méditerranées* 37 (1986).

Tanenbaum, Jan karl, 'France and the Arab Middle East 1914–1920', in *Transactions of the American Philosophical Society* 68 (1978).

Tarbayn, Ahmad, *Lubnan mundhu 'ahd al-mutasarrifiyya ila bidayat al-intidab, 1861–1920* (Cairo, 1968).

Taylor, Baron I., *La Syrie, La Palestine et la Judée: Pélerinage à Jerusalem et aux Lieux Saints* (Paris, 1860).

Temimi, Abdeljelil ed., *Les Provinces arabes et leurs sources documentaires à l'époque ottomane* (Tunis, 1984).

Thackston, Wheeler McIntosh Jr trans., *Murder, Mayhem, Pillage, and Plunder: the History of the Lebanon in the Eighteenth and Nineteenth Centuries*, trans. from *al-Jawab 'ala iqtirah al-ahbab* (Albany, NY, 1988).

Thobie, Jacques, *Intérêts et impérialisme français dans l'empire Ottoman, 1859–1914* (Paris, 1977).

Tilly, C., *From Mobilization to Revolution* (Reading, 1978).

Touma, Toufic, *Paysans et institutions féodales chez les Druzes et les Maronites du Liban du XVIIe siècle à 1914*, 2 vols (Beirut, 1971–2).

Travaux du séminaire de sociologie du développement 1981–1982, Université libanaise, Institut des sciences sociales (Rabiyeh, Lebanon).

Tucker, Judith, *Women in Nineteenth Century Egypt* (Cambridge, 1985).

Tuéni, Ghassan, *Une guerre pour les autres* (Paris, 1985).

Turner, Bryan S., *Marx and the End of Orientalism* (London, 1978).

Valensi, Lucette, *Fellahs tunisiens: l'économie rurale et la vie des campagnes* (Paris et La Haye, 1977).

Waltz, K. N., *Theory of International Politics* (Reading, Mass., 1979).

Waterbury, J., *The Egypt of Nasser and Sadat* (Princeton, NJ, 1983).

Yamak, L. Z., 'Party politics in the Lebanese political system', in L. Binder ed., *Politics in Lebanon* (New York, 1966).

Zamir, M., 'Emile Eddé and the territorial integrity of Lebanon', *Middle Eastern Studies* (May 1978) 232–5.

Zamir, Meir, *The Formation of Modern Lebanon* (London, 1985).

Index

French support for 84, 85
growth of power of 35–6, 84–5, 88
and political mobilization 184, 186, 189
reaction to 1861 reforms 74–5
role of 68, 70–1, 88
role of patriarch 66, 72–3, 75
Maronite College, Rome 35
Maronites
on Administrative Council 74, 80, 82
community in Beirut 288, 289
educational system 186
French connection 7, 27, 37, 38, 42, 71,
104, 106, 112
Kiyanism and 151
militias 264, 269
perceptions of Greater Lebanon 124–5:
see under Greater Lebanon
political mobilization among 184–6, 189
and presidency 245, 246, 253
in *qa'imaqamiyyatan* 312
reaction to *tanzimat* reforms 68–70, 71
in Republic 263
in revolt in Kisrawan 22–3, 24, 72–3
role in Lebanese history 7–8, 9, 10, 12,
14, 124
struggle for survival 75–6
Sunni alliance 24
uprisings in emirate 21, 22
Mas'ad, Patriarch Bulus 70, 74
Maysalun battle 151, 215, 216
Melkites 38
Mémoire de l'aube (Khoury) 213
Metternich, Prince Clement 38, 42
Meyrier, High Commissioner 141
Mikkawi, Jamil 160
military conscription 17, 22, 68
Millerand, Alexandre 128
Mishaqa, Mikha'il 51, 53, 56
Mishaqa family 53
Montville, Joseph 207–8
Moore, Barrington J. 15
Moubarak, Monseigneur 140
Mount Lebanon
Anglo-French rivalry over 101, 105–19,
265
Christian immigration and expansion
24–5
Council independence decree 76–7
election and politics during *muta-
sarrifiyyat* 84–90
European interests and intervention 6,
32, 37–9, 41, 45–7, 264

growth of Maronite strength in 34
Kiyanism and 151, 159
Maronite–Druze co-operation 33, 39,
43, 107
Maronite–Druze rivalry 6, 8, 11, 22, 31,
39, 41, 54, 101, 102
conflict of 1845 31, 44
conflict of 1860 44, 49–59, 109, 312
Ottoman role reaffirmed 41, 42: opposition to 43
political entity of 3–4, 32–4, 261
rebellion of 1821 18, 21
rebellion of 1840 21, 22, 39–40, 108
rebellion of 1858–61 22–4
role of Chehab amirs 33
Mousseitbe 281
Mufarrej, Fu'ad 155
Muhammad 'Ali 18, 64, 65, 69, 102
French support for 37
occupation by 22, 36, 37, 39, 41, 107,
108
rule in Egypt 33, 107
Muhsin, Muhammad 92
Multinational Force 264, 268
Murr, Du'aibis al- 155
Muslims
reaction to Western influence 9, 10
see also Shi'i Muslims, Sunni Muslims
Mustapha Pacha 42
mutasarrifiyya 44–5, 74–6, 77, 79, 109,
112–13, 133
Administrative Council 79–96: *see main
heading*
basis of modern state 6–7, 31, 126
confessionalism of 31
creation of 3–4, 6, 7, 11
Druze acceptance of 11
1912 protocol 94
Muzaffar Pasha 75, 90, 91

Nabatiyya 307
Naccache, Alfred 130
Nadi al-ahli, al- 154, 155
Nahhas Pacha 143
Najjades, les (Najjadeh, al-) 142, 160, 186
Nakhlé, Rachid 131
Na'mani, 'Arif 151
Napoleon I 104–5, 110
Napoleon III 110
Nasser Eddine, 'Ali 159
Nasserism 183, 184, 186, 187, 265, 266, 267
National Bloc 184

Index

335

National Liberal Party 184, 189
National Pact 11, 119, 124, 143, 144, 220, 227, 253, 263, 312–13
  economic significance of 166, 169
Na'um Pasha 89–90, 91
Nordlinger, Eric 229, 233
Nujaym, Bulus *see* Jouplain, M.
Nusuli, Muhi Eddine 154

Ohannes Pasha 94, 95
Omar Pacha 42, 43
Organization of Communist Lebanese 267
Orthodox church 38
Ossairan, 'Adel 159
Osseiran, Zouheir 143
Ottoman empire
  Anglo-French rivalry and 5, 37, 42, 101–5
  coup d'état, 1908 91
  disintegration of 111, 114
  financial stringency 82
  land tenure in 19
  post-first world war dismemberment 6, 212
  provincial administration 19
  public security 64, 68
  reaction to foreign intervention 5–6
  reforms of 19th century 64–9, 106, 217
  Sublime Porte 31, 32, 38, 41, 42, 59, 64, 81, 82, 83, 85, 94, 103
  succession problems 264, 265
  tanzimat reforms 17, 21 66, 68, 69, 70, 76

Palestine 18, 166, 170, 225, 262, 265
Palestine Liberation Organization (PLO) 269, 308
Palestinians 185, 192, 220, 266–9 *passim*, 289, 314
pan-Arabism 183, 186, 187
Pannikar, K. M. 121
Parti du Pacte national 130, 143
Parti du progrès 130
Parti national social syrien 142
patriotism and state loyalty 69–70
Peace Conference 1919 127, 128, 150
'Peace for Galilee' operation 307
Phalanges libanaises, les 142, 184, 185–6, 189, 219
  militias of 267, 268
Pharaon, Henry 143, 168

political mobilization *see under* urban networks
Ponsot, High Commissioner 134, 135, 136
Pontois, French ambassador 42
power sharing
  compensatory mechanisms 240, 244: attribution 240, 252, 255; rotation 240, 244, 251, 255; superposition 240, 255
  egalitarian strategy 240, 254–5
  multiple balance system 240, 243, 244–5: alternative mechanisms 240, 249–51, 252–5; ceiling system 240, 245–6; mille-feuille system 240, 246–9
  parliamentary representation 255
  presidencies 240, 244, 245, 250, 252–3
  proportionality rule 240–4, 249, 251
Progressive Socialist Party 267, 268
Protocol of Mount Lebanon *see Règlement organique*
protracted social conflict 201–9
Prussia 38, 42, 44

Qabadayat ('tough men') 25, 52, 183, 184, 187, 193
Qadi, Hasan al- 158
qa'imaqamiyyatan 4, 42–4, 46, 67, 109
  choice of *qa'imaqam* 43
  confessionalism in 31, 43–4, 312
  effects of 31, 46, 52–3
Qusa, Franco Pasha 81, 83, 84–5, 90
Qusa, Yusuf 90, 91, 95

Rabin, Yitzhak 310
Ras Beirut 282
Rashid 'Ali 163
rebellion of 1858–61 19, 21, 31
Règlement organique 21, 25, 31, 45, 59, 67, 79, 312
  Maronite–Sunni alliance sanctioned 24, 27
  Protocol revision of 1864 31, 45, 59, 79, 212
  Protocol of 1892 89
Republican Independence Party 154–5
Rida, Ahmad 160
Rihani, Amin 130, 141
Rose, Colonel, consul 38, 41, 51, 54
Russia 38, 42, 44
Rustam, Pasha, 82, 83, 84, 85, 88
Ryllo, Father Maximilien 40